Views from the Left
Fresh Sociological Insights

Mario R. Reda

Pearson Education

Cover art by Salvatore Reda.

Printed in the United States of America

10 9 8 7 6 5 4 3 2 1

ISBN 0–205–35875–6

BA 993719

ALLYN & BACON
75 Arlington Street, Suite 300, Boston, MA 02116
A Pearson Education Company

Copyright Acknowledgments

Contents

I. Culture

doing the sociological imagination
The Act of Interpretation   3
    Peter L. Berger and Hansfried Keller

ethnocentrism
Body Ritual among the Nacirema   22
    Horace Miner

Drill, Grill and Chill   26
    Maureen Dowd

popular culture
'Apocalypse' Then, and Now   28
    David Thomson

exploring the sociological imagination—reflection from cinema
Apocalypse Now   33
    Vincent Canby

culture and values
The Reflections on the Politics of Culture   36
    Michael Parenti

a polemic on social sanctions
The Virtues of Humiliation   43
    Amitai Etzioni, (with a response from) Carl F. Horowitz

II. Groups

power of collective behavior;
McCarthy era: a time of ostracism & negative social sanction
Miller Convicted in Contempt Case   49
    Joseph A. Loftus

Are You Now or Were You Ever? (II)   51
    Arthur Miller

Why I Wrote "The Crucible"   56
    Arthur Miller

Miller Is Cleared of House Contempt   62
    Anthony Lewis

The Myth of the Liberal Campus   64
    Michael Parenti

III. Belief System as a Social Institution

radicals
Jesus Causes Confusion   73
    Andrew M. Greeley

religion?
To the Dot-Com Station   75
    Thomas Frank

Religion and the Shape of National Culture   88
    Robert N. Bellah

IV. Economic Order

values and income
The Rise of Market Populism: America's New Secular Religion   99
    Thomas Frank

Executive Pay: A Special Report, How the Pay Figures Were Calculated   105
    Alan Cowell

globalization
Total Mobilization, Globalization and Individuation: The Contradictory Domination Logic of Postmodern Society, A Theoretical Note   113
    Christine Monnier

Globalization Under Siege   124
    Editorial

Labor Standards Clash with Global Reality   126
    Leslie Kaufman and David Gonzalez

V. Family as an Institution

Sex and Society   133
Robert T. Michael, John H. Gagnon,
Edward O. Laumann, and Gina Kolata

The Myth of Cohabitation   145
Willard F. Jabusch

grinding up middle-class prosperity
For the First Time, Nuclear Families Drop Below 25% of Households   148
Eric Schmitt

How to Define Poverty? Let Us Count the Ways   152
Louis Uchitelle

VI. Polity as an Institution

The Age of Entrapment   159
Alan Ehrenhalt

The Wooing of Our Judges   161
Abner Mikva

Overcoming the Oligarchy   163
Ralph Nader

Oil and Gas: Long-Term Contribution Trends   167
Center for Responsive Politics

*Mike's Message: Why Don't We All Just Cut the Crap Right Now;
The Sequel: The Crap Ends Here*   168
Michael Moore

VII. The Social Institution Education

Make This Natural Treasure a National Monument   175
President Jimmy Carter

Right Answer, Wrong Score: Test Flaws Take Toll   177
Diana B. Henriques and Jacques Steinberg

When a Test Fails the Schools, Careers and Reputations Suffer   186
Jacques Steinberg and Diana B. Henriques

VIII. Stratification and Class

The Super Rich Are Out of Sight   197
Michael Parenti

Types of Forced Labor   200
    USA TODAY staff

IX. Population and Demographics

Population Implosion Worries a Graying Europe   205
    Michael Specter

U.S. Population Has Biggest 10-Year Rise Ever   212
    Eric Schmitt

Demographics and Race by Charts and Maps   214
    The New York Times

X. Resource Tools in Sociology

Bookmarks, Current iSociology: 85 Annotated Web Sites on the Internet   235

U.S Census on Population 2000, Table T1   247

a basic method: inquiring into a nation's origins
Defining Moments and Recurring Myths: A Reply   249
    Seymour Martin Lipset

Mixed Paint   253
    Louis Menand

XI. Urban Collectivities

Café Utne Cities Conference
Are You Getting Enough Vitamin T?   261
    Nicholas Albery

The 10 Most Underrated Towns in America   264
    Peter Katz

XII. Social Forces Moving Toward Social Change

Building Wealth   271
    Lester C. Thurow

Globalization Theory: Lessons from the Exportation of McDonaldization   284
and the New Means of Consumption
    George Ritzer and Elizabeth L. Malone

The Culture of Liberty: An Agenda   303
    Peter L. Berger

Sovereign Corporations   315
    William Greider

Acknowledgments

I once was told that to dedicate a textbook is an exaggeration of its weight. If this were the case, for me to do this in this anthology would be an even greater overstatement. Yet, this work in its small way is my wish that more teachers will begin to question the social system and work to improve our societal model. Because this is a sincere effort I believe it proper to dedicate this work to my best friend, **Lisa Marie Reda,** who understood I would be gone for great periods of time and nevertheless tirelessly supported the completion of the project. I also must thank my little helpers Connie Reda and Franco Becket Reda who cheerfully accepted my engagement in this task.

There are many that we are all indebted to—if we make inquiry into our sociological past a list would become endless. I can think of the wonderful moments in William Simon's classes or the times with Malcolm Knowles and the episodes with political scientist Robert Lorinskas and at work with Eugene Fappiano. There have been wonderful times, ever so brief, with passing friends at great universities—SIU Carbondale, Nova Southeastern, and Southern Connecticut. I am grateful for these moments and have learned much from them.

Over the years I have enjoyed being in a wonderful company of seekers, all dear friends at the College of DuPage teaching inside the Behavioral Science: Alan Lanning, Richard Voss, Christine Monnier, and Joyce Adair Bullen. Outside this field are colleagues Keith Krasemann and especially Diana Fitzwater who was a constant and most able research associate.

I am amazed with the talent found at Pearson Education, long time associate and guide Frank Burrows who constantly has displayed thoughtful ideas and clear direction. I am indebted to Susan Meade who kept me on task—for this I am truly thankful. There were others of on going assistance: Marcella Tullio, Karen Corday, Liane Hill and able assistance from Kristen Kiley inside Pearson Custom's Art department—working on the cover design and assisting Salvatore Reda with the cover art. The folks at Allyn & Bacon helped this difficult task get launched: Jennifer Borchardt from Allyn & Bacon (Chicago) and Joyce E. Nilsen (Vice President of Marketing at Allyn & Bacon—Boston) who liked and acted on my ideas. Without Joyce, there would not have been *Views from the Left: Fresh Sociological Insights.*

Exculpations may be the rule in a last paragraph, and yet it is my heartfelt belief that my friends must stand apart from what I have chosen to place between the covers of this work. Finally, to all go my thanks.

Mario R. Reda
River Forest, Illinois
A.M.D.G.

Introduction

Mario Reda

A contemporaneous reporting of a view from the bridge regarding the current interaction of humankind cannot help but begin to bring balance to a culture that has shifted so quickly toward anomie. Social instability has resulted from unwanted career shifts inside the social institution "economic order." Corporate directors have made decisions to pursue globalization that have resulted in early and unwanted career changes through a dismissal termed "downsizing." Small towns have been gobbled-up by a mass society, the push–pull of leaving one area to pursue work in larger urban centers had seen dramatic shifts in social space. As towns, neighborhoods and communities have changed to respond to the dictates of new, highly mobile work roles, so to has the economic order changed bringing about a lack of standards and values dictated by the pursuit of corporate profit.

Witness now human disorganization resulting in unsocial behavior: the corporation, a commercial organization that is granted a charter from the people through its law, and having its own privileges and liabilities has lost sight of the body corporate—its citizen. The commercial organization has reversed its rank, one would believe it should be in the denizen position, with the power of the people being first, but somehow the corporation is now paramount and the social system and its actors have granted away privilege so much so that the people must submit to it.

"Imagination bodies forth the forms of things unknown,"[1] So to the multinational corporation along with turbo-capitalism now bodies forth a social system that is caught up in the service of a god unknown but unlike imagination we can conjure up a pattern of social interaction taking the nation in the direction of a new supreme, called: "profit." This new "belief system" is found anointing a chief executive officer who pronounces a ritual formula of worship called the quarterly report of earnings. This CEO can dictate what gets sold and what unit will close or move to a third world country, all in the name of bibulous profit. These social forces along with hierarchical role definition can take place only when power becomes concentrated by a few and those who minister the organization for the elite that C. Wright Mills and Max Weber introduced to us turns a blind eye to the purposelessness experienced by the shrinking middle-class. Witness now the upper 10% of the economic stratum being maintained so as to obtain ". . . meaningless rewards when they qualify—

---

[1] William Shakespeare, *A Midsummer Night's Dream. Act v. Sc. 1.*

like swamps of gadgets, oodles of choices and the plethora of things no one really wants or needs."[2] John Seeley's early insight into the 21st century continues by referring to this as all . . . "nonsense. But deadly serious."[3] His prophetic statements, written when he was the dean at the Center for the Study of Democratic Institutions, ring out loudly today with the examination the social institution: Economic Order. Social change is occurring at breakneck speed inside the nation-states of the first world as it affects our social psychology and physical well-being.

When this text attempts to present *Views* of sociology from this position, *The Left*, it is this writer's opinion that American sociologists have few other written choices to select from; most other publications claim to be part of "mainstream" and the works are far from a critique of society or even a centrist position but clearly a skew of an ethnocentric culture; worshipers at the altar of power, profit and order. *Views from the Left: Fresh Sociological Insights* are essays capturing the interactions of society so the reader may quickly see the timely and germane vision of the subject matter. The tradition of the intellectual left has been to effect change to the established order, usually for the well-being of the common citizen. This work therefore is a movement away from mainstream texts, which tender on the *status quo.*

After the desire for a progressive view of sociology became the coordinating concept in this anthology, it became clear during the last decade that a measurable number of scholars were writing works that present germane questions that call for examination: "Is There a Common American Culture?" A number of sociologists, including our recent past president of the American Sociological Association, are writing that the social bonds that would hold individuals together with the interactions that give meaning and purpose are melting away. Another, the current recipient of the National Humanities Medal, states that our house is divided and that "a great danger emanating from this powerful elite is its loss of civic consciousness, of a sense of obligation to the rest of society, which leads to a secession from society into guarded, gated residential enclaves and ultra-modern offices, research centers and universities. A sense of a social covenant, of the idea that we are all members of the same body, is singularly weak in this new elite." Robert Bellah stated in a speech on the topic: "why do we need a public mission? [change mine]" He continued his reference to this changing culture and its proponents as a "duty-free" elite—behavior of an aggregate population being manifested outside any sense of community.[4]

"Just when we are in many ways moving to an ever greater validation of the sacredness of the individual person, our capacity to imagine a social fabric that would hold individuals together is vanishing."[5] Robert Bellah states it "is in part because of the fact that our ethical individualism, deriving, as I have argued, from the Protestant religious tradition in

---

[2] John R. Seeley, "The Break-down Machine," *Focus on the Human Experience*, Mario Reda and Linda Kelly Beaver, Ginn and Company, Lexington, MA. 1982. p. 191

[3] Ibid

[4] Robert Bellah, *Why Do We Need a Public Affairs Mission? The Moral Crisis in American Public Life*, http://www.goodcommunity.smsu.edu./citizenship/robert_bellahs_remarks.htm Southwest Missouri State University © 1998, p. 1–10

[5] Robert Bellah, "Religion and the Shape of National Culture." *America*, July 31, 1999 p. 9.

America, is linked to an economic individualism that, ironically, knows nothing of the sacredness of the individual."[6] Bellah, the Protestant sociologist, is not condemning his culture; far be it, what he is pointing to is the hold that "doctrine" has on the culture long after that viewpoint is no longer applicable, he argues about "a deep cultural code . . ." with "its ominous side."

In the work "Mixed Paint" the essayist Louis Menand gives a useful report on labeling theory and the language of the metaphor, "culture wars." He concludes his work discussing thoughts about culture as a "Rubik's Cube of possibilities" and stands the individual outside and against social organizations, but to end with a conceptual label and a solo view of the self would leave us little to be rightly conceived thereafter. The individual is a unit but it must be seen in action with others giving and holding interaction; that social interaction can be seen in relationship to a social structure or as patterns of behavior in a social environment with an appreciation for interdependency.

The intention of *Views*, by way of various essays, is to introduce balance to the current record of study found in Introductory Sociology. The overwhelming force of the power elite over the various social institutions of society makes a critique of the world in which we hold membership most difficult. The drift is subtle and not overt, seldom do we have time to know what ails us, and yet theses forces are spewing societal change upon the social collectivity. Without sociology asking critical questions about this unique social system, our interdependent world, as we know it, will change beyond recognition.

---

[6] Ibid

Preface

Titus Andronicus

Scene I. Act III.

A Street. Rome.

Titus: "Why, 'tis no matter, man: if they did hear,
They would not mark me, or if they did mark,
They would not pity me, yet plead I must,
All bootless unto them.
Therefore I tell my sorrows to the stones,
Who, though they cannot answer my distress,
Yet in some sort they are better than the tribunes,
For that they will not intercept my tale.
When I do weep, they humbly at my feet
Receive my tears, and seem to weep with me;
And, were they but attired in grave weeds,
Rome could afford no tribune like to these.
A stone is soft as wax, tribunes more hard than stones;
A stone is silent, and offendeth not,
And tribunes with their tongues doom men to death."[1]

Sociology is about debunking and brings news to its protégés about the world we live in while we are in it. It is a discipline that does not have the luxury to stand apart and outside the subject matter that it attempts to understand. Many areas of the social sciences claim this cloak of neutrality, as in Titus' speech to the tribunes. A radical sociology does not allow us to be "tribunes," let alone "stones," outside and apart of the society in which we exam, we cannot stand over and against society with some clipboard in hand collecting information, it does not allow the assumption that we are separate and removed from the subject matter—"the society"—while we are studying it. John Seeley noted that self and society are similar terms, and one cannot be separated from the other. Also, the two are one and

---

[1] William Shakespeare, *Titus Andronicus*.

the same thing but in different manifestation, that they constitute one another, "without separability and without residue."[2] If this is so, then the collective-we, constitutes the world in which we are in as the world is in us. It affects us as we affect it, smaller though we are.[3] And when the "self" is seen collectively, then the collection of selves as multiples is seen as a societal force.

"When we say men live in society *that* is what we mean."[4] Our living in it cannot be anymore removed from society than our body can organically be detached from action. As society brings us into an important union of collective actions uniting individuals, so too does the self unite the many interacting voices inside us. And those interacting voices inside us are often altered by what others think of us.[5] We don't just influence our subject matter. We are a part of it as we study it.

It is clear, I am not asking the sociologist who should know better, to produce a world composed of tribune-like individuals that Shakespeare's Titus sadly faced. Our perspective is a liberating force calling attention to what must be done. Moreover, sociologists who hold themselves apart from the subject matter that is in them refuse to accept who they are as well as their unique socialization and to only embrace a lesser position in a lesser science.

---

[2] John Seeley, *Journal of Applied Behavioral Science*, Vol. 1, No. 4. Found in *Systems and Processes by* Mario Reda, Eugene Fappiano & Leon Czikowsky, College and University Press Publisher, New Haven, Conn. 1968. pp. 51.

[3] Ibid

[4] Ibid

[5] Ibid, pp. 53–4

I. Culture

The Act of Interpretation

Peter L. Berger and Hansfried Keller

All human beings have meaning and seek to live in a meaningful world. In principle, every human meaning is accessible to others. Indeed, this mutual accessibility is a decisive premise for the belief that there is something like a shared humanity. But, of course, some meanings are more accessible than others. Following the distinctions made by Alfred Schutz, two broad kinds of meanings may be distinguished: There are the meanings within the individual's own life-world, those that are actually or potentially "within reach" or "at hand," and that are usually self-understood in the natural attitude of everyday living. And then there are the meanings *outside* the individual's own life-world, meanings of other societies or less familiar sectors of one's own society, also meanings from the past; these are all meanings that are not immediately available in the natural attitude, are not "within reach" or "at hand," but rather must be appropriated through specific processes of initiation, be it through immersing oneself in a different social context or (especially in the case of meanings from the past) through specific intellectual disciplines. Further distinctions must be made: in all the aforementioned cases, there is a difference between the ordinary interpretation of meanings in everyday life and interpretations in terms of the social sciences. Further: one must distinguish between interpreting the meanings of individuals with whom one is in actual or potential face-to-face interaction (those whom Schutz called "consociates"), the meanings of individuals with whom such interaction is *not* taking place (called "contemporaries"—or, in the case of the past, "predecessors"), and finally meanings that are embodied in anonymous structures (such as the meaning of an institution with whose concrete human representatives no interaction may ever take place).

Even the reader not familiar with the more arcane zones of the Schutzian corpus will readily see that all of this can quickly get to be very complicated. Rather than spin out the complexities, let us immediately apply them to a concrete example. In other words, let us see how interpretation actually occurs in concrete social situations. As phenomenologists like to say, let us construct a world—or, in this instance, at least a miniworld:

I am a young woman, a graduate student of sociology in a less than elite state university in the Middle West. I am attending a sociology convention in a big hotel on the West Coast.

Source: Peter L. Berger and Hansfried Keller, *Sociology Reinterpreted: An Essay on Method and Vocation,* "The Act of Interpretation," Anchor Press/Doubleday. Garden City, N.Y., 1981, pp. 17–55.

Right now, in between sessions, I am engaged in conversation with another young woman, a graduate student at an elite university in California. We have been talking about (what else?) the job market and she has been giving me some interesting and potentially useful information about job openings in her part of the country. The conversation has been friendly, animated, and both in form and content very familiar to me—that is, although I have just met this particular individual, I have had such conversations before on quite a few occasions, and although some of the information conveyed by her is new and interesting to me, none of it is surprising. Then, suddenly and without warning, an element of stark, indeed alarming, unfamiliarity is injected into the conversation, a big surprise that abruptly changes the placid quality of the interchange. My conversation partner looks at her watch, apologizes, and says that she must really go now. I mumble something by way of regretful assent. She has already started to move away, turns back, gives me a searching look, and says: "I don't really know you at all. Perhaps I shouldn't say this. But some friends of mine from L.A. are having an orgy, up on the fourteenth floor. I'm sure they would be happy if you came along. I think we could use an additional woman. Why don't you come with me? Some of the men are really very nice."

Now, let us freeze this tableau for a moment. Just what is happening now? Never mind for now whether I'm shocked or titillated, tempted to accept the invitation or to quickly retreat from the encounter. This has never happened to me before and, quite apart from my feelings and from what I might eventually do about the situation, what is happening right now is clear and simple: *I have been presented with a communication that calls out for interpretation.* Indeed, as soon as I have recovered from the steep upsurge in my adrenalin level, a number of different possible interpretations are crowding into my mind: "This is a joke." Or: "This is not really an invitation to an orgy, but an attempt at lesbian seduction." Or even: "Maybe I didn't hear right?" Each one of these possible interpretations would, if given credence, pull the situation back from outrageous unfamiliarity into the safety of the familiar—some people have a somewhat strange sense of humor; I have been approached by lesbians before; some of these Californians do talk a little funny. Let us further assume, though, that I dismiss the aforementioned interpretations—there is nothing to indicate that she is joking; lesbians bent on seduction do not mention nice men; Californian or not, she was speaking standard American English, and there is nothing wrong with my hearing. I conclude, therefore, that the communication says what it seems to say:, I am indeed being invited to an orgy. This conclusion presents me, in a very concrete way, with a social world that is new to me. However I will eventually respond to this world, on the level of further actions, I'm also being presented with an intellectual challenge. I must, as it were, expand my cognitive map to incorporate this new item of social reality.

To say that I must expand my cognitive map is another way of saying that I must find a way of interpreting the new territory that I have just discovered. In other words, interpretation is also a kind of incorporation: I move to understand the new by relating it to the old in my own experience. Now, it so happens in this case, I don't have to start from scratch. Although such a communication has never been made to me before, it does fit into things I know or believe to know—about Californian life-styles, for one (I have read Cyra McFadden's *Serial*, I've even seen the movie). If I can do this credibly, what I'm doing is to subsume the new information under a cognitive rubric that is already "at hand": "So Californians *really* behave this way!" In that case, while the concrete situation is indeed new to me, my cognitive apparatus already contains the categories by which the situation can be incorporated into my view of the social world. One could also say, then, that the situation is new, but not *all that* new. (To bring this point home, imagine a different invitation: "Some friends of mine from L.A. are having a blood sacrifice, up on the fourteenth floor. We don't have the victim yet. Would you like to be it? . . .") But even though I can now subsume the new information under categories already available to me, minimally I must reconstruct these categories to accommodate what has just occurred: the phrase "They *really* behave this way!" already constitutes such a reconstruction. As I continue to talk with my conversation partner, the reconstruction is likely to become firmer and more elaborate.

Now, it is important to stress that, in this example, I have not entered this conversation in the course of a sociological research project; indeed, up to now my reactions have been altogether similar to those of an ordinary person not blessed with any training in sociology. The intellectual effort at understanding what is being said to me then does not proceed systematically, step by step. Rather, it seems to happen spontaneously, with whole chunks of information being rapidly absorbed and "worked into" my cognitive system. This ongoing activity of interpretation is taking place within my own mind while the external conversation is going on; that is, my interpretation takes place in an inner conversation, which is a crucial *sotto voce* accompaniment to the verbal exchanges. But it is time to push our little story one step ahead. After the invitation has been issued to me, and after I have concluded that it is indeed what it purports to be (a conclusion that I will have reached in a fraction of the time needed here to put its logic on paper), I don't respond to it right away, either positively or negatively. *My interest has been aroused.* And (even if this may be in part to gain a little time) I begin to ask questions: Who are these friends from L.A.? Do they often do this? Does my conversation partner participate often? Just what goes on at these events? And so on.

At this point, of course, I am doing much more than interpreting the meaning of a single communication by another person. I have begun an investigation that will allow me to interpret a larger, perhaps much larger, segment of the social world. This, still, need not be a properly sociological investigation; the questions I ask now are those that any ordinary individual whose interest is aroused would ask. These questions, then, need not issue from some logic of systematic inquiry, and they follow each other without much forethought and in no planned sequence. But, if my partner is ready to answer them, they will naturally enable me to embark on a much more comprehensive interpretation of the phenomenon. If this is to be the result, though, there is a simple but exceedingly important presupposition: *I must listen.*

Again in very ordinary terms, it is not hard to spell out what is involved in this: I must keep attentive to what this person is saying. I must not let my mind wander, and I must try to keep attuned to her communications. I must not interrupt. And I must especially not interrupt with judgments or opinions of my own, not only because this might make her angry or defensive, but because it will deflect my attention from what she is communicating to me. That is, I must try to control my impulses of distraction or emotional affect (positive *or* negative). All of this adds up to a willingness to be open-minded at least for the moment: in order to grasp her view of the world, I must bracket my own for at least as long as this exploratory conversation is going on.

Let us suppose that this effort at a more ample understanding has been successful. My conversation partner has delayed her departure for the delights of the fourteenth floor long enough to answer my questions. What has happened now is that, minimally, I have acquired firsthand knowledge about people who conduct orgies at scholarly conventions. However modestly, this has modified my cognitive map in terms of this particular feature— if you will, my cognitive map of the sexual mores of American society. The very fact that my interest has been aroused (a possibility, let it be noted, even if unaccompanied by any arousal of the libido whatever) implies that this new knowledge is relevant to me. Putting this in more precise Schutzian terms, what I have done in this act of interpretation is to accommodate my own *relevance structure* to that of this other person and of the group with which she is affiliated.

The longer this conversation goes on, the more elaborate will be this accommodation of relevance structures. I will get to know more about her and her friends' general view of the world—which will in all likelihood include matters not directly related to sexuality. Indeed, I will begin to obtain an understanding of a general view of the world *within which* these sexual practices make sense to these people. This general view is likely to include some sort of a theory of interpersonal relations, of intimacy, perhaps of politics, or of religion. As I continue to question, my questions will be the result of an ongoing correlation between what I already know, what I am finding out now and what I would like to find out. Very likely, this gathering stock of knowledge will allow me to "locate" this particular woman more exactly within some set of social categories—that is, I will *typify* her. Thus, for example, I will be able to go beyond classifying her as "a Californian" (an obviously imprecise typification when it comes to people who participate in orgies—think of all those Reagan voters!), but instead will be in the process of constructing a much more detailed type of person who engages in such activities.

Remember this, though: my own construction of this type is dependent on what she has been telling me. Put differently: it is *she* who is giving me a portrait of this sexual subculture— we haven't gone to the fourteenth floor, not yet anyway—we're still down here in the coffee shop! Thus there are two hypotheses emerging from the conversation. One: the type of person represented by this individual perceives this subculture in this particular way. Or two: her perception of the subculture is a valid one. If I am to choose between the two hypotheses, I must obviously, by whatever means, come to some sort of conclusion as to my informant's *reliability*. Depending on which choice I make, I will say one of two things (say to myself, that is): "I now understand how, perhaps why, this person perceives the world in this way"; or, "This is a perception I ought to take seriously" (not necessarily seriously in the sense of wanting to join her subculture, but of acknowledging that her account of it is valid). One can use two terms of Jean Piaget's here: in the first instance, I have *assimilated* her point of view—that is, I have absorbed it into my own viewpoint, which has not changed very much in consequence; in the second instance, I have *accommodated* my point of view to hers, thus changing the former substantially. In either case, though, I see the world differently now. Put simply: *I cannot interpret another's meaning without changing, albeit minimally, my own meaning system.*

To repeat: thus far, in this example, I have been in this situation as an individual with an interest in understanding an unaccustomed slice of social reality just presented to me, but not *qua* sociologist; everything said so far about my efforts at interpretation could also have been said if I were, say, a buyer for a Midwestern department store, or a housewife, or (these days at least) a nun. But let us now vary the example slightly: I am now in this same conversation *qua* sociologist—that is, my efforts are now directed toward a specifically sociological interpretation. To say that I'm in the conversation *qua* sociologist may mean one of two things: either, let us imagine, that I have been hanging around the coffee shop with precisely this research interest in mind—I'm writing my doctoral dissertation about the sexual mores of sociologists—presumably, then, we will also have to imagine that the aforesaid invitation to an orgy was not an altogether fortuitous event but was sought out and perhaps provoked by me in the pursuit of my research. Or, alternatively, we can leave the situation as previously described but simply imagine that, in the course of the conversation, my interest *as a sociologist* is aroused—that is, inwardly if not verbally, I now define myself as a sociologist engaged in doing research on an unexpectedly interesting situation. What changes as a result of this switch from ordinary participant to sociological investigator?

As a sociologist I must certainly continue to listen and to interpret, but both the listening and the interpreting now take on a peculiar character. The similarities with ordinary listening and interpreting are great; essentially the same procedures as those just described will continue to take place. But the differences are important, and they can be spelled out. To begin with, I now establish a greater kind of *distance* from the situation within my own mind. Deliberately, I step outside the situation, take on the role of an outsider (even if the other partner in the situation is not aware of my detachment). By the same token, this distancing right away gives me a greater sense of control over what is taking place. It is still essential that I retain an open mind in listening, but this *ad hoc* (or *pro tem*) open-mindedness is more systematic and disciplined than that of the ordinary listener. And, of course, if I have done sociological research before, I have acquired habits of listening in this way that will be "at hand" for me as soon as I define this particular situation as a research occasion. I will also have developed a habit of disengaging my own existential concerns from the situation as far as I'm able—in the example, say, moral disapproval or breathless libidinal excitement or the quasi-religious expectation that I'm on the brink of a salvific insight or experience— and I will look upon the situation as one in which such disengagement is appropriate (as against, say, a conversation with my fiancé or my husband, when a comparable disengagement of existential concerns would not only be inappropriate but a betrayal of the personal relationship).

As I explore the situation sociologically, there is also the previously described interaction of my own relevance structure with that of my conversation partner and, hopefully, with the relevance structure of the sexual subculture that is coming into view as a result of her communications. But my own relevance structure now is not only more systematic and explicit; it is a relevance structure *of a different kind*. This is because it has not been shaped merely by my own previous experiences and interpretations, but by the body of sociological theory and knowledge, and this lore of the discipline is constantly present in my own process of interpretation. The typifications and hypotheses that I now undertake are also both more systematic and different in content. For instance, in typifying my conversation partner and her circle of friends I may pay special attention to their *class*, and in doing this I bring into my interpretation an entire body of stratification theory and data derived from the work of other sociologists. Thus I may hypothesize, on the basis of studies made by this or that other sociologist, that this sexual pattern is typical of upwardly mobile lower-middle-class Evangelical Protestants whose parents are divorced—or (what the hell) downwardly mobile upper-middle-class Jews who suffered from hay fever in their teens. Put differently: as I interpret the situation, *sotto voce* in my role as sociologist, the entire discipline (or, rather, that segment of it that is theoretically relevant to this research material) is invisibly present in my own mind—a silent partner in the situation, as it were.

As a trained sociologist, I can readily draw upon a large body of knowledge without doing this explicitly step by step. In other words, this whole body of knowledge is at hand for me. Almost automatically there flash before my mind different *possible* interpretations of this particular situation. The decision as to which of these I will actually apply will depend on its "fit" with the data in question. I do this spontaneously and implicitly. At the moment, however, that the data do *not* seem to "fit" into one of these available schemes of interpretation, I will now turn to an explicit and systematic comparison of possible interpretations. At this point, I am, as it were, "juggling" a number of possible interpretations. If none of them "fits" sufficiently, I will then be constrained to construct a *new*, or at least greatly modified, interpretation of my own. In doing this, I make a deliberate effort to sort out, or "falsify," what is already known as against the new knowledge I'm attempting to acquire. This is a deliberate undertaking of construction. This point will be returned to below in the discussion of conceptualization. Suffice it to point out now that this procedure is a safeguard against becoming dogmatic (in the sense of adhering to my previous point of view and forcing the data into it) and also against overlooking certain data that do not subsume themselves readily under previously available schemes of interpretation.

Also, as a sociologist I have a different way of dealing with the possible validity of what this individual has been saying. On the spot, having typified her, I can immediately hypothesize that others of her type are likely to hold these particular views. But if I want to decide whether to accommodate these views into my own sociological perception of American sexual mores, there is only one course of action for me to pursue: *I must go out and do further research into this putative subculture.* This need not necessarily mean that I follow my conversation partner to the fourteenth floor to see whether there really is an orgy and whether it is what she has claimed it to be; it means even less that, having gone to the fourteenth floor, I now participate in the sexual goings-on. I might indeed, in the interest of science, decide to be a so-called participant-observer; in that case it will be all the more important to maintain some inner detachment from the situation, difficult though this may be (it has been determined that orgasm and stratification theory do not mix easily). Or, if they let me, I might decide to remain an observer, engaged in what an earlier generation of Catholics was advised to do when inescapably trapped in non-Catholic religious observances—"inconspicuous nonparticipation" (this too may be difficult at an orgy). But, of course, there are other avenues open to me. I can interview other likely informants. I can seek contact with the subculture under other conditions that may be more favorable to research. If funded, I can hire other people to do the research for me. But, whatever avenue of research I finally choose to follow, it is clear that the validity or invalidity of this individual's report will have to be subjected to a process of (in principle rigorous) *empirical testing*. Conversely, I cannot draw any conclusions about the matter of validity simply on the basis of whether this individual seems credible to me—let alone on the basis of *a priori* theoretical convictions of mine. *All* my hypotheses—about downwardly mobile Protestants, hay-fever-afflicted Jewish teenagers, and so on—will be subject to this process of empirical testing. And, if my research is honest, I must remain open to the possibility that some of the hypotheses will not be supported by my findings.

What we have described so far is the interpretation (be it in ordinary life or *qua* sociologist) of meanings presented in face-to-face interaction. However, meanings are also presented by anonymous means, where concrete other persons are not empirically available. For example, I may be sitting at home, reading a newspaper story about new sexual mores in California. If I want to interpret this story, how is this act of interpretation different from the previously described face-to-face conversation? Again, there are many similarities, but the differences are important. In the newspaper a view of the world is being presented to me in a highly organized way, as against the much looser presentation in conversation. Most people, after all, do not speak in carefully ordered paragraphs. This also means that this particular item of alleged information is placed in a wider context—minimally, in the context of what the editors of this newspaper consider to be news—but possibly also in the context of the newspaper's wider presentation of social reality. Thus, for example, this may be a conservative newspaper, and this particular story is part of an ongoing depiction of the degeneracy of American society; or, on the contrary, this is a newspaper sympathetic to the cultural revolutions of the age, in which case the story may be part of a series of reports from the frontiers of liberation.

Also, in reading the newspaper, I can "listen" to its view of the world, in the sense of being attentive to it and trying to be open-minded. But I cannot ask questions. Therefore, the interlocking between my own body of knowledge and that presented to me is more difficult. I cannot so readily (using George Herbert Mead's phrase) "take the role of the other" in trying to penetrate into an unfamiliar cognitive map. Consequently, what the newspaper presents to me lacks the immediacy of what William James called the "accent of reality"; it is much easier to "put down" (in *both* senses of the phrase) the newspaper than a person sitting across the table. If I read the newspaper *qua* sociologist—newspaper stories then are part of my "data"—I have one slight advantage: I can more easily withdraw from the situation and confront the knowledge presented by the newspaper with my own body of knowledge. Put differently, the newspaper cannot as easily "suck me into" this new viewpoint as can an individual who is in face-to-face interaction with me. But if I now want to interpret the newspaper story as a sociologist, I must also be very much on my guard— precisely because of the highly organized form of the presentation. Unlike the face-to-face conversation, the newspaper presents its view to me in what could be called a *protoscientific* form—that is, the story is in itself already a form of interpretation—or, more precisely, the way in which the story is told already contains an interpretation (to an extent, this is also true of a story told in conversation, but much less so). Hence it is important for me to take this implied interpretation apart, to subject it to critical analysis, in terms of my own *sociological* relevance structure.

There is yet another case of interpretation that can only be briefly mentioned here: the interpretation of altogether anonymous structures, regardless of how their meanings are conveyed. This is the problem of interpreting, not the meanings of individuals or groups of individuals (even such as may constitute a specific concrete subculture), but of large institutional constellations. Examples of this would be "the American family," or "the American state," or "the capitalist economy," or "Islamic law." While, of course, every one of these abstractions is represented by concrete human beings engaged in concrete actions, institutions can never be empirically available as such. This, though, by no means implies that institutions are meaningless entities. On the contrary, every human institution is, as it were, a sedimentation of meanings, or, to vary the image, a crystallization of meanings in objective forms. As meanings become objectivated, *institutionalized*, in this manner, they become common reference points for the meaningful actions of countless individuals, even from one generation to another. But these institutionalized meanings can also be interpreted—"retrieved," or "unwrapped," from their seemingly inert forms. The way in which *this* can be done, however, cannot be pursued here.

Instead, we may now turn to the other kind of meaning mentioned earlier—that is, one that is completely outside one's own life-world. Of course, in the example described at some length before the interpreting individual is indeed faced with an unfamiliar, surprising social situation, and the subculture adumbrated in that situation is one in which she has not previously participated. All the same, both the situation and the subculture were not completely unknown to her. As was indicated, she actually had ready-made interpretative schemas "at hand" to begin dealing with the unfamiliar social reality—as witness the ready-made typifications (or, if one prefers, stereotypes) of the Californian way of life. And, after all, the initial informant was an individual with whom conversation was possible in the first place, with whom large chunks of one's own social reality were already shared (as evidenced by the preceding conversation topic of the professional job market), and (last not least) with whom one could converse in standard English. If we had spun out further a variation of the example just alluded to before—about people engaged in some homicidal sacrificial ritual in the midst of an American convention hotel—the process of interpretation, needless to say, would have been different and much more difficult. But, obviously, the best example for the kind of interpretation at issue now is that of a visitor to a more or less completely foreign society.

Let us posit, then, that I am an anthropologist, finally doing fieldwork in one of the few truly untouched jungle spots left in the world (I'm a *lucky* anthropologist). My indigenous informants, across formidable linguistic barriers, are explaining one of *their* homicidal rituals to me (why not?)—say, throwing virgins into the volcano in order to assuage the rain god. Once again, when my efforts at interpretation of this quaint custom are compared with interpretations going on in ordinary situations in my home society, there are both similarities and differences.

As a fully socialized adult engaged in face-to-face interaction with other human beings there is always one possibility open to me (in this case, let us assume, I'm *not* a virgin myself and thus not eligible for fuller participation in the events in question): this is the possibility of "going native." What happens in that event is a process of resocialization, at the end of which I become a member of the meaning system I originally studied as an outsider. Such resocialization is a standing professional hazard for all anthropologists; some of them, of course, may welcome rather than try to avoid this outcome. Be this as it may, the anthropologist who "goes native" has now developed a new "natural attitude" in the originally alien situation. The problems of interpretation are then no different from the ones discussed before within one's own society. The interpreter will share an essentially common relevance structure and body of knowledge with the people whose actions are to be interpreted: "Who are these girls?"—"Going into the volcano"—"Ah yes, of course, it's that time of the year again. How many are there?" . . .

The more interesting case, though, is that of the anthropologist (or, for that matter, any outsider) who does *not* "go native" completely. That is my case, let us assume. I remain what I was before I arrived in the jungle (or so I think), and I seek to interpret the "native" meanings. Any outsider, even a casual tourist, will be constrained to make this effort, but, being an anthropologist, my own attempts are more systematic and self-conscious. Here, of course, everything said before about sociological as against ordinary interpretation will apply, *mutatis mutandis*: there is an anthropological body of theory and data, an anthropological relevance structure and so on. Needless to say, the process of *listening* here is more difficult: I barely understand the language, I fail to observe all sorts of relevant cues in people's statements and actions, there are large areas that completely mystify me—and, let us also assume, the prospect of watching these individuals being thrown into a volcano is at least mildly upsetting to me, so that I have some difficulty maintaining the necessary attitude of calm detachment, of not "interrupting" with my own emotional reactions and moral judgments. To use the familiar anthropological term, I'm likely to suffer from acute culture shock. It is important to point out, though, that such culture shock has some useful side effects. It *forces* me to be fully attentive to everything that is going on, precisely because it is all so shockingly unfamiliar. By contrast, much in my own society ongoingly escapes my attention because it takes place within a structure of familiarity. It may be true that familiarity breeds contempt; more relevantly for the interpreting social scientist, familiarity breeds inattention. The very alienness of the situation, then, is both a difficulty and an asset, cognitively speaking.

If I am to be successful in this situation as an anthropologist—which means *neither* remaining the incomprehending outsider *nor* "going native"—I must, in a very real sense, become a "plural person" (to an extent everyone is that up to a point, especially in a modern pluralistic society, but there is a qualitative jump here). That is, I am both inside and outside the situation, and my activity as a social-scientific interpreter ensures that I maintain this always tenuous balance. The anthropological field researcher is trained to achieve this curious trick, by a variety of techniques; for instance, the practice of keeping continuous field notes, beyond its obvious instrumental utility, is a ritual for maintaining the insider/outsider status. The details of this cannot concern us here. The further point to be made, though, is that the sociologist, even in her or his own society, resembles the anthropologist in this status, despite the fact that the latter is easier to maintain "at home" than in the jungle. One may say that the alienness, which is automatically given to the anthropologist, must be artificially constructed by the sociologist if the perils of inattention to the familiar are to be avoided. Put differently, the anthropologist has the problem of "going native"; the sociologist must strive to "go alien." Put differently again, any act of sociological interpretation introduces an artificial distance, or a strangeness, between interpreter and interpreted.

Increasingly, of course, it is not only anthropologists who study exotic cultures; sociologists have undertaken their own share of such studies. To that degree, the methodological differences between the two disciplines have diminished. But there is yet another point to be made in the matter of interpreting a very alien society. Two distinct cognitive goals are possible. One, I may simply want to *present* this society—as it were, for exhibition in an ethnographic museum. Or, two, I'm interested in *comparing* this society with my own society and with other societies, for the purpose of testing some broad hypotheses or theories. Within the discipline of anthropology there have long been debates as to the respective validity of these two approaches. Within sociology, by contrast, there has never been much debate. Sociology, by its very nature, is comparative and generalizing, and this cognitive goal will dictate the character of the questions to which answers will be sought. Max Weber's vast work in the cross-cultural sociology of religion is the prime example of this comparative and generalizing thrust, though by no means the only example.

Different again, of course, is the interpretation of *past* societies—say, the interpretation of sexual mores or religious practices in ancient Rome. There is much similarity in this to the problems of interpreting a greatly alien society in the present—the barriers of language and lack of information, and the consequent difficulties in grasping the relevance structures in operation. But there are also differences: the sources are much more limited, for one. In the aforementioned jungle society, even if it is illiterate, every living member of that society is a "text" open to interpretation; in the case of ancient Rome, the interpreter is limited to a more or less fixed quantity of written sources, augmented by archaeological evidence. (In that respect, of course, there is the more fortunate case of an interpreter of a society on which a lot of new archaeological discoveries are in process of being made.) Also, in a more radical sense than previously stated with regard to reading a newspaper story, the interpreter cannot ask any questions. There are no living survivors of the society to answer. This further implies that the meanings to be interpreted are "frozen"; they will never change again. By contrast, even in a "primitive" jungle society, meanings always change, are in some sort of flux, as long as there are living human beings who orient their existence by these meanings. One may also say that this "frozen" quality of the past gives it its awesomeness: there are no more Romans, and what they have done and meant is caught in an eternal tableau that will never move again; ancient Rome, unlike any living society, is a "once and for all" reality.

As in the case of anthropology, the interpreter of the past, notably the historian, may have two different cognitive goals: to interpret this past society for its own sake; and to interpret it in order to explain certain features of the present, or of other societies than this particular one. Once more, these are the goals of "ethnography" as against comparison and generalization. Indeed, ever since Edward Gibbon if not earlier, one of the foremost motives attracting scholars to the history of ancient Rome has been the expectation that the latter will furnish "lessons" for the present. And as in anthropology, historians have quarreled over this kind of interest, some sharing it, others arguing that every historical constellation is unique and should be studied for its own sake without pedagogical hindthoughts. The sociologist, whatever the historian may decide to do, will always be inclined to draw lessons from the past—not, of course, moral or philosophical lessons, but lessons in the sense of finding in the past evidence for this or that generalizing hypothesis about the way societies work. Again, Max Weber is the prime example of such sociological uses of the past.

It may be useful now to sum up the entire discussion of this chapter up to now: In *all* the cases discussed, even in the case of ordinary conversation in everyday life, what is involved is an interpretation of the meanings of others through a complex interaction and interpenetration of relevance structures, meaning systems and bodies of knowledge. What I, the interpreter, find interesting comes up against the others' interests; what I mean and believe to know must, as it were, struggle against their intentions and definitions of reality. If I am not an ordinary observer but a sociologist, the process of interpretation is different in that I am, or should be, much more aware of the dynamics of this interaction, and therefore more in control of it. Also, *qua* sociologist, I am subject to explicit and implicit rules as to how to proceed—the "rules of the game" of the discipline of sociology. Finally,

I will then bring into the situation specific *scientific* relevance structures and bodies of knowledge, which are different from those of ordinary persons.

What must be done now is to further clarify the character of this specifically sociological (or, generally, social-scientific) form of interpretation. Put differently, we must further clarify the "rules of the game" of sociology. This can be done conveniently by focusing on a number of key methodological issues.

The issue of conceptualization. There are no "raw facts" in science; there are only facts within a specific conceptual framework. It is important to see, though, that this can also be said of ordinary life. There too, there are no "raw facts," but facts embodied in structures of relevance and meaning. That is, ordinary life is also organized in the minds of all who participate in it, and this organization takes place by means of a conceptual framework—however unsophisticated or illogical this may be, and however dimly the participants may be aware of it. Thus, to go back to an earlier example, the individual (that is, the ordinary individual, not the observing social scientist) who says, "This is an orgy!" may indeed say this on the basis of observing "facts" of an indubitably empirical sort—say, by observing ten people, stark naked, engaging in patently sexual activities on the carpet of this hotel room. But (no pun intended) this "fact" is not "raw" either. It only becomes an observed fact in the first place because the observer *is attentive to it*: after all, our somewhat innocent pedagogue from the provinces might, just conceivably, pay no attention to the naked people on the floor, but instead have her gaze riveted with passionate intensity on the artistic productions hanging on the wall (she is, let us imagine, a connoisseuse of hotel art). Or, alternatively, she might blindly rush into the bathroom and inspect the plumbing, because she is, for whatever intellectual reasons, interested in the latest innovations in that area of modern technology. In other words, her interest in the sexual "facts" in the situation is the result of what psychologists like to call "selective perception"—that is, she perceives *these* particular facts because she is interested in them as against *other* facts that, at least for the moment, she is inattentive to. This interest presupposes a conceptual framework by which the continuous mass of data assaulting the senses is ordered. And, of course, the seemingly spontaneous designation of these particular perceived facts as "an orgy" is the direct application of a *concept* to what is being perceived. That concept presupposes a larger system of concepts relevant to the area of sexual activity. So that, to vary the example, if upon entering the hotel room our observer would have found just two naked individuals, one male and one female, lying on the bed rather than the floor, engaged in sexual activity—whatever she might have called *that* scene, it would hardly have been "an orgy." In that case, within the same overall conceptual framework of sexual activity, *another* concept would have seemed to be more applicable.

But these are not concepts in the strict scientific sense, because they are not sharply defined, their relations to each other are not clarified and their empirical validity is not rigorously tested by evidence—all characteristics of concepts within a scientific frame of reference. The quasi-concepts of ordinary life have an eminently pragmatic purpose—to provide a "map for living." These same quasi-concepts, pragmatically applied in everyday life, are what Alfred Schutz called *typifications*, and, as he amply demonstrated, ordinary social life would be impossible without them: people would not know "what is what."

Now, the sociologist cannot simply adopt the typifications as they are, but she or he must *take cognizance* of them. If this cognizance is missing, no interpretation of what is actually going on may occur. Back to the example: the observer, by saying "This is an orgy!" is applying a concept that, minimally, implies a collective breach of conventional sexual mores. But if she is going to stick by this conceptualization as her inquiry proceeds, it is essential that she take cognizance of what the *actors* in this scene mean by their activity. In other words, in some fashion (not necessarily using the same word) the actors too must be saying to themselves "We are staging an orgy!" If this is *not* what they are saying to themselves, the sociologist's designation of the scene as "an orgy" is doubtful. This can be seen most easily by imagining alternate meaning structures in this situation: suppose that, upon further investigation, it turns out that this hotel room is occupied by an Arabian potentate and his nine concubines, and what they are doing is their normal siesta routine. Or suppose that no real sexual activity is going on at all, but rather a rehearsal of an amateur theatrical group for a spoof of contemporary sex movies. Or that the first perception of the situation was altogether in error: these people are wearing flesh-colored leotards and are practicing for a highly decorous modern dance performance.

What follows from this consideration is simple but of great methodological importance: sociological concepts cannot be models of thought imposed from without (as positivists of all descriptions are wont to do), but rather must relate to the typifications that are already operative in the situation being studied. All human situations carry meaning—if one prefers, are illuminated by meaning from within themselves. The purpose of sociological interpretation is to "bring out" these meanings more clearly, and to relate them (causally and otherwise) to other meanings and meaning systems. Using Schutzian language, sociological concepts are second-order constructs (the first-order constructs, of course, being the typifications, that the sociologist already finds within the situation). Or, using Weberian language, sociological concepts must be meaning-adequate (*sinnadaequat*)—that is, they must retain an intelligible connection with the meaningful intentions of the actors in the situation.

This understanding of the nature of social-scientific concepts was developed in great detail in Weber's theory of *ideal types*. All concepts in sociology are "ideal types." Their construction entails a peculiar *translation* of ordinary typifications into the scientific frame of reference. Therefore, they are not "real"—not "really out there"—but are "artificially" constructed for specific cognitive purposes. Take as an example two of Weber's own conceptual creations: *bureaucracy* and *inner-worldly asceticism*. Both are ideal types, in that they were carefully constructed by Weber for purposes of interpretation; neither is nor was "really out there" in the manner defined by Weber. There is a difference between them, though. There have been many individuals in modern societies who would readily say to themselves and to others, "I am a member of a bureaucracy." By contrast, no Puritan entrepreneur ever said to himself, "I am an inner-worldly ascetic." Thus the second concept is at a greater distance from the typifications of the "real" social world than the first. Yet both concepts are "meaning-adequate." A bureaucrat can readily recognize himself in Weber's construction of bureaucracy. And a Puritan entrepreneur, transported by time machine from colonial New England into Weber's Heidelberg study, would certainly have been puzzled by the *term* "inner-worldly asceticism," but, again, he would have had little difficulty recognizing his own moral world in Weber's delineation of it. The difference between the two concepts, and in their respective distance from the typifications of ordinary life, is due to a difference in Weber's cognitive purpose in the two cases. In his analysis of bureaucracy Weber was concerned with a phenomenon specific to the modern world; but the concept of inner-worldly asceticism was constructed in order to undertake comparisons and generalizations of moral systems ranging from ancient India to twentieth-century America, and consequently a more "distanced" concept *had* to be constructed.

It further follows that all sociological concepts have an *ad hoc* quality. They are constructed for a specific cognitive purpose, and they might be discarded for other purposes. Also, the empirical evidence "out there" may force their abandonment or modification. Thus, if the human beings to whom a concept is applied can *not* "recognize themselves" in it—in the case of living persons, by protesting verbally through their own definitions of their situation; in the case of people in the past, by what could be called "protesting texts"—then the sociologist will be constrained to construct new concepts that will be more adequate to the situation in question.

What has been done in all of this is that the meanings of ordinary life have been transposed into a *different* world of meanings, namely that of the social scientist. This transposition is at the core of sociological interpretation. It also constitutes an incipient *explanation* of the situation in question: the sociological interpreter now not only understands something, but understands it in a new way that was not possible before the transposition took place.

The issue of the outcome of conceptualization. Sociology from its beginnings has been haunted by the positivist ideal. This calls for the establishment of universal laws, in the fashion of the natural sciences, allowing for a system of causally connected relationships under which specific phenomena can be subsumed. If these laws are empirically valid, then the specific phenomena can be deduced from them as cases and predictions can be made as to their future course.

The previous description of conceptualization shows the weakness of this ideal. Social phenomena will inevitably be distorted if their inherent meanings are ignored. But this insight has further implications: laws are supposed to have universal validity; human meaning systems do not.

Take by way of example a sociologist's attempt to interpret political actions, undertaken by a particular group in a particular situation. Suppose that this interpretation is to follow a putative law that people vote in order to maximalize their own interests. This, of course, is not altogether false. But what people consider to be their own interests depends on their meaning systems—and these can *not* be deduced from the aforementioned law. For example, an observer may conclude that candidate X in a particular election clearly represents the interests of the majority of the voters in the district—in terms, say, of the economic policies being proposed by this candidate. But it so happens that the voters are not primarily concerned with economic issues. Rather, their attention is focused on ethnicity—and a large number of them have defined as their primary interest the election of candidates belonging to their own ethnic group, an affiliation that candidate X lacks. In other words, the interests in the situation are not the interests posited by the observer. The observer may well believe that these people's definition of the situation is irrational, even morally reprehensible, but this belief will be of no help whatever in interpreting this situation (and, not so incidentally, in predicting the outcome of the election).

Conceptualization as here understood can indeed assist in the establishment of causal connections ("candidate X lost the election because he is not Italian"), but only if the meanings operative in the situation are taken into account. The same, of course, goes for prediction.

Somewhat different from positivism is the functionalist ideal. This calls for the discovery of functions independent of what the actors in a social situation intend (the "latent functions" of Robert Merton; to discover the "manifest functions," of course, no great sociological explorations are needed, at least not in one's own society). Back to another earlier example: the underlying function of the sacrificial ritual around the volcano is not to ensure continuing rain but rather to serve the economic interests of the priesthood—say, because the ceremonies require expensive equipment, which is monopolistically produced and rented out for the occasion by the priestly caste.

Once again, this type of explanation is not to be rejected out of hand. But a distinction will have to be made (based, of course, on the empirical evidence). One possibility is that the priests are fully aware of these economic ramifications, indeed that this is why they or their predecessors invented the ritual in the first place. In that case, the economic interest is not a "latent function" at all—not for the priests, that is—but the manifest meaning of what they are doing. The other possibility (not at all uncommon) is that the priests—along with the general populace and (who knows?) perhaps even the about-to-be-sacrificed virgins—sincerely believe that the sole purpose of the operation is to induce the rain god to continue making rain. That is, the priests themselves (like so many sincere people) are not aware of their economic interests, do not define such interests as motives either to themselves or to others, and would violently resent it if such motives were imputed to them. In that case, the sociologist may well use a term such as "latent function." Or, using Weberian language, the sociologist may say that the economic benefits are "unintended consequences" of these actions. Both usages are acceptable, as long as it is clear that this is an explanation in the mind of the scientific observer only and is not imputed in any way to the social reality "out there." This should be even clearer if, in the tradition of Emile Durkheim and Anglo-American functionalism, the "latent function" of the ritual is explained in terms of the maintenance of collective solidarity (an explanation in which all the specifics of the ritual turn out to be incidental). In all cases of explanation in terms of "latency," the actors, of course, will not recognize themselves in the explanation—which is acceptable, just as long as such self-recognition is not imputed to them on some empirically unavailable level. (The question as to whether there might be "unconscious motives," in the psychoanalytic sense, cannot be pursued here.)

The issue of evidence. Evidence in sociology must always be framed in terms of meaning. More precisely, the second-order constructs of the scientific observer must be ongoingly related to the first-order constructs of ordinary life. Consequently, the falsification of the sociologist's hypotheses must also be framed in terms of meaning.

Back to the example of the election campaign: I (the sociologist analyzing the campaign) am interested in the chances of candidate X. In order to explore any hypothesis I may have in the matter, I must seek to understand the meanings in play in this particular district. Thus I have hypothesized that candidate X will win, because he represents the economic interests of the North End. But now I have gone out and discovered that most of the voters in the North End do not define their political interests in economic terms at all. My hypothesis is falsified precisely because it did not take cognizance of the meanings operative in the situation. I now modify it, and say, "Although candidate X represents the economic interests of the North End better than either of his two opponents, he will lose because he is Irish." Needless to say, that is still a hypothesis and not a statement of apodictic truth, and the prediction may turn out to be false on election day (thus it may happen that, as they enter the voting booth, a lot of these Italians suddenly remember their economic interests and bracket their ethnic enthusiasms and antagonisms for the next three minutes). That is, any social-scientific hypothesis is a statement of *probabilities*. (My hypothesis, incidentally, will remain probabilistic even after election day: I definitely know now that candidate X has lost the election; I can still only hypothesize *why* he lost.)

Sociological interpretation is not a philosophical enterprise. It is always subject to testing by empirical evidence. Sociological propositions are never axioms, but empirically falsifiable hypotheses. In that they are similar to propositions in all sciences. But evidence and falsification in sociology are not the same as in the natural sciences—precisely because they always involve meanings.

There is the further question as to the manner in which the evidence is gathered—in the parlance of American sociology, the question of *methods* (as against the question of *method*, in the sense of a general intellectual approach). For a long time this question has been posed in terms of qualitative versus quantitative methods. It is unfortunate that the understanding of sociological interpretation being presented here has often been coupled with an antagonism toward quantitative methods. That is a misunderstanding. *Nothing whatsoever in the present statement should be construed as implying a preference for qualitative over quantitative methods of empirical research.* There is nothing wrong whatever with quantitative methods—*as long as* they are used to clarify the meanings operative in the situation being studied. The choice between the two kinds of methods should, at least ideally, be based on nothing but their respective chances of obtaining the evidence being sought. (We know that, in a less than ideal world, there are also considerations of available resources and skills, but these are not considerations of methodological principle.) Thus, in the example, the decision may be made that, in order to delve into the minds of North End voters, an elaborate survey may be necessary—with the most rigorously designed and pretested questionnaire, its administration to a stratified sample of the voting population and the application of the most sophisticated statistical techniques to the ensuing data (including the use of the latest computer hardware). On the other hand, it may be decided that two or three thoroughly trained researchers hanging around the bars, stores and church halls of the North End may be quite enough to obtain the desired information. The decision will depend on cognitive as well as practical considerations, about which one cannot generalize. The point to be made here is that *either* the quantitative *or* the qualitative option may fully satisfy the sociological "rules of the game" in the acquisition of evidence.

The issue of objectivity. Interpretation, as proposed so far, has been understood by some critics of a positivistic persuasion as implying "pure subjectivism," "intuition" or "empathy"—that is, as an attempt to acquire knowledge without controls or correctives. Perhaps enough has been said already to show that this is a misunderstanding and that interpretation is not a guessing game where anything goes. The issue here, of course, is that of the objectivity of sociological interpretation, and the character of this objectivity needs to be spelled out a little further—and not only against positivistic critics who want to introduce criteria of objectivity derived from the natural sciences, but also against critics of altogether different persuasion, who deny that objectivity of any sort is possible in the interpretation of social reality.

The social location, the psychological constitution and the cognitive peculiarities of an interpreter are inevitably involved in the act of interpretation, and all of them will affect the interpretation. Thus, as I interpret the orgiastic goings-on in that hotel, I must reckon with certain facts—such as that I am an upwardly mobile middle-class Protestant Midwesterner, that I am a woman in my late twenties just emerged from a painful love affair that has made me suspicious of academic men, that I will avoid statistical methods if at all possible because I can't add, and that I have a consuming desire to disprove the Schulze-Merriwether hypothesis on sexual deviance (Schulze is a former roommate of mine and I hate her guts). Now, it would clearly be foolish to assert that all such factors can always be controlled by the conscientious sociologist, and that objectivity means that factors of this kind have been antiseptically removed from the interpretative enterprise. That, however, is not the point.

Rather, the point is that the sociologist can control these factors, certainly in principle and to a large degree in fact, by adhering to the previously discussed rules of scientific relevance structure and evidence. The scientific relevance structure first of all means that I can tell myself, "I am now doing sociology"—and *ipso facto* am *not* expressing my petty-bourgeois morality, my resentments against *homo academicus*, or my wish to prove Schulze wrong. But much more is involved than a pious intention to be objective if I can. The scientific relevance structure brings with it a body of empirical knowledge that must be taken into account in any specific interpretation. The same relevance structure provides the context of any concepts generated by the interpreter. These concepts must have explanatory uses, bringing the new to-be-interpreted phenomena into a meaningful relation with comparable phenomena previously interpreted by other sociologists. This relation does not spring arbitrarily from the interpreter's subjectivity. It rests on a generally available body of theory and data, and it must be ongoingly established in interaction with new empirical evidence. The empirical data, my own and those of others, always "have their say," although they "speak" within the conceptual scheme that I (and others) have constructed. Objectivity, then, does *not* mean that the sociologist reports on "raw facts" that are "out there" in and of themselves. Rather, objectivity means that the sociologist's conceptual scheme is in a dialectical relationship with the empirical data.

The classical case of Max Weber's work on "inner-worldly asceticism" may once more be cited. Various biographers have tried to illuminate Weber's social, psychological and other extrascientific "interests" in the question of the relationship of religious morality to the origins of modern capitalism. Yet the concept and the vast assemblage of hypotheses it has generated have been used and continue to be used by social scientists and historians who share none of Weber's extrascientific concerns. And the question of whether the famous "Protestant ethic thesis" is or is not objectively valid as an interpretation of certain facets of modern history cannot be decided as a result of any amount of delving into Weber's biography or psyche.

Put differently, *scientific objectivity is a specific relevance structure into which an individual can shift in his or her consciousness.* Those who deny that such a shift is possible must also deny the *general* possibility of shifts of relevance within consciousness—but such a denial would be in palpable contradiction to ordinary experience as well as scientific evidence. Thus we know that such shifts do in fact occur all the time even in ordinary life. Sexuality once again may serve as a very clear example: I am talking about a matter of shared political interest with an individual of the opposite sex. As the conversation proceeds, I become aware of a strong, possibly mutual physical attraction. From that point on the relevance structure of the conversation shifts drastically, and what began as, say, a campaign planning session is transformed into a seduction strategy. Or, conversely, I may be engaged in a highly erotic exchange when the other individual voices a political opinion that I find highly objectionable. Since I am a person who is very *engagé* politically, I find it impossible to continue my erotic focus in the face of this suddenly revealed political disagreement. I begin to argue politically, and as I do this (no wonder) I lose the sensation of physical attraction (at least temporarily). In other words, in ordinary life sexuality provides a relevance structure *into which* and *out of which* I can move with considerable ease. One may add that, unless I am either a sex maniac or (in the aforementioned example) a political fanatic, I can control these movements to a considerable extent.

This is true *a fortiori* of the scientific relevance structure. It is characterized by a much higher degree of awareness and controls, which can be learned and internalized by the scientific interpreter. Indeed, just this is one of the most important things one should learn in the course of sociological training. But also, very importantly, this specific relevance structure is *institutionalized.* This happens in what Charles Peirce called the *community of investigators.* In the case of the sociologist, there is the community of sociologists, both living and dead, who are "present" in consciousness as a sort of scientific "generalized other." In slightly different language, the community of sociologists, "the discipline," provides a "reference group" with which every individual sociologist ongoingly interacts, both externally by means of social relations, but also within the mind. Objectivity, not just as an ideal but ever again as an experienced reality, is the result of this ongoing interaction between the individual sociologist and the community of sociologists. By the very nature of scientific activity, the body of objective knowledge thus accumulated is never finally fixed, is always tentative and subject to revision, even revision made necessary by the uncovering of extra-scientific interests. None of this revisionist activity, however, negates the methodological principle of objectivity. On the contrary, it bears witness to its perduring validity—for, if science did not strive for objectivity, no revisions would be necessary in the first place.

The objectivity of sociological interpretation is closely related to what Max Weber called *value-freeness*—a concept that has been endlessly and often confusedly debated. We know that in ordinary life people's interpretations are bound by their values. In principle, this is also true of sociologists. They are, after all, members of society and participate in its values. Clearly, in many cases these values will provide the motives by which a sociologist became interested in a particular phenomenon to begin with. Thus, for example, it is quite clear that many if not most American sociologists who studied phenomena of race did so because the racial patterns of American society offended their values. Not only is it not wrong that such motives affect the work of sociologists, but it is inevitable. That is not the point. Rather, the point is that once these sociologists embark on their scientific inquiry, they must "bracket" these values as much as possible—not, needless to say, in the sense of giving them up or trying to forget them, but in the sense of controlling the way in which these values might distort the sociological vision. If such bracketing is not done, the scientific enterprise collapses, and what the sociologist then believes to perceive is nothing but a mirror image of his own hopes and fears, wishes, resentments or other psychic needs; what he will then *not* perceive is anything that can reasonably be called social reality.

This bracketing cannot be guaranteed by rigorous research methods. These can be influenced by values as much as less rigorous methods—even resentments can be quantified! Value-freeness is a cognitive act of a different order. In a way, it is an ascetic ideal—a certain asceticism of the mind—and it is often hard to achieve, especially of course in cases where one's own values are strongly engaged. It is above all a *passion to see*, to see clearly, regardless of one's likes or dislikes, hopes or fears. The bracketing of one's own values implies a systematic openness to the values of others as they are relevant to the situation being studied—even if these values are quite repugnant to oneself: seeing is not approving, but I cannot see at all if I constantly voice my own disapproval.

To strive for objectivity and value-freeness is to erect a crucial safeguard against dogmatism in science. A useful rule for doing this is the one suggested by Karl Popper—the constant and systematic search for falsifying data: that is, when I propose a hypothesis—precisely because I know that there may be values of mine that are relevant to the proposition—the most important thing that I must do is to search for those data that may falsify rather than support my hypothesis. Summing up on this issue: we agree with the positivists that there is such a thing as scientific objectivity (even if in practice it is often difficult to achieve). We disagree with the positivists in insisting that the objectivity of an interpretative science cannot be the same as the objectivity of the natural sciences. As to the critics of sociological objectivity from the other side, radical antipositivists who deny the possibility of any separation of values from scientific inquiry (such as is common today among various people who would like to ideologize sociology and turn it into an instrument of advocacy), we agree with them that extrascientific interests often interfere with the act of interpretation, as we also agree that such interferences ought to be uncovered. We disagree that these facts negate either the principle or the practical possibility of an objective social science. Further aspects of this position of ours will be taken up again in the next chapter.

The issue of applicability. Almost all knowledge about society can be applied by somebody in the service of this or that pragmatic project. This is unavoidable. But it is all the more important to understand the following: sociological interpretation is the result of a very specific cognitive process, within the specific relevance structure outlined above. As soon as the contents of this interpretation are to be applied to *action* in society, this relevance structure is abandoned. All action presupposes an altogether different relevance structure. Among other things, what must be abandoned now is the bracketing of one's own values. All application is necessarily value-based. Thus, for example, I can write a sociological treatise detailing, say, the patterns of race relations in a particular American community while bracketing my own racial values—which, let us assume, are liberal and therefore in tension with various illiberal features of the *status quo*. Suppose that my inquiry has produced further knowledge of the situation. It is inconceivable that this knowledge can be applied to action without reference to my values; indeed the likelihood is that I will now act in order to maximize the realization of my liberal values in this particular situation. But it also follows that there is no way by which "what ought to be done" can be directly deduced from my previous sociological interpretation. Thus I may have discovered in my study that there is a specific income gap as between comparable groups of whites and blacks in this community, and my value position leads me to deplore this finding. But, as I want to move now from interpretation to action, a number of possible courses of action are open to me—legal action to enforce nondiscrimination laws or affirmative action guidelines, unionization, special training and retraining programs, encouraging black business enterprise, and yet others. My choice among these various possibilities will be affected by considerations of values as well as practical feasibility assessments, and my choice will of course *also* be affected by various other items of sociological knowledge. But it will not be possible for me to say, to myself or to others, "This is what I have found; *therefore*, this is what ought to be done."

One of the abuses of sociology has been the ignoring of this indirect relation between understanding and action, of the shift in relevance structure necessitated by the movement from the first to the second. It is in consequence of this confusion that sociological concepts or findings are then used as *legitimations* of courses of action that are based on particular values. That is, sociology has been used to hide the value-presuppositions of this or that course of action. For example, it is one thing to state that a majority of both whites and blacks disapprove, say, of interracial marriage, quite another thing to say that *therefore* there ought to be laws forbidding interracial marriage—or, on the contrary, that *therefore* there ought to be educational programs to promote them.

A methodological and a moral imperative come together here in certain requirements by which sociologists ought to abide: One, that it be made clear that sociological knowledge is of a peculiar kind, deriving from a specific scientific frame of reference that is *different* from the frame of reference of the man in the street, the political activist or anyone else. (This is not just an individual matter, but a concern of the vocation of sociologist as a profession.) Two, that sociologists cannot make recommendations except in an "if . . . then" form, which is itself an interpretative process—"If you want to achieve goal *x, then* these findings of mine are relevant to your choice of possible actions." Three, no normative implications can be directly drawn from sociological concepts or findings; in other words, the sociologist cannot be a moral guide.

It goes without saying that, lengthy though this chapter is, it has not exhausted the ramifications of what is involved in the act of sociological interpretation. One final point, though: interpretation, as described here, may be found in different schools of sociology—including various groupings of Marxists, Durkheimians and structural functionalists. Sociological interpretation, in other words, is not a "sectarian" property. Nevertheless, as has been made amply clear, we believe that the Weberian tradition offers the most satisfactory approach to this matter, as it also evinces the most sophisticated awareness of the precarious relations between understanding and values on the one hand, and of understanding and responsible action on the other.

Body Ritual among the Nacirema

Horace Miner

The anthropologist has become so familiar with the diversity of ways in which different peoples behave in similar situations that he is not apt to be surprised by even the most exotic customs. In fact, if all of the logically possible combinations of behavior have not been found somewhere in the world, he is apt to suspect that they must be present in some yet undescribed tribe. This point has, in fact, been expressed with respect to clan organization by Murdock (1949:71). In this light, the magical beliefs and practices of the Nacirema present such unusual aspects that it seems desirable to describe them as an example of the extremes to which human behavior can go.

Professor Linton first brought the ritual of the Nacirema to the attention of anthropologists twenty years ago (1936:326), but the culture of this people is still very poorly understood. They are a North American group living in the territory between the Canadian Cree, the Yaqui and Tarahumare of Mexico, and the Carib and Arawak of the Antilles. Little is known of their origin, although tradition states that they came from the east. According to Nacirema mythology, their nation was originated by a culture hero, Notgnihsaw, who is otherwise known for two great feats of strength—the throwing of a piece of wampum across the river Pa-To-Mac and the chopping down of a cherry tree in which the Spirit of Truth resided.

Nacirema culture is characterized by a highly developed market economy which has evolved in a rich natural habitat. While much of the people's time is devoted to economic pursuits, a large part of the fruits of these labors and a considerable portion of the day are spent in ritual activity. The focus of this activity is the human body, the appearance and health of which loom as a dominant concern in the ethos of the people. While such a concern is certainly not unusual, its ceremonial aspects and associated philosophy are unique.

The fundamental belief underlying the whole system appears to be that the human body is ugly and that its natural tendency is to debility and disease. Incarcerated in such a body, man's only hope is to avert these characteristics through the use of the powerful influences of ritual and ceremony. Every household has one or more shrines devoted to this purpose. The more powerful individuals in the society have several shrines in their houses and, in fact, the opulence of a house is often referred to in terms of the number of such ritual centers it possesses. Most houses are of wattle and daub construction, but the shrine

Source: Horace Miner, "Body Ritual among the Nacirema," *American Anthropologist*, Vol. 58, 1956, pp. 503–507.

rooms of the more wealthy are walled with stone. Poorer families imitate the rich by applying pottery plaques to their shrine walls.

While each family has at least one such shrine, the rituals associated with it are not family ceremonies but are private and secret. The rites are normally only discussed with children, and then only during the period when they are being initiated into these mysteries. I was able, however, to establish sufficient rapport with the natives to examine these shrines and to have the rituals described to me.

The focal point of the shrine is a box or chest which is built into the wall. In this chest are kept the many charms and magical potions without which no native believes he could live. These preparations are secured from a variety of specialized practitioners. The most powerful of these are the medicine men, whose assistance must be rewarded with substantial gifts. However, the medicine men do not provide the curative potions for their clients, but decide what the ingredients should be and then write them down in an ancient and secret language. This writing is understood only by the medicine men and by the herbalists who, for another gift, provide the required charm.

The charm is not disposed of after it has served its purpose, but is placed in the charm-box of the household shrine. As these magical materials are specific for certain ills, and the real or imagined maladies of the people are many, the charm-box is usually full to overflowing. The magical packets are so numerous that people forget what their purposes were and fear to use them again. While the natives are very vague on this point, we can only assume that the idea in retaining all the old magical materials is that their presence in the charm-box, before which the body rituals are conducted, will in some way protect the worshipper.

Beneath the charm-box is a small font. Each day every member of the family, in succession, enters the shrine room, bows his head before the charm-box, mingles different sorts of holy waters are secured from the Water Temple of the community, where the priests conduct elaborate ceremonies to make the liquid ritually pure.

In the hierarchy of magical practitioners, and below the medicine men in prestige, are specialists whose designation is best translated "holy-mouth-men." The Nacirema have an almost pathological horror of and fascination with the mouth, the condition of which is believed to have a supernatural influence on all social relationships. Were it not for the rituals of the mouth, they believe that their teeth would fall out, their gums bleed, their jaws shrink, their friends desert them, and their lovers reject them. They also believe that a strong relationship exists between oral and moral characteristics. For example, there is a ritual ablution of the mouth for children which is supposed to improve their moral fiber.

The daily body ritual performed by everyone includes a mouth-rite. Despite the fact that these people are so punctilious about care of the mouth, this rite involves a practice which strikes the uninitiated stranger as revolting. It was reported to me that the ritual consists of inserting a small bundle of hog hairs into the mouth, along with certain magical powders, and then moving the bundle in a highly formalized series of gestures.

In addition to the private mouth-rite, the people seek out a holy-mouth-man once or twice a year. These practitioners have an impressive set of paraphernalia, consisting of a variety of augers, awls, probes, and prods. The use of the objects in the exorcism of the evils of the mouth involves almost unbelievable ritual torture of the client. The holy-mouth-man opens the client's mouth and, using the above mentioned tools, enlarges any holes which decay may have created in the teeth. Magical materials are put into these holes. If there are not naturally occurring holes in the teeth, large sections of one or more teeth are gouged out so that the supernatural substance can be applied. In the client's view, the purpose of these ministrations is to arrest decay and to draw friends. The extremely sacred and traditional character of the rite is evident in the fact that the natives return to the holy-mouth-men year after year, despite the fact that their teeth continue to decay.

It is to be hoped that, when a thorough study of the Nacirema is made, there will be careful inquiry into the personality structure of these people. One has but to watch the gleam in the eye of a holy-mouth-man, as he jabs an awl into an exposed nerve, to suspect that a certain amount of sadism is involved. If this can be established, a very interesting pattern emerges, for most of the population shows definite masochistic tendencies. It was to these that Professor Linton referred in discussing a distinctive part of the daily body ritual which is performed only by men. This part of the rite involves scraping and lacerating the surface of the face with a sharp instrument. Special women's rites are performed only four times during each lunar month, but what they lack in frequency is made up in barbarity. As part of this ceremony, women bake their heads in small ovens for about an hour. The theoretically interesting point is that what seems to be a preponderantly masochistic people have developed sadistic specialists.

The medicine men have an imposing temple, or *latipso*, in every community of any size. The more elaborate ceremonies required to treat very sick patients can only be performed at this temple. These ceremonies involve not only the thaumaturge but a permanent group of vestal maidens who move sedately about the temple chambers in distinctive costume and headdress.

The *latipso* ceremonies are so harsh that it is phenomenal that a fair proportion of the really sick natives who enter the temple ever recover. Small children whose indoctrination is still incomplete have been known to resist attempts to take them to the temple because "that is where you go to die." Despite this fact, sick adults are not only willing but eager to undergo the protracted ritual purification, if they can afford to do so. No matter how ill the supplicant or how grave the emergency, the guardians of many temples will not admit a client if he cannot give a rich gift to the custodian. Even after one has gained admission and survived the ceremonies, the guardians will not permit the neophyte to leave until he makes still another gift.

The supplicant entering the temple is first stripped of all his or her clothes. In everyday life the Nacirema avoids exposure of his body and its natural functions. Bathing and excretory acts are performed only in the secrecy of the household shrine, where they are ritualized as part of the body-rites. Psychological shock results from the fact that body secrecy is suddenly lost upon entry into the *latipso*. A man, whose own wife has never seen him in an excretory act, suddenly finds himself naked and assisted by a vestal maiden while he performs his natural functions into a sacred vessel. This sort of ceremonial treatment is necessitated by the fact that the excreta are used by a diviner to ascertain the course and nature of the client's sickness. Female clients, on the other hand, find their naked bodies are subjected to the scrutiny, manipulation and prodding of the medicine men.

Few supplicants in the temple are well enough to do anything but lie on their hard beds. The daily ceremonies, like the rites of the holy-mouth-men, involve discomfort and torture. With ritual precision, the vestals awaken their miserable charges each dawn and roll them about on their beds of pain while performing ablutions, in the formal movements of which the maidens are highly trained. At other times they insert magic wands in the supplicant's mouth or force him to eat substances which are supposed to be healing. From time to time the medicine men come to their clients and jab magically treated needles into their flesh. The fact that these temple ceremonies may not cure, and may even kill the neophyte, in no way decreases the people's faith in the medicine men.

There remains one other kind of practitioner, known as a "listener." This witch-doctor has the power to exorcise the devils that lodge in the heads of people who have been bewitched. The Nacirema believe that parents bewitch their own children. Mothers are particularly suspected of putting a curse on children while teaching them the secret body rituals. The counter-magic of the witch-doctor is unusual in its lack of ritual. The patient simply tells the "listener" all his troubles and fears, beginning with the earliest difficulties he can remember. The memory displayed by the Nacirema in these exorcism sessions is truly remarkable. It is not uncommon for the patient to bemoan the rejection he felt upon being weaned as a babe, and a few individuals even see their troubles going back to the traumatic effects of their own birth.

In conclusion, mention must be made of certain practices which have their base in native esthetics but which depend upon the pervasive aversion to the natural body and its functions. There are ritual fasts to make fat people thin and ceremonial feasts to make thin people fat. Still other rites are used to make women's breasts larger if they are small, and smaller if they are large. General dissatisfaction with breast shape is symbolized in the fact that the ideal form is virtually outside the range of human variation. A few women afflicted with almost inhuman hypermammary development are so idolized that they make a handsome living by simply going from village to village and permitting the natives to stare at them for a fee.

Reference has already been made to the fact that excretory functions are ritualized, routinized, and relegated to secrecy. Natural reproductive functions are similarly distorted. Intercourse is taboo as a topic and scheduled as an act. Efforts are made to avoid pregnancy by the use of magical materials or by limiting intercourse to certain phases of the moon. Conception is actually very infrequent. When pregnant, women dress so as to hide their condition. Parturition takes place in secret, without friends or relatives to assist, and the majority of women do not nurse their infants.

Our review of the ritual life of the Nacirema has certainly shown them to be a magic-ridden people. It is hard to understand how they have managed to exist so long under the burdens which they have imposed upon themselves. But with the insight provided by Malinowski when he wrote (1948:70):

> Looking from far and above, from our high places of safety in the developed civilization, it is easy to see all the crudity and irrelevance of magic. But without its power and guidance early man could not have mastered his practical difficulties as he has done, nor could man have advanced to the higher stages of civilization.

References

Linton, Ralph. 1936. *The Study of Man*. New York, D. Appleton-Century Co.

Malinowski, Bronislaw. 1948. *Magic, Science, and Religion*. Glenco, The Free Press.

Murdock, George P. 1949. *Social Structure*. New York, The Macmillan Co.

Drill, Grill and Chill

Maureen Dowd

WASHINGTON—We want big. We want fast. We want far. We want now. We want 345 horsepower in a V-8 engine and 15 miles per gallon on the highway.

We drive behemoths. We drive them alone. This country was not built on H.O.V. lanes.

We don't have limits. We have liberties.

If we don't wear our seat belts, it doesn't matter, because we have air bags. If the air bags don't deploy, it doesn't matter, because our cars are so beefy, we'll never get bruised. If we need to widen the streets for our all-wheel drives, we will. If we need to reinforce all the bridges in the country, so that they don't buckle and collapse under our 5,800-pound S.U.V.'s, our engineers will do that.

We'll bake the earth. We'll brown & serve it, sauté it, simmer it, sear it, fondue it, George-Foreman-grill it. (We invented the Foreman grill.) We might one day bring the earth to a boil and pull it like taffy. (We invented taffy.)

If rising seas obliterate the coasts, our marine geologists will sculpt new ones and Hollywood will get bright new ideas for disaster movies. If we get charred by the sun, our dermatologists will replace our skin.

If the globe gets warmer, we'll turn up the air-conditioning. (We invented air-conditioning.) We'll drive faster in our gigantic, air-conditioned cars to the new beaches that our marine geologists create.

We will let our power plants spew any chemicals we deem necessary to fire up our Interplaks, our Krups, our Black & Deckers and our Fujitsu Plasmavisions.

We will drill for oil whenever and wherever we please. If tourists don't like rigs off the coast of Florida, they can go fly fishing in Wyoming. We won't be deterred by a few Arctic terns. We don't care about caribou. We don't care for cardigans. Give us our 69 degrees, winter and summer. Let there be light—no timers, no freaky-shaped long-life bulbs. (We invented the light bulb.)

We want our refrigerators cold and our freezers colder. Bring on the freon. Banish those irritating toilets that restrict flow. When we flush, we flush all the way.

We will perfect the dream of nuclear power. We will put our toxic waste wherever we want, whenever we waste it. We have whole states with nothing better to do than serve as

Source: Maureen Dowd, "Drill, Grill and Chill," *The New York Times*, May 20, 2001, Op-Ed-Page.

ancestral burial grounds for our effluvium. It can fester in those wide open spaces for thousands of years.

We will have the biggest, baddest missiles, and we will point them in any direction we like, across the galaxies, through eternity, forever and ever.

We will thrust as many satellites as we want into outer space, and we will surround them with a firewall of weapons for their protection.

We will guarantee broadband and fast connections to the Internet. We will not permit anybody, anywhere, at any time to threaten the delivery of all the necessities to computers, Palm Pilots and BlackBerrys: stock quotes, sports scores, real estate listings, epicurean.com recipes, porn. (O.K., so we didn't invent porn.)

By arming space, and protecting satellites, we ensure life, liberty and the pursuit of happiness—our 500 TV channels drawn from the ether.

We will secure the inalienable right of every citizen driving by himself in his big car to be guided by a global positioning system. Nobody should have to call in advance for directions to a party when the satellite can show the way.

We will modify food in any way we want and send it to any country we see fit at prices that we and we alone determine in the cargo ships we choose at the time we set.

Our international banking arm—the World Bank and the I.M.F.—will support whatever dictatorships suit us best.

We will fly up any coast of any nation on earth with any plane filled with any surveillance equipment and top guns that we possess.

We will build superduperjumbo jets so Brobdingnagian that runways will be crushed under their weight at the most congested airports in the history of aviation. (We invented aviation.)

We will buy, carry, conceal and shoot firearms whenever and wherever we want, as is our constitutionally guaranteed right. (We invented the Constitution.) We will kill any criminal we want, by lethal injection or electrocution. (We invented electricity.)

We are America.

'Apocalypse' Then, and Now

This work gives us a **view** of the complex aspects of the major art form of our culture

David Thomson

By 1976, Francis Ford Coppola had made the two parts of "The Godfather" and "The Conversation." He had won the Oscar for best picture twice and for best director once and, in 1974, he had had two films—"The Godfather Part II" and "The Conversation"—nominated for best picture. It was easy to think that he had made it in every way: whether he did something large, grand and public, or something small, private and artistic, he was a champion. He was very rich, still young, and he had become a kind of god in the San Francisco area. In an age crowded with film students, his protégé George Lucas had already made "American Graffiti" and was off to England to shoot a thing called "Star Wars."

Then something intervened. A time of war, hell and disaster; a time of madness. It was a kind of irony, Mr. Coppola reckoned, that Mr. Lucas had been in on it from the beginning, the late 1960's, when the Vietnam War had seemed out of control and a whole gang of them had been in Los Angeles, former students at U.C.L.A. or U.S.C. It was then that George Lucas and John Milius had started talking about a Vietnam picture. Mr. Milius, who loved heroes, guns, the military and great stories involving all of them, had wanted to tell a strong story about the ordinary American soldier in Vietnam. And he'd seen the 1902 Joseph Conrad novella "The Heart of Darkness" as a model—how a man named Marlow goes up a dark river in the Congo to find a trader named Kurtz, who has gone mad and become like a rogue emperor.

Mr. Milius would, he said later, work on the project longer than anyone. His story became that of Willard, a young officer, sent upriver in Vietnam to find and eliminate—"to terminate with prejudice"—the brilliant but mad Colonel Kurtz, who has set up his own kingdom. George Lucas was going to direct, at first. But there was a failing out between Mr. Lucas and Mr. Coppola. The protégé thought he was being patronized. So he elected to try "Star Wars" instead. There was a hunt for other directors, but somehow the project

Source: David Thomson, "'Apocalypse' Then, and Now," *The New York Times*, May 13, 2001. Arts Section.

had fallen to Mr. Coppola. His wife, Eleanor, marveled that once upon a time he had said that the Vietnam film would be such fun after the stress and intrigue of the "Godfather" movies. It would be a picnic. So they went to the Philippines.

Two years later, in April 1978, the Coppolas were living a steady hell, hardly noticing the beauty around their home in Rutherford, Calif., in the Napa Valley. On the 13th, Mr. Coppola's 39th birthday, she found a loving card from another woman in his life. A few days earlier, her husband had told Ms. Coppola that he felt paralyzed. She was asking him to sort out their marriage and their life. United Artists was saying hurry up, finish the film, it's costing us too much. But Mr. Coppola admitted to his wife that he couldn't find an answer or an ending—the more he reached out, the more it receded. "Working on the ending he said, "is like trying to crawl up glass by your fingernails."

The film was "Apocalypse Now," though some mocking articles had already called it "Apocalypse Never." No one was used to a film needing so much time, or being so endlessly talked about. It was back in November 1975, after all, that Steve McQueen had said that the role of Willard wasn't really right for him. Marlon Brando had declared that he had no interest in playing the small role of Kurtz. So they offered the part to McQueen, but he said he wanted $3 million. That was a deal they had to refuse. Willard was proposed to Al Pacino, James Caan, Jack Nicholson, Robert Redford.

By March 1976, when the Coppola family went to the Philippines for what was meant to be a relaxed, five-month shoot, Harvey Keitel was Willard and Mr. Brando had yielded to Kurtz. The film was budgeted at about $13 million—"The Godfather" had cost $6 million only four years earlier. But this time, Mr. Coppola was raising the money himself. He would own the picture. Mr. Brando was to get $1 million up front, $250,000 a week if his schedule ran over, and 11.3 percent of the gross receipts once they passed $8.85 million.

MAYBE it's only when you own a picture yourself that the troubles really pile up—or maybe it's the gods deciding you've done well enough already and designing a continent ready to trap rash Americans, but there was a devastating typhoon that destroyed sets. Mr. Keitel was replaced, not because he wasn't a good actor but because he had been miscast (no matter that he'd been a marine). Martin Sheen came on board, and worked so hard he had a heart attack. As for Mr. Coppola, he lost his way somehow—he ran into a heart of darkness in his own project. As the story became a metaphor for everything, for America and himself, he lost control. He wasn't sure what the story meant or how it should end. He became involved with other women. He began to use drugs. The crisis grew and spread. Five months turned into 238 days, and $13 million had become $30 million, much of it borrowed from United Artists, which felt bound to back up its initial gamble. (The studio had bought the United States distribution rights.) So Mr. Coppola owned not quite the movie but its huge debt.

On May 21, 1979, though still described as a work in progress, the movie had its premiere at the Cannes International Film Festival. At the news conference, Mr. Coppola issued a statement: "Apocalypse Now" was not "about" Vietnam.

"It is Vietnam," he said. "And the way we made it was very much like the way the Americans were in Vietnam. We were in the jungle, we had access to too much money, too much equipment, and little by little we went insane."

It was a bold (or desperate) admission that seemed to echo the foreboding in the American press commentaries that Mr. Coppola had attacked at Cannes. Several writers had picked up the war metaphor, saying the film had been made with just the muddle that doomed America in Vietnam. There were hints of Mr. Coppola's own turmoil, or break-down, and they would be filled out later in the year, when Eleanor Coppola published "Notes," her anguished diary on the making of the film. Mr. Coppola had once encouraged her to do the book, but it helped paint the picture of an exhausted, ruined man.

The Cannes jury had awarded the film its Palme d'Or (shared with Volker Schlöndorff's "Tin Drum"), but United Artists felt that the prize could be the kiss of death in the domestic market. They noted that the ending of the film shown at Cannes was unclear, even though the running time was already close to two and a half hours. No one doubted the impact of the spectacle or the vivid early sequence with Robert Duvall's Colonel Kilgore and the air cavalry destroying a village so they can surf on its beach. But what exactly was Mr. Brando's Kurtz doing or saying, and what did it mean? They weren't alone. In the spring of 1979, Mr. Coppola himself remained uncertain about the ending—and everyone was afraid of the film becoming too long. So cuts and compromises were made, and no one had the nerve to take more time or make the film slower.

The American premiere was set for Aug. 15, and the greeting was mixed. In Time magazine, Frank Rich called it "emotionally obtuse and intellectually empty." In The New York Times, Vincent Canby said the effect was of "something borrowed and not yet fully understood." This response was sharpened by one more unwitting sign of confusion in the movie itself: there were two endings—the death of Kurtz and Willard's escape on 70 millimeter (which had no credits), and then, on 35 millimeter, the credits playing over infrared footage of an air attack destroying the Kurtz compound. United Artists had urged that that costly shoot be used in some way, and the credits needed something. The critics felt that the confusion was characteristic.

For audiences, it didn't matter too much. There was such curiosity to see the movie—and so much of it was already stunning and moving. On its first American release, the film grossed $75 million. But before Mr. Coppola could get his own hands on any money, U.A. had to be paid off for its investment and for promotional costs. Also, by December 1984, the percentage paid to Mr. Brando totaled more than $6.5 million. Still, the picture would eventually turn a profit. It was also nominated for eight Oscars. But it was defeated for best picture and best director (by Robert Benton's "Kramer v. Kramer"), winning only for cinematography (Vittorio Storaro) and sound (Walter Murch, Mark Berger, Richard Marks and Nat Boxer).

Time passes. Francis and Eleanor Coppola are still married. Their home at Rutherford adjoins the successful Niebaum-Coppola winery. There were hard times in the early 80's, after the failure of his experimental romance "One From the Heart" and the closing of his studio in Los Angeles. Mr. Coppola was nearly bankrupt.

A son, Gio, died in a horrible boating accident. Their daughter, Sofia, became an actress and later, with "The Virgin Suicides," a director. Mr. Coppola is now 62, and it is a long time since he made a film as good as his best. Well, making films is hard, and there have been many great directors who have had glory years and then something less. Rutherford has become his plantation.

But now history asks to be amended.

Restored films and directors' cuts are too often a fraud, pretexts for commercial rerelease. The second thoughts don't amount to much and rather support the idea that it is part of being an artist to make the crucial decisions at the living moment. But what Mr. Coppola and his old friend and editor, Walter Murch, have now done is not simply to exercise calm and reflection when 1978–79 was a scene of dismay and uncertainty. Nor is it just that they've restored 53 minutes of original footage to "Apocalypse Now Redux," which Miramax will release on Aug. 15, 22 years after the original. It's rather more that they have finally trusted and freed the proper film. Even those who were never persuaded by the original may now find it not just a new film but a masterpiece. We all grow older.

Consider Aurore Clément. She is a French actress, and she was part of an entire sequence cut from the film—the French plantation scene. It took weeks to shoot, and it required a beautiful set—the plantation house that Willard and his crew discover as they go upriver. Like the rest of the sets, the interiors were designed by Dean Tavoularis; later, he and Ms. Clément were married. So she got that much out of the picture. But she later attended a preview and only then found that her work was all gone—because it seemed to get in the way of the action and broke the rule, "Don't get off the boat." She has had to wait 22 years to see what she was like—and now she's a middle-aged woman looking back on her own youth.

The plantation looms out of dense river fog. At first it is just a Frenchman's voice telling the Americans to lay down their arms. The place is like a dream, and its survival as a French enclave as late as 1969 is neither explained nor justified. There's nothing wrong with that: the journey upriver was meant to go beyond reality and into the *heart of darkness* [italics mine] and nightmare. So the plantation is the past, and the possibility of a future—and that's more palpable now, two decades later, when we can try Vietnam as tourists.

But the plantation is so much more. The Americans are invited to dinner—it is magical, with soft light and sophisticated sauces—and the patriarch, Philippe de Marais (Christian Marquand, who died last November) gives Willard, and the audience, a lesson in history. The French knew Indochina. They watched the Americans create the Vietminh in 1945 to undermine colonialism—and the Vietminh became the Vietcong. The French, he says, are part of the country: "We stay because this is ours. You Americans fight for the biggest nothing in history."

Mr. Coppola wrote those lines himself, to fit a scene from John Milius's original screenplay. The point surprises Willard, and it had not really been digested in 1979. But now it helps us place the war in history. It makes the ferocity of the men seem more futile—the soldiers whose language preferred the numbing "terminate with prejudice" to "kill." And it leaves breathing room for an older, less macho culture and a feminine touch.

Aurore Clément plays Roxanne (Marais's widowed daughter-in-law) as a watchful face during the meal. There are glances between her and Willard to suggest interest, but there is something else to Roxanne—the patience to wait until the men stop talking. Then she goes to Willard, by candlelight, for a brief love scene. It may sound obvious, but the feeling is subtle and merciful in a film hitherto marked by growing male frenzy. The change of tone is like a slow movement in a charged, rampant symphony. It does not halt the work, but it offers a gentleness that opens us up for the final explosion.

When the mission resumes, Willard is sadder, or more vulnerable, because of Roxanne. The hysteria of male posturing has been offset. In a crucial way, the title of the movie—"Apocalypse Now"—was always part of a lip-smacking male defiance. And as the story goes on we can believe that while something terrible is going to happen, still, "Apocalypse" is a strident, adolescent word for it. After all the sound and fury, something softer and more enduring abides—and we have felt it in Roxanne's presence.

The French plantation scene is not just fascinating and challenging in what it says. In its mood and emotion it evokes the largeness of life, like the sunlight that must have shone some days at Auschwitz. And if Mr. Coppola and Mr. Murch and the others could not quite see that in 1979, it's only because filmmakers can be like soldiers. They sometimes lose their minds and their judgment.

There are other restorations, and they are all significant. Early on, we see a little more of Mr. Duvall's Kilgore, and it helps tip him away from heroism and toward madness. Then Willard steals Kilgore's precious surfboard. That seems a small thing, but it endears him to his crew and it helps expose Kilgore (pursuing by helicopter) as a ranting demon.

There is more of the Playboy bunnies who arrive in the middle of hell to entertain the troops. Willard and the crew meet up with two of them after the dance number at a desolate, rain-drenched Medivac camp. He trades with their boss (Bill Graham): fuel for the women's sexual favors. Chef (Frederic Forrest) has a brief scene with one playmate (Colleen Camp) that is funny, touching and another reminder of the other side of life. This sequence was barely shot, and its place in the new version depends upon Walter Murch's ingenuity at making something with fragments.

And what of Kurtz? For most people, he—or Mr. Brando—was the biggest problem with the picture. No matter his remarkable deal, or his history with Mr. Coppola: the actor came to the Philippines out of condition and unprepared. He was hugely overweight and he had hardly looked at the Conrad text.

In his own book, "Brando: Songs My Mother Taught Me," Mr. Brando says Mr. Coppola was "alternately depressed, nervous and frantic," behind schedule and unable to end the film. It may have been so. Mr. Brando says he steered the material back toward Conrad. Mr. Coppola would say that the actor did amazing improv work. He shaved his head and urged that it be like a moon in the dark. Still, on screen, Kurtz was too far gone to be compelling or coherent. Mr. Brando adds in his book that he was good at conning Mr. Coppola. "And he bought it, but what I'd really wanted from the beginning was to find a way to make my part smaller so that I wouldn't have to work as hard."

WELL, it was all a long time and millions of dollars ago. There is one restored Kurtz scene—in which he reads to Willard from Time magazine. It shows an alert, intelligent, scathing man, and it helps link the Kurtz of darkness to the man whose dossier we have read on the way upriver. It fills in the arc of the man, and it makes his decline more poignant.

When you've seen "Apocalypse Now Redux," you should read Peter Cowie's "Apocalypse Now Book" (Da Capo Press) on the film as a whole. It has far richer detail than can be conveyed here. You should read "Notes." You could look at the 1991 documentary by Fax Bahr and George Hickenlooper, "Hearts of Darkness," based on footage shot by Eleanor. You may want to run both versions of "Apocalypse" side by side; this is an occasion when the ordinary viewer may want to be like a film scholar. That will demonstrate the jeweled beauty of Vittorio Storaro's cinematography, which is now enhanced by a fully revived version of the old dye-transfer Technicolor. The jungle is moist, blooming and alive.

It can be fairly asked whether Francis Coppola can, or needs to, make another film as good as this or the first two "Godfather" films. He suffered badly in the Philippines, and he made others suffer in ways he could not hide from. He had bad years afterward, and that can take away your youth and your drive. But the new version of "Apocalypse" (which had its world premiere in Cannes [3/11/2001]) is an unmistakably great film—and it is his third. All three offer a horrified and consistent view of modern America. He had great collaborators—from Brando and Pacino to Murch and Storaro. But in the 1970's he made movies that no one has since surpassed. And now, so many years later, he has gone back and rescued what may be the best of them all.

Apocalypse Now

Vincent Canby

Scene: Day. Jungle. A small United States Army patrol boat pushed its way up a river overhung with dense foliage. The member of the crew make no comment on the burnt-out ribs of an American helicopter that remain stuck in a tree like the struts of a child's forgotten kite.

Scene: Day. Jungle. The little patrol boat cuts through the water with uncharacteristic speed, drawing behind it an exultant crew member on water skis. The brown-skinned farmers on the riverbank watch impassively.

Scene: Day. Jungle. The patrol boat stops to search a Vietnamese dugout filled with people and produce. Are they friends, enemies, or, as is most likely, simply uncommitted? No way to know. No language to communicate in. A young Vietnamese woman makes a sudden move to protect a particular crate. An American, armed with a machine gun, begins to fire. In several seconds these boat people are dead. The one survivor is a puppy.

Scene: Night. Jungle. The patrol boat, now deep in hostile territory, rounds a bend in the river to come upon a brilliantly floodlit stadium preparing to receive a U.S.O. troupe of Playboy bunnies.

In dozens of such scenes Francis Ford Coppola's "Apocalypse Now" lives up to its grand title, disclosing not only the various faces of war but also the contradictions between excitement and boredom, terror and pity, brutality and beauty. Its epiphanies would do credit to Federico Fellini, who is indirectly quoted at one point.

"Apocalypse Now" is not about any war but about the disastrous United States involvement in Vietnam, which, probably because it was disastrous, seems now to have been different, but was it really? The technology was as up-to-date as the taxpayers' billions could buy, but everything else was essentially the same. At its confused heart: a fearful hunger to survive. No matter what.

When it is thus evoking the look and feelings of the Vietnam War, dealing in sense impressions for which no explanations are adequate or necessary, "Apocalypse Now" is a stunning work. It's as technically complex and masterful as any war film I can remember, including David Leans' "The Bridge on the River Kwai," which comes to mind, I suppose, because both productions were themselves military campaigns to subdue the hostile landscapes in which they were made. "Kwai" was shot in Ceylon; "Apocalypse Now" in the

Source: Vincent Canby, "Apocalypse Now," *The New York Times*, August 15, 1979. Cover page Arts Section.

Philippines, which became, for Mr. Coppola, his Vietnam, swallowing men, money, and equipment as voraciously as any enemy.

"Apocalypse Now," though, wants to be something more than a kind of cinematic tone poem. Mr. Coppola himself describes it as "operatic," but this, I suspect, is a word the director hit upon after the fact. Ultimately, "Apocalypse Now" is neither a tone poem nor an opera. It's an adventure yarn with delusions of grandeur, a movie that ends—in the all-too-familiar word of the poet Mr. Coppola drags in by the bootstraps—not with a bang, but a whimper.

I realize that a movie's ending should not deny all that has gone before, but almost from the beginning of "Apocalypse Now" there have been portents that the film means to deal with not only the looks and expressions of what but also with such heavy things as the human condition, good, evil, fate, and various other subjects who might, in an earlier century, demanded that they be capitalized.

Mr. Coppola and John Milius, with whom he wrote the screenplay, have taken as their source material "Heart of Darkness," Joseph Conrad's classic story about a mad ivory hunter in nineteenth-century Africa. This shadowy man, named Kurtz, comes to represent to Conrad's narrator, Marlow, all the terrible possibilities of a soul returned to some precivilized state. Conrad is rather vague about the terrible things that Kurtz is up to. We know only that he rules his local tribes with a bloody hand and charms them with his sorcery. The point of the story is Marlow's realization that Kurtz is a heretofore unrecognized aspect of himself, which, being known, is safely manageable.

Mr. Coppola and Mr. Milius have attempted to update Conrad, who really doesn't need updating, by placing this story more or less on top of the Vietnam War. Kurtz (Marlon Brando), whom we meet in the film's concluding section, is a renegade Green Berets officer who has taken refuge in the Cambodian jungles, where, to the fury of his superiors, he wages his own wars—for and against whom is left blurry—at the head of a group of ferocious Montegnard tribesmen.

The Marlow character is now a battle-scarred Special Services officer named Captain Willard (Martin Sheen), who is assigned by the commanding general to go into Cambodia, find Kurtz, and to "terminate" him "with extreme prejudice." This plot, which seems to have been imposed on the film from above, keeps interrupting the natural flow of Mr. Coppola's perfectly sound, sometimes incredibly beautiful, meditation upon war.

The major part of the film is occupied with Willard's adventures as he travels upriver in the small patrol boat provided by the Army. These sequences are often spellbinding, none more so than one in which Willard and his companions are forced to observe an assault on a Vietcong village by American fighter planes and helicopters under the command of an exuberantly manic officer who's also a surfing nut. This fellow, played with breathtaking force and charm by Robert Duvall, exhibits most of the qualities we miss in the foolish pretensions of the movie's Kurtz, whose actions and words, when they finally come, have little to do with the rest of the movie.

From time to time in the course of his upriver odyssey, Captain Willard muses on the nature of the man he seeks—soundtrack narration that makes one's flesh wet with embarrassment. When we hear Willard say, "Everything I saw told me that Kurtz had gone insane," it not only fails to establish a bond between the two men, it's also an understatement to break a camel's back.

With the exception of Mr. Brando, who has no role to act, the actors are superlatively right, beginning with Mr. Duvall and Mr. Sheen, and including Frederic Forrest, Albert Hall, Larry Fishburne, and Sam Bottoms, who play the members of the patrol boat's crew. Dennis Hopper, looking as wild and disconnected as ever, turns up briefly at the end as a freelance photographer who has fallen under Kurtz's spell, apparently because Kurtz reads T. S. Eliot aloud (though none too well).

Vittorio Storaro, who photographed "Last Tango in Paris," among other fine films, is responsible for the extraordinary camerawork that almost, but not quite, saves "Apocalypse Now" from its profoundly anticlimactic intellectual muddle.

APOCALYPSE NOW

Produced and directed by Francis Ford Coppola; written by Michael Herr, John Milius, and Mr. Coppola; cinematographer, Vittorio Storaro; edited by Richard Marks; music by Carmine Coppola; art designer, Angelo Graham; released by United Artists. Running time: 139 minutes.

WITH: Marlon Brando (Colonel Kurtz), Robert Duvall (Lieutenant Colonel Kilgore), Martin Sheen (Captain Willard), Frederic Forrest (Chef), Albert Hall (Chief), Sam Bottoms (Lance), Larry Fishburne (Clean), Dennis Hopper (Photo Journalist), G.D. Spradlin (General), Harrison Ford (Colonel), and Jerry Zeismer (Civilian).

The Reflections on the Politics of Culture

Michael Parenti

In the academic social sciences, students are taught to think of culture as representing the customs and mores of a society, including its language, art, laws, and religion. Such a definition has a nice neutral sound to it, but culture is anything but neutral. Much of what is thought to be our common culture is the selective transmission of class-dominated values. Antonio Gramsci understood this when he spoke of class hegemony, noting that the state is only the "outer ditch behind which there [stands] a powerful system of fortresses and earthworks," a network of cultural values and institutions not normally thought of as political.[1] What we call "our culture" is largely reflective of existing hegemonic arrangements within the social order, strongly favoring some interests over others.

A society built upon slave labor, for instance, swiftly develops a racist culture, replete with its own peculiar laws, science, and mythology, along with mechanisms of repression directed against both slaves and the critics of slavery. After slavery is abolished, racism continues to fortify the inequitable social relations—which is what Engels meant when he said that slavery leaves its "poisonous sting" long after it passes into history.

Culture, then, is not an abstract force that floats around in space and settles upon us—though given the seemingly subliminal ways it influences us, it can feel like a disembodied, ubiquitous entity. In fact, culture is mediated through a social structure. We get our culture from a network of social relations involving other people: primary groups such as family, peers, and other informal associations within the community or, as is increasingly the case, from more formally articulated and legally chartered institutions such as schools, media, churches, government agencies, corporations, and the military.

Linked by purchase and persuasion to dominant ruling-class interests, such social institutions are regularly misrepresented as politically neutral, especially by those who occupy command positions within them or are otherwise advantaged by them. What

---

[1] Antonio Gramsci, Selections from the *Prison Notebooks* (New York: International Publishers, 1971), p. 238.

Source: Michael Parenti, "The Reflections on the Politics of Culture," *An Independent Socialist Magazine*, February 1999, Vol. 50, Issue 9, p. 11–19.

Gramsci said about the military might apply to most other institutions in capitalist society: their "so-called neutrality only means support for the reactionary side."[2]

The Slippery Slope of Cultural Relativism

When culture is treated as nothing more than an innocent accretion of solutions and practices, and each culture is seen as something inviolate, then all cultures are accepted at face value and cultural relativism is the suggested standard. So we hear that we should avoid ethnocentrism and respect other cultures. To be sure, after centuries in which indigenous cultures have been trampled underfoot by colonizers, we need to be acutely aware of the baneful effects of cultural imperialism and of the oppressive intolerance manifested toward diverse ethnic cultures within our own society.

But the struggle to preserve cultural diversity should not give carte blanche to anyone in any society to violate basic human rights. Many patriarchal cultures, for example, are replete with "sacrosanct customs" that, on closer examination, promote the worst kinds of gender victimization, including the mutilation of female children through clitorectomy and infibulation, and the sale of young girls into sexual slavery. I once heard an official from Saudi Arabia demand that Westerners show respect for his culture: he was addressing critics who denounced the Saudi practice of stoning women to death on charges of adultery. He failed to mention that there were people within his own culture—including, of course, the female victims—who were not enamored of such time-honored traditions.

For most of U.S. history, slaveholders and then segregationists insisted that we respect the South's "way of life." In Nazi Germany, anti-Semitism was an integral part of the ongoing political culture. Many evildoers might rally under the banner of cultural relativism. The truth is, as we struggle for human betterment, we must challenge the oppressive and destructive features of all cultures, including our own.

In academic circles, postmodernist theorists offer their own variety of cultural relativism. They reject the idea that human perceptions can transcend culture. For them, all kinds of knowledge are little more than social constructs. Evaluating any culture from a platform of fixed and final truths, they say, is a dangerous project that often contains the seeds of more extreme forms of domination. In response, I would argue that, even if there are no absolute truths, this does not mean all consciousness is hopelessly culture-bound. People from widely different societies and different periods in history can still recognize forms of class, ethnic, and gender oppression in various cultures across time and space. Though culture permeates all our perceptions, it is not the totality of human experience.

At the heart of postmodernism's cultural relativism is an old-fashioned anti-Marxism, an unswerving ideological acceptance of existing bourgeois domination. Some postmodernists depict themselves as occupying "positions of marginality," taking lonely and heroic stands against hoards of doctrinaire hardliners who supposedly overpopulate the nation's campuses. *So the postmodernists are able to enjoy the appearance of independent critical thought without ever saying anything that might jeopardize their academic careers.*

---

[2] Ibid, p. 212.

The Limits of Culturalistic Explanations

Taught to think of culture as an age-old accretion of practice and tradition, we mistakenly conclude that it is not easily modified. In fact, as social conditions and interests change, much (but certainly not all) of culture proves mutable. For almost four hundred years, the wealthy elites of Central America were devoutly Roman Catholic, a religious affiliation that was supposedly deeply ingrained in their culture. Then, in the late 1970s, after many Catholic clergy proved friendly to liberation theology, these same elites discarded their Catholicism and joined Protestant fundamentalist denominations that espoused a more comfortably reactionary line. Their four centuries of "deeply ingrained Catholic culture" were discarded within a few years once they deemed their class interests to be at stake.

Generally, whenever anyone offers culturalistic explanations for social phenomena, we should be skeptical. For one thing, culturalistic explanations of third-world social conditions tend to be patronizing and ethnocentric. I heard someone explain the poor performance of the Mexican army, in the storm rescue operations in Acapulco in October 1997, as emblematic of a lackadaisical Mexican way of handling things: It's in their culture, you see; everything is mañana mañana with those people. In fact, poor rescue responses have been repeatedly evidenced in the United States and numerous other countries. And more to the point, the Mexican army, financed and advised by the U.S. national security state, has performed brilliantly in Chiapas, doing the thing it was trained to do, which is not rescuing people but intimidating and killing them, waging low-intensity warfare, systematically occupying lands, burning crops, destroying villages, executing suspected guerrilla sympathizers, and tightening the noose around the Zapatista social base. To say the Mexican army performed poorly in rescue operations is to presume that the army is there to serve the people rather than to control them on behalf of those who own Mexico. Culturalistic explanations divorced of political-economic realities readily lend themselves to such obfuscation.

The Commodification of Culture

As the capitalist economy has grown in influence and power, much of our culture has been expropriated and commodified. Its use value increasingly takes second place to its exchange value. Nowadays we create less of our culture and buy more of it, until it really is no longer our culture. We now have a special term for segments of culture that remain rooted in popular practice: we call it "folk culture," which includes folk music, folk dance, folk medicine, and folk mythology. These are curious terms, when you think about it, since by definition all culture should be folk culture. That is, all culture arises from the social practices of us folks. But primary-group folk creation has become so limited as to be accorded a distinctive label.

A far greater part of our culture is now aptly designated as "mass culture," "popular culture," and even "media culture," owned and operated mostly by giant corporations whose major concern is to accumulate wealth and make the world safe for their owners, the goal being exchange value rather than use value, social control rather than social creativity. Much of mass culture is organized to distract us from thinking too much about larger realities. The fluff and puffery of entertainment culture crowds out more urgent and nourishing things. By constantly appealing to the lowest common denominator, a sensationalist popular culture lowers the common denominator still further. Public tastes become still more attuned to cultural junk food, the big hype, the trashy, flashy, wildly violent, instantly stimulating, and desperately superficial offerings.

Such fare often has real ideological content. Even if supposedly apolitical in its intent, entertainment culture (which is really the entertainment industry) is political in its impact, propagating images and values that are often downright sexist, racist, consumerist, authoritarian, militaristic, and imperialist.[3]

With the ascendancy of mass culture we see a loss of people's culture. From the nineteenth century to the mid-twentieth century, a discernible working-class culture existed, with its union halls, songs, poetry, literature, theater, night schools, summer camps, and mutual assistance societies, many of which were organized by anarchists, socialists, and communists, and their various front groups. But not much of this culture could survive the twin blows of McCarthyism and television, both of which came upon us at about the same time.

The commodification of culture can be seen quite starkly in the decline of children's culture. In my youth, I and my companions were out on the streets of New York playing games of childhood's creation without adult supervision: ringalevio, kick-the-can, hide-and-seek, tag, Johnny-on-the-pony, stickball, stoopball, handball, and boxball. Today, one sees little evidence of children's culture in most U.S. communities. The same seems to have happened in other countries. Martin Large notes that in England, in the parks and streets that once were "bubbling with children playing," few youngsters are now to be seen participating in the old games. Where have they all gone? The television "has taken many of our children away" from their hobbies and street games.[4]

This process, whereby a profit-driven mass culture preempts people's culture, is extending all over the world, as third-world critics of cultural imperialism repeatedly remind us.

Limited Accommodations

There are two myths I would like to put to rest: first, the notion that culture is to be treated as mutually exclusive of, and even competitive with, political economy. A friend of mine who edits a socialist journal once commented to me: "You emphasize economics. I deal more with culture." I thought this an odd dichotomization since my work on the news media, the entertainment industry, social institutions, and political mythology has been deeply involved with both culture and economics. *In fact, I doubt one can talk intelligently about culture if one does not at some point also introduce the dynamics of political economy. This is why, when I refer to the "politics of culture," I mean something more than just the latest controversy regarding federal funding of the arts.*

The other myth is that our social institutions are autonomous entities, not linked to each other. In fact, they are interlocked by corporate law, public and private funding, and overlapping corporate elites who serve on the governing boards of universities, colleges, private schools, museums, symphony orchestras, the music industry, libraries, churches, newspapers, magazines, radio and TV networks, publishing houses, and charitable foundations.

---

[3] See my *Make-Believe Media: The Politics of Entertainment* (New York: St. Martin's Press, 1992), chapter I and passim.

[4] Martin Large, *Who's Bringing Them Up?* (Gloucester, England: M.H.C. Large, 1980), p. 35.

New cultural formations arise from time to time, usually within a limited framework that does not challenge dominant class arrangements. So we have struggles around feminism, ethnic equality, gay rights, family values, and the like—all of which can involve important, life-and-death issues. And if pursued as purely lifestyle issues, they can win occasional exposure in the mainstream media. Generally, however, the higher circles instinctively resist any pressure toward social equalization, even in the realm of "identity politics." Furthermore, they use lifestyle issues such as gay rights and abortion rights, among others, as convenient targets against which to misdirect otherwise legitimate mass grievances.

The victories won by "identity politics" usually are limited to changes in procedure and personnel, leaving institutional class interests largely intact. For instance, feminists have challenged patriarchal militarism, but the resulting concession is not an end to militarism but women in the armed forces.

Eventually we get female political leaders, but of what stripe? We get Lynn Cheney, Elizabeth Dole, Margaret Thatcher and—just when some of us were recovering from Jeane Kirkpatrick—Madeleine Albright. It is no accident that this type of woman is most likely to reach the top of the present politicoeconomic structure. While indifferent or even hostile to the feminist movement, conservative females reap some of its benefits.

Professions offer another example of the false autonomy of cultural practices. Whether composed of anthropologists, political scientists, physicists, doctors, lawyers, or librarians, professional associations emphasize their commitment to independent expertise, and deny that they are wedded to the dominant politico-economic social structure. In fact, many of their most important activities are directly regulated by corporate interests or take place in a social context that is less and less of their own making, as doctors and nurses are discovering in their dealings with HMOs.

Supply Creates Demand

We are taught that the "free market of ideas and images," as it exists in mass culture today, is a response to popular tastes. Media culture gives the people what they want. Demand creates supply. This is a very democratic-sounding notion. But quite often it is the other way around: *supply creates demand.* Thus, the supply system to a library can be heavily prefigured by all sorts of things other than readers' preferences. Discussions of censorship usually focus on limited controversies, as when some people agitate to have this or that "offensive" book removed from the shelves. Such incidents leave the impression that the library is struggling to maintain itself as a free and open system. Overlooked is the prestructured selectivity, the censorship that occurs even before anyone gets a chance to see what books are on the shelves, a censorship imposed by a book market dominated by six or seven conglomerates. There is a difference between incidental censorship and systemic censorship. Mainstream pundits sedulously avoid discussion of the latter.

Systemic repression exists in other areas of cultural endeavor. Consider the censorship controversies in regard to art. These focus on whether a particular painting or photograph, sporting some naughty thing like frontal nudity, should be publicly funded and shown to consenting adults. But there is a systemic suppression as well. The image we have of the artist as an independent purveyor of creative culture can be as misleading as the image we have of other professionals. What is referred to as the "art world" is not a thing apart from the art market; the latter has long been heavily influenced by a small number of moneyed persons like Huntington Hartford, John Paul Getty, Nelson Rockefeller, and Joseph Hirschorn, who have treated works of art not as part of our common treasure but, in true capitalist style, as objects of pecuniary investment and private acquisition. They have financed the museums and major galleries, art books, art magazines, art critics, university endowments, and various art schools and centers—reaping considerable tax write-offs in so doing.

As trustees, publishers, patrons, and speculators, they and their associates exercise influence over the means of artistic production and distribution, setting ideological limits to artistic expression. Artists who move beyond acceptable boundaries run the risk of not being shown. Art that contains radical political content is labeled "propaganda" by those who control the art market. Art and politics do not mix, we are told—which would be news to such greats as Goya, Degas, Picasso, and Rivera. While professing to keep art free of politics ("art for art's sake"), the gatekeepers impose their own politically motivated definition of what is and is not art. The art they buy, show, and have reviewed is devoid of critical social content even when realistic in form. What is preferred is Abstract Expressionism and other forms of Nonobjective Art that are sufficiently ambiguous to stimulate a broad range of aesthetic interpretations, having an iconoclastic and experimental appearance while remaining politically safe.

The same is true of the distribution of films and their redistribution as videos. Some are mass-marketed while others quickly drop from sight. Capitalism will sell you the camera to make a movie and the computer to write a book. But then there is the problem of distribution. Will a film get mass exposure in a thousand theaters across the nation, or will the producer spend the next five years of his or her life toting it around to college campuses, union halls, and special one-day matinee showings at local art theaters (if that)?

So it is with publications. Books from one of the big publishing conglomerates are likely to get more prominent distribution and more library adoptions than books by Monthly Review Press, Verso, Pathfinder, or International Publishers. Libraries and bookstores (not to mention newsstands and drugstores) are more likely to stock *Time* and *Newsweek* than *Monthly Review*, *Covert Action Quarterly*, or other such publications. A small branch library will have no room or funds to acquire leftist rifles but will procure seven copies of Colin Powell's autobiography or some other media-hyped potboiler.

It is not just that supply is responding to demand. Where did the demand to read about Colin Powell come from? The media blitz that legitimized the Gulf War also catapulted its top military commander into the national limelight and made him an overnight superstar. It was supply creating demand.

Imperfect Socialization

One hopeful thought remains: socialization into the dominant culture does not operate with perfect effect. In the face of all monopolistic ideological manipulation, many people develop a skepticism or outright disaffection based on the sometimes evident disparity between social actuality and official ideology. There is a limit to how many lies people will swallow about the reality they are experiencing. If this were not so, if we were all perfectly socialized into the ongoing social order and thoroughly indoctrinated into the dominant culture, then I would not have been able to record these thoughts and you could not have understood them.

Years ago, William James observed how custom can operate as a sedative while novelty (including dissidence) is rejected as an irritant.[5] Yet I would argue that after awhile sedatives can become suffocating and irritants can enliven. People sometimes hunger for the uncomfortable critical perspective that gives them a more meaningful explanation of things. By becoming aware of this, we have a better chance of moving against the tide. It is not a matter of becoming the faithful instrument of any particular persuasion but of resisting the misrepresentations of a thoroughly ideologized bourgeois culture. In class struggle, culture is a key battleground. The capitalist rulers know this—and so should we.

Michael Parenti's two most recent books are *Blackshirts and Reds: Rational Fascism and the Overthrow of Communism* and *America Besieged*, both published by City Lights.

(Editor's note: italicized lines have been introduced into the body of the article.)

---

[5] William James, "The Sentiment of Rationality," in his *Essays in Pragmatism* (New York: Hafner, 1948), p. 13.

The Virtues of Humiliation

Amitai Etzioni

Continuing the debate from "<u>The Shaming Sham</u>" by Carl F. Horowitz (March–April 1997).

Dear Dr. Horowitz:

After reading your commentary on public shaming ["<u>The Shaming Sham</u>," *TAP*, March–April 1997], I realized that to engage in an intelligent debate on this topic, we first need to distinguish shaming from honorable forms of argumentation. I hope that you'd agree that it is shameful to point to one attribute shared by two parties, and then blame the second party for the various failings of the first. Thus, it is wrongheaded to accuse liberals of being commies just because both shared a concern for the downtrodden. Likewise, it is quite unacceptable for Stephen Holmes to taint communitarians with the sins of authoritarians just because both groups are critical of liberals, as he does in his book *Anatomy of Antiliberalism*

Of course, if you agree with me on the above two examples, then surely you will see the ironic flaw of your essay: You have written a tirade against shaming in which you avoid making an honorable argument by instead relying on shaming tactics of your own. Rather than treat shaming, which can be an educational and pro-social device, on its own terms, you repeatedly conflate it with: physical violence, including public hangings and the beheading of convicted drug dealers; "godly fumigation" of the termites that Pat Robertson claims are running our institutions; blacklisting and boycotts; and—the least of the charges—turning "cultural enemies into feckless mush."

To separate fact from allegation, let's start at the beginning. Shaming entails symbolic acts that communicate disapproval, ranging from relatively gentle acts such as according a student a C+ or sending a disruptive kid to stand in the classroom's corner, to a more severe measure such as marking the cars of people convicted of repeat drunk driving with a glow-in-the-dark bumper sticker that reads, "Convicted DUI—Restricted License." Shaming thus differs sharply from many other modes of punishment—public spanking for instance—in that the latter inflict bodily harm, rather than being limited to psychic discomfort, which has untoward consequences of its own. True, violent punishments also inflict shame, but this is a side effect of the main abuse. To equate shaming with public hangings is like conflating the lowering of flags with funerals, and Radio Marti with the Bay of Pigs.

Source: Amitai Etzioni, "The Virtues of Humiliation," *The American Prospect*, vol. 8, no. 35, November 1, 1997–December 1, 1997.

The first step in determining whether shaming is morally appropriate is to recognize that shaming is only justified when those being shamed are acting out of free will. When people act inappropriately but cannot help themselves, such as when those with mental illnesses talk to themselves loudly, chiding them is highly inappropriate. Many progressives argue that it is wrongheaded to shame the poor, the disadvantaged, and the unemployed for antisocial behavior, because society is to blame for their condition. Social conservatives, by contrast, depict most everything from homosexuality to being on welfare as reflecting one's free choices, and hence blameworthy if the choices made do not suit social conservative beliefs. In either case, when there is no free will, shaming is highly inappropriate.

But while you see any attempt to censure people as a form of intimidation used by political tyrants, the true test of the merit of shaming is faced when the people the community seeks to deal with are those who command a significant measure of free choice. Think about Michael Milken, who made $550 million a year and then cheated and clawed his way to another $100 million.

How are we to deal with those whose antisocial behavior cannot be ignored, and who can behave differently? The answer depends greatly on your assumptions about human nature. The sanguine crowd tends to assume that people can be convinced to conduct themselves in a socially constructive manner solely by means of praise and other forms of encouragement, or by nondirective and nonjudgmental treatment, allowing the goodness of people to unfold. For those who share this view, shaming is indeed cruel and unusual and unnecessary punishment.

Once we realize, however, that a world of only positive reinforcements is wondrous but not within human reach, we must reluctantly turn to disincentives, sanctions, and other forms of punishment. True, we should first determine if the social demands are fair and reasonable, and to what extent we can rely on positive inducements. But, at the end of the day, some form of disincentive—hopefully sparing and mostly of the gentle kind—cannot be avoided.

When it comes to punishment, the less you are inclined to shame, the more you end up relying on much harsher means of control, such as jailing and caning (two examples of punishment you mistakenly conflate with shaming). Many of my progressive friends are horrified at the hypothetical suggestion that a youngster convicted for the first time for dealing hard drugs on a playground should be sent home without his pants and with his head shaved clean. The widely used alternative is to send the same youngster to a place in which he will typically be subject to gang rape and deeply inducted into the culture of crime—a vastly inferior option.

Finally, shaming has one feature that even you cannot dispute: Shaming reflects the community's values, and hence cannot be imposed by the authorities per se against the people. Thus, if being sent to the principal's office is a badge of honor in a person's peer culture, then no shaming will occur. A yellow star, imposed to mark and shame Jews in Nazi Germany, is now worn as a matter of pride in Israel.

In short, unlike all other forms of punishment, shaming is deeply democratic. It can be said with only the slightest of exaggeration that if punish we must, shaming should be at the top of the list.

Sincerely,

Amitai Etzioni

Dear Dr. Etzioni:

I must say that after reading your commentary, you have proved more insightful as a student of complex organizations than as an evangelist for community reinvigoration. Not only do you misrepresent any number of my points, but you also shoot yourself in the foot more than once.

From what I gather, the gravamen of your complaint is that I lump together disreputable proponents of shaming with reputable ones, thereby committing the cardinal sin of confusing the content of an idea with its source. My taking to task fevered extremists who call for, say, public floggings of adulterers, you argue, only will undermine efforts by wonderfully civic-minded folks who deal with wrongdoing more humanely and effectively. I reiterate my position: Using shame as public policy attracts extremists, and the "good cops" of the shaming patrol differ from the "bad" ones far more in strategy than in substance. And the goal of both camps is stringent control over individual expression, lest the immoral among us lead us further down some cultural slippery slope. Inasmuch as it's necessary to distinguish between extremists and moderates, let us also remember "moderate" versions of bad ideas have a way of getting out of hand, and becoming witch-hunts. It is poetic justice that those who start revolutions often get swallowed by them.

Extreme or not, supporters of shaming make two spurious claims: first, shaming precludes, rather than precedes, government censorship; and second, shaming is humane and benign in and of itself. Since you've chosen not to force my hand on the first point, I'll stick to the second.

Shaming, even to the supposedly prudent extent you favor, is not likely to be humane or effective. I chose *This Will Hurt* as the point of reference because it exemplifies the seductive power of a bad idea. It may not seem right to harp on Singapore's caning of an American vandal, but consider this: A prominent mainstream conservative, *National Review* senior editor Jeffrey Hart, in giving *This Will Hurt* advance publicity, not only praised Singapore's action, but called for similar measures here.

Let us hope that you are blessed with a milder disposition. Still, with few reservations, you think shaming a decent, stabilizing, and "deeply democratic" process. You delight in shocking your progressive friends in describing how you would humiliate a drug-dealing school kid. Leaving aside what type of drug was dealt, and in what quantity, I should like to know where such a strategy has worked.

In your zeal to shame, you propose a dragnet that would not only snag drug-dealing school kids, but would also nail financier Michael Milken. That poor dead horse, Mr. Milken, spearheaded the construction of the information superhighway, enabling companies such as Turner Broadcasting, McCaw Cellular, MCI, and TCI to bypass banks to acquire needed project capital. For his efforts, Milken did earn $1.1 billion during 1984–87 (as opposed to the more virtuous Sam Walton, who earned $4 billion in 1987 alone). But Milken during this period also paid an estimated $500 million in federal and state taxes, and donated $300 million to schools and charities. That's not including the $600 million he paid the federal government years later to settle his case, or, of course, his stretch in federal prison.

Nowhere do I imply we should avoid speaking difficult truths to egregious wrongdoers, or to those accommodating them. Personally, I wouldn't want to belong to any country club that would have O.J. Simpson as a member. What I object to in today's manifold calls for moral censorship is the reflexively punitive tone, and the refusal to consider the consequences of institutionalizing fear. Individualism is not a four-letter word, and America is better off for that fact. In the long run, to challenge shaming as public policy, it is crucial to debunk the notion of America as in a state of cultural collapse, and thus in need of a "culture war" to restore it to good graces. But then again, without such a war most advocates of shaming would be out of a job.

Sincerely,

Carl F. Horowitz

II. Groups

Miller Convicted in Contempt Case

Joseph A. Loftus

WASHINGTON, May 31—Arthur Miller, the playwright, was found guilty today of contempt of Congress.

He had refused to answer two questions at a hearing before the House Committee on Un-American Activities. Although he testified frankly about his own relationships with persons of Communist bent or membership, he said that his conscience had forbidden him to tell about others.

Both of the questions that he refused to answer dealt with other persons who had attended meetings with him.

Overruling the defense on what the court considered the main point in the case, Judge Charles F. McLaughlin said that both questions had been pertinent to the committee's inquiry. Therefore, he convicted Mr. Miller on both counts.

Judge McLaughlin tried Mr. Miller recently in United States District Court without a jury. He filed the opinion with the clerk of the court today.

Sentence will be pronounced later. The maximum sentence for contempt of Congress is a year in jail and a $1,000 fine. Judges seldom impose the maximum in these cases and no one has been imprisoned recently for refusing to talk about others when he has been frank about himself.

The 42-year-old playwright, whose wife is Marilyn Monroe, the motion picture actress, testified before the committee on June 21, 1956. He said that he had attended five or six meetings of Communist party writers.

Referring to a 1947 meeting, the committee asked him:

1. "Can you tell us who were there when you walked into the room?"

2. "Was Arnaud D'Usseau chairman of the meeting of the Communist party writers which took place in 1947 at which you were in attendance?"

The Government contended that both questions had been pertinent to the subject of the fraudulent procurement and misuse of American passports by persons in the service of the Communist conspiracy. This was the announced subject of the hearing at which Mr. Miller testified.

Source: Joseph A. Loftus, "Miller Convicted in Contempt Case," *New York Times,* June 1, 1957.

Judge McLaughlin ruled that the committee had met the requirement of having valid legislative purpose for its hearing. The Government had shown, he said, that American passports were being misused by persons connected with the Communist conspiracy.

"Since the Congress has power to legislate concerning passports," he said, "it is evident that Congress had the right to investigate the subject of passports."

The court said that Communist sympathizers had used passports unlawfully, that Miller had held a passport in 1947, that he had been denied one in 1954, and that he had had an application pending for one at the time of the Congressional hearing.

Mr. D'Usseau, said the opinion, had been a witness before the same committee in 1952 and had refused to answer all questions about Communist party membership or activity.

Judge McLaughlin ruled:

"In the circumstances, an inquiry directed to defendant as to the identity of the Communist party writers with whom he foregathered for discussions of the works of Communist writers would seem to be one logically calculated to produce information which could be of assistance to the committee in connection with its investigation of communistic passport activities in relation to the aforementioned matter of legislative concern."

Discussing Mr. Miller's motive for refusing to answer, the court said:

"However commendable may be regarded the motive of the defendant in refusing to disclose the identity or the official position of another with whom he was in association, lest said disclosure might bring trouble on him, that motive and that refusal have been removed from this court's consideration."

In support of this, the court cited an opinion of the Circuit Court of Appeals, District of Columbia, in a similar contempt case, Watkins v. United States. The Watkins case now is before the Supreme Court.

At his apartment, 444 East Fifty-seventh Street, Mr. Miller declined yesterday to comment on his conviction.

Mr. and Mrs. Miller left the apartment late yesterday for an undisclosed destination.

Are You Now or Were You Ever?(II)

Arthur Miller

On a lucky afternoon I happened upon *The Devil in Massachusetts*, by Marion Starkey, a narrative of the Salem witch-hunt of 1692. I knew this story from my college reading, but in this darkened America it turned a completely new aspect toward me: the poetry of the hunt. Poetry may seem an odd word for a witch-hunt but I saw there was something of the marvellous in the spectacle of a whole village, if not an entire province, whose imagination was captured by a vision of something that wasn't there.

In time to come, the notion of equating the red-hunt with the witch-hunt would be condemned as a deception. There were communists and there never were witches. The deeper I moved into the 1690s, the further away drifted the America of the 50s, and, rather than the appeal of analogy, I found something different to draw my curiosity and excitement.

Anyone standing up in the Salem of 1692 and denying that witches existed would have faced immediate arrest, the hardest interrogation and possibly the rope. Every authority not only confirmed the existence of witches but never questioned the necessity of executing them. It became obvious that to dismiss witchcraft was to forgo any understanding of how it came to pass that tens of thousands had been murdered as witches in Europe. To dismiss any relation between that episode and the hunt for subversives was to shut down an insight into not only the similar emotions but also the identical practices of both officials and victims.

There were witches, if not to most of us then certainly to everyone in Salem; and there were communists, but what was the content of their menace? That to me became the issue. Having been deeply influenced as a student by a Marxist approach to society, and having known Marxists and sympathizers, I could simply not accept that these people were spies or even prepared to do the will of the Soviets in some future crisis. That such people had thought to find hope of a higher ethic in the Soviet was not simply an American, but a worldwide, irony of catastrophic moral proportions, for their like could be found all over the world.

But as the 50s dawned, they were stuck with the past. Part of the surreality of the anti-left sweep was that it picked up people for disgrace who had already turned away from a pro-Soviet past but had no stomach for naming others who had merely shared their illusions. But the hunt had captured some significant part of the American imagination and its power demanded respect.

Source: Arthur Miller, "Are You Now or Were You Ever?(II)," *Guardian Unlimited* © Guardian Newspapers Limited, June 17, 2000.

Turning to Salem was like looking into a petri dish, an embalmed stasis with its principal moving forces caught in stillness. One had to wonder what the human imagination fed on that could inspire neighbors and old friends to emerge overnight as furies secretly bent on the torture and destruction of Christians. More than a political metaphor, more than a moral tale, *The Crucible*, as it developed over more than a year, became the awesome evidence of the power of human imagination inflamed, the poetry of suggestion, and the tragedy of heroic resistance to a society possessed to the point of ruin.

In the stillness of the Salem courthouse, surrounded by the images of the 1950s but with my head in 1692, what the two eras had in common gradually gained definition. Both had the menace of concealed plots, but most startling were the similarities in the rituals of defence, the investigative routines; 300 years apart, both prosecutions alleged membership of a secret, disloyal group. Should the accused confess, his honesty could only be proved by naming former confederates. The informer became the axle of the plot's existence and the investigation's necessity.

The witch-hunt in 1692 had a not dissimilar problem, but a far more poetic solution. Most suspected people named by others as members of the Devil's conspiracy had not been shown to have done anything, neither poisoning wells, setting barns on fire, sickening cattle, aborting babies, nor undermining the virtue of wives (the Devil having two phenomenally active penises, one above the other).

To the rescue came a piece of poetry, smacking of both legalistic and religious validity, called Spectral Evidence. All the prosecution need do was produce a witness who claimed to have seen, not an accused person, but his familiar spirit—his living ghost—in the act of throwing a burning brand into a barn full of hay. You could be at home asleep in your bed, but your spirit could be crawling through your neighbour's window to feel up his wife. The owner of the wandering spirit was obliged to account to the court for his crime. With Spectral Evidence, the air filled with the malign spirits of those identified by good Christians as confederates of the Beast, and the Devil himself danced happily into Salem village and took the place apart.

I spent 10 days in Salem courthouse reading the crudely recorded trials of the 1692 outbreak, and it was striking how totally absent was any sense of irony, let alone humor. I can't recall if it was the provincial governor's nephew or son who, with a college friend, came from Boston to watch the strange proceedings. Both boys burst out laughing at some absurd testimony: they were promptly jailed, and faced possible hanging.

Irony and humor were not conspicuous in the 1950s either. I was in my lawyer's office to sign some contract and a lawyer in the next office was asked to come in and notarize my signature. While he was stamping pages, I continued a discussion with my lawyer about the Broadway theater, which I said was corrupt; the art of theater had been totally displaced by the bottom line, all that mattered any more. Looking up at me, the notarizing lawyer said, "That's a communist position, you know." I started to laugh until I saw the constraint in my lawyer's face, and I quickly sobered up.

I am glad that I managed to write *The Crucible*, but looking back I have often wished I'd had the temperament to do an absurd comedy, which is what the situation deserved. Now, after more than three-quarters of a century of fascination with the great snake of political and social developments, I can see more than a few occasions when we were confronted by the same sensation of having stepped into another age.

A young film producer asked me to write a script about what was then called juvenile delinquency. A mystifying, unprecedented outbreak of gang violence had exploded all over New York. The city, in return for a good percentage of profits, had contracted with this producer to open police stations and schools to his camera. I spent the summer of 1955 in Brooklyn streets with two gangs and wrote an outline. I was ready to proceed with the script when an attack on me as a disloyal lefty opened in the *New York World Telegram*. The cry went up that the city must cancel its contract with the producer so long as I was the screenwriter. A hearing was arranged, attended by 22 city commissioners, including the police, fire, welfare and sanitation departments, as well as two judges.

At the conference table there also sat a lady who produced a thick folder of petitions and statements I had signed, going back to my college years, provided to her by the Huac. I defended myself; I thought I was making sense when the lady began screaming that I was killing the boys in Korea [this was during the Korean war]. She meant me personally, as I could tell from the froth at the corners of her mouth, the fury in her eyes, and her finger pointing straight into my face.

The vote was taken and came up one short of continuing the city's collaboration, and the film was killed that afternoon. I always wondered whether the crucial vote against me came from the sanitation department. But it was not a total loss; the suffocating sensation of helplessness before the spectacle of the impossible coming to pass would soon help in writing *The Crucible*.

That impossible coming to pass was not an observation made at a comfortable distance but a blade cutting directly into my life. This was especially the case with Elia Kazan's decision to cooperate with the Huac. The surrounding fears felt even by those with the most fleeting of contacts with any communist-supported organization were enough to break through long associations and friendships.

Kazan had been a member of the Communist party only a matter of months, and even that link had ended years before. And the party had never been illegal, nor was membership in it. Yet this great director, left undefended by 20th Century Fox executives, his longtime employers, was told that if he refused to name people whom he had known in the party—actors, directors and writers—he would never be allowed to direct another picture in Hollywood, meaning the end of his career.

These names were already known to the committee through other testifiers and FBI informants, but exactly as in Salem—or Russia under the Czar and the Chairman, and Inquisition Spain, Revolutionary France or any other place of revolution or counter-revolution—conspiracy was the name for all opposition. And the reformation of the accused could only be believed when he gave up the names of his co-conspirators. Only this ritual of humiliation, the breaking of pride and independence, could win the accused readmission into the community. The process inevitably did produce in the accused a new set of political, social and even moral convictions more acceptable to the state whose fist had been shoved into his face, with his utter ruin promised should he resist.

I had stopped by Kazan's house in the country in 1952 after he had called me to come and talk, an unusual invitation—he had never been inclined to indulge in talk unless it concerned work. I had suspected from his dark tone that it must have to do with the Huac, which was rampaging through the Hollywood ranks.

Since I was on my way up to Salem for research on a play that I was still unsure I would write, I called at his house, which was on my route. As he laid out his dilemma and his decision to comply with the Huac (which he had already done) it was impossible not to feel his anguish, old friends that we were. But the crunch came when I felt fear, that great teacher, that cruel revealer. For it swept over me that, had I been one of his comrades, he would have spent my name as part of the guarantee of his reform. Even so, oddly enough, I was not filling up with hatred or contempt for him; his suffering was too palpable. The whole hateful procedure had brought him to this, and I believe made the writing of *The Crucible* all but inevitable. Even if one could grant Kazan sincerity in his new-found anti-communism, the concept of an America where such self-discoveries were pressed out of people was outrageous, and a contradiction of any concept of personal liberty.

Is all this of some objective importance in our history, this destruction of bonds between people? I think it may be, however personal it may appear. Kazan's testimony created a far greater shock than anyone else's. Lee J. Cobb's similar testimony and Jerome Robbins's cooperation seemed hardly to matter. It may be that Kazan had been loved more than any other, that he had attracted far greater affection from writers and actors with whom he had worked, and so what was overtly a political act was sensed as a betrayal of love.

It is very significant that in the uproar set off by last year's award to Kazan of an Oscar for life achievement, one heard no mention of the name of any member of the Huac. One doubted whether the thought occurred to many people that the studio heads had igno-miniously collapsed before the Huac's insistence that they institute a blacklist of artists, something they had once insisted was dishonourable and a violation of democratic norms. Half a century had passed since his testimony, but Kazan bore very nearly the whole onus of the era, as though he had manufactured its horrors—when he was surely its victim.

The trial record in Salem courthouse had been written by ministers in a primitive shorthand. This condensation gave emphasis to a gnarled, densely packed language which suggested the country accents of a hard people. To lose oneself day after day in that record of human delusion was to know a fear, not for one's safety, but of the spectacle of intelligent people giving themselves over to a rapture of murderous credulity. It was as though the absence of real evidence was itself a release from the burdens of this world; in love with the invisible, they moved behind their priests, closer to that mystical communion which is anarchy and is called God.

Evidence, in contrast, is effort; leaping to conclusions is a wonderful pleasure, and for a while there was a highly charged joy in Salem, for now that they could see through everything to the frightful plot that was daily being laid bare in court sessions, their days, formerly so eventless and long, were swallowed up in hourly revelations, news, surprises. *The Crucible* is less a polemic than it might have been had it not been filled with wonder at the protean imagination of man.

The Crucible straddles two different worlds to make them one, but it is not history in the usual sense of the word, but a moral, political and psychological construct that floats on the fluid emotions of both eras. As a commercial entertainment the play failed [it opened in 1953]. To start with there was the title: nobody knew what a crucible was. Most of the critics, as sometimes does happen, never caught on to the play's ironical substructure, and the ones who did were nervous about validating a work that was so unkind to the same sanctified procedural principles as underlay the hunt for reds. Some old acquaintances gave me distant nods in the theater lobby on opening night, and even without air-conditioning the house was cool. There was also a problem with the temperature of the production.

The director, Jed Harris, a great name in the theatre of the 20s, 30s and 40s, had decided that the play, which he believed a classic, should be staged like a Dutch painting. In Dutch paintings of groups, everyone is always looking front. Unfortunately, on a stage such rigidity can only lead an audience to the exits. Several years after, a gang of young actors, setting up chairs in the ballroom of the McAlpin Hotel, fired up the audience, convinced the critics, and the play at last took off and soon found its place. There were cheering reviews but by then Senator McCarthy was dead. The public fever on whose heatwaves he had spread his wings had subsided.

The Crucible is my most-produced play. It seems to be one of the few surviving shards of the so-called McCarthy period. And it is part of the play's history that, to people in so many parts of the world, its story seems to be their own. I used to think, half seriously, that you could tell when a dictator was about to take power, or had been overthrown, in a Latin American country, if *The Crucible* was suddenly being produced in that country.

The result of it all is that I have come, rather reluctantly, to respect delusion, not least of all my own. There are no passions quite as hot and pleasurable as those of the deluded. Compared to the bliss of delusion, its vivid colours, blazing lights, explosions, whistles and liberating joys, the search for evidence is a deadly bore. My heart was with the left. If only because the right hated me enough to want to kill me, as the Germans amply proved. And now, the most blatant and most foul anti-Semitism is in Russia, leaving people like me filled not so much with surprise as a kind of wonder at the incredible amount of hope there once was, and how it disappeared and whether in time it will ever come again, attached, no doubt, to some new illusion.

There is hardly a week that passes when I don't ask the unanswerable question: what am I now convinced of that will turn out to be ridiculous? And yet one can't forever stand on the shore; at some point, filled with indecision, scepticism, reservation and doubt, you either jump in or concede that life is forever elsewhere. Which, I dare say, was one of the major impulses behind the decision to attempt *The Crucible*.

Salem village, that pious, devout settlement at the edge of white civilization, had displayed—three centuries before the Russo-American rivalry and the issues it raised—what can only be called a built-in pestilence in the human mind; a fatality forever awaiting the right conditions for its always unique, forever unprecedented outbreak of distrust, alarm, suspicion and murder. And for people wherever the play is performed on any of the five continents, there is always a certain amazement that the same terror that is happening to them or that is threatening them, has happened before to others. It is all very strange. But then, the Devil is known to lure people into forgetting what it is vital for them to remember—how else could his endless reappearances always come as such a marvellous surprise?

Why I Wrote "The Crucible"

An Artist's Answer to Politics

Arthur Miller

As I watched "The Crucible" taking shape as a movie over much of the past year, the sheer depth of time that it represents for me kept returning to mind. As those powerful actors blossomed on the screen, and the children and the horses, the crowds and the wagons, I thought again about how I came to cook all this up nearly fifty years ago, in an America almost nobody I know seems to remember clearly. In a way, there is a biting irony in this film's having been made by a Hollywood studio, something unimaginable in the fifties. But there they are—Daniel Day-Lewis (John Proctor) scything his sea-bordered field, Joan Allen (Elizabeth) lying pregnant in the frigid jail, Winona Ryder (Abigail) stealing her minister-uncle's money, majestic Paul Scofield (Judge Danforth) and his righteous empathy with the Devil-possessed children, and all of them looking as inevitable as rain.

I remember those years—they formed "The Crucible's" skeleton—but I have lost the dead weight of the fear I had then. Fear doesn't travel well; just as it can warp judgment, its absence can diminish memory's truth. What terrifies one generation is likely to bring only a puzzled smile to the next. I remember how in 1964, only twenty years after the war, Harold Clurman, the director of "Incident at Vichy," showed the cast a film of a Hitler speech, hoping to give them a sense of the Nazi period in which my play took place. They watched as Hitler, facing a vast stadium full of adoring people, went up on his toes in ecstasy, hands clasped under his chin, a sublimely self-gratified grin on his face, his body swivelling rather cutely, and they giggled at his overacting.

Likewise, films of Senator Joseph McCarthy are rather unsettling—if you remember the fear he once spread. Buzzing his truculent sidewalk brawler's snarl through the hairs in his nose, squinting through his cat's eyes and sneering like a villain, he comes across now is nearly comical, a self-aware performer keeping a straight face as he does his juicy threat-shtick.

McCarthy's power to stir fears of creeping Communism was not entirely based on illusion, of course; the paranoid, real or pretended, always secretes its pearl around a grain of fact. From being our wartime ally, the Soviet Union rapidly became a expanding empire.

Source: Arthur Miller, "Why I Wrote 'The Crucible,'" *New Yorker,* Oct. 21, 26, 1996, pp. 168–164.

In 1949, Mao Zedong took power in China. Western Europe also seemed ready to become Red—especially Italy, where the Communist Party was the largest outside Russia, and was growing. Capitalism, in the opinion of many, myself included, had nothing more to say, its final poisoned bloom having been Italian and German Fascism. McCarthy—brash and ill-mannered but to many authentic and true—boiled it all down to what anyone could understand: we had "lost China" and would soon lose Europe as well, because the State Department—staffed, of course, under Democratic Presidents—was full of treasonous pro-Soviet Intellectuals. It was as simple as that.

If our losing China seemed the equivalent of a flea's losing an elephant, it was still a phrase—and a conviction—that one did not dare to question; to do so was to risk drawing suspicion on oneself. Indeed, the State Department proceeded to hound and fire the officers who knew China, its language, and its opaque culture—a move that suggested the practitioners of sympathetic magic who wring the neck of a doll in order to make a distant enemy's head drop off. There was magic all around; the politics of alien conspiracy soon dominated political discourse and bid fair to wipe out any other issue. How could one deal with such enormities in a play?

"The Crucible" was an act of desperation, Much of my desperation branched out, I suppose, from a typical Depression—era trauma—the blow struck on the mind by the rise of European Fascism and the brutal anti-Semitism it had brought to power. But by 1950, when I began to think of writing about the hunt for Reds in America, I was motivated in some great part by the paralysis that had set in among many liberals who, despite their discomfort with the inquisitors' violations of civil rights, were fearful, and with good reason, of being identified as covert Communists if they should protest too strongly.

In any play, however trivial, there has to be a still point of moral reference against which to gauge the action. In our lives, in the late 1940s and early 1950s, no such point existed anymore. The left could not look straight at the Soviet Union's abrogations of human rights. The anti-Communist liberals could not acknowledge the violations of those rights by congressional committees. The far right, meanwhile, was licking up all the cream. The days of "J'accuse" were gone, for anyone needs to feel right to declare someone else wrong. Gradually, all the old political and moral reality had melted like a Dali watch. Nobody but a fanatic, it seemed, could really say all that he believed.

President Truman was among the first to have to deal with the dilemma, and his way of resolving itself having to trim his sails before the howling gale on the right turned out to be momentous. At first, he was outraged at the allegation of widespread Communist infiltration of the government and called the charge of "coddling Communists" a red herring dragged in by the Republicans to bring down the Democrats. But such was the gathering power of raw belief in the great Soviet plot that Truman soon felt it necessary to institute loyalty boards of his own.

The Red hunt, led by the House Committee on Un-American Activities and by McCarthy, was becoming the dominating fixation of the American psyche. It reached Hollywood when the studios, after first resisting, agreed to submit artists' names to the House Committee for "clearing" before employing them. This unleashed a veritable holy terror among actors, directors, and others, from Party members to those who had had the merest brush with a front organization.

The Soviet plot was the hub of a great wheel of causation; the plot justified the crushing of all nuance, all the shadings that a realistic judgment of reality requires. Even worse was the feeling that our sensitivity to this onslaught on our liberties was passing from us—indeed, from me. In "Timebends," my autobiography, I recalled the time I'd written a screenplay ("The Hook") about union corruption on the Brooklyn waterfront. Harry Cohn, the head of Columbia Pictures, did something that would once have been considered unthinkable: he showed my script to the F.B.I. Cohn then asked me to take the gangsters in my script, who were threatening and murdering their opponents, and simply change them to Communists. When I declined to commit this idiocy (Joe Ryan, the head of the longshoremen's union, was soon to go to Sing Sing for racketeering), I got a wire from Cohn saying, "The minute we try to make the script pro-American you pull out." By then—it was 1951—I had come to accept this terribly serious insanity as routine, but there was an element of the marvellous in it which I longed to put on the stage.

In those years, our thought processes were becoming so magical, so paranoid, that to imagine writing a play about this environment was trying to pick one's teeth with a ball of wool: I lacked the tools to illuminate miasma. Yet I kept being drawn back to it.

I had read about the witchcraft trials in college, but it was not until I read a book published in 1867—a two-volume, thousand-page study by Charles W. Upham, who was then the mayor of Salem—that I knew I had to write about the period. Upham had not only written a broad and thorough investigation of what was even then almost lost chapter of Salem's past but opened up to me the details of personal relationships among many participants in the tragedy.

I visited Salem for the first time on a dismal spring day in 1952; it was a side-tracked town then, with abandoned factories and vacant stores. In the gloomy courthouse there I read the transcripts of the witchcraft trails of 1692, as taken down in a primitive shorthand by ministers who were spelling each other. But there was one entry in Upham in which the thousands of pieces I had come across were jogged into place. It was from a report written by the Reverend Samuel Parris, who was one of the chief instigators of the witch-hunt. "During the examination of Elizabeth Procter, Abigail Williams and Ann Putnam"—the two who were "afflicted" teen-age accusers, and Abigail was Parris's niece—"both made offer to strike at said Procter, but when Abigail's hand came near, it opened, whereas it was made up into a fist before, and came down exceedingly lightly as it drew near to said Procter; and at length, with open and extended fingers, touched Proctor's hood very lightly. Immediately Abigail cried out her fingers, her fingers, her fingers burned . . ."

In this remarkably observed gesture of a troubled young girl, I believed a play became possible. Elizabeth Proctor had been the orphaned Abigail's mistress and they had lived together in the same small house until Elizabeth fired the girl. By this time, I was sure John Proctor had bedded Abigail, who had to be dismissed most likely to appease Elizabeth. There was bad blood between the two women now. That Abigail started, in effect to condemn Elizabeth to death with her touch, then stopped her hand, then went through with it, was quite suddenly the human center of all this turmoil.

All this I understood. I had not approached the witchcraft out of nowhere, or from purely social and political considerations. My own marriage of twelve years was teetering and I knew more than I wished to know about where the blame lay. That John Proctor the sinner might overturn his paralyzing personal guilt and become the most forthright voice against the madness around him was a reassurance to me, and, I suppose, an inspiration: it demonstrated that a clear moral outcry could spring even from an ambiguously unblemished soul. Moving crabwise across the profusion of evidence, I sensed that I had at last found something of myself in it, and a play began to accumulate around this man.

But as the dramatic form became visible, the one problem remained unyielding: so many practices of the Salem trials were similar to those employed by the congressional committees that I could easily be accused of skewing history for a mere partisan purpose. Inevitably, it was no sooner known that my new play was about Salem than I had to confront the charge that such an analogy was specious—that there never were any witches but there certainly are Communists. In the seventeenth century, however, the existence of witches was never questioned by the loftiest minds in Europe and America; and even lawyers of the highest eminence, like Sir Edward Coke, a veritable hero of liberty for defending the common law against the king's arbitrary power, believed that witches had to be prosecuted mercilessly. Of course, there were no Communists in 1692, but it was literally worth your life to deny witches or their powers, given the exhortation in the Bible, "Thou shalt not suffer a witch to live." There had to be witches in the world or the Bible lied. Indeed, the very structure of evil depended on Lucifer's plotting against God. (And the irony is that klatches of Luciferians exist all over the country today, there may even be more of them now than there are Communists.)

As with most humans, panic sleeps in one unlighted corner of my soul. When I walked at night along the empty, wet streets of Salem in the week that I spent there, I could easily work myself into imagining my terror before a gaggle of young girls flying down the road screaming that somebody's "familiar spirit" was chasing them. This anxiety-laden leap backward over nearly three centuries may have been helped along by one particular Upham footnote. At a certain point, the high court of the province made the fatal decision to admit, for the first time, the use of "spectral evidence" as proof of guilt. Spectral evidence, so aptly named, meant that if I swore that you had sent out your "familiar spirit" to choke, tickle, or poison me or my cattle, or to control my thoughts and actions, I could get you hanged unless you confessed to having had contact with the Devil. After all, only the Devil could lend such powers of invisible transport to confederates, in his everlasting plot to bring down Christianity.

Naturally, the best proof of the sincerity of your confession was your naming others whom you had seen in the Devil's company—an invitation to private vengeance, but made official by the seal of the theocratic state. It was as though the court had grown tired of thinking and had invited in the instincts: spectral evidence—that poisoned cloud of paranoid fantasy—made a kind of lunatic sense to them, as it did in plot-ridden 1952, when so often the question was not the acts of an accused but the thoughts and intentions in his alienated mind.

The breathtaking circularity of the process had a kind of poetic tightness. Not everybody was accused, after all, so there must be some *reason why you were.* By denying that there is any reason whatsoever for you to be accused, you are implying, by a virtue of a surprisingly small logical leap, that mere chance picked you out, which in turn implies that the Devil might not really be at work in the village or, God forbid, even exist. Therefore, the investigation itself is either mistaken or a fraud. You would have to be a crypto-Luciferian to say that—not a great idea if you wanted to go back to your farm.

The more I read into the Salem panic, the more it touched off corresponding images of common experiences in the fifties: the old friend of a blacklisted person crossing the street to avoid being seen talking to him; the overnight conversations of former leftists into born-again patriots; and so on. Apparently, certain processes are universal. When Gentiles in Hitler's Germany, for example, saw their Jewish neighbors being trucked off, or farmers in the Soviet Ukraine saw the Kulaks vanishing before their eyes, the common reaction, even among those unsympathetic to Nazism or Communism, was quite naturally to turn away in fear of being identified with the condemned. As I learned from non-Jewish refugees, however, there was often a despairing pity mixed with "Well, they must have done something." Few of us can easily surrender our belief that society must somehow make sense. The thought that the state has lost its mind and is punishing so many innocent people is intolerable. And so the evidence has to be internally denied.

I was also drawn into writing "The Crucible" by the chance it gave me to use a new language—that of seventeenth century New England. That plain, craggy English was liberating in a strangely sensuous way, with its swings from an almost legalistic precision to a wonderful metaphoric richness. "The Lord doth terrible things amongst us, by lengthening the chain of the roaring lion in a extraordinary manner, so that the Devil is come down in great wrath," Deodat Lawson, one of the great witch-hunting preachers, said in a sermon. Lawson rallied his congregation for what was to be nothing less than a religious war against the Evil One—"Arm, arm, arm!"—and his concealed anti-Christian accomplices.

But it was not yet my language, and among other strategies to make it mine I enlisted the help of a former University of Michigan classmate, the Greek-American scholar and poet Kimon Friar. (He later translated Kazantzakis.) The problem was not to imitate the archaic speech but to try to create a new echo of it, which would flow freely off American actor's tongues. As in the film, nearly fifty years later, the actors in the first production grabbed the language and ran with it as happily as if were their customary speech.

"The Crucible" took me about a year to write. With its five sets and a cast of twenty-one, it never occurred to me that it would take a brave man to produce it on Broadway, especially given the prevailing climate, but Kermit Bloomgarden never faltered. Well before the play opened, a strange tension had begun to build. Only two years earlier, the "Death of a Salesman" touring company had played to a thin crowd in Peoria, Illinois, having been nearly boycotted to death by the American Legion and the Jaycees. Before that, the Catholic War Veterans had prevailed upon the Army not to allow its theatrical groups to perform, first "All My Sons," and then any play of mine, in occupied Europe. The Dramatists Guild refused to protest attacks on a new play by Sean O'Casey, a self-declared Communist, which forced its producer to cancel his option. I knew of two suicides by actors depressed by the upcoming investigation, and every day seemed to bring news of people exiling themselves to Europe: Charlie Chaplin, the director Joseph Losey, Jules Dassin, the harmonica virtuoso Larry Adler, Donald Ogden Stewart, one of the most sought-after screenwriters in Hollywood, and Sam Wanamaker, who would lead the successful campaign to rebuild the Old Globe Theatre on the Thames.

On opening night, January 22, 1953, 1 knew that the atmosphere would be pretty hostile. The coldness of the crowd was not a surprise; Broadway audiences were not famous for loving history lessons, which is what they made of the play. It seems to me entirely appropriate that on the day the play opened, a newspaper headline read "ALL 13 REDS GUILTY"—a story about American Communists who faced prison for "conspiring to teach and advocate the duty and necessity of forcible overthrow of government." Meanwhile, the remoteness of the production was guaranteed by the director. Jed Harris, who insisted that this was a classic requiring the actors to face front, never each other. The critics were not swept away. "Arthur Miller is a problem playwright in both senses of the word," wrote Walter Kerr of the *Herald Tribune*, who called the play "a step backward into mechanical parable" *The Times* was not much kinder, saying, "There is too much excitement and not enough emotion in "The Crucible."" But the play's future would turn out quite differently.

About a year later, a new production, one with younger, less accomplished actors working in the Martinique Hotel ballroom, played with the fervor that the script and the times required, and "The Crucible" became a hit. The play stumbled into history, and today, I am told, it is one of the most heavily demanded trade-fiction paperbacks in this country; the Bantam and Penguin editions have sold more than six million copies. I don't think there has been a week in the past forty-odd years when it hasn't been on a stage somewhere in the world. Nor is the new screen version the first. Jean-Paul Sartre, in his Marxist phase, wrote a French film adaptation that blamed the tragedy of the rich landowners conspiring to persecute the poor. (In truth most of those hanged in Salem were people of substance, and two or three were very large landowners.)

It is only a slight exaggeration to say that, especially in Latin America, "The Crucible" starts getting produced wherever a political coup appears imminent, or a dictatorial regime has just been overthrown. From Argentina to Chile to Greece, Czechoslovakia, China, and a dozen other places, the play seems to present the same primeval structure of human sacrifice to the furies of fanaticism and paranoia that goes on repeating itself forever as though imbedded in the brain of social man.

I am not sure what "The Crucible" is telling people now, but I know that its paranoid center is still pumping out the same darkly attractive warning that it did in the fifties. For some, the play seems to be about the dilemma of relying on the testimony of small children accusing adults of sexual abuse, something I'd not have dreamed of forty years ago. For others, it may simply be a fascination with the outbreak of paranoia that suffuses the play—the blind panic that, in our age, often seems to sit at the dim edges of consciousness. Certainly its political implications are the central issue for many people; the Salem interrogations turn out to be eerily exact models of those yet to come in Stalin's Russia, Pinochet's Chile, Mao's China, and other regimes. (Nien Cheng, the author of "Life and Death in Shanghai," has told me that she could hardly believe a non-Chinese—someone who had not experienced the Cultural Revolution—had written the play.) But below its concerns with justice the play evokes a lethal brew of illicit sexuality, fear of the supernatural, and political manipulation, a combination not unfamiliar these days. The film, by reaching the broad American audience as no play can ever can, may well unearth still other connections to those buried public terrors that Salem first announced on this continent.

One more thing—something wonderful in the old sense of that word. I recall the weeks I spent reading testimony by the tome, commentaries, broadsides, confessions, and accusations. And always the crucial damning event was the signing of one's name in "the Devil's book." This Faustian agreement to hand over one's soul to the dreaded Lord of Darkness was the ultimate insult to God. But what were these new inductees supposed to have *done* once they signed on? Nobody seems to have thought to ask. But, of course, actions are irrelevant during cultural and religious wars as they are in nightmares. The thing at issue is buried intentions—the secret allegiances of the alienated heart, always the main threat to the theocratic mind, as well as its immemorial quarry.

Miller Is Cleared of House Contempt

Anthony Lewis

Arthur Miller's conviction of contempt of Congress was reversed today by the United States Court of Appeals for the District of Columbia.

The full nine-man court held unanimously that the House Committee on Un-American activities had not sufficiently warned the playwright of the risk of contempt if he refused to answer its questions. The court ordered him acquitted.

The opinion cited a 1955 Supreme Court ruling that a contempt conviction could not stand if the witness had not been clearly warned of the possible penalty for not answering a Congressional committee's questions.

The court did not mention that, a few days after the 1956 hearing, the House committee voted to give Mr. Miller ten more days to answer questions, with the implication that he would be cited for contempt if he did not. Mr. Miller, who is 42 years old, is regarded as one of the two or three most important living American playwrights. Among his plays are "All My Sons," The Crucible," "A View From the Bridge" and "Death of a Salesman," for which he won the Pulitzer Prize. His wife is Marilyn Monroe, the film actress.

The House Committee questioned Mr. Miller in the course of hearings about the use of passports by alleged communists.

The playwright testified freely about himself. He said he had never been a member of the Communist party but had had associations with many persons of Communist bent and had signed many communist-backed petitions.

His difficulties with the committee arose when he was asked to name other persons present at a meeting of "Communist writers" in 1947.

Mr. Miller refused to testify about other persons. He said he could not in good conscience do so, and he also argued that the questions were not pertinent to the committee's passport inquiry.

The House voted, 373 to 9, to cite him for contempt. He was convicted, fined $500 and given a thirty-day suspended jail sentence.

Because of the importance of the case and its expected controversial nature, all nine judges of the Court of Appeals sat in instead of the usual three. It was something of a surprise, therefore, when the decision came down today in a brief and cryptic unsigned opinion.

Source: Anthony Lewis, "Miller Is Cleared of House Contempt," *New York Times,* August 8, 1958.

The opinion noted that Mr. Miller had asked the House committee chairman, Representative Francis E. Walter, Democrat of Pennsylvania, "not to press the direction to answer the question and requested him to defer it until a later time. The chairman agreed."

The hearing ended shortly afterward, the court said, "without any unequivocally renewed direction or command to answer the 'suspended' question. On the whole record it seems clear that appellant had a right to leave the hearing thinking that the direction to answer was still suspended, if not abandoned."

Mr. Miller issued a statement through his lawyer here, Joseph L. Rauh Jr., that the decision made "the long struggle of the past few years fully worth while."

"I can only hope," the statement said, that the decision "will make some small contribution toward eliminating the excesses of Congressional committees and particularly toward stopping the inhuman process of making witnesses inform on long past friends and acquaintances."

William Hitz argued the case for the Government.

The Myth of the Liberal Campus

Michael Parenti

Abstract: *The existence of the liberal campus remains a myth in the U.S. Professors and students voicing radical ideologies continue to be repressed and even expelled by university management, who have their own personal agendas and interests to protect.*

For some time now, we have been asked to believe that higher education is being devalued by the "politically correct" tyrannies of feminists, African American nationalists, gays, lesbians, and Marxists. The truth is something else. In fact, most college professors and students are drearily conventional in their ideological proclivities. And the system of rule within the average university or college, be it private or public, owes more to Sparta than to Athens. The university is a chartered corporation ruled, like any other corporation, by a self-appointed, self-perpetuating board of trustees, composed overwhelmingly of affluent and conservative businesspeople.

Trustees retain final say over all matters of capital funding, investment, budget, academic curriculum, scholarships, tuition, and the hiring, firing, and promotion of administration and faculty personnel. At no time do they have to deal with anything that might be called democracy. *They face no free and independent campus press*, no elections, no opposing political slates, and no accountability regarding policy and performance. Conservative critics who rant about "politically correct" coercions appear to be perfectly untroubled by this oligarchic rule.

On these same campuses can be found faculty members who do "risk analysis" to help private corporations make safe investments in the Third World, or who work on marketing techniques and union busting, or who devise new methods for controlling rebellious peoples at home and abroad and new weapons systems and technologies for surveillance and counterinsurgency. (Napalm was invented at Harvard.) For handsome fees, these faculty offer bright and often ruthless ideas on how to make the world safe for those who own it.

On these same campuses, one can find recruiters from various corporations, the armed forces, and the intelligence agencies. In 1993, an advertisement appeared in campus newspapers promoting "student programs and career opportunities" with the CIA. Students

Source: Michael Parenti, "The Myth of the Liberal Campus," *The Humanist*, September–October 1995, vol. 55, no. 5, pp. 20–4.

"could be eligible for a CIA internship and tuition assistance" and would get "hands-on experience" working with CIA "professionals" while attending school. (The ad did not explain how full-time students could get experience as undercover agents. Would it be by reporting on professors and fellow students who voiced iconoclastic views?)

Without any apparent sense of irony, many of the faculty engaged in these worldly activities argue that a university should be a place apart from immediate worldly interests. In reality, many universities have direct investments in corporate America in the form of substantial stock portfolios. By purchase and persuasion, our institutions of higher learning are wedded to institutions of higher earning.

A Matter of Some History

Ideological repression in academia is as old as the nation itself. Through the eighteenth and nineteenth centuries, most colleges were controlled by religiously devout trustees who believed it their duty to ensure faculty acceptance of the prevailing theological preach meets. In the early 1800s, trustees at northern colleges prohibited their faculties from engaging in critical discussions of slavery; abolitionism was a taboo subject. At colleges in the South, faculty actively devoted much of their intellectual energies to justifying slavery and injecting white supremacist notions into the overall curriculum.

In the 1870s and 1880s, Darwinism was the great bugaboo. Presidents of nine prominent eastern colleges went on record as prohibiting the teaching of evolutionary theory. What is called "creationism" today was the only acceptable viewpoint on most of the nation's campuses.

By the 1880s, rich businessmen came to dominate the boards of trustees of most institutions of learning. They seldom hesitated to impose ideological controls. They fired faculty members who expressed heretical ideas on and off campus and who attended Populist Party conventions, championed antimonopoly views, supported free silver, opposed U.S. imperialism in the Philippines, or defended the rights of labor leaders and socialists.

During World War I, university officials such as Nicholas Murray Butler, president of Columbia University, explicitly forbade faculty from criticizing the war, arguing that in times of war such heresy was seditious. A leading historian, Charles Beard, was grilled by the Columbia trustees, who were concerned that his views might "inculcate disrespect for American institutions" In disgust, Beard resigned from his teaching position, declaring that the trustees and Nicholas Murray Butler sought "to drive out or humiliate or terrorize every man who held progressive, liberal, or unconventional views on political matters."

Academia never has been receptive to persons of anticapitalist persuasion. Even during the radical days of the 1930s, there were relatively few communists on college teaching staffs. Repression reached a heightened intensity with the McCarthyite witchhunts of the late 1940s and early 1950s. The rooting out of communists and assorted radicals was done by congressional and state legislative committees and, in many instances, university administrations. Administrators across the land developed an impressively coherent set of practices to carry out their purge.

Almost any criticism of the existing politico economic order invited suspicion that one might be harboring "communist tendencies." The relatively few academics who denounced the anticommunist witchhunts did so from an anticommunist premise, arguing that "innocent" (that is, noncommunist) people were being hounded out of their jobs and silenced in their professions. The implication was that the inquisition was not wrong, just overdone, that it was quite all right to deny Americans their constitutional rights if they were really "guilty" of harboring communist beliefs.

The Open and Closed University

The campus uprisings of the Vietnam era presented an entirely new threat to campus orthodoxy. University authorities responded with a combination of liberalizing and repressive measures. They dropped course-distribution requirements and abolished parietal rules and other paternalistic restrictions on student dormitory life. Courses in black studies and women's studies were set up, along with a number of other experimental programs that attempted to deal with contemporary and community oriented issues.

Along with these grudging concessions, university authorities launched a repressive counteroffensive. Student activists were disciplined, expelled, drafted into a war they opposed, and—at places like Kent State and Jackson State—shot and killed. Radicalized faculty lost their jobs and some, including myself, were attacked and badly beaten by police during campus demonstrations.

The repression continued throughout the 1970s and 1980s. Angela Davis, a communist, was let go at the University of California at Santa Cruz. Marlene Dixon, a Marxist feminist sociologist, was fired from the University of Chicago and then from McGill University for her political activism. Bruce Franklin, a tenured associate professor at Stanford, author of 11 books and 100 articles and an outstanding teacher, was fired for "inciting" students to demonstrate. Franklin later received an offer from the University of Colorado that was quashed by its board of regents, who based their decision on a packet of information supplied by the FBI. The packet included false rumors, bogus letters, and unfavorable news articles.

During the 1970s, eight of nine antiwar professors who tried to democratize the philosophy department at the University of Vermont were denied contract renewals in swift succession. Within a three-year period in the early 1970s at Dartmouth College, all but one of a dozen progressive faculty members (who used to lunch together) were dismissed. In 1987, four professors at the New England School of Law were fired, despite solid endorsements by their colleagues. All four were involved in the Critical Legal Studies movement, a left-oriented group that viewed the law as largely an instrument of the corporate rich and powerful.

One could add hundreds of cases involving political scientists, economists, historians, sociologists, and psychologists. Whole departments and even schools and colleges have been eradicated for taking the road less traveled. At Berkeley, the entire school of criminology was abolished because many of its faculty had developed a class analysis of crime and criminal law enforcement. Those among them who taught a more orthodox, mainstream criminology were given appointments in other departments. Only the radicals were let go.

One prominent Communist Party member, Herbert Aptheker, a stimulating teacher and productive scholar, was unable to get a regular academic appointment for over 50 years. In 1976, he was invited to teach a course at Yale University for one semester, but the administration refused to honor the appointment. Only after 18 months of protests by students and faculty did the Yale oligarchs give in. Even then, precautions were taken to ensure that Aptheker did not subvert too many Yalies. His course was limited to 15 students and was situated in the attic of a dingy building at a remote end of the campus. Aptheker had to travel from New York City to New Haven, Connecticut, for his once a week appearance; he was given no travel funds and was paid the grand sum of $2,000 for the entire semester. Yale survived the presence of a bona fide communist—but not without institutional officials trembling a bit. They were not afraid that Aptheker by himself would undermine the university, but that his appointment might be the first step in an opening to anticapitalist viewpoints.

Lefties Need Not Apply

The purging of dissidence within the universities continues to this day. More frequent but less visible than the firings are the nonhirings. Highly qualified social scientists who are also known progressives have applied for positions at places too numerous to mention, only to be turned down in favor of candidates who—as measured by their training, publications, and teaching experience—are far less qualified.

Scholars of a dissident bent are regularly discriminated against in the distribution of research grants and scholarships. After writing *The Power Elite*, C. Wright Mills was abruptly cut off from foundation funding. To this day, radical academics are rarely considered for appointments within their professional associations and are regularly passed over for prestigious lecture invitations and appointments to editorial boards of the more influential professional journals.

Faculty usually think twice about introducing a controversial politico-economic perspective into their classrooms. On some campuses, administration officials have monitored classes, questioned the political content of books and films, and screened the lists of campus guest speakers. While turning down leftist speakers, trustees and administrators have paid out huge sums for guest lectures by such right-wing ideologues as William F. Buckley and George Will, warmongers Henry Kissinger and Alexander Haig, and convicted felons G. Gordon Liddy and Oliver North.

Presumptions of Objectivity

The guardians of academic orthodoxy try to find seemingly professional and apolitical grounds for the exercise of their political repression. They will say the candidate has not published enough articles. Or if enough, the articles are not in conventionally acceptable academic journals. Or if in acceptable journals, they are still wanting in quality and originality or show too narrow or too diffuse a development.

Seemingly objective criteria can be applied in endlessly subjective ways. In an article in the January 1, 1983, Washington Post, John Womack, one of the very few Marxists ever to obtain tenure at an elite university, and who went on to become chair of the history department of Harvard, ascribes his survival to the fact that he was dealing with relatively obscure topics:

> "Had I been a bright young student in Russian history and taken positions perpendicular to American policy . . . I think my [academic] elders would have thought that I had a second rate mind. Which is what you say when you disagree with somebody. You can't say, 'I disagree with the person politically' You say, 'It's clear he has a second rate mind'"

Politically orthodox academics maintain that only their brand of teaching and research qualifies as scholarship. They seem unaware that this view might itself be an ideological one, a manifestation of their own self-serving, unexamined political biases. Having judged Marxist or feminist scholars as incapable of disinterested or detached scholarship, the guardians of orthodoxy can refuse to hire them under the guise of protecting rather than violating academic standards.

In fact, *much of the best scholarship comes from politically committed investigators*. Thus it was female and African American researchers who, in their partisan urgency, have produced new and rich critiques of the unexamined sexist and racist presumptions of conventional research. They have ventured into fruitful areas that most of their white male colleagues never imagined were fit subjects for study.

Likewise, it is *leftist intellectuals who have produced the challenging scholarship about popular struggles* and often the only revealing work on political economy and class power-subjects remaining largely untouched by "objective" centrists and conservatives. In sum, partisan concerns and a dissenting ideology can actually free us from long-established blind spots and awaken us to things overlooked by the prevailing orthodoxy.

Orthodox ideological strictures are applied not only to scholarship but to a teacher's outside political activity. At the University of Wisconsin at Milwaukee, an instructor of political science, Ted Hayes, an anticapitalist, was denied reappointment because he was judged to have "outside political commitments" that made it impossible for him to be an objective, unbiased teacher. Two of the senior faculty who voted against him were state committee members of the Republican Party in Wisconsin. There was no question as to whether their outside political commitments interfered with their objectivity as teachers or with the judgments they made about colleagues.

In a speech delivered in Washington, D.C., Evron Kirkpatrick, who served as director of the American Politic for 25 years, proudly enumerated the many political scientists who occupied public office, worked in electoral campaigns, or in other ways served officialdom in various capacities. His remarks evoked no outcry from his mainstream colleagues on behalf of scientific detachment. It seemed that there was nothing wrong with political activism as long as one played a "sound role in government" (Kirkpatrick's words) rather than a dissenting role against it. Establishment academics like Kirkpatrick never explain how they supposedly avoid injecting politics into their science while so assiduously injecting their science into politics.

How neutral in their writings and teachings were academics such as Zbigniew Brzezinski, Henry Kissinger, and Daniel Patrick Moynihan? Despite being blatant proponents of American military industrial policies at home and abroad—or because of it—they enjoyed meteoric academic careers and subsequently were selected to serve as prominent acolytes to the circles of power. Outspoken political advocacy is not a hindrance to one's career as long as one advocates the right things.

The Myth of the Radical Campus

To repeat, at the average university or college, the opportunities to study, express, and support (or reject) iconoclastic, antiestablishment views are severely limited. Conservatives, however, believe otherwise. They see academia as permeated with leftism. They brand campus protests against racism, sexism, and U.S. interventionism abroad as "politically correct McCarthyism." Thus the attempts to fight reactionism are themselves labeled reactionary and the roles of oppressor and oppressed are reversed. So is fostered the myth of a university dominated by feminists, gays, Marxists, and black militants.

In dozens of TV opinion shows and numerous large circulation publications across the nation, scores of conservative writers complain, without any sense of irony, of being silenced by the "politically correct." Their diatribes usually are little more than attacks upon sociopolitical views they find intolerable and want eradicated from college curricula. Through all this, one never actually hears from the "politically correct" people who supposedly dominate the universe of discourse.

Today, a national network of well-financed, right-wing campus groups coordinates most conservative activities at schools around the nation and funds over 100 conservative campus publications, reaching more than a million students. These undertakings receive millions of dollars from the Sciafe Foundation, the Olin Foundation, and other wealthy donors. The nearly complete lack of alternative funding for progressive campus groups belies the charge that political communication in academia is dominated by left wingers.

Accusations of partisanship are leveled against those who challenge—but rarely against those who reinforce—the prevailing orthodoxies. By implicitly accepting the existing power structure on its own terms, then denying its existence and all the difficult questions it raises, many academics believe they have achieved a scholarly detachment from the turmoil of reality. And in a way, they have.

Michael Parenti is the author of *Land of Idols: Political Mythology in America*. This article has been adapted from his soon-to-be-published book *Against Empire* (San Francisco: City Lights Books).

(Editor's note: italicized lines have been introduced into the body of the article.)

III. Belief System as a Social Institution

Jesus Causes Confusion

Andrew M. Greeley

Jesus was a difficult person. He had a very bad habit of refusing to fit into anyone's paradigms.

He learned a lot from the Pharisees, but he wasn't one of them. He may have hung out with the Essenes, but he was not a compulsive hand-washer. He was surely a Jew, steeped in the Torah, but he put a very different spin on it. He was charming and even witty and told wonderful stories but he refused to be a celebrity. He dealt politely with those in authority, but did not sign on with them. Half the time he reassured people and the other half the time he scared them. He told all the old stories but with new and disconcerting endings. He was patently a troublemaker. Which is why they had to get rid of him. He ended up alone with few, if any, friends.

It's been that way ever since. Everyone claims him for their own. He's on our side. He's doing things our way. He confirms what we say. Then when we think we've sewed him up, he's not there anymore. When we have domesticated Jesus, we may have a very interesting person on our hands, even a superstar maybe. Alas, it is not the real Jesus. He's gone somewhere else, preaching his contradictions about his father's kingdom and stirring up his kind of trouble.

Jesus is as troubling to us as he was to men and women in his own time. We find him attractive and want him as a friend. However, we don't like his elusiveness, his challenge, his paradoxes, his weird parables. We would rather that he settle down and be on our side, that he provide consolation indeed but no challenge, that he would fade into the soft glow of Christmas tree lights and, at least for the holiday season, refrain from stirring up trouble, especially in our consciences.

It is his birthday, after all; would he please play our game our way instead of presuming that we have to play his game? Why does he have to be larger than life during the joyous season? If he can't leave us alone, will he please go away with his trouble-making until after the first of the year?

A Jesus who does not disconcert and shake us up is not Jesus at all.

So, does he disconcert us at Christmas?

Does he challenge those who work themselves into a frenzy preparing for Christmas and then are so exhausted that they are mean to all those for whom they think they're working?

Source: Andrew Greeley, "Jesus Causes Confusion." *Daily Southtown.* Tinley Park, IL., Copyright © 2001 The Sun-Times Co. December 24, 2000, op-ed page.

Does he disconcert those of us who eat and drink too much?

Does he make those who prate about "happy holidays" on radio and television feel uneasy?

Does he trouble those who with superior sophistication dismiss this festival as nothing more than a trick of consumerist capitalism?

Does he embarrass those who use the feast to unearth all the sibling rivalries and parent-child conflicts of the past? And those who love to sink themselves into a swamp of self-pity?

Does the poverty of his birth disturb the CEOs who make a thousand times more money (not including bonuses!) than their employees?

Does his elusiveness trouble those politicians who claim him as a political philosopher—preaching their philosophy, of course?

Does he cause some guilt pains (minor, of course!) in those triumphalist religious leaders who think they have a monopoly on his wisdom and truth? Does he make all of us wonder about how much money we are spending on Christmas?

Does he cause us to worry about how stingy our gifts are?

Does he challenge us in the depth of our soul about how we live in the world and how we make use of our goods and of creation?

Does he make us ask ourselves whether, in our relations with those who love us, we might have hearts as cold as the sub-zero wind-chill index?

If he does not wish us an uneasy as well as a merry Christmas, he may be a wonderful guest at the party, but don't trust him because he's not the one whose birth we are celebrating.

If the cute little baby Jesus in the crib with the angels and shepherds and oxen and sheep hovering around and the wise men struggling across the desert doesn't make us ask questions like this, then he remains a cute little kid; only he's not the baby Jesus anymore.

Andrew M. Greeley is a Roman Catholic priest, author and sociologist. He teaches at the University of Chicago and the University of Arizona. His column on political, church and social issues appears each Sunday in the *Daily Southtown*. Father Greeley's e-mail address is Agreel@aol.com and his home page, which includes homilies for every Sunday, is http://www.agreeley.com.

To the Dot-Com Station

Thomas Frank

Whatever can be done, will be done.
If not by incumbents, it will be done by emerging players.
If not in a regulated industry, it will be done in a new industry born without regulation.
Technological change and its effects are inevitable.
Stopping them is not an option.

—Andy Grove of Intel[1]

One is tempted to add, "resistance is futile."

—Kevin Kelly, 1998[2]

The Wages of Reaction

If it was a bad decade for journalistic "adversarialism," the nineties were disastrous for more specifically critical traditions. Journalists learned to "listen" while intellectuals of all kinds were advised to let go the stubborn egotism of ideas and feel the market pulsate through them. Americans were warned that badmouthing the market—loose lips sink stocks!—could very well bring on crash, disaster, war. They were informed that the accumulated economic knowledge of the centuries, along with all our ideas about what democracy looked like, were as nothing to the "New Economy." And, as if to give concrete form to the market's hostility to ideas, the crisis in academic labor shredded the aspirations of an entire generation of young scholars. [Ed. note: And with the recent crash, we paid the price.]

But while it was bucket-kicking time for some ideas, it was a seller's market for others. If you were the lucky proprietor of a quirky new intellectual technique for reaching the decade's favorite ideological conclusion—that the market was the highest and the greatest and the most enviable form of human organization—then it was a great time to be in the intellectual business. The bookstores and the magazines blossomed with zany new meta-theories, each one purporting to explain how all of human history merely led up to the victory of the free-market "New Economy" over the government-laden old. George Gilder profited by describing class conflict as the battle between new money and old while Tyler Cowen divided us all up into cultural pessimists and cultural optimists.

Source: Thomas Frank, *One Market Under God: Extreme Capitalism, Market Populism, and the End of Economic Democracy.* Doubleday, New York, 2000 pp. 341–358 & footnotes 397–398.

But in this glamorous new marketplace of bad ideas, few could match the achievement of Virginia Postrel, editor of the libertarian magazine *Reason* and a contributor to *Forbes ASAP*. Hers was the provocative thesis that the great, transhistorical conflict of Business Man with his traditional enemies—critics and government regulators (she made almost no mention of labor unions, a fairly common oversight by 1998)—was in fact a titanic battle between "dynamists" and "stasists," between those who believe in the people and will let them do whatever they want (provided they do it through the market and with duly signed contracts), and those who think they know better and who thus favor a world ordered by technocrats. At least, that's how Postrel tells it. But so lopsidedly does she heap praise on her "dynamists" and shower abuse on her "stasists" that one feels they might more appropriately be labeled "saints" and "the worst assholes ever." The motley assortment of blowhard politicians, environmentalists, and griping naysayers who make up the "stasist" camp are not only elitists in the usual market-populist sense (they believe in expertise, they're skeptical of the market, and hence they're hostile to the tastes and preferences of the people), but they seem to have profoundly evil designs on the world. Postrel charges them with despising beach volleyball and with secretly wishing to "forever yoke the world's peasants behind a water buffalo." The stasist rogues gallery, it turns out, contains a truly astonishing assortment of hate-figures: Ur-regulator Louis Brandeis, there for his sins against the railroads, is joined bizarrely with the southerners who passed Jim Crow laws. They are teamed up with the Unabomber, Jean-Marie Le Pen, the French in general, Robert Moses, and the grasping, ill-clad hairdressing regulators of New York State who so persecuted Vidal Sassoon back in the sixties. Pol Pot, making a cameo appearance as the greatest "stasist" of them all, is said to differ from other members of that monstrous fraternity—like the meddling legislators who passed affirmative action and who are mentioned a few sentences later—only in degree.[3] It is a scheme for understanding history so daft it's worthy of John Perry Barlow himself.

But Postrel's object isn't to understand the subtleties of history. Nor is it really to equate business with democracy, although that is, of course, an important theme. Her goal is to lay claim to the one idea that Americans hold in even higher esteem than democracy itself: the future. "The central question of our time," she writes, "is what to do about the future." Should we take the route of the fiendish "stasists," with their government regulation, their lousy clothes, and their killing fields? Or should we follow the "dynamists," those true believers in human promise (who turn out when Postrel names them mainly to be captains of industry, management theorists, and Republican politicians)? The decision is easy to make; in fact, it's been made for us. We *can't* follow the "stasists" to the future, because by definition *that's not where they are going.* Since "the future" and "free markets" are essentially the same thing, to wish to restrain the latter is to set oneself fully against the former. "Stasists" are thus, in addition to all their other crimes, "enemies of the future."[4]

Readers who are put off by such casual stinging of Stalinoid accusation should know that Postrel's 1998 book, *The Future and Its Enemies* (for that was its title as well as its signature idea), was highly acclaimed by thinkers like Tom Peters and James Glassman, who would soon distinguish himself with *Dow 36,000*. It even earned Postrel a gig as an occasional columnist for the business section of the *New York Times*. Few in those exalted circles found it unseemly to hear a colleague arraign critics of business as "enemies of the future." By 1998 this was a style of accusation and of analysis that friends of the "New Economy" found perfectly comfortable, if not reassuring. That markets had a special connection to "the future" just as they did to "the People" was, if not a universal given of the late nineties, a proud conviction of the true believers.

Zeitgeist and Weltgeist

Usually this connection between the market and the future was explained by business thinkers in the language of technological and demographic determinism: The triumph of markets over everything else was not only democratic, it was "inevitable" because computers were growing faster and cheaper, because bandwidth was doing its miraculous tricks, because the kids just wouldn't stand for it, because globalization was so overwhelmingly, unthinkably, authoritatively global. That determinism of any kind flatly contradicted the everyone-will-be-free promise of the Internet and of market populism generally seems to have bothered no one. In fact, the two ideas were often connected rhetorically, in a kind of good cop/bad cop routine: The market will give you a voice, empower you to do whatever you want to do—and if you have any doubts about that, then the market will crush you and everything you've ever known.

In the "grand argument" in which business literature imagines itself engaged, "inevitability" served as a sort of logical atom bomb to be dropped on foes like unions, liberals, and environmentalists when conventional talk of "democracy" failed. It was a technique for putting over a backward social system through simple cocksureness about the future, a rhetorical maneuver we haven't seen so much of on these shores since the heyday of thirties-style Marxism and the appearance on best-seller lists of John Strachey's *The Coming Struggle for Power*.[5]

The tactic grew increasingly common toward the end of the decade. When economist Lester Thurow ran into narrative problems in his 1999 work of "New Economy" evangelism, *Building WEALTH*, he simply escalated right away up to "inevitability." Regardless of what you may think about genetic engineering, for example, it will "inevitably" triumph over its doubters; whatever reservations you might have about billionaire proliferation, "trying to defend" old standards of income equality "is impossible"; whatever those Europeans might think they're up to, they "will have to adjust to the realities of a global economy," as "wishing for a different game is a waste of time."[6]

Thus Thomas Friedman imagined the secretary of the treasury whipping it out to bring the prime minister of Malaysia back into line ("Ah, excuse me, Mahathir, but what planet are you living on? . . . Globalization isn't a choice. It's a reality.") and fantasizes how political systems the world over will be transformed by means of a "golden straitjacket" into replicas of our own.[7]

Thus the first sentence in Kevin Kelly's 1998 book, *New Rules for the New Economy*: "No one can escape the transforming fire of machines." The point of the book is that we must act at once to remake the world in the image of the Internet, but it's probably better to read it as a primer on the dark science of passing off really bad ideas—bad ideas that nevertheless happen to be making all your friends really rich—through mystification, superstition, and panic. "The net is our future," Kelly writes, "the net is moving irreversibly to include everything of the world," and, finally, this imperative: "Side with the net." That is, unless you fancy being run over by the freight train of history.[8]

To discover the origins of this strategy, though, we must turn again to George Gilder, fully transformed by the late nineties from griping backlasher into "radical technotheorist."

Although Gilder bears much responsibility for launching the market-populist project, he also seems never really to have believed in its power to put laissez-faire across all by itself. Something much more intimidating would be required to suppress the liberal impulse, and all the way back in 1989 he set about finding it. So even as he was discovering that the microchip endorsed by its very architecture the class politics of the entrepreneur, he was also finding that the microchip revealed to mankind a number of new *laws of the universe*. In the mid-eighties Gilder had written that entrepreneurs "know the rules of the world and the laws of God"; by 1989 the entrepreneurs were writing the laws themselves, revealing them to the world through their intermediary, the Moses of the Microchip, descended from the heights of Sand Hill Road: "Moore's Law," "Metcalfe's Law," Gilder's own "Law of the Microcosm," and the awe-inducing "Law of the Telecosm," all of them as unrepealable as the old laws of gravity and of diminishing return.[9]

New laws of nature—*that specifically affirmed the politics of Gilder's beloved entrepreneur!* Now here was an idea to conjure with. Gilder could now simply inform us that we had either to bow to the freemarket way or die. Not because he was still hostile toward those who doubted the market—good gracious, no!—but because there was simply no power on earth that could prevent the microchip from realizing its colossal market-populist ambitions. What Gilder called the "microcosm" was thus a foolproof device (literary if not factual) by which the imperatives of the free market could be made to triumph over all the peoples and all the ideas of the world. *Inevitably, inexorably, remorselessly, universally.* "The laws of the microcosm are so powerful and fundamental that they restructure nearly everything else around them," he wrote. And again: "However slowly theory catches up to practice, the microcosm will increasingly dominate international reality, subduing all economic and political organizations to its logic."[10]

But "subduing all economic and political organizations" wasn't enough for Gilder. Finally throwing caution to the wind he went all the way: "The logic of the microcosm" was becoming the very "*logic of history*," getting set to deliver all of mankind to that luminous reverse communism in the sky where the state really does wither away and the dreams of the heroic soda pop bottlers and real estate operators who inhabited Gilder's earlier books would come true at last. *Inevitably* would the meddling feds lose control. *Inevitably* would labor unions decline into irrelevance. And *inevitably* would all the vaunted forms and receipts and regulations of the bureaucrat crumble like so much soggy paper.[11] Those who humbly imbibed the wisdom of the market profited immensely; those who arrogantly defied it declined in a slow death spiral that was encoded in the very weft of nature.

"These are not mere prophecies," the ever-humble Gilder wrote. "They are the imperious facts of life." Equipped with the microchip the capitalist is "no longer entangled in territory, no longer manacled to land, capital, or nationality."[12] The chosen of history but also free of history, free of corporeality, he is free of the laws of man and nature. He is pure idea, pure spirit, a god in his own right.

From New Times to New Economy

In Britain, where the "New Economy" was embraced in the late nineties as the miracle-worker that would snap the country out of its long decline, "inevitability" was put to much more rigorous uses. At the London think tank Demos, the thought of Gilder, Tom Peters, and Kevin Kelly was spun into the finest gold of "New Labour" industrial policy. For all its commitment to the Silicon Valley way, though, Demos was the kind of organization that would probably send old Gilder into a red-seeing rage. Martin Jacques, who helped to found the think tank in 1993, was an editor of both the Communist Party magazine *Marxism Today* and the 1989 *New Times* collection of essays that foreshadowed the periodical's termination. Geoff Mulgan, a writer who came with him from *Marxism Today*, served as director of Demos until 1998, when he began working for the prime minister. Charles Leadbeater, who contributed to both *New Times* and *Marxism Today*, is its reigning deep thinker, producing practical-looking policy booklets whose titles seem to return again and again to a mystic link between entrepreneurship and national identity (*Civic Entrepreneurship, The Rise of the Social Entrepreneur, The Independents: Britain's New Cultural Entrepreneurs*, and *Britain: The California of Europe?*). Both Mulgan and Leadbeater wrote much-celebrated works on the standard "New Economy" themes; Mulgan's book *Connexity* was published in the US by the Harvard Business School Press in 1998, while Leadbeater's book *Living on Thin Air* came out in Britain in 1999. The two men were very much the intellectuals of the "New Labour" moment: Demos held seminars at Downing Street, Mulgan became a member of Blair's "policy unit," and Leadbeater, who was once rumored to be the prime minister's very favorite political thinker, boasted blurbs from Blair as well as Peter Mandelson, the New Labour spinmeister, on the dust jacket of his book.

When I was a student the *New Times* group was a theoretical force to be reckoned with; their 1989 anthology was the product of a scholarly sophistication far beyond the ken of a Midwestern kid like myself. And the various Demos publications initially inspired the same feeling of awestruck inadequacy. Again the authors spoke with an authority that seemed to arise from intimate familiarity with the massive, overwhelming forces that are remaking our world and determining our fates. The favorite label in the nineties, "New Economy," was slightly more specific than the older "New Times," and the grand historical themes which the Demos writers summon up—entrepreneurship, technology, and the market— were quite different from the big picture of 1989. Instead of Marx's dialectic they now had Moore's Law.

The head-swimming effect was the same as ever, though, with the Demos gang nimbly condemning "the conventions, laws, codes, and organizations we have inherited from industrial society" and tossing about the usual end-of-everything-you've-ever-known concepts like "the knowledge economy" and "weightless work." The reader reeled before the array of outrageous facts that were rattled off to show the obsolescence of the material world: The stock market valuation of Microsoft, the number of computers in a car, Nike's massive subcontracting network (*they don't make the shoes themselves!*). The "old economy" was not only "old," it was as dead and gone and forgotten and irrelevant as the five-year plans of the thirties. We can never go back.[13]

But if you read far enough into the works of Demos, you would discover that what the authors had actually done was simply round up various clichés from popular management literature and, adopting a tone of extreme historical righteousness, recast them as political advice. It was all there: The flattened, antihierarchical corporation as the way of the future, attacks on Taylorism, breathless praise for the "learning organization," the magic of "networks," even talk about "free agents." "Branding" emerged as the weightiest concept of all, the Demos solution to nearly everything that ailed Britain. Branding was what would survive as material industry dissolved into insignificance in the "weightless" years to come, they argued; branding was what justified companies' bizarre stock market valuations; branding was now something of a science; and what's more, building brands just happened to be what the British people were good at! In 1997, Demos actually suggested that the UK "rebrand" itself, purposely set about altering the world's perception of the country the same way that, say, Oldsmobile has tried to shake off its association with wealthy oldsters.[14]

Unfortunately, mixing high state seriousness with the inanity of management literature sometimes yielded some pretty stupid stuff. In *Living on Thin Air*, Leadbeater illustrated certain aspects of the rise of the "New Economy"—speedy entrepreneurs vs. slow moving big companies; cool brands vs. square brands—by comparing them to Princess Diana's struggle with the royal family and then taking an entire chapter to work out every absurd angle of this preposterous analogy. In a 1999 policy pamphlet titled *The Independents*, Leadbeater and a coauthor wrote a document that could easily pass as a parody of misguided think-tankery: Noting how important young creative rebels were to the British economy— the British music industry alone, another pamphlet noted, was the country's "strongest export sector"—they soberly, seriously, judiciously laid out a program by which cities could plan and develop thriving urban bohemias, "rebranding" themselves in an attractive manner and replacing dying heavy industry with colonies of profitable nonconformists. As if this spectacle of authorized dissidence and scientifically validated government schemes to promote "innovation in pop music" weren't enough, the pamphlet ended by soberly reporting a truly world-class bit of market idiocy: Like American towns bidding for a peripatetic NFL franchise, one dying Midlands city was finding its efforts to attract bohemians to its run-down former industrial district undermined by the even more aggressive boho-policies of *another* dying Midlands city only forty miles away![15]

In America, when leftists change sides and come around to the virtues of the business civilization, it is a privileged moment, a political set piece of great symbolic significance. Not only do we reward leftist apostates such as Whittaker Chambers and David Horowitz with undying literary fame or lifelong ideological sinecures, but we find in their movement from left to right an especially satisfying confirmation of the goodness of the corporate order. Having fought the market on behalf of the common people, on behalf of the workers, on behalf of equality, they now constitute living proof that the market is the true and correct protector of those noble causes. Their enthusiasm for capitalism is thus a special enthusiasm, an enthusiasm that somehow ranks above that of the poolside loungers at the country club or the traders in the Merc's pork-belly pit.

Demos offered a curious twist on this classic narrative. What they brought to the market wasn't so much the blessing of the workers, or even the sacred cause of equality, but the aura of "radicalism" itself. The value of this was obvious in a commercial climate like that of the nineties, when "radical," "subversive," and "extreme" were terms of approbation in everyday commercial use. Just as Diana was a different sort of royal than the queen, it was a different thing entirely when "radicals" approved of the market system than when Tories did. Demos's affirmations were worth something because Demos was cool. The Demos people wanted to build bohemia, not tear it down out of some misguided dedication to "tradition." They liked rock bands, they referred casually to rave scenes, they knew in which neighborhoods and even in which bars the cool people of Glasgow, Sheffield, and Manchester could be found. It was never very convincing when Tories talked about the creativity required for entrepreneurship; it was considerably more so when former leftist Leadbeater called for a "constitution which encourages experimentation, diversity, and dissent."[16] And it was infinitely more credible when a genuine revolutionary saluted the "revolutionary business model" of the hot advertising agency du jour than when *Advertising Age* did the same.

But it was in the eternal battle to uphold the truths of the market order that Demos really shone. While the world's telecom firms, software makers, and online brokerages fought an ideological bidding war, each one striving to top the others' association of the market with freedom, with democracy, Demos provided the theoretical ammunition. The democracy of markets was a fantasy that Mulgan, in particular, proved skillful in affirming. Writing in his book *Connexity*, he discredited the various traditional bête noirs of the business class—taxation and government economic planning—by linking them (and quite wrongly, especially in the American case) to "the era of absolute monarchy." He blamed not overweening, overpolluting, lying corporations for the vast tide of popular disaffection one found both in the UK and the US, but instead what he called "governmental hubris"—the bureaucrat's fatal impulse to fix everything. And he informed readers that "the upper classes in England resisted the telephone," thereby setting up communications technology as an automatic subverter of the power of "elites."[17]

Ah, but the Internet-empowered world of "connexity": Here was a place, Mulgan believed, where those hated "absolute hierarchies of culture" disappeared along with the "automatic respect" once paid to political leaders and aristocrats. Here was a land where the leftist dreams of yore were being swiftly accomplished, where new means of communication "liberate people from the bonds of settled agriculture and industry." In fact, so democratic were the market forces that gave us this wondrous "connexity" that Mulgan found it useful to reverse the traditional comparison: Electoral democracy was only democratic insofar as it operated according to the market principles of choice and competition.[18] (According to those standards, ironically, New Labour's much celebrated rapprochement with the market, as well as Clinton's "triangulations," could be understood as offenses against democracy itself, since they essentially deprived voters of any real political choice.)

Demos's greatest contributions were its thoughts on inevitability. Columnist Nick Cohen, who had some experience with the Demos crowd when they were briefly in charge of editing *The Independent* newspaper, recounts that "Leadbeater and the rest had lost their faith in socialism, but in their conversation you could still hear the sharp accents of Marxist teleology. . . ."

> History was moving down the tracks; questioning the inevitable was pointless. After being given a long lecture in this vein, an old hand staggered out of an editorial conference. "These People used to go to Moscow and say, 'I've seen the future—and It Works!'" he bellowed. "Now they go to Singapore and cry: 'I've seen the future—and Gosh!'"[19]

Even in their dry policy booklets a tone of historical smugness seemed to be the Demos house literary conceit: Anthologies bore titles like *Tomorrow's Politics* and *Life After Politics*; blurbs asserted that "to read Mulgan is to read the future"; authors tended to slip nonchalantly into the future tense, to reason that, as "the future" will be requiring X, we'd better be doing Y in order to prepare. For Leadbeater, especially, all arguments about globalization and markets boiled down to questions of being in synch with our historical epoch. He began *Living on Thin Air* by warning that "we are on the verge of the global twenty-first century knowledge economy, yet we rely on national institutions inherited from the nineteenth-century industrial economy"; he made its narrative go by giving us hints of "what the knowledge-creating company of the future will look like." Strangely, Leadbeater also believed that the heroic entrepreneurs who populated his works shared his ability to predict the future. Thus he attributed the success of the great Bill Gates to his powers of "precognition," his ability "to discern the emerging shape of competition . . . before everyone else."[20] It was as though the sage of Seattle had been by his side all along, from the days of *New Times* even, marching with the People as they advanced to meet their Future.

Looking back after ten years at the *New Times* anthology with which all this began, what impresses one most is the then-Marxist authors' powerful need to define the historical "epoch" that the Western world was then entering. In the book's introduction a name for the big change is suggested (the world was moving from "Fordism" to "post-Fordism") and leftists were warned of the dangers of being "overtaken by history." A "Manifesto for New Times" further noted that new ideas were necessary because "socialism has always claimed to speak for the future." Before it was anything else, according to this view, socialism was the custodian of historical periodicity, the movement responsible for understanding where we were going and what would have to be done when we arrived.[21]

Reading through the Demos books one can't help but marvel at the grip that historical determinism still held on the authors, even after its political polarities had been reversed. For Leadbeater and Mulgan, at least, it seemed to have drowned out every other consideration, every other value. They dumped the once-beloved working class, for example, like so much industrial slag, opting instead to cheer for the "cultural entrepreneurs." Does Marxism, like Jesuitism, leave its imprint on the soul even after apostasy?

Maybe, but a more likely explanation of the Demos shift is the same "New Economy" magnetism that sparked a brain drain in the world's consultancies and a gold rush in Silicon Valley, that sent everyone with even modest bullshit-slinging skills west to take their shot—any kind of shot—at that magic options/IPO combination. Forget the proletariat, forget the dialectic: Think NASDAQ. The only power worth considering in the world of the late nineties was the size of the rewards being handed out to the "New Economy" winners—the McMansions, the overnight 200 percent gains, the seven-figure bonuses. And the people from Demos were simply doing what they could—give 'em democracy! give 'em inevitability!—to ensure that the IPO Santa Claus made a stop in their country as well. For these were prizes for which we would gladly surrender anything, sink seventy years of social advance, lock up two million of our fellow citizens, send our heavy industry up in flames, *anything—just to keep that ticker spiking upward.*

The Pump and Dump Future

What does a capitalist ideologue do when she finds herself, by some twist of fate, driving the train of history? For some it is just another way to win that "grand argument."* Virginia Postrel, who apparently can sometimes pick out "enemies of the future" by their personality type alone,[22] doesn't do so in order to hustle us (for I am named as one of those "enemies") off to reeducation camps, where we might be made more amenable to "plenitude,"

---

* Note: for a detailed discussion of the "grand argument" see Chapter 1 of Thomas Frank's *One Market Under God: Extreme Capitalism, Market Populism, and the End of Economic Democracy.*

to beach volleyball, to popular music, and to the wacky "fun" enjoyed so abundantly in the office complexes of Silicon Valley. The point is, rather, to use "the future" as another weapon to pummel critics—costly, troublemaking critics—in the here and now.[23] For all Postrel's erudition, her writing sometimes reads less like a serious theory of politics than an extended new-business presentation to the nation's industrialists: These are the tools I can deploy on your behalf. With just a few references to "elitism," "the future," and the grand tale of "progress," we can put those dirty regulators and nasty critics back in their place.

But leave that battle to the true believers. Most readers of business literature just want to get rich. For them knowledge of the future is valuable only insofar as the seer can use it to make miraculous investments—the same golden promise that drives the plot of Hollywood movies dealing with time travel. And this is where capitalist inevitability has done its finest service, keeping the brokers busy and the mutual fund money flowing. Thus Rich Karlgaard, writing in the summer of 1999 as the publisher of *Forbes*, used "Moore's Law" and its allied principles to reassure investors suffering from cold feet:

> Hold the phone. The pace *can* go on. The physics of the Information Age is a sure bet. Chips *are* headed toward infinite speed at zero cost. So is bandwidth. The radical new software and e-commerce business models that will follow in their wake can only be guessed at. But their arrival is a sure bet. Zany zooms in the underlying power are locked in.[24]

Locked in. If, as John Kenneth Galbraith charged, runaway bull markets are propelled onward and upward by "incantation" of a particularly reverent sort, this was the incantation to top them all. That was no bubble on Wall Street; it was the future itself, generously whispering its secrets into the ears of the faithful and making us all wealthy beyond our wildest dreams.

Leave it to the great Gilder, the man who popularized the concept of "locked-in" progress in the first place, to come up with the most enterprising way to capitalize on this gift of prophecy. In 1996 he began issuing a pricy tip-sheet for investors anxious to cash in on the mad stock appreciations that theories like his had made possible. Here at last was the business end of Gilder's clairvoyance, what all his "laws" and "paradigms" and "inevitabilities" came down to in the end: Subscribers to his $295-a-year *Gilder Technology Report* could "grow rich on the coming technology revolution." As a mail solicitation for the newsletter promised, they would learn why "the Law of the Telecosm" would cause certain stocks to climb so rapidly that even Microsoft would be left in the dust. They would learn about "the Gilder paradigm," find out "why the bandwidth revolution is inevitable!" And for those who weren't sure about this Gilder fellow, the solicitation included the spellbound endorsement of his publisher, Tim Forbes: "I am convinced that the future as George sees it will happen."[25]

Strangely, the future as George saw it *did* happen, again and again. Not because of Gilder's psychic powers, but because the overheated stock market had transformed him from the man who talked to the microchip into the object of one of the long prosperity's most peculiar manias. "Listen to the technology," Gilder liked to say. "Listen to Gilder," chanted the rest of the world, logging on to his website on the day a new issue was scheduled to appear and desperately buying shares in whatever company the great man had touted. By the year 2000, financial journalists were discussing the "Gilder effect," the massive and immediate movement in a company's share price that the ideologue was capable of setting in motion with even the most indirect pronouncements. Novell, a maker of network software, saw its market capitalization leap by $2 billion one day in December 1999 after Gilder wrote favorably of it in his newsletter. When Gilder steered his followers towards Xcelera.com in February 2000, its price climbed 47 percent in one day; when he touted NorthEast Optic Network a month later, its price nearly doubled. And Qualcomm, which he had boosted for years, became one of the great bubble stocks of the late nineties, appreciating some 2,618 *percent* over the course of 1999 as investors rushed to be a part of the future. And when Gilder pooh-poohed a technology, its makers discovered themselves on the wrong side of history in no uncertain terms, shunned by investors and their share price plummeting.[26] Having conjured the "New Economy" up out of the backlash mud, having transformed the lexicon of social class into the language of free markets, Gilder himself was now transformed into the archetypal character of the new era: the stock picker infallible, the bubble-blower as *philosophe.*

And perhaps the "New Economy" itself—this new order in which ideas trumped things—was nothing but the "Gilder effect" writ large, a colossal confusion of ideology with production, of populism with profit, of unprecedented good times for the rich with real social advance.

This Age of Incantation

The distant aerial view is one of the favorite conceits of the market-populist consensus. When human civilization is observed from far, far up, it occurs to several of the deepest thinkers of the nineties, a curious fundamental truth about us becomes evident: Life is in fact a computer. Everything we do can be understood as part of a giant calculating machine. The cars proceeding down the highways, the weave of our fabrics, even the fish in the ocean—all of us doing little sums, suspending judgment, surrendering control, participating in the hive mind. It's a Norman Rockwell image for the age of the Internet billionaire: the little people going happily about their business as tiny monads in the great swarm of humanity. From high up in the clouds, preferably from a seat in "business class," it can be seen that the "New Economy," the way of the microchip, is writ into the very DNA of existence.

I propose, though, that we imagine how all these things will appear from a historical distance rather than a high altitude. As the free money dries up and the euphoria cools off, as the pages yellow and the commercials get pulled and the websites are disconnected and the high-flying shares settle down for a thirty-year flat-line stretch at one-seventieth of their 1999 prices, we will look back at this long summer of corporate love and wonder how it was that we ever came to believe this stuff. We will shake our groggy heads and muddle on with our lives.

Unfortunately, though, we won't be able to shake off the material aspects of the "New Economy" quite as easily. The new era came with a real-world price tag, and the things we permitted to happen just so that we could live in its brilliant light for a few years are things we may never be able to undo or escape. In other lands where the advance of free trade is cheered on by our columnists as the greatest sort of empowerment, the battle to make the world safe for outsourcing has turned as bloody as any of our own nineteenth-century labor wars. In Colombia, recipient of a billion-dollar Clinton administration military aid package, union organizers have been assassinated every year in such numbers (around three thousand overall since 1987) that in 1997 they accounted for fully 50 percent of the trade union activists murdered worldwide.[27] Our political thinkers imagined our money frolicking open-mindedly through the economies of the world, chasing the best return without regard for color or creed. But what ensured those returns was not the "inevitability" of the microchip but the guns and the muscle and the hard unanswering face of economic power. Wherever one turned, old-fashioned coercion was the silent partner of "New Economy" ebullience.

Here at home the price was the destruction of the social contract of mid-century, the middle-class republic itself. Our portfolios may have appreciated graciously, but they did so only to the extent that we countenanced the reduction of millions to lives of casual employment without healthcare or the most elementary sort of workplace rights. We caught the tail end of the Qualcomm wave and pretended not to notice as sweatshops reappeared on our shores. We wondered like tots at the majesty of Cisco, at the generosity of Gates, and we stood by as the price of a good education for our kids ascended out of our reach.

The less tangible cost of consensus was the atrophy of the idea of conflict. Economic fairness, many of us came to believe, was something that just happened, that materialized at the mall like a new line of Pokémon products. Democracy was a thing served up to us like a Happy Meal; it required no effort on our part. To be sure, it had a mysterious, counter-intuitive quality to it: If we unilaterally gave up our power to compel humane treatment from the boss, like magic there would come some karmic payoff, some shower of money from heaven, some ten-bagger in Yahoo! If we acquiesced to the holy process of deregulation, to the tossing of millions of single mothers out into the labor force, we would one day stumble upon some vast picnic spread out just for our gratification by the Archer Daniels Midland Company or JDS Uniphase. Someday we, too, would be invited to help ourselves to the complimentary after-dinner mints. To board at our leisure.

But for others of us—the ones with no access to the Senator's ear or the hip ad agencies or the prime commercial time on CNBC—the nineties only sharpened the sense that something had gone drastically wrong. To the casualization of work, to the destruction of the social "safety net," to the massive prison roundup, the powers of commerce added the staggering claim of having done it all on our behalf. Out of the roaring chaos of everyday speech, they told us, they could hear the affirmations rolling up; from the chirped warnings of the car alarms to the screeching of the modems they could hear America singing. But the great euphoria of the late nineties was never as much about the return of good times as it was the giddy triumph of one America over another, of their "New Economy" over our New Deal. Though they banged the drum with a fervor almost maniacal, the language of the euphoria still rang so patently false, sounded so transparently self-serving that it threatened to collapse in on itself almost as quickly as it bubbled up from the talk shows and the celebrated think tanks. And in the streets and the union halls and the truck stops and the three-flats and the office blocks there remained all along a vocabulary of fact and knowing and memory, of wit and of everyday doubt, a vernacular that could not be extinguished no matter how it was cursed for "cynicism," a dialect that the focus group could never quite reflect, the resilient language of democracy.

Endnotes

1 As quoted in *Wired*, January 1998. Curious line breaks in original.

2 Kevin Kelly, *New Rules for the New Economy: 10 Radical Strategies for a Connected World* (New York: Viking, 1998), p. 77.

3 Virginia Postrel, *The Future and Its Enemies: The Growing Conflict over Creativity, Enterprise, and Progress* (New York: The Free Press, 1998), pp. xvii, 50, 114, 128, 171, 192. I have no idea why Postrel feels she must point out that the members of the "state cosmetology board" who antagonized the stylish Sassoon wore crappy clothing (one might even remark here that, from a certain perspective, polyester can be regarded as a liberator just as easily as Sassoon himself), but nonetheless she quotes a favorite source, anthropologist Grant McCracken, who celebrates Sassoon's victory thusly: "Some 30 years after his tangle with that angry little bureaucrat swathed in wash and wear, Sassoon's empire continues to grow." One wonders if Pol Pot might seem more of a "dynamist" when his stylish black cotton pajamas are taken into account.

4 Ibid., pp. xiv. Postrel equates the future with markets by pointing out that the enemies of the one are the enemies of the other, p. xv. She also defines the two "processes" (future and market, that is) in strikingly similar terms, cf. pp. xiv, 35.

5 The argument could be made that the entire "New Economy" literature is a descendent of Stalinist rhetoric. Francis Fukuyama, the foreign policy thinker whose 1989 article about the "End of History" ignited this feeling of world-historical infallibility among American intellectuals, based his argument on the interpretation of Hegel proposed by the Russo-French intellectual Alexandre Kojève. In 1999 the DST, the French equivalent of the FBI, announced that Kojève had in fact been a KGB agent for some thirty years before his death in 1968. Although this revelation has since been disputed by friends and biographers of Kojève, his fondness for Stalin was already well known. "La DST avait identifié plusieurs agents du KGB parmi lesquels le philosophe Alexandre Kojève," *Le Monde*, September 16, 1999; Dominique Auffret, "Alexandre Kojève: du trompe-l'oeil au vertige," *Le Monde*, September 24, 1999; Edmond Ortigues, "Pour l'honneur d'Alexandre Kojève," *Le Monde*, October 4, 1999; Daniel Johnson, "Europe's Greatest Traitor," *Daily Telegraph*, October 2, 1999, p. 22.

6 Thurow, *Building WEALTH*, 33, 45, 97.

7 Friedman, *Lexus*, p. 93. Imagining national leaders talking like hardguys to one another is one of Friedman's trademark conceits. Strangely, Friedman also makes a big fuss over the mountainously arrogant notion that affluence is a matter of a choice, since it has been so fully figured out by us here in America. Any country, it seems, can ditch their history, can ditch the shitty hand nature has dealt them and "choose prosperity" as easily as that (p. 167). In this respect the "New Economy" revolution is not as inevitable as was the dictatorship of the proletariat, since a country can opt not to don the "golden straitjacket" and remain mired in poverty But if a country wants a decent standard of living, it has no choice.

8 Kelly, *New Rules for the New Economy*, pp. 1, 8, 73, 81.

9 Kevin Kelly describes Gilder in these words on page 52 of *New Rules*. He also describes the "Law of the Microcosm," whose provisions are described in chapter 2 (along with Moore's Law) as "Gilder's Law." "Metcalfe's Law," which Gilder revealed to the world in an article in *Forbes ASAP* ("Metcalfe's Law and Legacy," September 13, 1993) seems to be interchangeable with what Gilder calls the "Law of the Telecosm," which is defined thus in Gilder's 1992 work, *Life After Television*: the "total value" of *n* linked computers "rises in proportion to the square of 'n,'" p. 19. It should be noted that Gilder's fondness for "laws" and inevitabilities was not a passing taste: He stuck with it quite doggedly in his *Forbes ASAP* "Telecosm" writings in the nineties.

[10] Gilder, *Microcosm*, pp. 319, 344.

[11] Ibid., p. 369.

[12] Ibid., p. 369.

[13] Kimberly Seltzer and Tom Bentley, *The Creative Age: Knowledge and Skills for the New Economy* (London: Demos 1999), p. 13; Geoff Mulgan, *Connexity*, pp. 30, 223; Leadbeater, *Thin Air*, p. 38.

[14] Mark Leonard, *Britain™: Renewing Our Identity* (London: Demos, 1997).

[15] Leadbeater, *Thin Air*, pp. 19–23; Leonard, *Britain™*, p. 54; Charles Leadbeater and Kate Oakley, *The Independents: Britain's New Cultural Entrepreneurs* (London: Demos, 1999), p. 74.

[16] Leadbeater, *Thin Air*, 224.

[17] Mulgan, *Connexity*, pp. 35–36, 168, 183.

[18] Ibid., pp. 76, 44, 167.

[19] Nick Cohen, "There is no alternative to becoming Leadbeater," *London Review of Books*, October 28, 1999, p. 33.

[20] Mulgan, *Connexity*, back cover; Leadbeater, *Thin Air*, pp. viii, 80; Ian Hargreaves and Ian Christie, eds., *Tomorrow's Politics: The Third Way and Beyond* (London: Demos, 1998), p. 16.

[21] Stuart Hall and Martin Jacques, eds., *New Times: The Changing Face of Politics in the 1990s* (London: Verso 1990 [1989]), pp. 12, 16, 452.

[22] Postrel discusses "dynamism," "stasism," and their related personality types, as these were revealed to her by a friendly economist on p. xv of *The Future and Its Enemies*.

[23] Postrel seems to have a problem generally with criticism. While she makes a great fuss over the tolerance of "dynamists" (see p. 142) and the intolerance of "stasists," the grand theme of the book is that "stasist critics," if left to do their criticizing, will ruin "the future" for all of us. Evidently criticism is of a different nature entirely when it issues from a "dynamist" and a "stasist": "Dynamists" always limit their criticism to questions of taste or contract violation, while whenever a "stasist" opens his mouth he is demanding, implicitly if not overtly, government intervention of the most loathsome sort. "Stasist criticism," therefore, is ipso facto intolerant, and must be beaten back.

[24] Kelly, *New Rules*, p. 81. Karlgaard, *Forbes*, August 23, 1999. Emphasis in original.

[25] Mail solicitation for *The Gilder Technology Report*, "A Joint Publication of Forbes magazine and the Gilder Group," dated "Winter 2000," collection of the author.

[26] "Technically, Gilder's Words Carry Weight," *Wall Street Journal*, January 7, 2000, p. C1; Fred Barbash, "Market Guru Puts Acolytes on Wild Ride," *The Washington Post*, March 5, 2000, p. H1; Aaron Zitner, "Sage of the Berkshires," *Boston Globe*, March 20, 2000, p. C1; George Gilder and Richard Vigilante, "AT&T's Wireless Debacle," *Wall Street Journal*, May 1, 2000, p. A34. As for Gilder's personal holdings, the *Journal* reports, "He says he owns about seven of the companies on his list, and he doesn't sell."

[27] See the various reports on Colombia produced by the International Confederation of Free Trade Unions. http://www2.icftu.org.

Religion and the Shape of National Culture

Robert N. Bellah

David Hollenbach, in a recent paper entitled "Is Tolerance Enough? The Catholic University and the Common Good," suggests why the idea of the common good is so important for public discussion in the United States today and why Catholics have a special responsibility for putting it forward. He emphasizes the virtue of solidarity as Pope John Paul II defines it, "a firm and persevering determination to commit oneself to the common good, that is to say, to the good of all and of each individual," and argues that such a position is not one to be merely tolerated, which is to say ignored, in the public sphere, but one that is rightfully central to the common civic project. And he argues that "engaged conversation about the good life," while central to the Catholic tradition, can reach out "across the boundaries of diverse communities" and actually lead to the development of larger, more inclusive communities as well.

I want to take up Hollenbach's suggestion and ask why it is so hard for Americans to understand the idea of the common good, much less engage in conversation about it. Then I want to tackle the really hard question: How could we change this situation so that concern for the common good might become more central in our society and beyond. I will speak frankly about the specifically Catholic contribution to a revitalized commitment to the common good and why Protestants often have a hard time even understanding the idea. Since I am not a Catholic, but a Protestant layman, one raised in the Presbyterian Church but presently an Episcopalian, perhaps I can be forgiven if I put the issue sharply and critically: The dominance of Protestantism, for historical reasons, in what I will be calling the American cultural code, is responsible for many of our present difficulties. We badly need an infusion of what the Rev. Andrew Greeley in *The Catholic Myth* (1991) calls the Catholic imagination if we are to overcome those difficulties. (See also his *The Enchanted Imagination*, forthcoming.) Greeley speaks of a Catholic imagination in a way that is congruent with what I mean by a cultural code and he argues that it is different from the Protestant imagination. He paints the contrast in stark terms:

The Catholic tends to see society as a "sacrament" of God, a set of ordered relationships, governed by both justice and love, that reveal, however imperfectly, the presence of

Source: Robert N. Bellah, "Religion and the Shape of National Culture." *America*, vol. 181 issue 3, July 31, 1999.

God. Society is "natural" and "good," therefore, for humans and their "natural" response to God is social. The Protestant tends to see society as "God-forsaken" and therefore unnatural and oppressive. The individual stands over against society and not integrated into it. The human becomes fully human only when he is able to break away from social oppression and relate to the absent God as a completely free individual.

This is not entirely fair, as it overlooks the community-forming capacity of Protestantism so evident earlier in our history, but it does help us understand Margaret Thatcher's otherwise nearly unintelligible remark, "There is no such thing as society," a quintessentially Protestant thing to say.

The Protestant Imagination

I want to take the argument of *Habits of the Heart* and *The Good Society* about American individualism and put it in the context of a Protestant-Catholic contrast, left implicit but perhaps evident to the discerning reader of those books. But before pursuing this line of argument further I want to make more explicit the general argument about the contribution of religion to the shape of national cultures. David Vogel in an as yet unpublished article argues that, in the formation of a national culture, a historical Protestant heritage may override the presence of a large number of Catholics in the society. As examples he cites Germany, the Netherlands and the United States. Drawing on Ronald Inglehart's values studies for corroboration, Vogel argues that historically Protestant culture overrides religious pluralism. As Vogel puts it, "for the purpose of my analysis all Americans are Protestants regardless of what particular religion they practice, just as are all Germans." Vogel seems to be confirming G. K. Chesterton's famous remark that "in America, even the Catholics are Protestants." Conversely, Vogel quotes Inglehart as saying, "The societies that are historically Catholic still show very distinct values from those that are historically Protestant—even among segments of the population who have no contact with the church today. These values persist as part of the cultural heritage of given nations. . . ." With the help of Andrew Greeley, I will have to qualify the notion that all Americans are Protestants, but it is part of the truth.

To sum up what I think to be the connection between Protestantism and our national cultural code, let me quote the historian Donald Worster: "Protestantism, like any religion, lays its hold on people's imagination in diverse, contradictory ways and that hold can be tenacious long after the explicit theology or doctrine has gone dead. Surely it cannot be surprising that in a culture deeply rooted in Protestantism, we should find ourselves speaking its language, expressing its temperament, even when we thought we were free of all that" (*The Wealth of Nature*, 1993, p. 200). I think what Worster is pointing to here is what Greeley would call the Protestant imagination.

Flaw in the Cultural Code: Radical Individualism

Far be it from me to condemn the Protestant cultural code altogether. It has contributed to many of our greatest achievements. But the idea of a deep cultural code is not without its ominous side. A genetic code can produce a highly successful species, successful because specialized for a particular environment. But then, even at its moment of greatest success, because of a dramatic change in that environment, the code can lead to rapid extinction. In the same way, a cultural code that has long enjoyed remarkable success in many fields can lead a civilization into abrupt decline if it disables society from solving central problems, problems perhaps created by its own success. And yet the cultural code, however deep, is not a genetic code: It can be changed, although sometimes it takes a catastrophe to change it.

What, then, is the flaw in the cultural code that could produce, perhaps is already producing, the gravest consequences?

The flaw in our cultural code was really the primary subject of both *Habits of the Heart* and *The Good Society*, although we did not call it that. In *Habits* we used the metaphor of "language" rather than "cultural code," and we argued that America has a first language, composed of two complementary aspects, utilitarian and expressive individualism, and also second languages, namely biblical and civic republican languages. These second languages have tended to get pushed to the margins. Already in the introduction to the 1996 paperback edition of *Habits*, my coauthors and I suggested that the individualism that forms America's dominant cultural orientation was not solely derived from 18th-century Utilitarianism and 19th-century Romanticism, but had roots in both of our second languages as well. In my November 1997 address to the American Academy of Religion, titled "Is There a Common American Culture?" (published in the academy's journal in summer 1998), I took the argument a step further. There I argued that beyond the homogenizing effect of television, education and consumerism, and deeper even than utilitarian and expressive individualism, there was a still, small voice, a tiny seed, from which our current cultural orientation derives.

Nestled in the very core of utilitarian and expressive individualism is something very deep, very genuine, very old, very American, something we did not quite see or say in *Habits*. Its core is religious. In *Habits* we quoted a famous passage in Alexis de Toqueville's *Democracy in America*: "I think I can see the whole destiny of America contained in the first Puritan who landed on those shores." Then we went on to name John Winthrop, following de Toqueville's own predilection, as the likeliest candidate for being that first Puritan. Now I am ready to admit, although regretfully, that we and de Tocqueville were probably wrong. That first Puritan who contained our whole destiny might have been, as we also half intimated in Habits, Anne Hutchinson; but the stronger candidate, because we know so much more about him, is Roger Williams.

Roger Williams, banished from the Massachusetts Bay Colony by John Winthrop and founder of Providence and of the Rhode Island Colony, was a Baptist. The Baptists in 17th-century New England were a distinct minority, but they went on to become, together with other dissenting Protestants, a majority in American religious culture from the early 19th century on. As Seymour Martin Lipset has recently pointed out, we are the only North Atlantic society whose predominant religious tradition is sectarian rather than an established church (*American Exceptionalism*, 1996, p. 19–20). I think this is something enormously important for our culture.

What was so important about the Baptists, and other sectarians such as the Quakers, was the absolute centrality of religious freedom, of the sacredness of individual conscience in matters of religious belief. We generally think of religious freedom as one of many kinds of freedom, many kinds of human rights, first voiced in the European Enlightenment and echoing around the world ever since. But Georg Jellinek, Max Weber's friend and, on these matters, his teacher, published a book in 1895 called *The Declaration of the Rights of Man and of Citizens*, which argued that the ultimate source of all modern notions of human rights is to be found in the radical sects of the Protestant Reformation, particularly the Quakers and Baptists. Of this development Weber writes: "Thus the consistent sect gives rise to an inalienable personal right of the governed as against any power, whether political, hierocratic or patriarchal. Such freedom of conscience may be the oldest Right of Man—as Jellinek has argued convincingly; at any rate it is the most basic Right of Man because it comprises all ethically conditioned action and guarantees freedom from compulsion, especially from the power of the state. In this sense the concept was as unknown to antiquity and the Middle Ages as it was to Rousseau. . . ." Weber then goes on to say that the other rights of man were later joined to this basic right, "especially the right to pursue one's own economic interests, which includes the inviolability of individual property, the freedom of contract, and vocational choice."

My fellow sociologist of religion, Phillip E. Hammond, has written a remarkable book, *With Liberty for All: Freedom of Religion in the United States* (1998), detailing the vicissitudes of this sectarian Protestant concern for the sacredness of the individual conscience as it got embodied in the First Amendment to the Constitution and has been given ever wider meaning by the judicial system, especially the Supreme Court, ever since.

Roger Williams was a moral genius, but he was a sociological catastrophe. After he founded the First Baptist Church, he left it for a smaller and purer one. That, too, he found inadequate, so he founded a church that consisted only of himself, his wife and one other person. One wonders how he stood even those two. Since Williams ignored secular society, money took over in Rhode Island in a way that would not be true in Massachusetts or Connecticut for a long time. Rhode Island under Williams gives us an early and local example of what happens when the sacredness of the individual is not balanced by any sense of the whole or concern for the common good.

Predestination and the Divinization of the Self

Let me make two suggestions about how certain central Protestant beliefs have strengthened our radical individualism. The Reformers, fearing idolatry and magic, attacked the doctrine of transubstantiation and other Catholic practices. Afraid of the idea of the sacred in the world, they, in effect, pushed God out of the world into radical transcendence. With the doctrine of predestination Calvin (or if not Calvin, as some scholars now believe, then some of his followers) described a God who had preordained everything that can occur before the beginning of time. It was natural for some philosophers and scientists to move from that idea to a deterministic physical universe without a personal God at all: "I have no need of that hypothesis," as one of them said. So Calvin's powerful doctrine of divine transcendence paradoxically opened the door to atheistic naturalism. Even more ominously, into the empty space left by the absence of God came an understanding of the self as absolutely autonomous that borrows an essential attribute of God to apply to the self. Since Calvinism as a consistent doctrine hardly survived the 18th century, I am arguing that this aspect of the Protestant cultural code made its ambiguous contribution quite some time ago.

There is a second Protestant religious source of our problem that is, however, very much alive and well today. This is the near exclusive focus on the relation between Jesus and the individual, where accepting Jesus Christ as one's personal lord and savior becomes almost the whole of piety. When this happens, then the doctrine of the God-Man easily slips into the doctrine of the Man-God. The divinization of the self is often called Gnosticism, and Harold Bloom, in *The American Religion* (1993), sees Gnosticism as the quintessentially American religion. He says so not as a critic but as a believer, for he proclaims himself a Gnostic. He sees the Evangelical Protestant focus on the personal relation of the believer to Jesus as one of the major sources of American Gnosticism.

If I may trace the downward spiral of this particular Protestant distortion, let me say that it begins with the statement, "If I'm all right with Jesus, then I don't need the church," which we heard from some of the people we interviewed for *Habits of the Heart*. It progresses, then, to the "Sheilaism" that we described in that book. A woman named Sheila Larson defined her faith thus: "Its Sheilaism. Just my own little voice." But Sheilaism seems positively benign compared to the end of the road in this direction that comes out with remarkable force in an interview recounted in Robert Wuthnow's *Loose Connections* (1998). A man in his late 20s who works as a financial analyst describes the individualism that "you're just brought up to believe in" as follows: "The individual is the preeminent being in the universe. There's always a distinction between me and you. Comity, sharing, cannot truly exist. What I have is mine, and its mine because I deserve it, and I have a right to it." Let us hope he knows not what he says. The general tendency of American Evangelicalism toward a private piety pulls everyone influenced by it very much in this direction. Some may think that Jesus-and-me piety is quite different from the individual as the preeminent being in the universe, but I am suggesting that they are only a hair apart

Loose Connections and Porous Institutions

The flaw in our cultural code becomes most evident when the radical religious individualism I have just described is joined with a notion of economic freedom that holds that the unrestrained free market can solve all problems. Through much of our history a variety of associations, often created by Protestant or Catholic initiative, together with still vibrant extended families, provided a protective barrier against the creative destruction of the market economy. But since the early 70s many of these groups and associations have fallen into sharp decline, the churches themselves holding out the longest, but even they are now beginning to show signs of weakening. One recent study reported by Wuthnow found that 75 percent of the public said that the "breakdown of communities" is a serious national problem. Although 90 percent said it is important to participate in community organizations, only 21 percent said they did so, according to Wuthnow. What has been happening to us can be summed up in the title of Wuthnow's book: *Loose Connections*. People are not plugged in very tightly to groups and associations. They may volunteer a few hours a week for a while, but they will not join an organization that expects their loyalty and commitment for the long haul, or at least they are much more reluctant to do so than they once were. Loose connections is a powerful metaphor and I cannot help drawing a conclusion from it that Wuthnow does not stress: Loose connections can be dangerous, can lead to a fire, can lead to catastrophe.

Wuthnow pairs the metaphor of loose connections with another metaphor that partly explains it: porous institutions. Porous institutions are institutions that do not hold individuals very securely; porous institutions leak. In a world of porous institutions it is hard to have any connections that are not loose. One thinks of the family. Whereas in 1960 one in four marriages would fail, today one in two will. And a lot of things go along with that. The fastest growing category of households is those with one member, which now amount to 25 percent of all households. Families, as we know, do not necessarily consist of two parents and their children. Husbands and wives drift in and out, often bringing children from a former marriage with them, resulting in what is called "blended families." However successfully families are coping with these conditions, there is always the uncertainty: Will this marriage last? Will my parents divorce?

Work, the other great source of personal identity besides family for most Americans, has also become increasingly porous. Arlie Hochschild, in her book *The Time Bind* (1997), reports the statement of a factory worker in a corporation she studied: "In the last 30 years while I've had this job, I have had two marriages, both of which broke up, and several girlfriends in between. This job is my family." Unfortunately, Hochschild reports, this man was about to be downsized. In *Habits of the Heart* we talked about jobs, careers and callings as three increasingly engaged ways of thinking about work. But not only have jobs become transient and insecure; careers are increasingly vulnerable to change. Wuthnow writes: "The median number of different careers listed by people aged 45 or over in the U.S. labor force is now three; the traditional pattern of working in only one career now typifies only 21 percent of all workers aged 45 or over." If job and career are uncertain, then we may wonder how many people actually find a calling,

These symptoms suggest that there may be aspects of our deep cultural code that are a significant part of the problem. Just when we are in many ways moving to an ever greater validation of the sacredness of the individual person, our capacity to imagine a social fabric that would hold individuals together is vanishing. This is in part because of the fact that our ethical individualism, deriving, as I have argued, from the Protestant religious tradition in America, is linked to an economic individualism that, ironically, knows nothing of the sacredness of the individual. Its only standard is money, and the only thing more sacred than money is more money. What economic individualism destroys and what our kind of religious individualism cannot restore is solidarity, a sense of being members of the same body. In most other North Atlantic societies, including other Protestant societies, a tradition of an established church, however secularized, provides some notion that we are in this thing together, that we need each other, that our precious and unique selves are not going to make it all alone.

The Catholic Contribution: Solidarity/Communion

It is in this context that, I believe, we can turn to a Catholic cultural tradition in America that has never been completely Protestantized after all. If our deep cultural code in its Protestant version combines privatized piety with economic freedom in a way that leads to loose connections and porous institutions and has inundated us with the incessant language of freedom and responsibility but is virtually inarticulate about the common good, how can an alternative Catholic code help us? The resources of the Catholic tradition of the virtues and Catholic social teaching as embodied in papal encyclicals are invaluable. David Hollenbach and other Catholic ethicists are right to bring these traditions into public discussion. But the cultural code that we need to change is deeper than ideology or policy analysis; it is rooted in what Greeley calls the religious imagination, which operates on a partly unconscious level. I believe we need at this moment to reconstitute our cultural code by giving much greater salience to the sacramental life (Greeley uses the terms Catholic imagination and sacramental imagination interchangeably), and, in particular, to the Eucharist.

The most fundamental practice that tells us who we are as Christians is worship. The very concreteness of the sacramental tradition is difficult for free-floating middle-class Americans, even Catholics, to understand. If I find that I live in porous institutions with loose connections, how can I understand that this bread and this wine is the actual body and blood of Christ and that by participating in the Eucharist I become immediately and physically one with the body of Christ, and so one with the whole of God's creation? Yet for Protestants, as for Catholics, not only the word but the sacraments are necessary for our salvation. The sacraments pull us into an embodied world of relationships and connections, a world in which, to quote Greeley, "humans [are] integrated into networks, networks that reveal God," rather than a world in which individuals attempt to escape from society.

Some concrete examples and the voices of Catholic believers will illustrate my point better than abstract analysis. I would like to turn first to a parish where the sacramental imagination has been enacted. David Roozen and his associates in their book *Varieties of Religious Presence* describe a Catholic parish, St. Margaret's, largely made up of Puerto Ricans, in the poorest neighborhood of Hartford, Conn., which was deeply involved in a justice ministry. Here a sacramental theology has formed the life and worship of the whole parish. As one of the members put it:

> The Mass is the reenactment of the moment of Redemption. In every Mass, the Cross of Calvary is transplanted into every corner of the world, and humanity is taking sides, either sharing in that Redemption or rejecting it, by the way we live. We are not meant to sit and watch the cross as something done and ended. What was done on Calvary avails for us only in the degree that we repeat it in our lives. All that has been said and done and acted during Holy Mass is to be taken away with us, lived, practiced, and woven into all the circumstances and conditions of our daily lives. (p. 161)

"Life at St. Margaret's," in the words of a deacon, "begins and ends with the Mass." Priests and parishioners share a common eucharistic theology. "Mass is the center of everything," the senior priest states emphatically.

> The Eucharist is the living presence of Christ. In sharing that presence, the call is to go out to make that presence operational, living in the world. That going out wears us out, so the Eucharist is both the beginning and the end. It draws us to it, pushes us out into the world, and then draws us back. It is an overflow of the Lord's presence. The Mass is part of the world and the world is part of the Lord. (p. 162)

Roozen sums up his account of this parish as follows:

> The expressed goal of the leadership—clerical and lay—is to work within the world to make it Christian, a world in which love toward God and neighbor is the maxim. Energy for this task, in the St. Margaret's view, comes from the Mass. The model is Christ on the cross, and there is a firm belief that human nature can be shaped into the formations of love. (p. 176)

The Roozen book is some 20 years old now, but just last year I learned of things going on near my home that confirm the current vitality of that sacramental understanding of life. I was fortunate to sit on the Graduate Theological Union doctoral dissertation committee of a Jesuit from India named Matthew Jayanth, whose thesis was titled "Eucharist and Social Ethics." While conducting interviews in several East Bay communities, he found lay persons whose understanding was quite similar to that of the parishioners at St. Margaret's. A number of them, not necessarily aware of one another, had adopted a simple mode of life in which they worked only to maintain their necessities and spent most of their time in the voluntary service of the destitute. They are a kind of contemporary third order Franciscans without the formality of it. Several of them used a phrase with which I was not previously familiar: They spoke of "being eucharist for others." One of them said, "That's what life is for me, being eucharist for others. It is not about martyrdom, it's about life; its about giving life to others." Another put it this way:

> The commission to "go in the peace of Christ to love and serve one another" means that this is what the Mass has nourished us to do. And yet when he says the Mass is ended, that is only true in one sense. . . . It is not ended, it is continuing. It is an invitation to go out and put it into practice now. To do what you said you were going to do. What you tried to focus yourself on so that you can function as a whole person, united with Christ and then as the whole body of Christ. So now you have to go out and incarnate that, that is what life is about.

And a final voice:

> To become eucharist. I mean to become willing to give ourselves, to be willing to risk all that we have, willing to bring new life to others, willing to break open our bodies. . . . The full sense of the Eucharist would be to understand the totality of our lives as eucharist. . . . The major connection between Eucharist and the life of commitment to justice is that in the eucharistic celebration we are nourished and empowered and we are sent forth to become eucharist for others.

What these people are talking about is that tangible, physical act of participating in the body and blood of the crucified and risen Christ. It is in that moment that we become members one of another, that we not only partake of the Eucharist but can actually become eucharist, ourselves completing "what is lacking in Christ's afflictions," as Paul says in Colossians, by self-giving love for the whole world.

Because the Catholic and the Protestant imaginations are rooted in a common tradition, they are both available to all American Christians. But our most urgent need at the moment is to open up our deep cultural code so that the sacramental imagination will have a more pervasive influence over our lives. That would probably require a severe reality-challenge to our present apparently successful way of life, something like a major depression, and, in response, a combination of the Catholic imagination with a kind of Evangelical revivalism, Catholic content in a Protestant form if you will. It is that improbable but not impossible scenario that I have attempted to describe.

Robert N. Bellah is Professor of Sociology Emeritus, University of California, Berkeley. He is co-author of *Habits of the Heart* (1985) and *The Good Society* (1992). A somewhat longer version of this article was recently given as a talk at Regis University in Denver.

IV. Economic Order

The Rise of Market Populism:
America's New Secular Religion

Thomas Frank

When Richard Hofstadter wrote thirty years ago that "conflict and consensus require each other and are bound up in a kind of dialectic of their own," he was offering advice to historians examining the American past, but he might as well have been describing the culture of the 1990s. If there was anything that defined us as a people, we came to believe in that decade, it was our diversity, our nonconformity, our radicalism, our differentness. It was an era of many and spectacular avant-gardes, of loud and highly visible youth cultures, of emphatic multiculturalism, of extreme sports, extreme diets and extreme investing.

But even as Americans marveled at the infinite variety of the Internet and celebrated our ethnic diversity, we were at the same time in the grip of an intellectual consensus every bit as ironclad as that of the 1950s. Across the spectrum, American opinion leaders in the nineties were coming to an unprecedented agreement on the role of business in American life. The leaders of the left parties, both here and in Britain, accommodated themselves to the free-market faith and made spectacular public renunciations of their historic principles. Organized labor, pounded by years of unionbusting and deindustrialization, slipped below 10 percent of the US private-sector work force and seemed to disappear altogether from the popular consciousness. The opposition was ceasing to oppose, but the market was now safe, its supposedly endless array of choice substituting for the lack of choice on the ballot. Various names were applied to this state of affairs. In international circles the grand agreement was called the "Washington Consensus"; economics writer Daniel Yergin called it the "market consensus"; *New York Times* columnist Thomas Friedman coined the phrase "golden straitjacket" to describe the absence of political options. While once "people thought" there were ways to order human affairs other than through the free market, Friedman insisted, those choices now no longer existed. "I don't think there will be an alternative ideology this time around," he wrote in August 1998. "There are none."

It is this intellectual unanimity about the nature and the purpose of economies, as much as the technological advances of recent years, that we refer to when we talk so triumphantly about the "New Economy." It is this nearly airtight consensus—this assurance that no matter what happens or who wins in November, a strong labor movement and an

Source: Thomas Frank, "The Rise of Market Populism: America's New Secular Religion," *The Nation*, Oct. 30, 2000, Vol. 271, i13, p. 13–18.

interventionist government will not be returning—that has made possible the unprecedented upward transfer of wealth that we saw in the Clinton years, that has permitted the bull market without end, and that has made the world so safe for billionaires.

This is not to say that in the nineties Americans simply decided they wanted nothing so much as to toil for peanuts on an assembly line somewhere, that they loved plutocracy and that robber barons rocked after all. On the contrary: At the center of the "New Economy" consensus was a vision of economic democracy as extreme and as militant-sounding as anything to emanate from the CIO in the thirties. From Deadheads to Nobel-laureate economists, from paleoconservatives to New Democrats, American leaders in the nineties came to believe that markets were a popular system, a far more democratic form of organization than (democratically elected) governments. This is the central premise of what I call "market populism": that in addition to being mediums of exchange, markets are mediums of consent. With their mechanisms of supply and demand, poll and focus group, superstore and Internet, markets manage to express the popular will more articulately and meaningfully than do mere elections. By their very nature markets confer democratic legitimacy, markets bring down the pompous and the snooty, markets look out for the interests of the little guy, markets give us what we want.

Many of the individual components of the market-populist consensus have been part of the cultural-economic wallpaper for years. Hollywood and Madison Avenue have always insisted that their job is simply to mirror the public's wishes, and that movies and ad campaigns succeed or fail depending on how accurately they conform to public tastes. Similarly, spokesmen for the New York Stock Exchange have long argued that stock prices reflect popular enthusiasm, that public trading of stocks is a basic component of democracy. And ever since William Randolph Hearst, newspaper tycoons have imagined themselves defenders of the common man.

But in the nineties these ideas came together into a new orthodoxy that anathematized all alternative ways of understanding democracy, history and the rest of the world. An example of the market-populist consensus at its most cocksure can be found in "Fanfare for the Common Man," the cover story that *Newsweek* used to mark the end of the twentieth century. The story's title comes from a Depression standby (a 1942 work by Aaron Copland), and its writing recalls the militant populism of that era. Looking back on the events of the "people's century," it occurred to Kenneth Auchincloss, the story's author, that for once in the human experience "ordinary folks changed history." To nail it down he singled out a succession of popular heroes who changed things: suffragettes, feminists, the antiwar and civil rights movement, and, finally, "the entrepreneurs"—this last group illustrated with a drawing of Bill Gates. Even while hailing the richest man in the world as a champion of the common people, Auchincloss took pains to point out that the New Deal wasn't nearly as wonderful as everyone thought it was. The other hero of the thirties, the labor movement, was not mentioned in the story at all.

This may seem egregious, but it was hardly atypical. Wherever one looked in the nineties entrepreneurs were occupying the ideological space once filled by the noble sons of toil. It was businessmen who were sounding off against the arrogance of elites, railing against the privilege of old money, protesting false expertise and waging relentless, idealistic war on the principle of hierarchy wherever it could be found. Their fundamental faith was a simple one: The market and the people—both of them understood as grand principles of social life rather than particulars—were essentially one and the same. As journalist

Robert Samuelson wrote in 1998, "the Market 'R' Us." This is how a "Fanfare for the Common Man" could turn into yet another salute to Bill Gates and his fellow billionaires; how the New York Stock Exchange, long a nest of privilege, could be understood in the nineties as a house of the people; how any kind of niche marketing could be passed off as a revolutionary expression—an empowerment, even—of the demographic at which it was aimed.

And as business leaders melded themselves theoretically with the people, they found that market populism provided them with powerful weapons to use against their traditional enemies in government and labor. Since markets express the will of the people, virtually any criticism of business could be described as an act of "elitism" arising out of despicable contempt for the common man. According to market populism, elites are not those who, say, watch sporting events from a skybox, or spend their weekends tooling about on a computer-driven yacht, or fire half their work force and ship the factory south. No, elitists are the people on the other side of the equation: the labor unionists and Keynesians who believe that society can be organized in any way other than the market way. Since what the market does—no matter how whimsical, irrational or harmful—is the Will of the People, any scheme to operate outside its auspices or control its ravages is by definition a dangerous artifice, the hubris of false expertise.

This fantasy of the market as an anti-elitist machine made the most sense when it was couched in the language of social class. Businessmen and pro-business politicians have always protested the use of "class war" by their critics on the left; during the nineties, though, they happily used the tactic themselves, depicting the workings of the market as a kind of permanent social revolution in which daring entrepreneurs are endlessly toppling fat cats and picking off millions of lazy rich kids. Wherever the earthshaking logic of the "New Economy" touched down, old money was believed to quake and falter. The scions of ancient banking families were said to be finding their smug selves wiped out by the streetwise know-how of some kid with a goatee; the arrogant stockbrokers of old were being humiliated by the e-trade masses; the WASPs with their regimental ties were getting their asses kicked by the women, the Asians, the Africans, the Hispanics; the buttoned-down whip-cracking bosses were being fired by the corporate "change agents"; the self-assured network figures were being reduced to tears by the Vox Populi of the web. A thousand populist revolts shook the office blocks of the world, and the great forums of market ideology overflowed with praise for in-your-face traders from gritty urban backgrounds, for the CEO who still retained the crude manners of the longshoreman.

How did populism ever become the native tongue of the wealthy? Historically, of course, populism was a rebellion against the corporate order, a political tongue reserved by definition for the nonrich and the nonpowerful. It was a term associated with the labor movement and angry agrarians. But in 1968, at the height of the antiwar movement, this primal set piece of American democracy seemed to change its stripes. The war between classes somehow reversed its polarity: Now it was a conflict in which the patriotic, blue-collar "silent majority" (along with their employers) faced off against a new elite, a "liberal establishment" with its spoiled, flag-burning children. This new ruling class—a motley assembly of liberal journalists, liberal academics, liberal foundation employees, liberal politicians and the shadowy powers of Hollywood—earned the people's wrath not by exploiting workers or ripping off the family farmers but by contemptuous disregard for the wisdom and values of average Americans.

Counterintuitive though it may have been, the backlash vision of class conflict was powerful stuff. Until recently American politics remained mired in the cultural controversies passed down from the late sixties, with right-wing populists forever reminding "normal Americans" of the hideous world that the "establishment" had built, a place where blasphemous intellectuals violated the principles of Americanism at every opportunity, a place of crime in the streets, of unimaginable cultural depravity, of epidemic disrespect for the men in uniform, of secular humanists scheming to undermine family values and give away the Panama Canal, of judges gone soft on crime and politicians gone soft on communism. The thirty-year backlash brought us Ronald Reagan's rollback of government power as well as Newt Gingrich's outright shutdown of 1995. But for all its accomplishments, it never constituted a thorough endorsement of the free market or of laissez-faire politics. Barbara Ehrenreich, one of its most astute chroniclers, points out that the backlash always hinged on a particular appeal to working-class voters, some of whom were roped into the Republican coalition with talk of patriotism, culture war and family values. Class war worked for Republicans as long as it was restricted to cultural issues; when economic matters came up the compound grew unstable very quickly. Lee Atwater, an adviser to Presidents Reagan and Bush, is said to have warned his colleagues in 1984 that their new blue-collar constituents were "liberal on economics" and that without culture wars to distract them "populists were left with no compelling reason to vote Republican."

Fortunately for the right, as the culture wars finally began to subside in the aftermath of the impeachment fiasco, a new variation on the populist theme was reaching its triumphant zenith. Market populism was promulgated less by a political party than by business itself—through management theory, investment literature and advertising—and it served the needs of the owning community far more directly than had the tortured populism of the backlash. While the right-wing populism of the seventies and eighties had envisioned a scheming "liberal elite" bent on "social engineering"—a clique of experts who thought they knew what was best for us, like busing, integration and historical revisionism—market populism simply shifted the inflection. Now the crime of the elite was not so much an arrogance in matters of values but in matters economic. Still those dirty elitists thought they were better than the people, but now their arrogance was revealed by their passion to raise the minimum wage; to regulate, oversee, redistribute and tax.

There are critical differences between market populism and the earlier right-wing dispensation, of course. While the backlash was proudly square, market populism is cool. Far from despising the sixties, it broadcasts its fantasies to the tune of a hundred psychedelic hits. Its leading think tanks are rumored to pay princely sums to young people promising to bring some smattering of rock-and-roll street cred to the market's cause. And believing in markets rather than God, it has little tolerance for the bizarre ideas of the Christian right or the Moral Majority. Market populism has also abandoned the overt race-baiting of the backlash: Its "Southern strategy" involves shipping plants to Mexico or Guatemala and then describing this as a victory for the downtrodden Others of the planet. Market populists generally fail to get worked up about the persecution of Vietnam vets (they sometimes even equate new-style management theories with the strategy of the Vietcong); they have abandoned the "family values" of Reagan; they give not a damn for the traditional role of women or even of children. The more who enter the work force the merrier.

By the middle of the nineties, this was a populism in the ascendancy. Leftoid rock critics, Wall Street arbitrageurs and just about everyone in between seemed to find what they wanted in the magic of markets. Markets were serving all tastes, markets were humiliating the pretentious, markets were permitting good art to triumph over bad, markets were overthrowing the man, markets were extinguishing discrimination, markets were making everyone rich.

In the right hands, market populism could explain nearly any social phenomenon. The "tiger economies" of Asia had collapsed, market populists told us, because they had relied on the expertise of elites rather than the infinite wisdom of the people. Similarly, the economies of Western Europe were stagnant because the arrogant aristocrats every red-blooded American knows run those lands were clinging to old welfare-state theories. Meanwhile, the NASDAQ was soaring because the buy-and-hold common man had finally been allowed to participate. And when the House of Morgan was swallowed up by Chase Manhattan, we were told this was because it was a snooty outfit that had foolishly tried to resist the democracy of markets.

More important, market populism proved astonishingly versatile as a defense of any industry in distress. It was the line that could answer any critic, put over any deregulatory initiative, roll back any tax. Thus economist Stanley Lebergott used it to blast a 1998 warning by Hillary Clinton against the values of consumerism. The consumer culture, he informed the First Lady from the *New York Times* Op-Ed page, and by extension the free market generally, was the righteous collective product of the people themselves. "Who creates this 'consumer-driven culture' but 270 million Americans?" he asked. Taking an indignant swipe at the carping snobbery of the "best and the brightest," Lebergott then asserted that criticism of business was in fact criticism of "other consumers," and that simply by participating in American life—by driving "a 1-ton car to the theater" or by "accumulat[ing] books and newspapers printed on million-dollar presses"—we authorize whatever it is that the market chooses to do.

On the *Wall Street Journal* editorial page, where the behavior of markets is consistently understood as a transparent expression of the will of the people, one saw market populism wheeled out to defend the advertising industry, to defend the auto industry, to bolster demands that the software industry be permitted to import more workers, to hail stock options as the people's true currency and, most remarkably, to defend Microsoft from its antitrust pursuers. Since a company's size (like the value of a billionaire's pile) was simply a reflection of the people's love, antitrust itself was fundamentally illegitimate, a device used by elitist politicians, the *Journal* once proclaimed, "to promote the interests of the few at the expense of the many." Even after the Microsoft verdict had been announced, the *Journal* continued to assert that the company "should have argued that we have a monopoly because our customers want us to have one." And when Al Gore began annoying the men of privilege with his recent attacks on big business, the paper responded in the most direct manner imaginable. "Mr. Bush should tell Americans," online *Journal* executive James Taranto opined in an Op-Ed late last summer, "when my opponent attacks 'big corporations,' he's attacking you and me."

Market populism can seem quite absurd at times. We are, after all, living through one of the least populist economic eras in the past hundred years. The "New Economy" has exalted the rich and forgotten about the rest with a decisiveness that we haven't seen since the twenties. Its greatest achievement—the booming stock market of recent years—has been based in no small part on companies' enhanced abilities to keep wages low even while CEO compensation soars to record levels. Market populism is, in many ways, the most blatant apologia for economic inequality since social Darwinism. But there can be no doubting the intensity of the true believers' faith. Only a few paragraphs after identifying "you and me" with "big corporations," for example, the *Journal's* Taranto went on to declare that "thanks to the democracy of the market" and the widespread ownership of stock, "the U.S. is now closer to [the] Marxian ideal than any society in history." And unless you have a spare billion to tell the world otherwise with a thirty-second spot during the Super Bowl, you can count on listening to proclamations like that for years to come.

Thomas Frank, a founding editor of *The Baffler,* is the author of *The Conquest of Cool* (Chicago) and coeditor of *Commodify Your Dissent: Salvos From The Baffler* (Norton). This essay is adapted from his new book, *One Market, Under God: Extreme Capitalism, Market Populism and the End of Economic Democracy* (Doubleday).

Executive Pay: A Special Report, How the Pay Figures Were Calculated

Alan Cowell

To measure executive compensation, *Money & Business* studied 200 large public companies that had filed proxies for their 2000 fiscal year by March 27. Executive Compensation Advisory Services, an Alexandria, Va., division of Drake Beam Morin that analyzes and sells information on executive pay, collected the data. Eric Legg, the senior project manager, conducted the research.

Pay can be calculated in many ways. Pay critics tend to cite the biggest possible numbers, while executives often try to minimize the reported size of pay packages. The biggest differences stem from the way stock options are valued.

Any value assigned to an option is a guess; the real worth of a chance to buy a stock four years from now at, say, $30 a share depends on the trading price of that stock in four years. The data in the tables on the following two pages recognizes this uncertainty by valuing options in two ways.

One method, using the widely accepted Black-Scholes formula, estimates the ultimate value of the options based on the stock's price on the day of the grant and the stock's historical volatility. The other method estimates the value of options based on current prices for each stock—the value that an executive would have in mind if he had an eye on the stock ticker.

Income from options that executives exercised in 2000 but received in previous years appears in a separate column. It is not included in the pay statistics in the main article in this section, since this money is pay from a previous year.

For executives who served only part of the fiscal year as chief executives, the study prorated their cash pay based on their time in the job. The value of stock and stock options were not prorated.

Here are definitions for the columns in the tables.

Direct Compensation

Salary. Base annual pay that does not depend on company results. By law, any amount exceeding $1 million is not tax deductible.

Source: Alan Cowell, "Executive Pay: A Special Report, How the Pay Figures Were Calculated," *The New York Times*, pp. 9–11, April 1, 2001.

Bonus. A cash payment that depends on the company's performance.

Long-Term Incentive and Other. Incentive payments that most companies set approximately three years in advance and pay out based on a company's results, plus miscellaneous items like moving expenses, insurance payments or fees covering personal use of a corporate jet.

Total Direct Compensation. The sum of the three previous categories.

At-Risk Compensation

Restricted Stock Awards. The value, as reported by the company, of shares conditionally granted to an executive. Typically, executives get to keep these shares only if they remain with the company for a predetermined period. Values are shown only for executives who received restricted stock.

2000 Options, Grant-Date Value. An estimate of the value of the stock options granted to an executive, using the Black-Scholes formula.

2000 Options, Estimated Current Value. An estimate of the value of those stock options based on the closing price of the stock on Wednesday. For an executive who received 100,000 options on a stock that traded on the grant date at $30, the current value would equal $200,000 if the current stock price was $32. If the stock was trading at $29, the options would have no current value.

Accumulated Wealth

Options Profits Realized in F.Y. 2000. The gain that executives saw in the 1999 fiscal year by exercising options from previous years. This gain is the difference between the exercise price and the share price at the time of exercise. (Some executives immediately sell the underlying shares, while others hold onto the stock.)

Value of Stock Beneficially Held. The value of shares held outright by an executive, based on the closing stock price at the end of the company's fiscal year. In some cases, executives may disclaim beneficial ownership of a portion of the shares they are reported as owning—because, for instance, shares are held in trust for a child.

Value of Options, Fiscal Year-End. Value, at the end of a company's fiscal year, of both exercisable and nonexercisable options held by the executive.

Total Value of Equity. The sum of the previous two numbers.

Ownership Stake. Beneficial stock holdings, plus exercisable options and options exercisable within 60 days, as a percentage of the company's total shares outstanding, as reported in the company's proxy.

Performance

Stock Performance Vs. S.&P. 500. The amount in percentage points, by which the company's performance trailed or exceeded the stock index during fiscal 2000.

Averages and Medians

For each column, these figures take into account only executives for whom values were reported. For example, the averages for restricted stock grants include only those executives who received restricted stock. "Average" is the arithmetic mean; "median" is the figure in the middle of the series of numbers.

The performance statistics were calculated by Money & Business, based on data provided by Bloomberg Financial Markets.

Executive Pay: A Special Report

Company	Chief executive	Salary	Bonus	Long-term incentive and other	Total direct compensation	Restricted stock awards	Grant date value	Est. current value	Profits realized in 2000	Value of stock beneficially held	Value of options, end of fiscal year	Total value of equity	Owner-ship stake	Company's 1-year stock performance vs. S.&P. 500-stock index
3Com	Eric A. Benhamou	$750,000	$275,316	0	$1,025,316	0	$39,528,068	$320,433	$30,952,592	$483,293,461	$153,779,600	$514,246,053	0.35%	+ 10.47
7-Eleven	James W. Keyes	437,500	99,563	0	537,063	0	4,966,620	0	0	79,625	0	79,625	0.19	+ 7.35
Abbott Laboratories	Miles D. White	1,390,961	1,800,000	68,881	3,259,842	0	7,866,000	5,085,000	229,558	13,477,153	12,336,236	13,706,711	0.08	+ 44.95
Advanced Micro Devices	W. J. Sanders III	1,000,000	5,143,236	417,284	6,560,520	0	23,136,000	5,100,000	85,057,766	3,253,010	16,866,000	88,310,776	1.00	+ 4.56
AES Corporation	Dennis W. Bakke	0	0	12,133	12,133	0	7,276,000	0	12,820,283	1,834,609,190	70,134,592	1,847,429,473	7.05	+ 57.26
Aetna	Dr. John W. Rowe*	1,000,000	375,000	0	1,375,000	1,367,188	13,420,262	4,783,617	0	6,521,054	38,868,924	6,521,054	0.11	– 0.23
Aflac	Daniel P. Amos	995,000	1,626,825	172,898	2,794,723	0	8,702,000	2,899,856	16,836,319	337,936,613	102,262,632	354,772,932	2.40	+ 63.07
Agilent Technologies	Edward W. Barnholt	1,000,000	660,000	0	1,660,000	46,908	12,450,000	2,250,000	0	3,885,633	25,354,579	3,885,633	0.17	– 20.08
Air Products & Chemicals	Harold A. Wagner	1,003,462	1,181,000	0	2,184,462	0	1,120,900	1,124,200	971,295	5,995,007	8,147,372	6,966,302	0.50	+ 12.68
Airborne	Robert S. Cline	650,000	0	0	650,000	0	926,820	0	247,393	2,968,193	0	3,215,586	1.37	– 46.09
Allegheny Technologies	Robert P. Bozzone*	800,000	0	0	57,143	602,862	136,050	0	0	1,244,169	0	1,244,169	0.20	– 17.28
Alltel	Joe T. Ford	825,000	1,237,500	778,750	2,841,250	0	16,577,500	0	5,702,538	80,602,192	53,209,374	86,304,730	0.77	– 13.71
Ameren	Charles W. Mueller	660,000	235,200	0	895,200	0	438,886	972,900	0	490,469	3,232,562	490,469	0.07	+ 60.41
American Electric Power	E. Linn Draper Jr.	850,000	485,775	0	1,335,775	0	7,014,000	6,562,500	0	5,380,794	7,612,500	5,380,794	0.04	+ 63.99
American Express	Harvey Golub	1,000,000	3,200,000	2,922,865	7,122,865	0	23,839,398	0	43,225,200	231,396,951	228,965,284	274,622,151	0.72	+ 8.80
American Home Products	John R. Stafford	1,640,000	1,968,000	0	3,608,000	0	17,665,200	444,906	22,606,763	40,506,516	67,130,769	63,113,279	0.19	+ 73.88
AmeriSource Health	R. David Yost	525,000	592,250	0	1,117,250	0	615,750	2,592,188	720,000	9,118,000	8,917,501	9,838,000	1.09	+ 55.22
AmSouth Banoration	C. Dowd Ritter	900,000	810,000	8,935,565	10,645,565	0	3,404,420	828,998	832,601	16,909,617	1,196,268	17,742,218	0.32	– 7.43
Anadarko Petroleum	Robert J. Allison Jr.	1,125,000	2,600,000	0	3,725,000	0	18,480,000	10,102,500	25,257,318	45,139,709	89,206,001	70,397,027	0.55	+118.18
Anheuser Busch	August A. Busch III	1,152,600	3,000,000	37,944	4,190,544	0	12,780,000	0	24,998,982	226,920,162	56,286,890	251,919,144	0.79	+ 39.59
Aon Corporation	Patrick G. Ryan	1,125,000	0	180,304	1,305,304	0	3,213,000	1,265,610	0	1,048,723,972	11,746,667	1,048,723,972	11.97	– 2.72
Apple Computer	Steven P. Jobs	1	0	90,000,000**	90,000,001	0	685,000,000	0	0	168	855,000	168	4.29	– 31.93
Applied Materials	James C. Morgan	835,769	3,000,000	0	3,835,769	0	5,232,000	1,188,000	44,350,183	215,645,180	36,957,484	259,995,363	0.39	– 30.60
Archer Daniels Midland	G. Allen Andreas	2,373,972	500,000	69,419	2,443,391	0	1,923,334	653,335	0	227,419,760	0	227,419,760	3.93	– 39.37
ArvinMeritor	Larry D. Yost	700,000	500,000	328,263	1,528,263	0	902,010	0	0	2,044,674	0	2,044,674	0.70	– 15.14
Ashland	Paul W. Chellgren	881,588	1,370,631	480,697	2,732,916	0		0	128,125	5,860,556	623,125	5,988,681	0.82	– 9.77
Automatic Data Processing	Arthur F. Weinbach	687,500	560,000	0	1,247,500	2,002,020	2,918,400	1,804,800	7,224,557	27,739,305	38,042,000	34,963,862	0.17	+ 15.31
Avnet	Roy Vallee	750,000	515,000	0	1,265,000	128,250	2,298,000	0	221,550	4,880,140	14,735,941	5,101,690	1.28	+ 11.83
Ball	George A. Sissel	740,000	1,050,413	491,535	2,281,948	0	1,082,400	477,500	0	7,246,620	11,521,916	7,246,620	2.76	+ 28.3
Bank Of America	Hugh L. McColl Jr.	1,500,000	2,500,000	0	4,000,000	0	0	0	0	57,250,113	0	57,250,113	0.12	+ 4.40
Baxter International	Harry M. Kraemer Jr.	880,000	1,320,000	2,795,562	4,995,562	2,150,126	17,857,125	5,026,125	293,985	27,187,798	19,489,797	27,481,783	0.18	+ 58.09
BB&T	John A. Allison IV	771,600	906,090	557,440	2,235,130	0	1,680,996	2,496,109	997,375	10,460,037	12,360,581	11,457,412	0.22	+ 49.68
Bear Stearns	James E. Cayne	200,000	11,665,172	0	11,865,172	9,577,402	2,775,828	0	0	211,239,597	520,569	211,239,597	4.30	+ 18.07
BellSouth	F. Duane Ackerman	1,200,000	2,200,000	1,499,800	4,899,800	6,345,300	12,318,484	0	0	24,033,014	62,848,200	24,033,014	0.22	– 1.98
Bergen Brunswig	Robert E. Martini	675,000	245,900	105,475	1,026,375	10,316	318,020	437,625	0	50,355,529	1,735,576	50,355,529	7.70	– 27.45
Berkshire Hathaway	Warren E. Buffet	100,000	0	0	100,000	0	0	0	0	33,878,786,000	0	33,878,786,000	35.53	+ 34.66
Black & Decker	Nolan D. Archibald	1,100,000	1,250,000	1,311,320	3,661,320	0	20,740,000	0	0	12,711,191	26,596,250	12,711,191	1.11	– 14.81

Column group headers: 2000 COMPENSATION (Direct compensation; At-risk Compensation — Valuations of 2000 options; Options) · ACCUMULATED WEALTH (Equity Holdings) · PERFORMANCE

2000 COMPENSATION / ACCUMULATED WEALTH / PERFORMANCE

Company	Chief executive	Salary	Bonus	Long-term incentive and other	Total direct compensation	Restricted stock awards	Grant date value	Est. current value	Profits realized in 2000	Value of stock beneficially held	Value of options, end of fiscal year	Total value of equity	Owner-ship stake	Company's 1-year stock performance vs. S. & P. 500-stock index
Boeing	Philip M. Condit	1,359,231	1,978,200	12,191,135	15,528,566	3,068,596	0	0	1,122,905	21,096,805	15,443,163	22,219,710	0.09	+ 70.3
Boise Cascade	George J. Harad	875,010	120,422		995,432	0	2,634,147	1,531,300	344,728	1,542,581	9,938,676	1,887,309	3.35	– 6.18
Bristol-Myers Squibb	Charles A. Heimbold Jr.	1,376,983	1,287,587	800,000	3,464,570	0	19,999,800	0	0	230,354,036	423,424,560	230,354,036	0.48	+ 26.28
Brunswick	George W. Buckley	660,625	1,410,000	856,120	2,926,745	0	3,033,000	110,250	0	646,898		646,898	0.12	– 14.97
Campbell Soup	David W. Johnson*†	500,000	713,514	0	1,213,514	500,000	0	0	0	119,903,536	1,668,240	119,903,536	1.78	– 46.96
Capital One Financial	Richard D. Fairbank	0	0	0	0	0	1,574,518	510,523	27,206,848	45,506,657	500,587,392	72,713,505	3.91	+ 45.98
Cardinal Health	Robert D. Walter	949,231	1,836,517	64,835	2,850,583	0	25,650,000	42,987,500	1,979,910	245,526,833	51,235,461	247,506,743	1.52	+ 8.38
Caterpillar	Glen A. Barton	967,500	780,000	352,778	2,100,278	0	1,804,800	1,214,992	0	4,323,253	2,932,975	4,323,253	0.09	+ 13.26
Chevron	David J. O'Reilly	862,500	2,000,000	390,750	3,253,250	0	3,054,000	825,000	0	2,932,975	3,542,646	2,473,512	0.05	+ 9.67
Chubb	Dean R. O'Hare	1,004,751	800,000	0	1,804,751	0	5,786,347	5,476,512	0	3,542,646	136,405,230	82,861,875	2.62	+ 65.53
Cigna	H. Edward Hanway	896,200	4,375,000	0	5,271,200	0	9,894,550	5,136,214	16,620,175	66,241,700	152,221,840	142,757,806	1.55	+ 75.42
Cinergy	James E. Rogers	1,050,000	990,000	874,138	2,914,138	0	1,833,190	3,779,633	16,219,736	126,538,070	25,769,874	20,715,599	1.24	+ 65.92
Cisco Systems	John T. Chambers	323,319	1,000,000	0	1,323,319	0	117,760,000	0	155,980,290	20,715,599	1,125,999,350	311,813,388	0.24	+ 101.69
Citigroup	Sanford I. Weill	1,000,000	18,484,414	449,404	19,933,818	8,687,442	286,471,364	2,401,940	3,728,597,715	155,833,098	1,139,580,043	28,315,621,316	11.27	+ 32.71
Clear Channel Comm.	L. Lowry Mays	1,000,000	3,000,000	0	4,000,000	0	14,726,250	0	0	24,587,023,601	6,868,690	1,418,629,653	5.27	– 36.63
Clorox	G. Craig Sullivan	937,500	0	261,451	1,198,951	0	0	0	0	1,418,629,653	36,414,864	5,084,918	0.67	– 21.81
Coca-Cola	Douglas N. Daft	1,268,750	3,000,000	131,554	4,400,304	0	19,285,500	0	0	5,084,918	69,042,188	130,036,786	0.10	– 40.90
Coca-Cola Enterprises	S. K. Johnston Jr.	25,000	232,652	848,615	1,106,267	87,281,250	0	0	0	130,036,786	54,614,505	544,290,834	6.85	+ 4.33
Compaq Computer	Michael D. Capellas	1,234,641	3,806,330	139,293	5,180,264	24,444,000	606,034	0	348,595	544,290,834	0	30,985,903	0.16	– 35.04
Conagra	Bruce Rohde	950,705	2,440,000	1,185,660	4,576,365	24,444,000	9,749,500	765,000	0	30,985,903	0	6,717,437	0.13	– 18.78
Conoco	Archie W. Dunham	1,200,000	3,000,000	124,168	4,324,168	0	1,122,425	0	2,833,038	6,717,437	6,868,690	84,887,906	1.74	+ 29.1
Cooper Industries	H. John Riley Jr.	910,000	932,500	1,258,351	3,100,851	750,019	4,842,474	4,764,825	0	82,054,868	48,415,926	11,917,014	0.54	+ 27.41
Costco Wholesale	James D. Sinegal	356,731	175,000	0	531,731	0	2,670,000	0	0	11,917,014	1,944,090	135,013,415	1.13	– 24.17
CSX	John W. Snow	1,100,008	0	705,665	1,805,673	0	5,005,500	0	796,225	134,664,820	22,734,234	39,625,060	1.58	+ 3.89
Cummins Engine	Theodore M. Solso	900,000	486,000	142,500	1,528,500	1,085,013	1,643,066	48,644	0	38,828,835	1,471,222	10,901,265	1.51	+ 9.58
CVS	Thomas M. Ryan	975,000	1,600,000	0	2,575,000	5,500,000	3,714,000	3,487,500	8,032,009	10,901,265	118,788	36,460,944	0.43	+ 60.24
Dana	Joe M. Magliochetti	850,000	0	98,363	948,363	0	5,200,000	0	0	28,428,935	65,505,888	1,798,037	0.28	– 36.6
Darden Restaurants	Joe R. Lee	738,557	1,107,800	28,846	1,875,203	553,900	3,044,250	567,188	1,850,855	1,798,037	1,798,037	12,044,851	1.66	– 29.48
Dean Foods	Howard M. Dean	700,000	677,408	0	1,377,408	0	1,271,940	0	0	10,193,996	1,480,624	12,080,867	2.48	– 38.27
Delphi Automotive Systems	J.T. Battenberg III	1,387,500	2,600,000	1,845,655	5,833,155	0	5,675,500	0	0	12,080,867	1,376,287	2,406,128	0.26	– 18.03
Delta Air Lines	Leo F. Mullin	745,833	1,400,000	66,629	2,212,462	0	17,614,000	0	0	2,406,128	2,406,128	1,827,883	1.47	– 19.32
Dominion Resources	Thomas E. Capps	925,000	1,495,528	1,667,129	4,087,657	0	978,511	4,778,467	0	1,827,883	13,437,400	22,707,506	0.63	+ 89.32
Dover	Thomas L. Reece	920,000	1,250,000	1,265,485	3,435,485	0	1,409,678	0	0	22,707,506	9,933,885	12,379,507	0.37	+ 0.51
Dow Chemical	Michael D. Parker	703,717	930,000	12,006	1,645,723	0	4,468,800	0	0	12,379,507	7,305,082	25,107,570	0.09	+ 5.61
Duke Energy	Richard B. Priory	954,164	1,908,328	300,384	3,162,876	0	944,000	6,275,000	1,021,906	25,107,570	19,430,011	15,060,228	0.14	+ 85.09
DuPont	Charles O. Holliday Jr.	1,040,000	1,700,000	0	2,740,000	0	8,994,000	0	0	14,038,322	179,990	20,608,132	0.28	– 15.12
Eastman Kodak	David A. Carp	1,000,000	598,500	0	1,598,500	0	1,670,000	0	408,576	20,608,132	50,409	10,671,591	1.25	– 29.51
Eaton	Alexander M. Cutler	797,940	636,043	929,978	2,363,961	0	1,951,424	870,810	2,388,738	10,263,015	8,780,046	18,032,550	1.23	+ 15.22
Electronic Data Systems	Richard H. Brown	1,500,000	3,412,800	0	4,912,800	465,610	0	0	0	15,643,812	16,250,000	19,090,475	0.16	+ 3.72
Eli Lilly	Sidney Taurel	1,300,000	1,487,294	3,226,371	6,013,665	0	16,191,000	0	12,697,033	19,090,475	19,090,475	78,127,788	0.13	+ 51.03
EMC	Michael C. Ruettgers	1,000,000	1,809,880	87,216	2,897,096	0	12,387,500	0	67,181,800	65,430,755	62,902,788	228,566,660	0.21	+ 30.84
Emerson Electric	Charles F. Knight	1,400,000	6,000,000	42,349	7,442,349	3,203,125	1,168,000	1,843,750	1,708,956	161,384,860	265,925,868	89,690,346	0.42	– 4.50
FedEx	Frederick W. Smith	1,093,754	1,048,000	2,131,163	4,272,917	0	9,147,000	9,147,000	0	87,981,390	6,065,868	707,550,216	7.39	– 45.70
Fifth Third Ban	George A. Schaefer Jr.	976,732	1,462,500	0	2,439,232	0	4,401,000	3,849,990	0	707,550,216	16,435,911	104,056,179	1.10	+ 33.02
First Data	Henry C. Duques	950,000	836,000	1,895	1,787,895	0	4,326,335	0	32,573,996	775,100	141,842,046	33,349,096	1.49	+ 16.13

Company	Chief executive	Salary	Bonus	Long-term incentive and other	Total direct compensation	Restricted stock awards	Grant date value	Est. current value	Profits realized in 2000	Value of stock beneficially held	Value of options, end of fiscal year	Total value of equity	Owner-ship stake	Company's 1-year stock performance vs. S & P 500-stock index
First Union	G. Kennedy Thompson	$940,000	$0	$30,834	$970,834	$697,531	$5,112,909	$1,802,981	$18,780	$27,683,339	$1,426,996	$27,702,119	0.26%	– 0.78
Fleet Boston Financial	Terrence Murray	992,200	5,000,000	122,582	6,114,782	0	15,020,000	4,735,000	0	61,289,281	46,413,800	61,289,281	0.49	+ 20.49
Fleetwood Enterprises	Glenn F. Kummer	99,000	1,348,275	556,548	2,003,823	0	265,720	0	0	541,125	0	541,125	2.07	– 58.77
FMC	Robert N. Burt	928,175	1,439,042	0	2,367,217	535,669	1,410,486	1,175,107	0	5,317,749	8,615,089	5,317,749	1.46	+ 34.18
Fortune Brands	Norman H. Wesley	800,000	1,020,000	841,388	2,661,388	0	1,954,000	1,900,000	0	1,463,010	2,234,824	1,463,010	0.28	+ 3.19
Gannet	John J. Curley	1,100,000	2,000,000	4,800	3,104,800	0	0	0	5,814,500	27,917,293	34,248,250	33,731,793	0.67	– 12.48
General Electric	John F. Welch Jr.	4,000,000	12,700,000	54,019	16,754,019	48,715,625	79,020,000	0	57,112,560	141,663,414	341,518,062	198,775,974	0.10	+ 3.06
General Mills	Stephen W. Sanger	696,150	1,264,600	0	1,960,750	316,138	5,164,170	4,610,366	3,699,939	10,798,611	112,027,905	34,498,550	18.31	– 8.79
Genuine Parts	Larry L. Prince	655,000	799,376	0	1,454,376	0	187,500	578,125	0	10,856,657	1,012,970	10,856,657	0.55	+ 20.04
Gillette	Edward F. DeGraan¶	642,083	715,000	0	1,357,083	0	5,286,400	67,000	0	6,920,863	18,752,760	6,920,863	0.20	– 1.55
Goldman Sachs	Henry M. Paulson	600,000	14,056,600	0	14,656,600	3,866,533	5,881,329	577,356	0	331,341,046	0	331,341,046	0.83	+ 23.27
Goodrich B. F.	David L. Burner	900,000	1,375,938	554,069	2,830,007	0	1,466,448	928,233	137,812	4,682,226	2,344,861	4,820,038	0.49	+ 45.61
Goodyear Tire & Rubber	Samir G. Gibara	1,100,000	175,562	9,000	1,284,562	0	584,800	1,074,400	0	422,211	902,700	422,211	0.19	– 4.32
Hartford Financial Srvs.	Ramani Ayer	995,833	1,752,000	2,638,844	5,386,677	25,042	5,522,879	9,803,928	2,440,500	15,562,007	46,737,312	18,002,507	0.69	+ 61.01
H. J. Heinz	William R. Johnson	900,000	1,776,864	0	2,676,864	0			0	10,833,541	14,975,539	10,833,541	0.52	– 34.71
Hershey Foods	Kenneth L. Wolfe	775,000	640,584	234,847	1,650,431	0	1,858,416	3,956,950	7,847,514	25,786,629	14,038,752	33,634,143	0.83	+ 47.80
Hewlett Packard	Carleton S. Fiorina	1,000,000	1,766,250	205,113	2,971,363	0	38,235,477	0	0	92,292,462	7,187,544	92,292,462	0.09	– 55.56
Household International	William F. Aldinger	1,000,000	4,000,000	154,242	5,154,242	7,999,962	12,612,000	5,868,000	9,070,325	123,771,226	84,905,558	132,841,551	2.71	+ 59.12
Ikon Office Solutions	James J. Forese	825,000	712,800	0	1,537,800	129,250	977,920	947,250	0	724,195	0	724,195	0.41	– 85.74
Illinois Tool Works	W. James Farrell	899,990	1,309,500	0	2,209,490	0	12,231,000		650,566	4,348,416	18,786,932	4,998,982	0.25	+ 1.56
Ingersoll Rand	Herbert L. Henkel	950,000	850,000	992,536	2,792,536	187,410	3,637,500	0	0	7,506,848	0	7,506,848	0.47	– 13.62
I.B.M.	Louis V. Gerstner Jr.	2,000,000	8,000,000	3,681,807	13,681,807	0	40,300,000	0	59,887,423	76,739,445	269,023,076	136,626,868	0.30	– 11.73
International Paper	John T. Dillon	1,089,375	975,000	5,387,391	7,451,766	0	4,597,000	668,700	0	29,071,478	2,300,000	29,071,478	0.44	– 16.45
Interstate Bakeries	Charles A. Sullivan	815,385	0	0	815,385	0	289,200	60,000	1,153,809	8,519,939	267,125	9,673,748	1.22	– 54.04
ITT Industries	Travis Engen	1,090,962	1,484,010	1,295,023	3,869,995	0	2,204,000	469,000	3,693,481	11,228,123	34,927,700	14,921,604	2.15	+ 27.26
Johnson & Johnson	Ralph S. Larsen	1,435,000	1,550,287	1,653,620	4,638,907	0	31,972,500	0	2,921,800	71,228,474	64,679,046	74,150,274	0.12	+ 23.37
Johnson Controls	James H. Keyes	1,082,505	2,260,000	972,000	4,314,505	0	2,932,500	538,500	0	3,657,380	13,546,826	3,657,380	0.89	+ 31.43
Kellogg	Carlos M. Gutierrez	806,250	127,500	0	933,750	0	1,327,500	695,250	0	3,159,371	290,000	3,159,371	0.15	– 2.35
Kerr-McGee	Luke R. Corbett	892,596	0	66,750	959,346	1,897,500	3,508,500	220,305	29,644	5,392,686	4,868,786	5,422,330	0.44	+ 35.98
KeyCorp	Henry L. Meyer III	687,501	526,500	0	1,214,001	0	981,000	581,200	850,000	8,538,503	14,507,500	9,388,503	0.40	+ 42.55
KeySpan	Robert B. Catell	786,000	336,000	0	1,122,000	0	1,530,080	7,678,841	4,916,444	10,949,531	43,581,246	15,865,975	2.70	+103.21
Kimberly-Clark	Wayne R. Sanders	950,000	1,110,304	31,477	2,091,781	0	7,588,000	6,450,000	1,253,880	25,006,729	34,542,584	26,260,609	0.27	+ 19.10
Lear	Robert E. Rossiter	880,000	0	41,024	921,024	155,124	2,583,000	1,963,000	0	7,993,446	3,935,126	7,993,446	0.84	– 13.36
Lehman Brothers	Richard S. Fuld Jr.	750,000	8,750,000	0	9,500,000	13,572,896	9,552,000	26,700,000	42,950,000	190,993,901	111,998,085	233,943,901	2.87	+ 34.63
Lennar	Stuart A. Miller	600,000	2,817,300	0	3,417,300	1,843,750	110,040	255,100	0	10,833,196	22,042,082	10,833,196	2.19	+ 79.05
Lexmark International	Paul J. Curlander	704,671	0	0	704,671	0	16,258,000	0	0	24,603,216	50,326,850	24,603,216	1.61	– 49.05
Litton Industries	Michael R. Brown	725,005	696,005	0	1,421,010	0	0	0	0	1,077,345	1,274,265	1,077,345	0.39	+ 66.87
Lockheed Martin	Vance D. Coffman	1,292,643	2,500,000	117,856	3,910,499	1,931,250	4,266,000	9,900,000	0	7,630,025	9,525,750	7,630,025	0.30	+ 66.95
Lucent Technologies	Richard A. McGinn	1,100,000	0	137,384	1,237,384	0	127,765,932	0	0	116,608,149	177,847,206	116,608,149	0.35	– 41.63
Lyondell Chemical	Dan F. Smith	1,018,004	1,546,552	359,592	2,924,148	0	2,366,733	1,117,773	0	2,545,305	1,285,104	2,545,305	0.57	+ 38.29

110

Column groups: **2000 COMPENSATION** — *Direct compensation* (Salary, Bonus, Long-term incentive and other, Total direct compensation) and *At-risk Compensation / Valuations of 2000 options* (Restricted stock awards, Grant date value, Est. current value). **ACCUMULATED WEALTH** — *Options* (Profits realized in 2000) and *Equity Holdings* (Value of stock beneficially held, Value of options end of fiscal year, Total value of equity, Ownership stake). **PERFORMANCE** — Company's 1-year stock performance vs. S. & P. 500-stock index.

Company	Chief executive	Salary	Bonus	Long-term incentive and other	Total direct compensation	Restricted stock awards	Grant date value	Est. current value	Profits realized in 2000	Value of stock beneficially held	Value of options, end of fiscal year	Total value of equity	Ownership stake	1-year stock perf. vs. S&P 500
Marriott International	J. W. Marriott Jr.	1,000,000	1,166,000	0	2,166,000	233,310	0	0	0	2,469,001,482	76,955,936	2,469,001,482	24.91	+ 43.83
MBNA	Alfred Lerner	2,000,000	4,000,000	0	6,000,000	10,900,000	7,456,000	9,700,000	0	3,646,918,865	255,520,704	3,646,918,865	12.56	+ 46.06
McGraw-Hill	Harold W. McGraw III	900,000	1,400,000	1,270,973	3,570,973	0	3,417,500	0	54,815	25,076,961	11,621,796	25,131,776	0.50	+ 5.90
Mead	Jerome F. Tatar	820,838	530,000	383,950	1,734,788	383,950	1,579,835	0	0	1,931,320	1,666,894	1,931,320	0.74	– 16.92
Mellon Financial	Martin G. McGuinn	800,000	1,500,000	1,377,163	3,677,163	4,152,000	3,888,348	755,491	20,604,834	231,172,003	81,757,830	251,776,837	0.97	+ 56.86
Merck	Raymond V. Gilmartin	1,283,340	1,700,000	0	2,983,340	0	9,808,000	3,800,000	0	16,296,859	164,775,937	16,296,859	0.08	+ 50.84
Merrill Lynch	David H. Komansky	700,000	15,550,000	0	16,250,000	8,380,400	13,595,017	0	0	123,567,508	0	123,567,508	1.59	+ 74.54
MetLife	Robert H. Benmosche	1,000,000	3,400,000	4,484,200	8,884,200	0	0	0	0	12,250	0	12,250	0.00	+121.85
Micron Technology	Steven A. Appleton	656,827	2,541,793	0	3,198,620	0	7,600,000	1,015,000	39,569,779	26,432,738	33,738,475	66,002,517	0.10	+101.39
Microsoft	Steven A. Ballmer	428,414	200,000	0	628,414	0	0	0	0	14,991,653,677	0	14,991,653,677	4.47	– 18.54
Morgan Stanley Dean Witter	Philip J. Purcel	775,000	12,612,500	113,178	13,500,678	8,531,064	24,841,461	0	156,105,651	97,502,889	293,671,155	253,608,540	1.56	+ 21.28
Murphy Oil	Claiborne P. Deming	691,674	650,000	0	1,341,674	0	605,700	210,936	187,030	7,356,604	2,087,765	87,543,634	3.51	+ 17.07
National City	David A. Daberko	998,333	400,000	664,389	2,062,722	764,750	3,002,928	3,684,150	5,196,891	292,215	26,971,890	5,489,106	0.96	+ 37.83
Navistar International	John R. Horne	975,000	0	0	975,000	4,990,375	6,393,033	0	61,578,253	148,266,962	13,572,350	209,845,215	8.08	– 27.36
NCR	Lars Nyberg	1,033,846	418,243	7,166	1,459,255	0	6,893,600	0	0	6,009,805	16,730,862	6,009,805	1.28	+ 38.80
Nike	Philip H. Knight	1,205,300	1,330,651	0	2,835,951	0	0	0	0	12,303,791,202	0	12,303,791,202	106.42	– 39.44
NiSource	Gary L. Neale	800,000	1,060,000	2,350,650	4,210,650	0	1,376,250	2,417,813	0	26,828,297	13,257,630	26,828,297	0.89	+ 90.61
Northwestern	Merle D. Lewis	734,208	247,000	80,676	1,061,884	0	863,170	591,689	0	4,097,126	361,078	4,097,126	0.75	+ 19.62
Occidental Petroleum	Ray R. Irani	1,250,000	2,125,000	202,575	3,577,575	596,000	5,452,500	2,953,125	0	36,819,357	21,768,730	36,819,357	1.36	+ 26.45
Oracle	Lawrence J. Ellison	208,000	0	0	208,000	0	216,200,000	329,000,000	75,024,427	47,623,120,781	3,433,812,105	47,698,145,208	24.39	+468.88
Paccar	Mark C. Pigott	1,070,000	0	607,903	1,677,903	0	964,563	294,920	0	37,356,864	3,322,533	37,356,864	0.58	+ 25.45
Parker Hannifin	Duane E. Collins	1,035,000	854,186	942,575	2,831,761	0	2,280,579	146,023	10,226,812	11,110,886	9,082,962	21,337,698	1.00	– 31.16
PepsiCo	Roger A. Enrico	1	4,000,000	200,744	4,200,745	0	10,276,949	5,479,416	4,403,727	19,127,160	124,194,726	23,530,887	0.29	+ 51.52
Pfizer	William C. Steere Jr.	1,616,000	3,232,000	9,431,600	14,279,600	2,688,600	13,560,000	5,648,000	23,044,101	103,039,172	124,371,808	126,083,273	0.08	+ 52.18
Pharmacia	Fred Hassan	1,250,006	2,005,600	51,499	3,307,105	0	26,225,140	5,932,150	0	122,013,786	163,241,664	122,013,786	0.62	+ 82.19
Philip Morris	Geoffrey C. Bible	1,750,000	3,000,000	8,661,278	13,411,278	0	16,529,142	32,335,546	7,445,160	82,748,424	143,027,030	90,193,584	0.60	+114.4
Pitney Bowes	Michael J. Critelli	919,000	600,000	873,400	2,392,400	0	4,485,500	1,335,000	2,007,256	76,177,563	25,010,966	78,184,819	1.58	– 20.26
PNC Financial Services	James E. Rohr	836,120	2,601,000	3,690	3,440,810	3,862,500	2,997,415	5,596,709	11,033,320	58,831,276	72,499,304	69,864,596	0.77	+ 79.23
PPG Industries	Raymond W. LeBoeuf	840,000	850,000	9,703	1,699,703	308,740	4,889,418	8,606,179	0	5,676,477	0	5,676,477	0.45	– 14.2
PPL	William F. Hecht	788,270	571,170	0	1,359,440	0	5,416,000	2,225,000	0	27,478,812	12,655,975	27,478,812	0.46	+114.04
Praxair	Dennis H. Reilley*	789,565	660,000	161,179	1,610,744	25,000	1,821,951	2,225,000	0	2,995,845	1,975,000	2,995,845	0.04	– 1.33
Progressive	Peter B. Lewis	623,077	275,057	59,822	957,956	0	2,041,662	2,041,662	5,977,010	989,569,943	40,761,684	995,546,953	12.99	+ 51.27
Public Service Enterprise	E. James Ferland	890,000	1,001,300	361,440	2,252,740	0	2,991,000	0	58,000	10,933,823	7,595,001	10,991,823	0.48	+ 56.91
Qwest Comm. International	Joseph P. Nacchio	854,615	1,963,736	1,107,913	3,926,264	5,281,250	3,522,400	5,425,125	93,454,973	23,079,251	352,381,408	116,534,224	0.44	+ 4.16
Raytheon	Daniel P. Burnham	973,500	1,750,000	76,606	2,800,106	1,163,497		0	0	33,078,527	22,049,595	33,078,527	0.89	+ 29.80
RJ Reynolds Tobacco	Andrew J. Schindler	900,000	1,250,000	880,604	3,030,604	0	7,540,500	0	10,911,542	40,214,460	18,915,474	51,126,002	1.62	+218.31
Rockwell International	Don H. Davis Jr.	900,000	1,300,000	30,179	2,230,179	0	1,565,098	0	0	6,467,668	5,222,772	6,467,668	1.21	– 54.18
Rohm & Haas	Rajiv L. Gupta	787,500	323,962	316,911	1,428,373	0		0	102,456	2,999,921	600,977	3,102,377	0.09	+ 0.50
Safeco	Roger H. Eigsti	900,000	0	0	900,000	0	0	0	22,543	3,921,955	903,460	3,944,498	0.36	+ 49.81
Safeway	Steven A. Burd	870,000	1,657,000	0	2,527,000	0	58,220,000	330,000	0	28,578,188	302,488,443	28,578,188	1.04	+ 83.93
SBC Communications	Edward E. Whitacre Jr.	1,886,667	4,500,000	4,289,740	10,676,407	0	13,259,928	1,787,525	65,347,515	78,297,012	146,047,584	143,644,527	0.24	+ 9.21
Schering-Plough	Richard Jay Kogan	1,338,000	1,872,000	0	3,210,000	6,304,250	12,529,860	645,750	23,103,970	30,818,542	36,546,324	53,922,512	0.13	+ 44.70
Schlumberger	D. Euan Baird	1,500,000	1,500,000	0	3,000,000	0	0	0	0	55,954,403	66,063,142	55,954,403	0.40	+ 52.91
Schwab, Charles	Charles R. Schwab	800,004	8,101,000	0	8,901,004	0	5,208,000	0	19,122,628	7,551,632,608	118,209,377	7,570,755,236	19.08	+ 20.52
Schwab, Charles	David S. Pottruck	800,004	8,101,000	0	8,901,004	0	5,208,000	330,000	63,404,959	187,690,619	240,348,283	251,095,578	0.96	+ 20.52

Company	Chief executive	Salary	Bonus	Long-term incentive and other	Total direct compensation	Restricted stock awards	Grant date value	Est. current value	Profits realized in 2000	Value of stock beneficially held	Value of options, end of fiscal year	Total value of equity	Owner-ship stake	Company's 1-year stock performance vs. S.&P. 500-stock index
		Direct compensation				At-risk Compensation (Valuations of 2000 options)			Options	Equity Holdings				
SCI Systems	A. Eugene Sapp Jr.	$ 777,308	$1,967,350	$1,967,350	$ 4,712,008	$ 0	$ 3,340,000	$ 0	$ 0	$ 10,910,880	$ 26,289,426	$ 10,910,880	0.72%	+ 48.05
Sears, Roebuck	Alan J. Lacy	675,000	1,041,247	7,950	1,724,197	0	7,950,675	1,223,888	0	2,979,986	2,073,680	2,979,986	0.10	+ 26.86
Sempra Energy	Stephen L. Baum	913,231	1,560,000	174,643	2,647,874	0	7,048,650	4,393,050	0	9,173,660	10,618,988	9,173,660	0.51	+ 50.06
Sherwin-Williams	Christopher M. Connor	749,821	490,000	0	1,239,821	0	1,398,600	1,075,000	0	2,556,891	3,450,001	2,556,891	0.23	+ 37.55
Smithfield Foods	Joseph W. Luter III	620,000	2,528,316	0	3,148,316	0	0	0	0	100,707,923	1,956,200	100,707,923	7.87	− 30.28
Sodexho Marriott Srvs.	Michel Landel	419,617	180,000	18,705	618,322	0	1,033,000	1,243,750	211,982	190,125	402,107	402,107	0.10	− 11.76
State Street	David A. Spina	821,276	1,168,200	8,385,029	10,374,505	0	7,473,840	0	0	62,624,322	49,554,860	62,624,322	0.60	+ 80.14
Sun Microsystems	Scott G. McNealy	103,846	4,767,500	0	4,871,346	0	28,060,000	0	19,968,740	1,104,840,435	848,753,239	1,124,809,175	2.28	+ 156.82
Sunoco	John G. Drosdick	757,692	1,128,000	530,515	2,416,207	0	2,754,300	421,875	0	5,198,171	6,431,876	5,198,171	0.74	+ 57.69
SunTrust Banks	L. Phillip Humann	808,750	0	308,775	1,117,525	0	2,830,500	1,781,250	111,787.5	36,395,856	2,213,550	36,507,644	0.35	+ 3.27
Sysco	Charles H. Cotros	750,000	1,243,003	0	1,993,003	1,101,569	239,580	354,915	437,018	7,788,105	2,042,751	8,225,123	1.32	+ 35.39
Temple-Inland	Kenneth M. Jastrow II	567,308	785,000	0	1,352,308	0	2,166,000	0	0	18,073,448	107,880	18,073,448	0.76	− 7.34
Tenet Healthcare	Jeffrey C. Barbakow	1,124,000	1,802,115	65,596	2,991,711	0	0	0	0	28,496,358	43,097,000	28,496,358	1.75	− 5.83
Texas Instruments	Thomas J. Engibous	796,200	1,300,000	0	2,096,200	0	25,389,000	0	35,314,454	12,286,913	101,660,800	47,601,367	1.60	+ 7.30
Textron	Lewis B. Campbell	1,000,000	1,937,500	1,635,551	4,573,051	0	1,074,000	782,813	70,313	20,784,245	681,609	20,854,658	0.72	− 28.71
TransMontaigne	Donald H. Anderson*	300,000	0	0	300,000	0	1,869,600	0	0	1,755,000	160,000	1,755,000	9.85	− 65.73
TRW	Joseph T. Gorman	1,366,154	1,882,595	93,218	3,341,967	1,202,500	10,265,000	0	1,343,125	10,440,606	5,624,650	11,783,731	1.29	− 13.91
Tyco International	L. Dennis Kozlowski	1,350,000	2,800,000	0	4,150,000	21,207,540	179,802,582	6,401,270	1,099,090,784	4,863,129,455	117,813,520	5,962,220,239	20.29	− 12.68
Tyson Foods	John H. Tyson	650,000	0	132,886	782,886	483,750	0	0	0	5,741,740	0	5,741,740	0.28	− 11.24
UAL	James E. Goodwin	843,528	225,000	60,877	1,129,405	3,600,000	4,417,200	0	963,000	8,759,431	1,304,125	9,722,431	0.73	− 81.47
Union Pacific	Richard K. Davidson	962,504	0	96,442	1,058,946	0	0	0	0	24,377,966	7,687,720	24,377,966	0.67	+ 27.56
Unisys	Lawrence A. Weinbach	1,320,000	396,000	566,920	2,282,920	0	9,956,000	0	0	3,726,362	2,843,200	3,726,362	0.46	− 45.11
United Technologies	George David	1,200,000	2,400,000	87,985	3,687,985	499,375	9,415,250	3,412,500	14,647,600	35,285,013	236,907,056	49,932,613	0.90	+ 31.72
US Industries	David H. Clarke	750,000	0	0	750,000	675,000	1,791,545	0	0	19,640,912	802,816	19,640,912	5.00	− 59.42
V.F.	Mackey J. McDonald	834,000	878,000	211,000	1,923,000	0	1,201,500	1,320,000	0	3,791,972	6,077,440	3,791,972	8.31	+ 34.01
Verizon Communications	Charles R. Lee	1,490,400	2,620,800	87,900	4,199,100	6,614,200	12,861,819	2,379,000	3,248,800	53,817,709	67,634,000	57,066,509	0.20	− 7.21
Verizon Communications	Ivan G. Seidenberg	1,350,000	2,577,000	148,700	4,075,700	6,562,500	17,127,834	2,379,000	0	56,527,968	28,645,000	56,527,968	0.15	− 7.21
Wachovia	Leslie M. Baker Jr.	990,000	0	54,817	1,044,817	2,240,000	3,038,000	0	125,218	16,919,839	3,334,025	17,045,057	0.49	− 1.98
Walgreen	L. Daniel Jorndt	950,000	543,115	86,513	1,579,628	352,617	1,726,436	2,610,225	0	4,018,216	39,641,324	4,018,216	0.14	+ 26.22
Walt Disney	Michael D. Eisner	13,462	8,500,000	800,000	9,313,462	0	39,060,000	4,680,000	60,531,000	1,124,717,906	266,765,100	1,185,248,906	12.34	+ 34.95
Wells Fargo	Richard M. Kovacevich	995,000	5,475,000	280,799	6,750,799	0	11,032,341	10,017,650	0	86,122,055	83,365,904	86,122,055	0.24	+ 49.82
Weyerhaeuser	Steven R. Rogel	1,000,000	1,900,000	291	2,900,291	0	3,584,000	0	0	54,560	23,906	54,560	0.13	− 17.87
Whirlpool	David R. Whitwam	1,080,833	850,000	644,711	2,575,544	0	2,558,400	0	223,895	9,303,402	566,057	9,527,297	1.09	− 15.39
Winn-Dixie Stores	Allen R. Rowland*	700,000	210,000	0	910,000	0	4,615,000	500,000	0	790,625	0	790,625	0.39	− 66.61
Average		926,749	1,883,757	1,082,860	3,889,688	1,696,771	14,899,165	3,673,069	33,730,242	838,071,393	78,039,814	870,465,784	0.67%	
Median		900,000	1,168,200	64,835	2,575,000	0	3,508,500	32,335,546	60,000	20,715,599	12,384,600	23,530,887	0.67%	

*Indicates annualized compensation †Waived first six months' salary for restricted stock; Salary reported here represents half of annual salary.

¶Acting chief executive **Represents the value of an aircraft with a total cost to the company of approximately $90 million awarded as a special bonus for serving as the interim chief executive for the past 2 1/2 years without compensation.

Total Mobilization, Globalization and Individuation: The Contradictory Domination Logic of Postmodern Society, A Theoretical Note

Christine Monnier*

Few media eyebrows went up the other day when the World Bank canceled a global meeting set for Barcelona in late June—and shifted it to the Internet. Thousands of street demonstrators would have been in Spain's big northeastern port city to confront the conference. Cyberspace promises to be a much more serene location. (. . .) If hackers can be kept at bay, the few hundred participants in the Annual Bank Conference on Development Economics will be able to conduct a lovely forum over the Internet. The video conferencing system is likely to be state-of-the-art, making possible a modern and bloodless way to avoid uninvited perspectives. (. . .) Top officials of the World Bank are onto something. In a managerial world, disruption must be kept to an absolute minimum. If global corporatization is to achieve its transnational potential, then **discourse among power brokers and their favorite thinkers can happen everywhere at once—and nowhere in particular** *(emphasis added). Let the troublemakers try to interfere by doing civil disobedience in cyberspace."*[1]

When I read this column written by media critic Norman Solomon, it seemed to me that it powerfully summed up some of the most important socio-political aspects of our times. The idea of power brokers making far-reaching decisions that will affect millions of people, completely remote from social realities experienced by these same people, while, at the same time, being everywhere and nowhere, in cyberspace, constitutes both a very real

Source: Christine Monnier, "Total Mobilization, Globalization and Individuation: The Contradictory Domination Logic of Postmodern Society, A Theoretical Note." *Views from the Left: Fresh Sociological Insights*, Mario Reda, editor (Boston: Allyn & Bacon/Pearson Education, 2002).

113

aspect of, and a metaphor for, postmodern society: the disintegration of time and space and replacement with a sort of virtual reality, which nonetheless has concrete consequences.

In the paragraphs that follow, I would like to try to delineate some of the recent theoretical contributions provided by progressive social thinkers on the issues confronting us in terms of political economy, domination and the possibilities of social change. But before addressing the issues involved with the above quote, we need to question the very notion of the "postmodern society" as a new form of social organization.

What Is Postmodern Society?

Defining Modernity

It is impossible to talk about postmodernity without defining "modernity." Modernity refers to a series of political, cultural, economic and social transformations experienced by Western countries. Modernity is often associated with the transformations brought about by the Industrial Revolution. It involved new ways of producing, organizing and thinking that constituted a radical break with traditional societies that had preceded industrialization.

The new discourses or ways of thinking associated with modernity are often referred to as the Enlightenment. The project of the Enlightenment and modernity emphasized reason and science as the only true sources of knowledge and progress, against superstition and other non-rational modes of knowledge. If societies were organized according to the principles of reason, progress would follow. Positivist social thinkers such as Auguste Comte, who initiated positivism, proposed such arguments. In other words, modernization involves the reorganization of societies according to rational principles.

The optimistic prospects, when contrasted with the historical reality of modernity, reveal a different picture. The Industrial Revolution produced as much misery as it produced wealth. Modes of organizations and production based on rational and scientific principles, such as Taylorism or Fordism, far from being emancipatory, revealed themselves to be profoundly alienating and debilitating for the people subjected to their rule.

The Dialectic of The Enlightenment

The rationalization of society and its horrific consequences have been studied at length by thinkers who witnessed these phenomena, namely, Karl Marx and Max Weber. Marx's analysis of alienation, and Weber's descriptions of bureaucracies as iron cages, and the expansion of instrumental reason laid the ground for a re-examination of the project of modernity.

This re-examination was fully developed by Frankfurt School founders Max Horkheimer and Theodor Adorno in their now classic "Dialectic of the Enlightenment."[2] While not denying the progress brought about by modernization, they also describe how modern principles can give birth to their exact opposites: alienation rather than emancipation, more powerful modes of domination rather than increased freedom. In this sense, the Holocaust can be interpreted as the first and unique modern genocide: a genocide based on principles of efficiency and scientific rationalization. Just as modernity provided the conditions of possibility for mass production and mass consumption, it engendered mass murder.

Postmodern Critique of Modernity

Postmodern theorists adopt this idea of modernity and modern modes of thinking as regimes of oppression and terror as their first justification to re-examine Enlightenment claims. For instance, Michel Foucault, in his studies on the birth of the asylum and the birth of prison[3] (both institutions traditionally conceived as humanitarian and rational improvements in the way societies treat its deviants), shows how the logic of instrumental reason ends up creating a disciplinary society in which behavior is observed, regulated, and, if necessary, normalized.

Contrary to the Marxian tradition of social theory that divides society between the base structure and the superstructure, Foucault argues that power, in modern society, is not located in one domain (the economy) and in the hands of a few (the capitalist class, the state), but dispersed throughout society, incarnated in many different institutions (police, education, health care) under the form of micro-power. Therefore, overthrowing the economic system through revolution would not do away with other forms of power, located in other domains of society. This is why Foucault advocated local political struggles, directed at these micro-sources of power (he, himself, espoused the cause of prisoners' rights). In Foucault's analyses, power has no center, it is decentered and incarnated in pluralities of settings.

And contrary to the Enlightenment movement as a whole, Foucault demonstrates that scientific knowledge and reason, far from emancipating subjects, actually provides new capacities of domination and surveillance. The real transformation operated by modernity is that power becomes a productive force, all the more efficient that it does not operate from above (the capitalist class, the power elite, the state) but in a capillary form that pervades society and the subject. Subjectivity itself becomes an effect of power.

But Foucault is somewhat a unique case because he does not so much analyze postmodern society as he advocates new forms of knowledge (which he calls archeology of knowledge, and later in his career, genealogies of power) to provide a critique of modernity and the project of the Enlightenment.

Theorizing Postmodernity

The bulk of postmodern analysis has mainly consisted in proclaiming the end of modernity (and the end of history, and the end of politics, and the end of ideologies), and the birth of a new (dis)order of things. In this sense, postmodern theorists focus their analyses on what they see as a radical break with previous historical stage: the postmodern society.

Contemporary society, characterized by widespread use of information and communication technologies, the globalization of trade, the decline in the legitimacy and power of the nation-state (a typical product of modernity) and its corresponding notion of citizenry, the uninterrupted flow of images and cultural representations, and the compression of time and space constitute unprecedented social conditions and modes of social (dis)organization that cannot be adequately addressed by traditional (mostly Marxian) modes of analysis, especially since the end of Soviet communism. Therefore, these conditions require a whole new epistemology, characterized by an emphasis on disintegration, implosion, difference, diversity, discontinuity, relativism, and, for extreme forms of postmodern social theories, nihilism.

Postmodern social theory is extremely diverse, and almost every postmodern social theorist creates his own concepts and frame of analysis, which makes it oversimplified to group postmodern theorists all under the same banner since they may share very little except a rejection of modern reason, humanism, the Enlightenment, totalizing theories (here again, Marxism is the primary target) and a political cynicism that very often turns conservative. Moreover, having pronounced politics, the subject, history and ideologies dead, there is for them no further need to address these issues.

We will later show that it is possible to integrate insights from postmodern theorists into a reconstructed critical theory of postmodern society; however, from the outset, we should discard what Ben Agger calls *New York Times* postmodernism.[4] *New York Times* postmodernism is political discourse that conceals its political nature and is really critical of the left any critical attempt directed at the current trends. For Agger, *New York Times* postmodernism. has four characteristics:

1. *New York Times* postmodernism considers political discourse as out-of-date;
2. *New York Times* postmodernism strongly supports consumer capitalism;
3. *New York Times* postmodernism is enthusiastic about popular culture without grasping political aspects of mass commodification.
4. *New York Times* postmodernism adopts irony or cynicism at its political posture contributing to the general cynicism of Americans toward politics, and therefore to a greater individualistic withdrawal from the public sphere.

This is postmodern theory at its worst. At its best, postmodern theory has provided some important critical insights that should be integrated into a critical theory to offer the most accurate guide to postmodern social reality. Indeed, modern theories, such as traditional Marxism, have focused issues of power and political economy around class struggle, neglecting other loci of power and political struggle: women's movements, struggles for racial and ethnic equality, gay/lesbian movements, environmental groups.

It is one of the most important contributions of postmodern theories, through their emphasis on diversity, and contextualization of specific microstructures of power, to have decentered class struggle to shed light on the other forms of struggles and resistance to power. Where we strongly disagree with postmodern theory is when this decentering process involves a complete rejection of class struggle and large-scale social forces at work in postmodern society.

In other words, modern theories, because of their totalizing tendencies, have neglected micro-phenomena of power; postmodern theories, because of their deconstructive tendencies, neglect macro-social aspects of postmodern society. Following Best and Kellner,[5] we suggest, that both aspects have to be taken into account if we are to provide an accurate mapping of postmodern social reality.

Mapping Postmodern Society

One of the most central aspects of postmodern society is precisely how it involves changing complex social processes and how traditional notions may be useless to grasp its constituent aspects. Actually, an important question for social theory is to what extent postmodern society differs from modern society, does it represent a radical break with modernity or is there a continuity between the two. It is our view that we can identify both elements of rupture and continuity in postmodern society.

Time-Space Compression

For instance, unprecedented globalization of trade and use of information and communication technologies certainly represent a rupture; however, at the same time, accelerating economic globalization, made possible by these technologies, has pushed the logic of capitalism to a new stage, late capitalism or global capitalism. In this sense, there is a continuity: the collapse of modernity opened a new phase in the evolution of the capitalist economy.

To be precise, David Harvey, in his foundational work on postmodernity,[6] suggested that one important aspect of this new social condition was what he called "time-space compression." Time-space compression has been made possible by the technologies of communication and information. Through these technologies, it became easier for companies to sub-contract and outsource, in the search for cheaper labor all over the world. Products, information and capital now circulate at a much faster speed all over the globe. Financial investors have the capacity to instantly scan the globe in search of rewarding investments, through computerized trading and electronic banking. As Harvey puts it:

> "It is now possible for a large multi-national corporation like Texas Instruments to operate plants with simultaneous decision-making with respect to financial, market, input costs, quality control, and labour process conditions in more than fifty different locations across the globe. Mass television ownership coupled with satellite communication makes it possible to experience a rush of images from different spaces almost simultaneously, collapsing the world's spaces into a series of images on a television screen. The whole world can watch the Olympic Games, the World Cup, the fall of a dictator, a political summit, a deadly tragedy. (. . .) The image of places and spaces becomes as open to production and ephemeral use as any other."[7]

But, as Harvey underlines, the compression of space has not made places irrelevant: when outsourcing and investment decisions are made, the content of specific places is examined, in terms of natural resources, local political power, workforce skill level, fiscal policies, environmental and labor regulations. Spatial barriers may have collapsed, but they have not annihilated the relevance of places in global capitalism; on the contrary, specificities have become more relevant than ever. At the same time, this phenomenon could be interpreted as part of a neocolonialist logic, a continuation of an exploitation system that is not born with postmodern society. Again, Harvey beautifully summarizes this dialectic of space and place:

> "We thus approach the central paradox: the less important the spatial barriers, the greater the sensitivity of capital to the variations of place within space, and the greater the incentive for places to be differentiated in ways attractive to capital. The result has been the production of fragmentation, insecurity, and ephemeral uneven development within a highly unified global space economy of capital flow. The historic tension within capitalism between centralization and decentralization is now being worked out in new ways."[8]

As is well known, the consequences of this flexibility of production and accumulation have been devastating for the workforces in high-income countries. Indeed, one product of modernity was the nation-state, along with the welfare state, pensions systems, specific forms of labor/capital relations, a citizenship as the main source of identity, and clearly defined national borders. All these components of the nation-state have been or are being dismantled; as consequences, there have been an increasing gap between rich and poor, downward pressure on the welfare state, crisis of legitimacy for the polity, crisis of identity for large numbers of people.

As Ulrich Beck[9] describes, global capitalism generates massive unemployment—capitalism without work—, increasing inequality in the distribution of wealth. In other words, the Western model that included the project of modernity, the welfare state is being liquidated. Beck defines these changes as opening a second modernity based on globalism and globalization.

Globalism refers to an ideology of rule by the world market and neoliberalism, at the expense of political action. Culture, social policies, politics, that is, the multidimensionality of the nation-state, are reduced to a single economic dimension: the market economy, understood now as a world-market system; national complexities are flattened and running a company becomes the model for running every other institution (government, schools, families). Globalism also involves a different set of players: in the first modernity, the main player was the state and actors in the political sphere; under globalism, global actors, multinational corporations and global institutions (IMF, World Bank, WTO and NATO) become dominant. Globalization refers to the process through which dimensions of the nation-state, and the nation-state itself are undermined and liquidated by these global players.

Another important consequence of this time-space compression and its corresponding effects is the inability of individuals to position themselves individually and collectively in postmodern society. As we have seen, loci of power have been multiplied and decentered (as opposed to the unique state entity). And, as we see in Solomons' column, power can disappear altogether in virtual reality, thereby maintaining its dominance but offering no grasp for collective movements to organize protests. If the target disappears, against what can political collective action be directed? What is needed, then, is the provision of what Fredric Jameson calls "cognitive mapping";[10] he privileges a politics of alliances where the multiple experiences of repression by women, racial/ethnic minorities, gays and lesbians and other oppressed groups can provide such a mapping. By combining critical analysis of these different forms of oppression, we can determine the major structures of constraint within late capitalism. This gets Jameson close to the topic of new social movements, to which we will return later.

At the same time that collective action is made more difficult by the time-space compression, workers face conditions in an individual manner, without the traditional protection of unions or other bargaining organizations. The liquidation of the power of labor, as a counter-force to capital, involves the individuation of workers, as Manuel Castells eloquently showed in his masterpiece on the information age.[11]

One-Dimensionality and Total Mobilization

This reduction to one dimension—neoliberal version of economy—has been examined previously by other thinkers. For instance, Herbert Marcuse, in his work on one dimensionality,[12] combining Marxism and Freudian analysis, describes how capitalism has penetrated deeper and deeper into our personalities. For Marcuse, capitalism can only protect itself against its own contradictions (falling rate of profits and crisis tendencies) by mobilizing the totality of human experience, not just the productive part of such experience.

In early capitalism, as analyzed by Marx, work time and leisure time were defined as two separate dimensions, the former being subject to alienation, but not the latter, which constituted the basis for critical thinking, the emergence of class consciousness, and ultimately, the revolutionary subject.

Drawing on Freud's work, Marcuse argues that, in late capitalism, even the leisure dimension has been coopted, hence reducing reality and human experience to one dimension. From Freud, Marcuse derives the notion that civilization is based on basic repression of biologically grounded, infantile desires; these desires are channeled through sublimation into socially useful activities (work, production of goods, elimination of scarcity), internalized through the reality principle.

But for Marcuse, capitalism has penetrated deeper into the very structure of subjects' personalities through what he calls surplus repression, based on the performance principle that goes beyond basic repression necessary for civilization. Late capitalist societies are not characterized by scarcity (which justified repression and sublimation), but by material abundance; therefore, there is need for additional repression (surplus repression) to maintain social control and domination over human beings. This is achieved through what Marcuse calls repressive desublimation: superficial release of desire in ways that support the capitalist mode of consumption.

The leisure dimension becomes another locus of alienation through false needs: needs that subjects need to satisfy in ways that reinforce the system and its total domination. These needs are false because they are arrived at through free self-reflection but based on an additional repression (surplus repression). False needs transform human beings into obedient consumers and give human beings the illusion that mass consumption makes up for the injustices suffered in the work place.

In other words, capitalism achieves complete domination by extending repression of desires to the leisure domain and permitting their release in specifically channeled ways (through false needs) that reinforce the capitalist logic. If the work dimension is characterized by mass production, the leisure dimension is characterized by frantic, ultimately unsatisfying, and never ending mass consumption. There is no place to turn to for liberation from alienation. Alienation has become total and complete. The potential for liberation, located in the leisure dimension, has been liquidated through false needs that channel subjects' desublimation not toward emancipation, but toward further alienation.

Through surplus repression, false needs and repressive desublimation, late capitalism has achieved a continuum of domination that is all the more powerful; that domination runs deeper in the unconscious layers of our personalities.

This notion of the deepening of capitalist penetration has also been analyzed by Jurgen Habermas, under the notion of colonization of the lifeworld.

Colonization of the Lifeworld

Habermas[13] uses Weber's notion of instrumental reason (rationalization) to describe the development of modern society; but, for Habermas, this conception of reason is too narrow and must be broadened to incorporate a more basic form of reason: communicative rationality. Communicative rationality, incarnated in communicative action, is intersubjective. A most basic aspect of action is not necessarily instrumental, but communicative, that is, the achievement of intersubjective understanding, free from an instrumental logic of domination. No interaction is possible unless common understanding is achieved. Basic co-operation in encounters (which can involve conflict and disagreement) is grounded in communicative reason and action; subjects interact by putting forth validity claims for their position. For Habermas, there are three types of validity claims:

1. claims based on objective and factual observations of the external world;
2. claims based on social norms that regulate interpersonal relations;
3. claims based subjective experiences.

This typology does not reflect the much messier nature of everyday interactions, but it enables Habermas to analyze these components. In real situations of interaction, participants make claims and counter-claims which deepen mutual understanding and basic agreement (people may agree that they disagree and that no further discussion is possible). Of course, in real life, people may try to deceive or manipulate others, but this can only be achieved through shared communicative basis.

On the other hand, instrumental reason involves strategic action, that is, action informed by instrument purpose and persuasion is achieved, not by consensus, but by sanctions or gratification, force or money.

Communicative actions themselves are supported by a background of cultural assumptions, norms (see validity claims above), cultural knowledge that we share with other members of society, references to the institutional, cultural, political aspects of society, and on which we rely in our interactions. This cultural background and the foreground of our interactions constitute what Habermas calls the lifeworld (in that, his position is close to that of phenomenological thinkers, such as Alfred Schutz).

For Habermas, the lifeworld is one component of modern society. The second component, borrowed from Talcott Parsons, is the system, increasingly complex and differentiated into specialized spheres. The lifeworld is social reality as intersubjectively constituted by participants' interactions. The system is social reality as an external and objective entity. Both components are essential for the reproduction of society.

In modern society, lifeworld and system become uncouples, the system becoming independent from the lifeworld; for instance, the economy becomes independent and exclusively based on rationalization (as we have seen at the beginning) or instrumental reason and operating "behind the backs" of social actors. At the same time that the logic of the system becomes independent of the lifeworld, there is no separation; rather, the system elements reshape the lifeworld in their own instrumental terms; instrumental reason invades or colonizes all aspects of social organizations (remember Beck, every domain of society should be organized and run like a company). Money and power penetrate areas of the lifeworld that require communicative action, cultural activities, education, and socialization in general. The colonization of the lifeworld also disrupts value systems—morality or religion, for instance—and replaces them with instrumentality. Human relationships themselves become dominated by market/rational (Foucault) logic (individuation again).

These analyses, as different as they are, all point to something common: the market logic has penetrated, invaded or colonized larger and larger areas of social life, including our unconscious life. Is there any hope?

New Social Movements

For Habermas, prospects are not as bleak as they were for Max Weber. System elements can be forced out of the lifeworld. The colonization has not eliminated the capacity for protests and social change. Indeed, the colonization of the lifeworld has created a legitimacy crisis (part of postmodern society and globalization) and generates new forms of protests, as the ones we witnessed in Seattle and Montreal.

These forms of protest are "new social movements" in the sense that they group together different elements, organizations that used to be opposed (labor versus environment). All these movements are, one way or the other, protesting these very mechanisms of colonization: the exploitation of the environment, the pitting of poor nations against one another to attract financial investment, the potential for economic exploitation in biogenetic developments (the decoding of the human genome).

The new social movements also protest the impersonal, undemocratic and evasive nature of new forms of power. The World Trade Organization is a particular target precisely because this institution presents such characteristics. And as the column from Norman Solomon shows, the reaction of these new institutions of power to street protests is to become even more remote (uncoupled) from concrete social reality while, at the same time, expanding its colonization.

These new social movements also focus on what sociologist Kai Erikson calls "new species of trouble":

> "The first thing to say about this new species of trouble is that it is a product of human hands. The ancients feared pestilence, drought, famine, flood, plague and all the other scourges that darken the pages of the Bible. These miseries trouble us yet, to be sure, but it is fair to say that we have learned ways to defend ourselves against many of the worst of them. (. . .) The irony, though, is that the technological advances that have afforded us this degree of protection from natural disasters have created a whole new category of events that specialists have come to call technological disasters—meaning everything that can go wrong when systems fail, humans err, designs prove faulty, engines misfire, and so on. (. . .) Technological disasters have clearly grown in numbers as we humans test the outer limits of our competence."[14]

In other words, what new social movements are protesting against are, on the one hand, values that reflect unbridled market economy and its limitless exploitation of people (women, minorities, children, etc.), that is the colonization of human relations (humans to humans or humans to nature, or humans to institutions) by an economic logic; on the other, they, very often, warn of the potential for large-scale technological disasters (already seen in Chernobyl and Three-Mile Island) inherent in the globalization logic.[15]

Conclusion

In this paper, I have by no means been exhaustive about the issues involved with postmodernity and globalization; and I have most certainly not done justice to the social thinkers mentioned. What I have modestly tried to provide is a first step to the cognitive mapping of postmodernity, to refer to Jameson again. As we have seen, one of the problems associated with postmodernity is the elusive nature of new, and far- and deep-reaching forms of power and domination, as illustrated by Solomon's opening statement.

Postmodern social theories are useful in this task when they emphasize diversity and differentiation in these new forms of domination, but they fail to grasp the totalizing implication of this multidimensional domination logic. Modem theories do the reverse: by focusing on systems, they neglect the micro-physics of power.

It is my contention here, that it is possible to build a critical theory that incorporates the best of modern and postmodern theories. Such an integration is already present in new social movements; they represent a clear indication of the possibilities for progressive social change as well as the resistances, obstacles and challenges that will have to be addressed (again, as Solomon's column indicates). But in the final instance, there is too much at stake to withdraw into apolitical cynicism, as some postmodern thinkers have done.

Endnotes

* Christine Monnier currently teaches Sociology at the College of DuPage, in Glen Ellyn, Illinois. Her research interests are in social theory, sociology of the mass media and globalization issues.

1 Solomon, N. (2001), *Simulating Democracy Can Be a Virtual Breeze*, www.creators.com, (May 26–27, 2001).

2 Horkheimer, M & Adorno, T. (1972), *Dialectic of the Enlightenment*, New York, Seabury.

3 Foucault, M. (1973), *Madness and Civilization*, New York: Vintage Books.

Foucault, M. (1979), *Discipline and Punish*, New York: Vintage Books.

4 Agger, B. (1992), *The Discourse of Domination. From the Frankfurt School to Postmodernism*, Evanston: Northwestern University Press, pp. 73–82.

5 Best, S. & Kellner, D. (1991), *Postmodern Theory*, New York: Guilford.

6 Harvey, D. (1989), *The Condition of Postmodernity*, London: Blackwell.

7 Harvey, D. (2000), "Time-Space Compression and the Postmodern Condition," in David Held & Anthony McGrew (eds.), *The Global Transformation Reader*, Cambridge: Polity Press, pp. 82–91, p. 84.

8 *Ibid*, p. 86.

9 Beck, U. (2000), "What is Globalization?," in David Held & Anthony McGrew (eds.), *The Global Transformation Reader*, Cambridge: Polity Press, pp. 99–103.

10 Jameson, F. (1984), "Postmodernism or the Cultural Logic of Late Capitalism," *New Left Review*, no. 146, pp. 53–93.

11 Castells, M. (1998), *End of Millenium*, Volume 3 of the *Information Age Trilogy*, Oxford: Blackwell.

12 Marcuse, H. (1964), *One-Dimension Man*, Boston: Beacon Press.

13 Habermas is an extremely complex thinker and we do not pretend to exhaust interpretation and understanding of his theoretical work; for our own purposes, we will just borrow some elements that fit the current discussion. Our arguments will be based mainly on secondary sources on Habermas:

Dodd, N. (1999), *Social Theory and Modernity*, London: Polity, pp. 106–127.

Layder, D. (1994), *Understanding Social Theory*, London: Sage, pp. 186–206.

Cuff, E.C, Sharrock, W.W. & Francis, D.W. (1998), *Perspectives in Sociology*, 4th Edition, London: Routledge, pp. 327–338.

[14] Erikson, K. (1995), A New Species of Trouble. The Human Experience of Modern Disasters, London: W.W. Norton, pp. 141–142.

[15] See Held, D., McGrew, A., Goldblatt, D. & Perraton, J. (1999), *Global Transformations*, Stanford: Stanford University Press, especially Chapter 8, "Catastrophe in the Making: Globalization and the Environment," pp. 376–412.

Globalization Under Siege

Editorial

THERE IS A SEASON FOR EVERYTHING—for planting and building, and for uprooting and tearing down. The protesters who swarmed through the streets of Washington, D.C., over the weekend of April 14–16, during the meeting of the International Monetary Fund and the World Bank, seemed more interested in tearing down. They represented an unlikely coalition—labor unions, environmentalists, human rights activists, anarchists, economic nationalists and isolationists—that had first assembled in Seattle last December to protest the World Trade Organization.

The problem is that for two decades now the I.M.F., the World Bank and the W.T.O. have lined up behind the so-called Washington consensus—the belief that privatization, deregulation and open capital markets are all that is needed to create jobs, make companies more competitive, lower consumer prices, supply foreign capital and technology to poor countries and, by spreading prosperity, establish the conditions in which democracy and respect for human rights flourish.

Critics of this laissez-faire doctrine do not dispute all its claims, but they tell another side of the story—of weak economies (witness Thailand, Indonesia, Russia and Brazil) overwhelmed by easy money and vulnerable to volatile shifts in capital flows, of jobs less secure than the livelihoods abolished by globalization, of sweatshops and child labor, of environmental devastation, of wealth not enlarged but distributed upward to local elites and multinational corporations, and of intensified social and political conflict. In addition the critics point out that the I.M.F., private bankers and brokerages demand accountability in the form of "transparency" and "due diligence" from the governments and banks of developing countries while exempting themselves from the same requirements.

At their best, the protesters in Seattle and Washington are part of a sensible movement to civilize the global economy. At their worst they are playing into the hands of people like Senator Phil Gramm of Texas, chairman of the Senate Banking Committee, who would eviscerate the I.M.F. and the World Bank and in the process derail the effort to relieve poor nations of crushing debt.

The W.T.O., which makes and enforces the rules of international commerce, espouses an exclusive faith in supposedly self-adjusting markets. In practice, the doctrinaire deregulation of international trade often means that the biggest corporations are free to enter mar-

Source: Editorial, "Globalization Under Siege." *America*, New York, N.Y., Vol. 182, No. 16:3 (May 6, 2000).

kets and extract resources without worrying much about health, safety or environmental constraints. As for the International Monetary Fund, it makes loans to troubled nations to prevent financial panics and in return demands sound management and transparent bookkeeping (all very sensible). But its bailouts also enable big Western banks like Chase and Citigroup—and offshore banking centers in places like the Cayman Islands, which specialize in laundering "dirty money" and avoiding national taxes—to walk away unscathed from reckless investments.

Meanwhile the I.M.F.'s one-size-fits-all austerity programs undercut local government programs that protect people from the harshness of the market. The recent I.M.F. structural adjustment program in Indonesia, for instance, did not revive the economy but plunged it into depression, sending half its businesses into bankruptcy, provoking massive social and political disorder and making it harder than ever to restore the confidence of customers of Merrill Lynch and Goldman Sachs.

IT IS TIME, THEREFORE, for some rebuilding of international financial institutions. The neoliberal dogma that national governments must refrain from asserting themselves in the new global economy is unrealistic and counterproductive. For some time now, Chile has saved itself from economic, social and political havoc by imposing controls on short-term capital flows. We also need better programs to prevent sharp swings in currency values from feeding speculative frenzies. And a new international bankruptcy court should be established to set rules for equitable settlements between creditors and defaulting nations so that the fallen country is not scavenged of its remaining assets while foreign investors walk away scot-free. We also need international environmental and labor regulations to limit unbridled exploitation of developing countries.

Most immediately, generous funding for aid programs, especially for educational and social services, is needed so that the disruptive impact of stabilization programs does not fall disproportionately on workers and the poor, who are not responsible for the bad policies and corruption of their government and business elites.

None of this will make a theme for a Broadway hit, but it is a work whose season has clearly come.

Labor Standards Clash with Global Reality

Leslie Kaufman and David Gonzalez

SAN SALVADOR—Six years ago, Abigail Martínez earned 55 cents an hour sewing cotton tops and khaki pants. Back then, she says, workers were made to spend 18-hour days in an unventilated factory with undrinkable water. Employees who displeased the bosses were denied bathroom breaks or occasionally made to sweep outside all morning in the broiling sun.

Today, she and other workers have coffee breaks and lunch on an outdoor terrace cafeteria. Bathrooms are unlocked, the factory is breezy and clean, and employees can complain to a board of independent monitors if they feel abused.

The changes are the result of efforts by **Gap**, the big clothing chain, to improve working conditions at this independent factory, one of many that supply its clothes.

Yet Ms. Martínez today earns 60 cents an hour, only 5 cents more an hour than six years ago.

In some ways, the factory, called Charter, shows what Western companies can do to discourage abuse by suppliers. But Gap's experience also demonstrates the limits to good intentions when first-world appetites collide with third-world realities.

Ms. Martínez's hours are still long, production quotas are high, and her earnings are still not enough to live on. She shares a two-room concrete home with a sister, two brothers, her parents and a grandmother.

Yet the real alternative in this impoverished nation is no work. And government officials won't raise the minimum wage or even enforce labor laws too rigorously for fear that employers would simply move many jobs to another poor country.

The lesson from Gap's experience in El Salvador is that competing interests among factory owners, government officials, American managers and middle-class consumers—all with their eyes on the lowest possible cost—make it difficult to achieve even basic standards, and even harder to maintain them.

"Some have suggested that there are simple or magic solutions to ensure that labor standards are applied globally," said Aron Cramer, director of human rights at Business for Social Responsibility, a nonprofit advocacy group that receives support from business. "In fact, it takes a great deal of work."

Source: Leslie Kaufman and David Gonzalez, "Labor Standards Clash with Global Reality" *The New York Times,* April 24, 2001.

Fed up with abusive conditions, Ms. Martínez and a small group of other workers organized and began to hold strikes at the factory, then called Mandarin International, in 1995. As tension rose, workers took over the factory and shut down power to the plant. Security guards forcibly ejected strikers; union members said the guards dragged women out by their hair and clubbed them with guns. The factory's owners fired hundreds, including Ms. Martínez.

It might have ended that way, except that it occurred just as concern about sweatshops was rising in the United States. Groups like the National Labor Committee, a union-backed, workers advocacy group based in New York, had formed to oppose sweatshops. Mandarin offered a media-ready case of abuse, and the revolt was widely publicized.

Still, two of the four retailers using Mandarin left after the protests—**J. C. Penney** and Dayton Hudson (now **Target**). Eddie Bauer, a unit of **Spiegel** Inc., suspended its contract. Gap Inc., which is based in San Francisco, intended to quit, too, but a group of Mandarin workers pleaded with the company to save their jobs. Some blamed union organizers for the trouble. "Problems were made to look worse by the union," said one employee, Lucía Alvarado, who has worked at the factory for eight years.

Gap executives chose to stay after deciding that all the groups involved—workers, labor activists and factory owners—were willing to make changes. The workers were expected to stop disrupting the plant, and managers had to agree to more humane practices and to accept outside monitors.

To make sure the changes stuck and to arbitrate disputes, Gap decided to try the then innovative idea of hiring local union, religious and academic leaders as independent monitors who would meet regularly with workers to hear complaints, investigate problems and look over the books.

"It's not a paradise," said Carolina Quinteros, co-director of the Independent Monitoring Group of El Salvador, as the monitors call themselves. "But at least it works better than others down here. They don't have labor or human rights violations."

The push for change ranges far beyond the Charter factory, or El Salvador. Today, activists on college campuses are calling for an end to sweatshops everywhere. [As recently as this past weekend in Quebec, world trade officials debated how to clean up those operations, and the United States has pushed developing countries to raise pay and working conditions in thousands of plants from Bangladesh to Brazil.]

Results, however, have been negligible. The basic problem is that jobs and capital can move fast these days, as the president of El Salvador, Francisco Flores, is keenly aware. "The difficulty in this region is that there is labor that is more competitively priced than El Salvador," he said.

Here, as in many other countries, labor advocates say the problem is made worse by the government's cozy ties with factory owners. When a Labor Ministry committee issued a report critical of forced overtime, poor safety and threats against labor organizers, factory owners complained. The government swiftly withdrew and disowned it.

Salvadoran officials and business leaders have also objected to monitors Gap has hired to police working conditions. They contend that the group is a tool of unions that want to keep jobs from leaving the United States—or a leftist anti-government front, a suspicion left over from El Salvador's long civil war, which ended in 1992.

Then there is practicality. Gap spends $10,000 a year for the independent monitors at Charter, which is owned by Taiwanese investors, and thousands more for management time to arbitrate disputes and for its own company monitors to recheck the facts on the ground. For the company to duplicate these intensive efforts at each of the 4,000 independent factories it contracts with would have taken about 4.5 percent of its annual profit of $877 million last year.

In a world where costs are measured in pennies, that percentage would be a significant burden. **Wal-Mart** and **Kmart** are praised by investors for relentlessly driving down costs, but they have much less comprehensive monitoring programs.

Gap says that expense and staff time are not even its main concerns. The experiment in El Salvador has only reinforced the company's conviction that companies cannot substitute for governments indifferent to enforcing laws. Also, it said, retailers have limited power over their independent contractors. Either they pull out, which would punish innocent workers, or they must accede to a slow process where they must cajole and bully for every bit of progress.

"We are not the all-powerful Oz that rules over what happens in every factory," said Elliot Schrage, Gap's senior vice president for global affairs. "Do we have leverage? Yes. Is it as great as our critics believe? Not by a long shot."

Sitting Down: Monitoring Effort Enlists Outsiders

Still, monitoring is the sweatshop opponents' great hope. Watchdog groups say that only people outside of the company can win the trust of workers and evaluate complaints. "That is where you get problems that won't show up in paper records and interviews with management," said Sam Brown, executive director of the Fair Labor Association, a labor advocacy group in Washington.

At the time, however, no one had ever done it, said Mr. Brown, who is a former Ambassador to the Organization for Security and Cooperation in Europe and past director of Action, federal domestic volunteer agency.

Gap's efforts are still in many ways a blueprint for the international labor advocacy movement—since 1995 other companies like **Liz Claiborne** and **Reebok** have attempted to start similar programs. But what has actually happened in El Salvador is a process that lasted longer, cost more and achieved less than what many people had hoped for. "We knew it would be hard," Mr. Schrage said. "But it's been harder than we ever imagined."

The company has found that no aspect of its efforts escapes local politics. On the recommendation of Charles Kernaghan, the director of the National Labor Council, Gap turned to the legal aid office of the Archdiocese of San Salvador and to the Jesuit University here. Earlier, both institutions had helped uncover abuses in the plant, which to Gap demonstrated their experience and independence from management. But both also had a history of sympathy for the Farabundo Martí National Liberation Front, a coalition of rebel groups and political parties during the civil war. The coalition is known as the F.M.L.N., its initials in Spanish.

"When companies see me, they see someone to the left of the F.M.L.N.," said Benjamín Cuéllar, the director of the Institute for Human Rights at the University of Central America here who is also on the board of independent monitors. That view manifests itself in mistrust and resistance by managers, he said.

Beyond politics, Gap says it is not easy to impose its will on contractors simply because it is a major customer. Pedro Mancía, the factory's manager, indicated that he looks on the monitors as an annoyance, not a threat. In his view, the only meaningful role they played was in easing tensions among the workers themselves after the 1995 strike.

That event "was not between management and workers," Mr. Mancía argued. "We had two warring factions of unions and they could not sit down together."

Factory managers agreed to accept monitors mostly to avoid losing Gap and going out of business. Still, trust is tenuous and the managers have found ways—subtle and not so subtle—to resist, monitors say.

It took about a year to rehire all of the workers fired during the 1995 strike, for example. And 30 of those rehired in 1997 were fired again recently, not because they were strikers but because the company said they were not productive enough. "They are playing by the rules of the game," said one member of the monitoring group. "But I'm not much in agreement with the rules of the game."

Gap says that this project has taught it the limit of its own influence. "We can't be the whole solution," Mr. Schrage said. "The solution has to be labor laws that are adequate, respected and enforced. One of the problems in El Salvador is that that was not happening and is not happening."

Moving On: Economic Obstacles Impede Reforms

Before dawn each day, Flor de María Hernández leaves her three children in the tent where they have lived since an earthquake leveled her home earlier this year and begins her two-hour commute to the Charter clothing factory.

She and the others, like Ms. Martínez, must be at work before 7 a.m. Managers close the gate precisely on the hour and dock the pay of anyone who is late.

Inside, rows of sewing machines face blackboards on which supervisors have written the daily quotas for shirts and trousers, roughly 2,000 a day for each line of 36 machines. The pace is relentless, but by local standards it is a pleasant place to work. There are lockers, tiled bathrooms, a medical clinic and an outdoor cafeteria. Large fans and high ceilings keep temperatures down.

But Ms. Martínez remembers just what it took to get this far. She was among the workers who protested the abusive conditions in 1995. "Workers would bring in permission slips from their doctors to go to the hospital," she recalled, "and supervisors would rip it up in their faces."

Of the 70,000 garment workers in El Salvador, 80 percent are women. Few earn enough to take care of their families. Ms. Hernández, for example, earns about $30 a week inspecting clothes. It is not enough to feed her children; to make ends meet, she relies on help from her ex-husband.

She keeps her job because the most common alternative is to work as a live-in maid or a street vendor. Jobs cutting sugar cane in the searing sun, once plentiful, are difficult to find now, and wages have fallen in recent years along with commodity prices.

El Salvador, never a wealthy country, is struggling every bit as hard as its people. Roughly 75,000 people were killed and thousands wounded in the civil war. The war also drove away foreign investment, shuttered relatively high-paying electronics factories and left roads, power lines and other basic services in tatters.

Earlier this year, two powerful earthquakes compounded the difficulties by wrecking hundreds of thousands of buildings. Economists estimate that 180,000 Salvadorans are jobless. Almost half of the population lives in poverty.

The government has gone out of its way to attract investment and jobs. Government leaders pin the country's future on the optimistic hope of doubling the number of factories making clothes for the United States, to more than 400, in three years. "Maquilas have been a source of significant economic growth in recent years," President Flores said using the Spanish term for the plants that enjoy tax and trade benefits. "They are the most dynamic economic sector in the country."

That growth, however, has not been matched by the budget of the Labor Ministry, which is among the worst-financed agencies. It employs only 37 labor inspectors to enforce regulations—1 for every 10 factories, not including coffee plantations, construction sites or other places of business in this country, which has 6.1 million people.

The limits of the government's willingness to be an advocate for labor was illustrated last summer when it suppressed the report critical of factory working conditions. The labor minister, Jorge Nieto, said that the report was technically flawed, and insists that the government intends to modernize his agency and improve inspector training. "We want investment, but only with respect and fairness," he said. "Only when workers' rights are respected can we generate more contracts with American companies."

But to get those contracts, El Salvador must compete with neighbors like Honduras and Nicaragua, where wages are lower and the population even poorer and more eager for work. Government officials and factory managers concede that El Salvador's current minimum wage is not enough to live on—by some estimates it covers less than half of the basic needs of a family of four—but they are wary of increasing it.

"We cannot be satisfied with the wage, but we have to acknowledge the economic realities," Mr. Nieto said.

Since Gap pioneered the independent monitoring effort, few other American companies have followed. They cite costs, politics and questionable effectiveness. Gap executives echo those worries when they assess the experience at Charter.

"We are in a very competitive marketplace," said Mr. Schrage of Gap. "Consumers make decisions on lots of factors, including price. There is no clear benefit in having invested in independent monitoring to a consumer and it is not clear if we were to make it more broad policy that consumers would get a benefit or care at all."

As she shopped at the Gap flagship store at Herald Square in Manhattan, Claire Cosslett fingered an aqua cotton T-shirt made in El Salvador to check for quality. Ms. Cosslett, a legal recruiter, said she reads labels and sometimes worries that her garments are "made by some child chained to a sewing machine."

American companies dread comments like that. Yet for all their fears, they ultimately have to balance their concern over image, and any feelings they have about third-world workers, with customers' attitudes. Then there are the competitive pressures to keep costs low. Would the cost of raising working standards in El Salvador raise the price of a T-shirt enough to drive off customers?

Among several shoppers who were interviewed at the Manhattan store, Ms. Cosslett was the only one to say that reports of sweatshop conditions had stopped her from buying a particular brand. She said she would be willing to pay more for a garment made under better working conditions.

But then she paused and hedged. "It would depend how much," she said.

V. Family as an Institution

Sex and Society

Robert T. Michael, John H. Gagnon, Edward O. Laumann, and Gina Kolata

In private and in public, within our families and among our friends, most of us are living the sexual lives that society has urged upon us. Social networks match up couples, sexual preferences are learned or mimicked within networks, social forces push Americans toward marriage and so richly reward wedded couples that marriage turns out to be the best way to have regular sex and the best way to have a happy sex life.

But there is more to social forces than social networks, social scripts, and a widespread conviction that marriage is the ultimate goal for nearly everyone. There also are social attitudes and beliefs, the very beliefs that show up in many of the contradictory messages that we all hear about the power and the pleasure—and the shame—of sexuality.

These attitudes and beliefs underlie some of the bitter social debates of our day. Should there be limits on a woman's right to an abortion? Should sex education be taught in schools? Should we treat homosexuality as just another lifestyle or should we consider it a sin or abnormality?

One way to look at the roots of these arguments is to ask whether there is any relationship between sexual behavior and deep-seated feelings about sexual morality. And if there is a relationship between behavior and beliefs, who is likely to hold which attitudes? Are highly educated people more likely to be libertarians? Do religious people have fewer sexual partners? Do people who view sex as a form of recreation do different things in bed than people who say their sexual behavior is guided by their religious beliefs?

In a broader sense, looking for such a relationship tests our entire thesis that sexual behavior is a social behavior, determined, shaped, and molded by society like other more visible behaviors—religious practices or recreational habits, for example. If sexual behavior were a completely independent force, not subject to conscious thoughts but controlled instead by hormones, or whipped up by drives, then it should matter little what a person's attitudes are.

We asked our respondents about their attitudes and beliefs about sexual behavior, and, separately, we asked them what appealed to them sexually and what they did. This enabled

Source: Robert T. Michael, John H. Gagnon, Edward O. Laumann, and Gina Kolata, "Sex and Society," *Sex in America: A Definitive Survey,* Little, Brown and Company, Boston, MA., 1994. pp. 230–246.

133

us to put the pieces together. We found that there is a strong, robust link between attitudes and sexual behavior, and that it suggests why so many social issues related to sex are so contentious. Not only do people's underlying attitudes about questions of sexual morality predict what sort of sex they have in the privacy of their bedrooms, but they even predict how often people *think* about sex.

From the different attitudes and, correspondingly, different behavior of men and women, of older and younger people, and of people of different religions, we can suggest why it is that there is a war between the sexes, why it is that many women complain that men will not commit themselves to marriage, and why it is that many older people are dismayed by the sexual practices of the young.

To learn about attitudes and beliefs, we asked several questions about opinions regarding sexual behavior and other related topics, nine of which we discuss below. For example, we asked respondents to tell us how they felt about premarital sex. Was it always wrong, almost always wrong, sometimes wrong, or not wrong at all? We asked about sex between people of the same gender. Was it always, almost always, sometimes, or never wrong? We asked respondents if their religious beliefs guided their behavior. Then, with the replies to nine such questions in hand, we used a method called cluster analysis to divide the population into groups according to their opinions about those nine issues. Although people in each group varied, overall they had a general set of similar beliefs about key issues.

Cluster analysis is a frequently used tool of social scientists who often need to find patterns in masses of data and are not aided by strong theory in their quest. In our case, we did not know ahead of time how people would sort themselves out by their answers to these questions, and we knew, at the outset, that there were a large number of possible combinations of answers to our nine questions. Since each person answered all nine questions about his or her attitudes and beliefs, and since we are focusing here on whether the respondents agreed or disagreed with each statement, there are a total of 29 or 512 ways to answer the set of nine questions. But, we reasoned, if there are logical or belief-driven patterns to the answers, there should be certain clusters of replies among all these possibilities. A man, for example, who says his religious convictions guide his views toward sexuality might also say that sex outside of marriage is always wrong, that teenage sex is always wrong, that extramarital sex is always wrong, and that abortions should be prohibited.

Cluster analysis underlies many studies in which people are categorized according to their replies to an array of questions rather than a single one. For example, a cluster analysis looking for voting patterns might group people according to their replies to such questions as: Should capital punishment be abolished? Should all companies be required to practice affirmative action? Should handguns be outlawed? Should women have the right to an abortion for any reason? Should states provide vouchers for parents who choose to send their children to private schools? People in each group would have similar answers to the questions. While no one question characterizes a person's political views, and while each person in a cluster will not give exactly the same answers as every other person in the cluster, the pattern of their replies could be a good indication of their political leanings.

In this particular analysis, we divided the respondents into three broad categories on the basis of their attitudes. First is the *traditional* category, which includes about one-third of our sample. These people say that their religious beliefs always guide their sexual behavior. In addition, they say that homosexuality is always wrong, that there should be restrictions on legal abortions, that premarital sex, teenage sex, and extramarital sex are wrong.

Second is what we call the *relational* category, whose members believe that sex should be part of a loving relationship, but that it need not always be reserved for marriage. These people, who make up nearly half of our sample, disagree with the statement that premarital sex is always wrong, for example. Most, however, say that marital infidelity is always wrong and that they would not have sex with someone they did not love. The third group is the *recreational* category, who constitute a little more than a quarter of the sample. Their defining feature is their view that sex need not have anything to do with love. In addition, most of those in this third group oppose laws to prohibit the sale of pornography to adults.

Within each of these categories, however, people varied in their attitudes, and so we subdivided the categories to further characterize our respondents. A man would be part of the relational group, for example, if he thinks extramarital sex is always wrong and that he would not have sex with anyone unless he loved her. But he might also say that same-gender sex is always wrong. A woman who is in a different group in that category might agree with him about extramarital sex, and sex with a partner she loved, but disagree about same-gender sex being wrong.

Table 1 shows how the groups are categorized, according to people's replies to the nine questions on attitudes.

The columns show the percentages of our population who agree with the statements in the column on the left. We divided the traditional category into "conservative" and "pro-choice" groups essentially according to their opinions on abortion. Although people in this category nearly all believe that premarital sex among teenagers, same-gender sex, and extramarital sex are always wrong, they split on whether a woman should be able to have an abortion.

The relational category breaks down into three groups, which we have labeled as religious, conventional, and contemporary religious. Those in the religious group said that religious beliefs shape their sexual behavior and tended to say that they oppose sex between people of the same gender and they oppose abortions. The conventional group is more tolerant than the religious group toward teenage sex, pornography, and abortion and are far less likely to say they are influenced by religious beliefs. But most think that same-gender sex and extramarital sex are always wrong. The contemporary religious group is much more tolerant of homosexuality but people in this group say that they are guided by their religious beliefs.

In the recreational category there are two groups. One, which we call pro-life, consists of people who oppose both homosexuality and abortion for any reason but who are more accepting of teenage sex, extramarital sex, and pornography. The second group is the libertarian group. They have the most accepting position on all the items. None of this libertarian group considers religion as a guide to their sexual behavior.

Just dividing the respondents into these groupings on the basis of their opinions, however, tells only part of the story. We also want to know how the groups differ by social characteristics. Men and women gravitate to different groups, as seen in Table 2. So do older and younger people and so do blacks and whites. The distribution of people into groups reveals why the formation of social policy regarding sexual issues is so contentious and so complex.

The top rows of Table 2 tell us that women are more likely to have the opinions we labeled "traditional" and are much less likely to have the views we called "recreational." By age, we see that the older men and women are disproportionately "traditional" and much less likely to hold the "recreational" views.

Table 1: Description of Seven Normative Orientations Toward Sexuality Relational

	Traditional		Relational			Recreational		Total sample
	Conserv.	Pro-Choice	Religious	Conventional	Contemp. religious	Pro-life	Libertarian	
1. Premarital sex is always wrong	100.0†	23.6	0.0	0.4	0.8	6.5	0.0	19.7
2. Premarital sex among teenagers is always wrong	99.5	90.3	78.6	29.1	33.6	65.7	19.7	60.8
3. Extramarital sex is always wrong	98.2	91.0	92.1	94.2	52.1	59.3	32.0	76.7
4. Same-gender sex is always wrong	96.4	94.4	81.9	65.4	6.4	85.9	9.0	64.8
5. There should be laws against the sale of pornography to adults	70.6	47.2	53.1	12.2	11.7	14.9	6.4	33.6
6. I would not have sex with someone unless I was in love with them	87.5	66.0	98.0	83.8	65.3	10.1	19.5	65.7
7. My religious beliefs have guided my sexual behavior	91.3	72.9	74.7	8.7	100.0	25.0	0.0	52.3
8. A woman should be able to obtain a legal abortion if she was raped	56.3	98.6	82.3	99.1	99.3	84.3	99.8	88.0
9. A woman should be able to obtain a legal abortion if she wants it for any reason	0.5	100.0	0.0	87.4	84.9	9.3	88.6	52.4
N = 2,843	15.4%	15.2%	19.1%	15.9%	9.3%	8.7%	16.4%	100.0%

Oversample was excluded from analysis, as were respondents who had missing values for one or more items. Clusters were derived by minimizing the squared Euclidean distance between members within each cluster. All items were dichotomized before clustering. Column percentages.

†Indicates the percentage of persons in the "Conservative Traditional" cluster who believe that premarital sex is always wrong.

With distributions like this it is no wonder that the battle between the sexes rages. Lance Morrow, a columnist for *Time* magazine, bemoaned men's fate. Women, he complained, have a particularly pejorative view of hapless men, thinking and saying something like "Men-are-animals-I-don't-care-if-they're-not-doing-anything-at-the-moment-they're-thinking-about-it-and-they-will-when-they-have-a-chance." Some women, on the other hand, have sniped that men are not so blameless, pointing out that many men still leer at women when they walk down the street, and some men act like they have to be dragged kicking and screaming into marriage, behaving as if marriage is a ball and chain.

The distribution of men and women in the attitude clusters tells us, at least, that many more women than men are looking for love and consider marriage to be a prerequisite for sex. When women bitterly complain that the men they meet are not interested in long-term commitments, their laments have a ring of truth. Many more men than women are looking for sexual play and pleasure, with marriage or even love not necessarily a part of it. After all, men in the recreational category may be unlikely to feel that linking sex with marriage is high on their list of priorities. When men note that their girlfriends are always trying to lure them into making a commitment to exclusivity or that their relationships seem to end with an ultimatum—marry me or get out—there is a good reason for it.

The conflicting goals of men and women—and particularly young men and young women—are played out in the lines the men may use when they meet women. And at no time is this more true than in adolescence and young adulthood, the very time that men are most likely to be part of all-male groups who have recreational attitudes toward sex.

Elijah Anderson, a sociologist at the University of Pennsylvania, tells how black teenagers in an inner-city neighborhood take on these roles: "The lore of the streets says there is a contest going on between the boy and girl before they even meet. To the young man, the woman becomes, in the most profound sense, a sexual object. Her body and mind are the object of a sexual game, to be won for his personal aggrandizement." And to win a young woman, Anderson says, the young man devises a rap, "whose object is to inspire sexual interest."*

The young women, on the other hand, want "a boyfriend, a fiancé, a husband, and the fairy-tale prospect of living happily ever after with one's children in a good house in a nice neighborhood," Anderson says. So the young man, trying to have sex with a woman, "shows her the side of himself that he knows she wants to see, that represents what she wants in a man." He may take the young woman to church, visit her family, help her with chores. But after the young man has sex with the young woman, he often leaves her for a new conquest.

The teenage woman "may know she is being played but given the effectiveness of his rap, his presentation of self, his looks, his age, his wit, his dancing ability, and his general popularity, infatuation often rules," Anderson notes.

Put differently, we see in this typical script the competitive marketplace for sexual partners. The young man is emphasizing those of his attributes that he thinks will attract the young woman. He engages in negotiations and interchanges designed, with all his strategic skills, to persuade her that a friendship that includes sex will be to her liking. She, similarly, emphasizes her attributes that she thinks might attract the most appealing guy. She carefully calibrates her encouragement and insists on behavior that wraps sex into the bundle of activities that she desires.

Table 2: Distribution of Normative Orientations within Demographic Groups

Social Characteristics	Normative Orientation		
	Traditional	Relational	Recreational
GENDER			
Men	26.9%	40.1%	33.0%
Women	33.7	47.6	18.7
AGE			
Men			
18–24	17.4	46.9	35.7
25–29	21.0	46.2	32.9
30–39	26.2	38.6	35.2
40–49	31.2	38.2	30.5
50–59	40.1	31.3	28.6
Women			
18–24	23.0	51.8	25.3
25–29	27.5	54.6	17.9
30–39	34.6	46.6	18.8
40–49	34.5	44.9	20.6
50–59	47.0	43.4	9.6
MARITAL/RESIDENTIAL STATUS			
Men			
Noncohabiting	18.4	39.7	42.0
Cohabiting	8.6	48.4	43.0
Married	36.4	39.0	24.5
Women			
Noncohabiting	31.9	46.8	21.3
Cohabiting	23.9	50.4	25.6
Married	36.2	48.1	15.8
EDUCATION			
Men			
Less than high school	31.6	39.5	28.8
High school graduate or equivalent	28.3	40.9	30.8
Any college	25.0	39.8	35.2
Women			
Less than high school	36.6	47.6	15.9
High school graduate or equivalent	38.3	46.0	15.7
Any college	30.4	48.7	20.9
RELIGION			
Men			
None	11.7	39.1	49.2
Mainline Protestant	24.2	43.8	32.0
Conservative Protestant	44.5	30.1	25.3
Catholic	17.8	49.6	32.6
Women			
None	10.4	44.4	45.2
Mainline Protestant	30.9	51.4	17.7
Conservative Protestant	50.5	38.4	11.2
Catholic	22.2	58.0	19.8

Social Characteristics	Normative Orientation		
	Traditional	Relational	Recreational
RACE/ETHNICITY			
Men			
White	26.1	41.6	32.3
Black	32.4	25.4	42.3
Hispanic	25.3	45.1	29.7
Women			
White	30.5	48.3	21.2
Black	45.3	45.8	8.9
Hispanic	40.7	43.2	16.1

Note: Percentages in rows total 100 percent.

Whether the outcome is a single sex episode or a more steady dating relationship or even a longer-term sexual partnership, each of these young people offers and withholds, explores and considers, and reaches agreement about the sex. The strategic behavior by each, designed to attract the partner and achieve the objective that each seeks, embeds the individual's endeavor in a social context that typically involves competition.

The table also shows us that the married men and women are least likely to hold the recreational view of sexuality, while the not-married men are far more likely to hold that set of views. The cohabiting men and women, on the other hand, are least likely to hold the traditional views of sexuality. Of course, these unmarried men and women are also likely to be younger than those who are married, so the pattern by marital status partly just mirrors the pattern we noted above that older (and married) people hold more traditional views while the younger (unmarried) people are more likely to be in the recreational category. This contributes to the battle of the generations. Older people, often the parents of teenagers or of people in their twenties, tend to have a very different view of the purpose of sex.

The age distribution also suggests the possibility that people change their attitudes over the years (though our data cannot confirm this), moving from times, in their youth, when they thought love need have nothing to do with sex to times, when they grow older, when loving relationships become more central to sexuality. People seem to move along the spectrum from libertarian toward conservative as they age. This could be one reason why 58 percent of our respondents who said premarital sex is always wrong also told us that they themselves had had sex before they were married. And it could explain why 26 percent of our respondents who told us that teenage sex is always wrong also said that they had had sex when they were teenagers. These differences by age might, on the other hand, reflect lifelong held differences of opinion of those born in the 1930s, the 1940s, and so on, but we speculate that these opinions change with age.

When we look at the relationship between race, religion, and education and attitudes about sex, we can see why people tend to feel more comfortable when they choose partners like themselves. The table shows, for example, that few who are not religious are part of the traditional category, but 48 percent of conservative Protestants are traditionalists. People with no religion are most likely to be part of the recreational category—nearly half are found here.

Our findings also show that the clichéd strife between black men and black women may, in fact, reflect fundamentally different attitudes about sex. Black women are more likely than white or Hispanic women to be traditionalists and are noticeably less likely than other women to be in the recreational category—fewer than 10 percent of black women have recreational views toward sex. But black men are noticeably more likely than other men to be in the recreational group—more than 40 percent have recreational views.

The pattern seen in Table 2 by education level is not dramatic, but it is quite systematic. Those with less than a high school level of education are more likely to hold traditional views about sexuality and less likely to hold recreational views; those with college education are just the opposite: they are more likely to hold the recreational views, and least likely to hold the traditional views.

We did not have strong expectations or theories about how people's views of sexuality might be related to their social characteristics. But our findings seem to confirm the notion that people's beliefs about sexual morality are part of a much broader social and religious outlook that helps define who they are. Their orientations are reinforced by their friends and family and others in their social networks.

The next question is whether what people believe about sexual behavior is linked to what they actually do sexually. It is one thing to have a certain set of attitudes, but it is another thing to have those attitudes determine your most private acts, wishes, and thoughts. Yet that is what we find, as seen in Table 3. Membership in a particular attitudinal group is closely associated with what their sexual practices are. It is even correlated with how often people think about sex and how often they have sex.

The top portion of both panels of Table 3 shows the number of sex partners in the past year for the men and women who are not living with a partner. We see there that those who have traditional views about sexuality mostly have zero or one partner and only a relatively small percentage had two or more sex partners in the past year: about 30 percent of the men and about 14 percent of the women have that many. But of those who held recreational views of sexuality, about 60 percent of the men and nearly 50 percent of the women had two or more sex partners in the past year. Their attitudes and opinions, as characterized by the three categories of traditional, relational, and recreational, do in fact distinguish these unmarried and noncohabiting respondents quite effectively in terms of their number of sex partners in the past year.

To be sure, there are a few of those with a traditionalist view who have several sex partners, and a few of those with a recreationalist's view who have no sex partner or one partner, but in the main, the views they held are very consistent with the number of partners they had in the past year.

The same is true of those who are married, as seen in the second set of rows in Table 3. For the men who were traditionalists or relationalists, only 3 or 4 percent had more than one sex partner in the past year, but as many as 15 percent of those who were recreationalists had more than one. The same pattern is seen for the married women where only 1 or 2 percent of the traditionalists and relationalists had more than one partner but more than 7 percent of the recreationalists had more than one. The tremendous influence of marital status on the number of sex partners is seen here, with a vast majority of the married men and women having zero or one sex partner in the past year, and the unmarried much more likely to have several, but within both marital statuses the influence of these opinions shines through.

In contrast, people's views about sex had little bearing on how often they had sex. Roughly half of those in each of the three categories report having sex once a week or more. Although somewhat fewer recreationalists said they did not have sex at all last year, the difference between them and those in other groups was not very great. We suspect it reflects the fact that people in the recreational group are more likely to be young and may not have yet found a sexual partner, however much they may want to.

Whether they are actually having sex or not, people who are recreationalists are much more likely than traditionalists to think about sex every day and are much more likely to masturbate. Those in the recreational group are twice as likely as those in the traditionalist group to report that they masturbated once a week or more.

Oral and anal sex and sex with someone of the same gender follow the same patterns, as is seen in the bottom three rows of Table 3. Recreationalists are more likely than traditionalists to have had oral sex in the last year with their partner. They also are more likely to have had anal sex. And they are more likely to have had same-gender sex. In fact, as we move along the scale from traditionalist to recreationalist, the frequency of oral sex, anal sex, and same-gender sex increases.

Overall, people's sexual opinions and their behavior mesh quite closely. We cannot tell whether the opinions prompted the behavior or whether the behavior prompted the opinions, or both, but the relationship is clear.

From these findings on attitudes, beliefs, and sexual behavior along with our findings on sexual networks and choices of sexual partners, we can start to see why America has such heated social policy debates about sexual issues such as abortion, public nudity, gay rights, and pornography.

As Table 2 showed, opinions and social characteristics seem to go hand in hand. The young have one set of opinions about sexuality while older adults have another; conservative Protestants have one set of views while those without religious affiliations have another; the less educated tend to have different views than the well educated. Table 3 showed that people's attitudes are reflected in their behavior, so different groups really do act differently.

In chapter 3 of the text *Sex in America*, we saw that people tend to choose sexual partners who are just like themselves in education, religion, and race or ethnicity. Now we see that we have probably paired off with someone who has many of our own opinions about sexuality. That is, in fact, probably a key reason why we choose partners from our own social group. Of course, opinions also may shift and become more similar as the partnership continues, but when that happens, it only makes the partnership stronger. It can be very difficult to maintain a sexual relationship with someone who strongly disagrees with you about such matters as whether abortion or extramarital sex is always wrong or whether religious beliefs always guide sexual behavior.

Our friends and families, the members of our social networks, also tend to be like us in social characteristics, and so they are likely to share many of our opinions about sexual behavior. Consequently, when we have discussions with our friends we tend to be speaking to people who are like us and who agree with us about sex. So we tend to get reinforcement for our views. That is probably one of the main reasons why our opinions are so internally consistent and so well reflected in our sexual behavior.

But all this reinforcement and consistency makes it very threatening to change our views, to become convinced by an outside argument or to change an opinion about one aspect of sexual behavior, such as whether extramarital sex is always wrong, without changing any other opinions. Our opinions, behavior, and social networks all tend to encourage us to hold to those views that help tie all these opinions, beliefs, and behavior together.

And when we see these sets of behaviors as woven together by our religious beliefs and our ethical principles, we are, quite understandably, reluctant to give ground. So the national debates on so many of these sexual issues become heated and all sides become entrenched. No wonder we are a nation that is deeply conflicted about sexual matters and that the disputes seem to go on forever, with no compromises in sight.

And with this we have traveled full circle, going from an investigation of what people do and who they are to who they are and what they do, and what they believe about sex. We began our study by asking whether sexual behavior could be studied in the same way

Table 3: Selected Sexual Behaviors within Normative Groups

Panel A: Men

	Normative Orientation		
Sexual Behaviors	Traditional	Relational	Recreational
PARTNERS LAST YEAR: NONCOHABITING			
None	40.6%	22.4%	12.8%
One	30.2	41.0	27.9
Two or more	29.2	36.6	59.4
PARTNERS LAST YEAR: MARRIED			
Zero or one	97.0	96.0	84.9
Two or more	3.0	4.0	15.1
LAST YEAR SEX FREQUENCY			
None	12.5	8.8	8.4
Three times a month or less	31.4	34.2	35.9
Once a week or more	56.1	57.1	55.7
THINK ABOUT SEX			
Twice a month or less	13.4	14.1	7.1
Twice a week or less	40.8	35.3	27.0
Daily or more	45.8	50.6	65.9
MASTURBATE			
Never	50.2	35.5	25.6
Three times a month or less	32.1	38.5	39.4
Once a week or more	17.7	26.0	35.0
HAD ORAL SEX (ACTIVE OR PASSIVE) WITH PRIMARY PARTNER IN LAST YEAR			
Yes	56.4	78.2	80.7
HAD ANAL SEX DURING LIFETIME			
Yes	18.7	23.1	32.3
EVER HAD SAME-GENDER PARTNER SINCE AGE 18			
Yes	2.6	4.5	7.8
PARTNERS LAST YEAR: NONCOHABITING			
None	46.7	25.2	14.6
One	39.1	52.6	36.6
Two or more	14.1	22.2	48.8

Panel B: Women

Sexual Behaviors	Normative Orientation		
	Traditional	Relational	Recreational
PARTNERS LAST YEAR: MARRIED			
Zero or one	98.0	98.5	92.5
Two or more	2.0	1.5	7.5
LAST YEAR SEX FREQUENCY			
None	18.5	10.8	8.0
Three times a month or less	31.5	34.0	39.6
Once a week or more	50.0	55.1	52.4
THINK ABOUT SEX			
Twice a month or less	45.0	36.8	30.1
Twice a week or less	40.6	44.0	39.0
Daily or more	14.3	19.2	30.8
MASTURBATE			
Never	69.0	56.6	37.5
Three times a month or less	26.0	35.4	50.2
Once a week or more	5.0	8.1	12.3
HAD ORAL SEX (ACTIVE OR PASSIVE) WITH PRIMARY PARTNER IN LAST YEAR			
Yes	55.9	73.9	83.6
HAD ANAL SEX DURING LIFETIME			
Yes	13.2	19.5	37.5
EVER HAD SAME-GENDER PARTNER SINCE AGE 18			
Yes	0.8	3.0	8.6

Note: Percentages in columns total 100 percent within the categories; the "no" percentages are omitted in the last three.

as other social behaviors and, if so, whether it followed any social rules. We asked whether the privateness of sexual behavior and the powerful myths put it in a class apart from other social behaviors or whether, when we drew back the curtain and looked at what really happens, sexual behavior would turn out to be not so mysterious after all.

In every instance, our data has shown that social forces are powerful and persistent in determining sexual behavior. We have found that our society constrains us, nudging us toward partners who are like ourselves. But, at the same time, it frees us, putting us together with people who have the same sorts of general understandings about sex that we do, and so easing our way into sexual intimacies and revelations. We also found that although America may not be as sexy a place as it is often portrayed, most people are satisfied with the sexual lives they have chosen or that were imposed upon them.

America is not the golden land of eroticism where everybody who is young and beautiful has a hot sex life. Nor is it a land where vast hordes of miserable people, kicked out of the sexual banquet, lick their wounds in silence and resentment. Instead, it is a nation that uses social forces to encourage sexual norms and whose sexual behavior is, in large measure, socially determined. It is a nation of people who are for the most part content, or at least not highly dissatisfied, with the sexual lots they have drawn.

And, for those who feel the status quo is far from ideal, we have found that the costs of breaching the social pressures may be high, and the rewards of going along may be great. But by seeing where and how the pressures are brought to bear, we can break away from the myths and magical thinking that have captured us in the past. With unclouded eyes, we can ask whether we really want changes in sexual behavior and, if so, what the benefits and costs of these changes might be.

Endnote

* Elijah Anderson, *Streetwise: Race, Class, and Change in an Urban Community* (Chicago: University of Chicago Press, 1990).

The Myth of Cohabitation

Willard F. Jabusch

Every parish priest and university chaplain knows the story. The young couple visits their pastor to make arrangements for their wedding. The pastor begins to ask the questions on the prenuptial questionnaire. The young man gives his address and later the young woman. It appears they live at the same address and in the same apartment. Like so many others, they have been living together, perhaps for some time. There is, however, no embarrassment or apology, not the slightest hint of shame. Cohabitation has become so common that it seems it is the rare couple, at least in the big cities, who have not been living together before marriage. In fact, the common wisdom is that this is helpful for a future wedded life, since both man and woman will certainly get to know each other's follies and foibles, virtues and vices as they have breakfast and supper together every day, share a bathroom, take out the garbage and vacuum the rug. It is, supposedly, a sort of dress rehearsal for married life.

But is it true that you can improve your chances of having a successful marriage by living together to see what it's like? Not according to two recent studies, one by a sociology professor, Linda Waite of the University of Chicago, and another by the National Opinion Research Center, a University of Chicago research facility. According to Professor Waite, cohabiting couples lack both specialization and commitment in their relationships. And although these couples are abundant in today's society, they are also more prone to make less money and are more likely to abuse one another physically than are married couples.

"Cohabitation isn't marriage," says Professor Waite, "and cohabitation people don't act the same way as married people. They don't have the same characteristics; they don't get the same benefits; and they don't get to pay the same costs."

Unlike Scandinavian countries, where cohabiting relationships tend to be long-term, Waite has observed that in the United States they are usually short-term and lead to a lack of committed marriages. Thomas W. Smith, director of the National Opinion Research Center survey, also notes that cohabitation remains in the United States a short-term phenomenon, but that it is, both before the first marriage and between marriages, the general rule. He remarks that the average duration of cohabitation is a little over a year, and these temporary relationships usually end in break-ups or marriage.

Source: Willard F. Jabusch, "The Myth of Cohabitation." *America*, New York, N.Y., Vol. 183, No. 10:14–16 (October 7, 2000).

Statistics show that almost two-thirds of Americans choose to cohabit before getting married. According to Census Bureau figures, four million heterosexual couples are currently involved in these relationships, eight times more than in 1970.

"One of the things people get out of marriage is insurance," Waite remarks. "If you think of the Christian marriage vow—in sickness and in health—it seems that people will stay together even if one gets M.S. or cancer or gets disabled. It's insurance, and insurance is expensive. Emotionally, it's important in that if you get sick, there's someone who will take care of you."

When cohabitation is short-term, as in the United States, there is a lack of what might be called specialization. Waite points out that in marriage "you can say, I like to cook and you like to clean, and I'll get to be a terrific cook because I'll never have to clean. Two people together produce more. They can have a high quality life because they have two specialists, whereas people who live alone don't specialize." Also, according to Professor Waite, cohabiting couples do not pool their money, and those with separate incomes must pay separate taxes. They lack the shared financial resources upon which married couples rely.

In her article "The Negative Effects of Cohabitation," written for *The Responsive Community*, an academic journal, she writes that partners in the typical cohabitation relationship are also less likely to connect with their mate's family and to take care of their mate's children. "The parenting role of a cohabiting partner toward the child(ren) of the other person is extremely vaguely defined. The non-parent partner—the man, in the substantial majority of cases—has no explicit legal, financial, supervisory, or custodial rights or responsibilities regarding the child of his partner." Since many religions disapprove of cohabitation, it is not surprising that cohabiting couples are frequently not involved with any church.

The cohabiting man and woman are also more likely to lead separate lives and are less likely to have a monogamous sexual relationship than those who are married. Waite observes: "Four percent of married women had a secondary sex partner, compared to 20 percent of cohabiting women and 18 percent of dating women."

Her study indicates that "to preserve their exit option, they are not really working in a partnership. They are being two separate people—it is trading off freedom and low levels of commitment for fewer benefits than you get from commitment." It also seems that many unmarried mothers remain in cohabiting relationships because they fear the domestic violence of marriage. Yet the study reports that married women are half as likely as women in cohabiting relationships to acknowledge physical abuse. "When it comes to 'hitting, shoving, and throwing things,' cohabiting couples are more than three times more likely than the married to say things that get far out of hand; people who live together are 1.8 times more likely to report violent arguments than married people."

Research at N.O.R.C. has shown, according to Smith, "the surprising result that people who cohabit before marriage are more likely to divorce. A trial marriage that would allow people to pick a lifetime partner and therefore lead to a better marriage doesn't work." Professor Waite attributes this to the non-committal attitude created during cohabitation. She says, "There is sort of a myth that you can improve your chances of having a successful marriage by living together to see what it's like, and there is no evidence at all that that helps people make a better decision; so it's not a good reason for living with somebody." She points out that her findings do not apply to couples living together who are engaged. "They are not planning an easy exit; they are planning to get married, they just have not done it yet." Since engaged couples are truly planning on spending the rest of their lives together, they are able to specialize and have fewer reasons for friction and distrust.

The full text of the study, a synthesis of Smith's work during the past 10 years, will be published in her new book *Strengthening American Marriage: A Communitarian Perspective* (Rowman and Littlefield). Social scientists have studied the cohabiting relationship for some time, ever since they began to wonder if it is just "marriage without the paper, or something else."

"I think," says Linda Waite, "we are pretty convinced that it is something else."

Willard F. Jabusch is the director of Calvert House, the Catholic student center at the University of Chicago.

For the First Time, Nuclear Families Drop Below 25% of Households

Eric Schmitt

WASHINGTON, May 14—For the first time, less than a quarter of the households in the United States are made up of married couples with their children, new census data show.

That results from a number of factors, like many men and women delaying both marriage and having children, more couples living longer after their adult children leave home and the number of single-parent families growing much faster than the number of married couples.

Indeed, the number of families headed by women who have children, which are typically poorer than two-parent families, grew nearly five times faster in the 1990's than the number of married couples with children, a trend that some family experts and demographers described today as disturbing.

The new data offer the 2000 census' first glimpse into the shifting and complicated makeup of American families and carry wide-ranging implications that policy makers and politicians are already struggling to address.

With more communities having fewer households with children, public schools often face an increasingly difficult time gathering support for renovating aging buildings and investing in education over all. Voters in Cleveland last week approved $380 million in levies to fix city schools, but only after two months of exhaustive lobbying by civic leaders.

"This may have something to do with why our education system is not up to snuff," said Isabel Sawhill, a senior fellow at the Brookings Institution. "Oftentimes, those parents who still are invested in the schools don't have the money or influence to change things."

Demographers expressed surprise that the number of unmarried couples in the United States nearly doubled in the 1990's, to 5.5 million couples from 3.2 million in 1990. Some of those couples have children.

Many conservative groups point to the increase as well as the statistics on single-parent households as troubling indicators of deeper societal problems.

"This data shows we need to regain the importance of marriage as a social institution," said Bridget Maher, a marriage and family policy analyst at the conservative Family

Source: Eric Schmitt, "For the First Time, Nuclear Families Drop Below 25% of Households," *The New York Times,* May 15, 2001, p. 1.

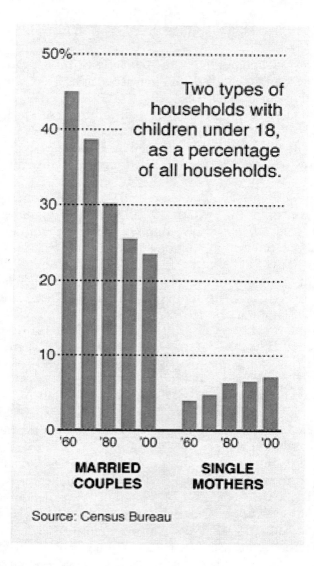

50%

Two types of
households with
children under 18,
as a percentage
of all households.

40

30

20

10

0

'60   '80   '00   '60   '80   '00

MARRIED   SINGLE
COUPLES   MOTHERS

Source: Census Bureau

Research Council. "People are disregarding the importance of marriage and the importance of having a mother and father who are married."

Ms. Maher and other conservatives point to the findings as justification for the enactment of policies that they say would strengthen the family, like eliminating the so-called marriage penalty in the tax code.

The decades-long decline in the overall number of American households with children slowed during the 1990's as two of the most troubling trends—divorce and out-of-wedlock births—moderated, demographers said.

But even with that slowdown, the percentage of married-couple households with children under 18 has declined to 23.5 percent of all households in 2000 from 25.6 percent in 1990, and from 45 percent in 1960, said Martin O'Connell, chief of the Census Bureau's fertility and family statistics branch. The number of Americans living alone, 26 percent of all households, surpassed, for the first time, the number of married-couple households with children.

William H. Frey, a demographer at the University of Michigan, said, "Being married is great but being married with kids is tougher in today's society with spouses in different jobs and expensive day care and schools."

The number of married-couple families with children grew by just under 6 percent in the 1990's. In contrast, households with children headed by single mothers, which account for nearly 7 percent of all households, increased by 25 percent in the 1990's.

The new census data paint a more detailed picture of the American family in other ways.

Unmarried couples represent 9 percent of all unions, up from 6 percent a decade ago.

"It's certainly consistent with what we've all been noting, the growth in cohabitation in this country, but it also tells us how complex American families are becoming," said Freya L. Sonenstein, director of population studies at the Urban Institute in Washington and a visiting fellow at the Public Policy Institute of California.

The number of nonfamily households, which consist of people living alone or with people who are not related, make up about one-third of all households. They grew at twice the rate of family households in the 1990's.

Demographers pointed to several factors to explain the figures. People are marrying later, if they many at all. The median age of the first marriage for men has increased to 27 years old from 22 in 1960; for women, it has increased to 25 years old from 20 in 1960, said Campbell Gibson, a Census Bureau demographic adviser.

The booming economy has allowed more younger people to leave home and live on their own. Divorce, while leveling off, has left many middle-age people living alone—at least temporarily. Advances in medicine and bulging stock portfolios have permitted many elderly people to live independently longer.

"It's easier for a young person to start out on his own or live in a group home," said Mr. O'Connell. "And the elderly population is healthier and economically better off."

Census officials said the median age of the country's population increased to 35.3 years old, the highest it has ever been. This reflects the influence of the so-called baby boom generation, born between 1946 and 1964. The most rapid increase in size of any age group was the 49 percent jump in the population 45-to-54 years old.

While an influx of immigrants and other foreign-born residents with larger, younger families held down this aging indicator, several other statistics underscore the demographic and marketing power the baby boomers wield as they enter their peak earning years. For example, the share of owner-occupied housing increased to 66 percent in 2000 compared with 64 percent in 1990.

"Baby boomers are driving the increase in owner-occupied housing," said Jeffrey S. Passel, a demographer at the Urban Institute, a social policy research organization. "Ten years from now, they will be pushing pre-retirement homes, and 20 years from now they will cause the Social Security crisis."

The new census data also show that while there are still about 5 million more women than men in the United States, men are narrowing the gap partly because of improved medicine and greater health awareness by men, but also because of slightly higher rates of lung-related deaths among women, primarily due to increased smoking among them, demographers said.

The number of men for every 100 women increased to 96.3 in 2000 from 95.1 in 1990, largely because men are closing the life-expectancy gap with women. As of 1998, the latest figures available from the National Center for Health Statistics, women on average live 79.5 years, up from 78.8 years in 1990.

Men can expect to live 73.8 years, up from 71.8 years in 1990, Mr. Gibson said.

Within the refined demographic profile, there were also intriguing trends among specific racial groups. For instance, the overall Asian population in the United States grew by 48 percent in the 1990's, but the number of Chinese, Indians and Vietnamese doubled or nearly doubled in the decade.

How to Define Poverty?
Let Us Count the Ways

Louis Uchitelle

The Census Bureau each fall goes through a ritual that is as Americana as the World Series. A press conference is convened and senior officials, illustrating their numbers with colorful charts, disclose to the nation the latest income data. None gets more attention than the poverty level. A family of four that falls below $17,062 in annual income falls into poverty, the bureau declared last September.

Federal aid programs indexed to the poverty line—Head Start, food stamps and children's health insurance, among others—are then doled out accordingly, which is a lot of power for a statistic that is out of touch with reality.

In public opinion polls, most Americans say poverty begins north of an annual income of $20,000 for a family of four. Not even the Census Bureau believes its poverty numbers. Since 1995 the bureau has been developing a new measure, one pegged more closely to the actual cost of getting by. A progress report is due in July, but building the new income and expenditure procedures and testing them take time, Census Bureau officials say. A final proposal is not likely to reach the White House for approval in President Bush's current term.

Not that he minds. His predecessor didn't. "Whenever the question of the poverty data came up informally," said Robert B. Reich, who was President Bill Clinton's first secretary of labor, "the consensus was not to change the standard for fear the poverty rate would look worse"—although the present poverty figures, as Mr. Reich put it, "are almost meaningless."

Defining poverty is not easy. Even if the Census Bureau's new measure calculates necessary expenditures more accurately than the current formula, the new approach, like the current one, still uses income as the single criterion for judging who is poor. That leaves out neighborhoods, for instance. Is a ghetto family impoverished because of its crime-ridden surroundings and poor schools, although the family has enough income to rise above the official poverty threshold? And there is the issue of responsibility. Should the family of a hardworking full-time employee earning the minimum wage be blamed for poverty because the minimum no longer lifts the worker's income above the poverty level, as it did in the 1960's and early 70's?

Source: Louis Uchitelle, "How to Define Poverty? Let Us Count the Ways," *The New York Times,* May 26, 2001. pp. A15 & 17.

"Poverty is really the lack of freedom to have or to do basic things that you value," said Amartya Sen, the Nobel laureate in economics. By that definition, a ghetto family that wants to move to an adequate neighborhood but cannot afford to do so or is prevented by discrimination from doing so is impoverished.

Or try this definition from Benjamin I. Page and James R. Simmons, political scientists at Northwestern University and the University of Wisconsin, Oshkosh, respectively, and the authors of "What Government Can Do." (University of Chicago Press): "A person deprived of things that everyone around him has is likely to suffer a sense of inadequacy, a loss of dignity and self-respect."

That brings state of mind into the mix, introducing all kinds of judgments that few people agree on. For all their concern about living standards, Americans have left the definition of poverty to politicians, who have defined it narrowly.

Income levels have been the only criterion since 1965, when President Lyndon B. Johnson adopted the present poverty formula. The latest figures show that 11.8 percent of the population lived in poverty in 1999, the lowest percentage in 20 years. The formula is not merely a statistical statement, however; it carries a particular viewpoint as well, about who is responsible for poverty—government, society or the individual.

You neutralize poverty "by keeping the focus on the characteristics of poor people rather than on the economy, politics and society more broadly construed," writes Alice O'Connor, a historian at the University of California in Santa Barbara and the author of the recently published "Poverty Knowledge" (Princeton University Press).

For Lawrence Katz, a Harvard economist, and William Julius Wilson, a sociologist at Harvard, ghetto neighborhoods reinforce poverty and contribute to it. But dismantling ghettos and integrating neighborhoods, a hugely complicated endeavor, has not been high on the agenda of any administration in 20 years. Nor has the minimum wage. Adjusted for inflation, it has declined from more than $6 an hour in the 1960's to $5.25 today.

"Rather than a single poverty measure, what you really want is to develop multiple measures of deprivation and look at them on a regular basis," said Rebecca Blank, dean of the University of Michigan's School of Public Policy. "For example, you might have a level of neighborhood crime that is some threshold level of acceptability, and then you determine how many people live in neighborhoods where the crime rate is above the acceptable level."

That is certainly not the current approach. The present system is based on a minimally nutritious food budget devised decades ago by the Department of Agriculture. The food budget is multiplied by three because back in the 1950's and 60's food was considered one-third of an average family's outlays.

Neither the food budget nor the multiplier have changed in all these years, although food is less than 20 percent of the average family budget today. Poverty thresholds have remained static, as a result, since 1965, except for the annual inflation adjustment, which the Census Bureau ceremoniously announces at the fall news conference. So every time household incomes have risen faster than inflation—and thus faster than the Census Bureau's poverty level incomes—the percentage of households in poverty has naturally fallen. That happened in the Johnson years and in the late 1990's, which helped President Bill Clinton.

Some poverty experts see virtue in the present system despite its faults. "There is a reason to have a dozen poverty lines, including the one we have, which tells us many things," said Douglas Besharov, a resident fellow at the American Enterprise Institute.

"There is a political battle, a minor skirmish, going on here," he added, "with a number of people favoring the new measure because it would raise the count of poor and thus the need for more programs and more spending."

The Census Bureau's experimental measure, based on the six-year-old recommendations of a panel on poverty organized by the National Academy of Science, is likely to raise the poverty rate, many experts say. The reason is embedded in its structure.

The new measure relies on actual expenditures for food, clothing, shelter and utilities plus "a little bit more," as the Census Bureau puts it, for life's other necessities. The bureau would draw on the Labor Department's annual survey of consumer expenditures, not on an outdated, unchanging food budget.

"Basically we are asking the question, if we look back to last year, how many families were not able to purchase food, clothing, shelter, utilities and a little bit more—that basic bundle," said Kathleen Short, a senior researcher at the Census Bureau. She is working on a way to adjust the new poverty measure also for regional differences in living costs, particularly for housing.

A special calculation would keep the initial poverty rate in line with the current one to avoid alarming politicians, but the new poverty rate would fluctuate more than the current one as expenditures rose and fell with the business cycle. It would probably average one or two percentage points above what the current formula produces, based on the Census Bureau's preliminary calculations.

"If consumer expenditures go up 10 percent," said Angus Deaton, a Princeton University economist, "then the poverty rate will drift up 5 percent, because food, shelter and clothing do not go up as fast as other expenditures."

That is all straightforward enough. Calculating income is not. The current system counts only cash wages before taxes and other cash payments as income. The new system would also count noncash benefits like food stamps. "The rationale is that because we are allowing for food stamps and so on, we are taking account of public policy," Ms. Short said. "Under the current system, you can distribute billions in noncash benefits and it does not count."

While those benefits would raise a family's official income, some expenses would be subtracted, lowering it. Taxes, child care, other work-related expenses and out-of-pocket medical outlays would all be excluded from income. But there are still gaps, say poverty researchers. For example, 40 million Americans do not have health insurance, not even Medicaid. With enough income, many of these people can rise above the official poverty threshold, although in Mr. Sen's view, they are not "free" to afford quality medical care.

While the Census Bureau struggles to give birth to a poverty formula more realistic than the present one, ad hoc poverty measures pop up frequently from academics, nonprofit organizations and regional development groups. Nearly all conclude that a family of four needs at least $25,000 a year to afford the basics, including a car to commute to work, an item overlooked in the Census Bureau's new measure. At least $25,000 is the income featured in the "basic needs" budget developed by Indiana's Economic Development Council, one goal being to draw jobs to the state that pay at least that much.

The United Way of Central Indiana now uses the basic needs budget as a guideline in awarding grants. The Urban League of Indianapolis just got $97,000 to develop a training program that will qualify black men for jobs paying at least $25,000.

"That is self-sufficiency," said David Weinschrott, a United Way director. "Poverty is all about stereotypes. Families with less than $25,000 fall below self-sufficiency."

Adam Smith would have agreed. There's more to poverty than lacking the bare necessities, he argued. "A linen shirt, for example, is, strictly speaking, not a necessary of life," Smith wrote in 1776.

"The Greeks and Romans lived, I suppose, very comfortably though they had no linen. But in the present times, through the greater part of Europe, a creditable day laborer would be ashamed to appear in public without a linen shirt, the want of which would be supposed to denote that disgraceful degree of poverty which, it is presumed, nobody can well fall into without extreme bad conduct."

VI. Polity as an Institution

The Age of Entrapment

Alan Ehrenhalt

WASHINGTON—A few weeks ago in Chicago, an Alderman named Rafael Frias was acquitted of bribery. The jury's verdict surprised many of those who had followed the trial: Mr. Frias had been caught accepting cash from a crooked waste-hauler in exchange for help in winning approval for a rock-crushing site in Mr. Frias's neighborhood.

It was all on tape. The rock-crushing deal was a scam created by the Federal Bureau of Investigation and the United States Attorney in Chicago. The hauler, John Christopher, was working as an F.B.I. informer. To most of the people who read about it, the indictment was one more depressingly familiar token of the moral climate of Chicago public life.

But the jurors, having heard all the evidence, decided it was something else: a case of inexcusable law enforcement excess. They heard the tape of the money changing hands, but they also heard Mr. Frias, obviously troubled, trying to extricate himself from the mess and refusing any more money, only to have the undercover agents try to force it on him over and over again.

At one point, Mr. Christopher pulled $500 out of his pocket and started waving it at Mr. Frias. "Do you want this or not?" he asked.

No, Mr. Frias said, "that's not what I'm looking for."

This happened 17 times. The informer never managed to coax Mr. Frias into making a second misstep.

"He kept saying no, no, he didn't want it," one of the jurors explained after the trial, "but they kept coming after him. And that, really, is entrapment."

I don't suppose Bill Clinton has ever heard of Ray Frias, and I certainly wouldn't argue that their situations are similar. Nobody has tricked the President into doing anything. It is the presumed witness against him, Monica Lewinsky, who has been the victim of entrapment. But in a peculiar way, the two cases have something in common. The Alderman of the 12th Ward and the leader of the free world have both become enmeshed in a 1990's law enforcement culture whose underlying premise is that in the investigation of public officials, all the rules are suspended. Any tactic of deception is permissible, as long as a judge somewhere will allow it.

When it comes to the investigation of public officials, we are living in an age of entrapment. We have been living in it for the better part of two decades. Whatever its

Source: Alan Ehrenhalt, "The Age of Entrapment," *The New York Times,* February 4, 1998, Op-Ed Page.

contributions to justice may be in individual cases, it is not doing the country as a whole any good. Perhaps it is time to think about a moratorium.

In 1980, the F.B.I. began the current era with the use of ersatz Arab sheiks and hidden tape recorders in the Ab scam investigation that resulted in the conviction of seven members of Congress. In the ensuing years similar sting operations with exotic names like Boptrot and Azscam and Greylord and Lost Trust have brought down elected officials at every level of government—mayors, city managers, county commissioners, state House speakers, state senators.

I have no doubt that in the vast majority of these cases, the departure of the ensnared has raised the overall moral quality of the institutions they served in. But the game is not worth the rules. In their zeal against public corruption, agents and prosecutors have grown comfortable using tactics that violate most Americans' instinctive sense of fair play. Sometimes they violate simple common sense. Few of us would profess any desire to live in a society where the Government, on the basis of undocumented allegations by known criminals, went around testing its citizens to determine their propensity to commit manufactured crimes. Or in a society where a prosecutor, hired to investigate one set of allegations, is given carte blanche to look into just about any character weaknesses that happen to interest him.

Fortunately, most of us do not have to live under those rules. We have chosen in the past 20 years to apply them to just one class of people: the people we elect to public office.

We have done that, I suppose, out of a well-meaning societal belief that these officials shouldn't just be morally equivalent to the rest of us, they should be better than we are. They are entrusted with the public welfare, and in return they should be held to the loftiest possible standard of conduct, not the standard of ordinary human weakness. If upholding the highest standard requires some deceptive tactics that we would never want used on private citizens, then so be it.

That's the theory. The reality, as we are learning in education, is that higher standards don't necessarily guarantee higher performance. We have representative government in this country, not only in the sense that the people we elect mirror our preferences and values but also in the sense that they mirror our personal frailties. Exposing those frailties with a hidden tape recorder does nothing in the end to improve the quality of government's performance, and no matter how many politicians it humiliates, it does not strengthen public confidence in government. It corrodes it.

Recapturing healthy democracy in this country will require, among other things, a public recognition that the Government is not an alien force and its officials are not alien creatures. They do not deserve special privileges or special treatment, but neither do they deserve to be subjected to an intrusiveness that would be considered manifestly unjust if applied to the rest of us in private life. In the absence of compelling evidence of misconduct, they should be left alone to do their jobs, and then held accountable at election time.

I know this isn't what most reporters or syndicated columnists believe, or what the Federal judiciary believes. But it is what the jury in the Chicago bribery case believed, and I think it is part of what the poll numbers on President Clinton are trying to tell us.

Alan Ehrenhalt is the executive editor of *Governing Magazine* and the author, most recently, of "The Lost City: The Forgotten Virtues of Community in America."

The Wooing of Our Judges

Abner Mikva

CHICAGO—In a lifetime as a judge, lawyer and lawmaker, I can safely say I've encountered few judges guilty of outright dishonesty. Even when I started practicing law in Chicago in the bad old days, the number of crooked judges was small. But that is not what people believed then or believe now.

That is why so much is built into our judicial system—from the black robe and "all rise" custom to lifetime tenure for federal judges—to help foster the notion of judicial integrity. It all becomes meaningless, however, when private interests are allowed to wine and dine judges at fancy resorts under the pretext of "educating" them.

Between 1992 and 1998, according to a report from the Community Rights Counsel, a nonprofit public-interest law firm, more than 230 federal judges took one or more trips each to resort locations for legal seminars paid for by corporations and foundations that have an interest in federal litigation on environmental topics.

In the seminars devoted to so-called environmental education, judges listened to speakers whose overwhelming message was that regulation should be limited—that the free market should be relied upon to protect the environment, for example, or that the "takings" clause of the Constitution should be interpreted to prohibit rules against development in environmentally sensitive places.

Judges who attended the seminars wrote 10 of the most important rulings of the 1990's curbing federal environmental protections, including one that struck down habitat protection provisions of the Endangered Species Act and another that invalidated regulations on soot and smog. In six of these cases, according to the report, the judge attended one of the seminars while the case was pending before the court. And, the report reveals, many judges failed to disclose required information about these seminars on their financial disclosure forms.

If an actual party to a case took the judge to a resort, all expenses paid, shortly before the case was heard, the judge and the host would be perceived to be acting improperly even if all they discussed was their grandchildren. The conduct is no less reprehensible when an interest group substitutes for the party to the case.

Of course it may be a coincidence that none of the seminars financed by private interests take place in Chicago in January or in Atlanta in July. It may be a coincidence that the

Source: Abner Mikva, "The Wooing of Our Judges," *The New York Times,* August 28, 2000, Op-Ed page.

judges who attend usually come down on the same side of important policy questions as those who financed the meetings. It may even be a coincidence that environmentalists are seldom invited to speak. But surely any citizen who reads about judges attending fancy meetings under questionable sponsorship will have well-founded doubt about their objectivity.

I know one federal judge who has been on a dozen trips sponsored by the three most prominent special interest seminar groups. I remember at least two occasions where judges on judicial panels where I also served took positions that they had heard advocated at seminars sponsored by groups with particular interest in the litigation.

The federal judiciary has a Federal Judicial Center that provides educational seminars for judges on a wide range of legal topics. Since it uses taxpayer funds and answers to Congress, the program locales are not exotic, but the presentations are balanced.

Unfortunately, the United States Judicial Conference, the governing body for all federal judges, has punted the propriety of privately funded seminars, advising that judges assess their appropriateness "case by case."

Short of requiring judges to stick to federally sponsored seminars, the government could, at least, require that whenever a judge attends any professional seminar, the government must pay his or her way. Then citizens might begin to ask questions about what they were paying for—and whether it was really likely to promote judicial fairness.

Abner Mikva, a former member of Congress and chief judge of the United States Court of Appeals for the District of Columbia circuit, was counsel to President Clinton in 1994 and 1995.

Overcoming the Oligarchy

Ralph Nader

Abstract: *Alan Greenspan says that the US economy is thriving, yet he is using the measures of corporate profit, gross national product, and stock market conditions. In real terms, consumer debt is at an all-time high, earnings are lower than in 1973, and child poverty is at 25%. A priority of the progressive agenda should be to create an economy driven by consumers, not corporations.*

The struggle for consumer justice is, in many ways, the most comprehensive of economic reform drives. If the government does not enforce adequately the consumer protection laws covering food, drugs, autos, anti-trust, and occupational safety and health, then consumer well-being is diminished.

- If workers are unable to earn a livable wage for their families, consumer well-being is diminished.
- If the environment is polluted or damaged, consumer well-being is diminished.
- If all Americans do not have health insurance, consumer well-being is diminished.
- If the media are controlled by a few media barons, they will not regularly expose corporate crimes, fraud, and abuses, and consumer well-being is again diminished.

We need to decide which yardsticks we are going to use when we measure the health of our society. When Federal Reserve Chairman Alan Greenspan testifies that the economy could hardly be better, he is using a corporate yardstick, which emphasizes profits and the stock prices he is so intent on boosting. Notice how he ignores other yardsticks: 25 percent child poverty (by far the highest in the Western world), 80 percent of workers are earning less than they were in 1973 when you adjust their wages for inflation, and consumer debt is at record levels while the GNP and corporate profits are rising to new highs year after year.

Throughout this century in America, progress for consumer justice has come when we held up more important standards. At the turn of the century, activist women started the consumer movement, aided by great muckraking articles in the new women's magazines

Source: Ralph Nader, "Overcoming the Oligarchy," *The Progressive*, January 1999, vol. 63, #1. pp. 58–9.

like the *Ladies' Home Journal* and *McClure's* about price-gouging by monopolies like Standard Oil and dishonest labeling of medicines by pharmaceutical companies. The populist-progressive surges in American politics further highlighted the dangers from phony medicines, contaminated foodstuffs, and the evils of price-rigging and monopolistic practices. This activism led to the creation of the Food and Drug Administration and the Federal Trade Commission.

After a quiet 1920s (recall Calvin Coolidge's "the business of America is business"), the 1930s saw a revival of consumer activism. Led by President Franklin Delano Roosevelt, who accused Big Business of being "malefactors of wealth," more regulatory agencies were established (covering banking, securities, and airline industries) and others strengthened. The Congress of Industrial Organizations got started and so did Consumers Union, both of which had a consumer/worker protection philosophy. Consumers Union urged and informed customers to take working conditions of employers into account when deciding from whom to buy their products.

Nonetheless, consumer rights and protection remained society's poor cousin—rarely on any electoral agenda, comparatively bereft of theoretical development by scholars, ignored by data gatherers within the government, and avoided as a steady reportorial beat by newspapers.

Until the 1960s. In 1962, Rachel Carson's *Silent Spring* exposed to the public the peril that pesticides were causing to the environment and to consumers' health. In 1965, my book *Unsafe at Any Speed* pressed for democratizing technology that protects the safety of motorists. These books—along with a sharp expansion of consumer reporting by some enterprising journalists and a few influential Congressional hearings—helped usher in a new set of consumer laws, regulatory agencies, and private-sector consumer groups.

The sweep of change was dramatic. Under pressure from a reawakened consumer movement, the government imposed tougher standards on motor vehicles, meat and poultry inspection, flammable fabrics, product safety, and drinking water. The government also set occupational safety and health regulations, product recall and labeling obligations, and some state-of-the-art safety standards for products like cars. When issued in a timely way and enforced, safety regulations saved many lives, prevented many injuries, and spared enormous expense. In 1965, for example, the fatality rate per 100 million vehicle miles traveled was about 5.5; in 1997, it was about 1.7. More people turned to nutritious diets or stopped smoking as those incremental consumer advances informed and aroused the public.

In the early 1970s came the notorious memorandum by Lewis Powell, then a corporate attorney in Virginia, to the business lobby. After noting that the pressures for corporate accountability had reached new heights, Powell (who would later become a Justice of the Supreme Court) urged a large counterattack. He advised business to expand corporate-funded "think tanks" and beef up lobbying and political activity.

It took a few years before the leaders of Big Business got their propaganda and political machines geared up, but then they were rolling. The oil crisis and inflation helped turn the tables in their favor. Global capital mobility and weaknesses in labor law diminished the power of the trade unions. The elections of Nixon, Reagan, and Bush congealed the corporatist character of the federal government. An acquiescing Bill Clinton followed suit. (I call him George Ronald Clinton because many of the regulatory agencies under his regime are as bad, if not worse, than they were under his predecessors.)

Clinton placed a layer of autocratic federal law, called NAFTA and GATT, over our democratic processes, courts, and domestic health and safety laws. Under NAFTA and GATT, the commercial imperative of international trade is supreme. Health, safety, environmental, and other policies deemed "trade restrictive" by secret tribunals within the World Trade Organization (WTO) can be overturned.

The WTO's mandate is trade uber alles. Its order is the "harmonization" of safety and environmental standards among member nations. This works to the disadvantage of American consumers because standards here are often higher than those in many of the 120 member countries. Harmonization procedures call for secrecy. Like the tribunals, they have no public transcript and no independent appeals. And the United States, like Saint Kitts or Luxembourg, has only one vote and no veto inside the WTO. The downward pressure of harmonization keeps the United States and any other countries from being first with safety standards.

While the corporate architects of these global trade agreements incrementally work their will over our domestic jurisdictions, multinational companies are using legislators and bureaucrats to twist the processes of regulation, litigation, shareholder rights, the voting franchise, and tax-payer rights. They are trying to turn the tools of democracy against the citizenry. The very laws of contracts and torts are falling into corporatist control. Consumers are now facing a corporate assault on their right to have a full day in court against corporations charged with wrongful injury (an assault grotesquely called "tort reform"). Contrary to corporate propaganda, nine out of ten wrongfully injured people do not even file a lawsuit. There are already too many hurdles. There is no civil litigation explosion except for businesses suing businesses.

The rights of consumers in the marketplace are also under siege. Every day, millions of consumers enter into insurance, banking, credit, landlord, or employer contracts on a take-it-or-leave-it basis—a veritable mass of fine print blaring forth non-negotiable demands by vendors.

If the consumer movement is to overcome domination by the pro-corporate oligarchy, we need to build consumer power in three dimensions.

First, consumers must band together for group buying. In addition to more traditional efforts such as co-ops, we can use the Internet to pool purchase orders so that skilled negotiators can put these orders out for competitive bidding. Whether for buying household hardware, motor vehicles, or a variety of services, the new technology affords rapid point-of-sale pooling of consumer orders that could reshape the quality of competition among vendors.

Second, consumers can use the same technologies for group negotiating and advocacy. Consumer groups with large memberships can negotiate standard contracts with the giant banks, insurance companies, or cable conglomerates, much as trade unions negotiate their contracts with General Motors or Exxon. This could involve better-equipped cable channels for public constituencies such as a consumer channel or a labor channel.

Whether by negotiation or by legal requirement, paper or electronic inserts in billing envelopes, bank statements, or government mailings at the state and federal level can invite consumers to choose among member-based consumer associations. This dramatically reduces the costs of banding together and reaches audiences of millions of people at peak interest times—as when they receive their HMO or utility bills. This "insert" concept has worked in Illinois, where some 200,000 residential utility ratepayers belong to a Citizens' Utility Board that has a fifteen-year record of victories against electric, telephone, and gas companies.

Third, group negotiating where there are many buyers with similar complaints—as with the same lemon car model—can win redress from companies that sell faulty products.

Corporations have eroded standards of living—and sometimes living itself—due to medical malpractice and HMO abuses, defective or dangerous products, the corporate-induced addiction of youngsters to tobacco and alcohol, systematic price gouging, and many other market manipulations. People's livelihoods suffer from the effects of concentrated power and wealth.

In place of an economy ruled by corporations, we must create a consumer-sovereign economy. Consumers need to be able to decide not only what to buy but what not to buy. We need the wherewithal to protect the environment and to connect economic democracy to a resurgent political democracy that applies law and justice to corporations.

Creating this consumer-sovereign economy should be a higher priority on a progressive agenda.

Ralph Nader, the consumer advocate, is the founder of *Public Citizen*. Its web page is citizen.org. You can access additional information on consumer rights at another web page: essential.org.

Oil and Gas:
Long-Term Contribution Trends

Center for Responsive Politics

SECTOR:
Energy/Natural Resources > INDUSTRY / CATEGORY: Oil & Gas > PAGE: Totals

INDUSTRIES HOME

DATA FOR THIS INDUSTRY:

- Totals
  Background
  Top Contributors
  Top Recipients

SEE ALSO:

Alert: The Defense Industry and Oil Prices

Issue Profile: Oil & Gas

GO TO INDUSTRY:

[Go!]

opensecrets.org

THE CENTER
FOR RESPONSIVE
POLITICS

FORMAT TO PRINT

Oil & Gas:
Long-Term Contribution Trends

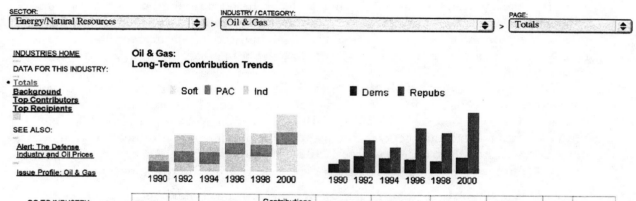

Soft ▮ PAC ▮ Ind   ▮ Dems ▮ Repubs

1990 1992 1994 1996 1998 2000   1990 1992 1994 1996 1998 2000

Election Cycle	Rank†	Total Contributions	Contributions from Individuals	Contributions from PACs	Soft Money Contributions	Donations to Democrats	Donations to Republicans	% to Dems	% to Repubs
2000	9	$32,612,717	$10,450,517	$6,646,868	$15,515,332	$6,608,099	$25,502,564	20%	78%
1998	7	$21,677,051	$6,372,834	$6,542,204	$8,762,013	$4,864,258	$16,732,696	22%	77%
1996	7	$24,847,230	$8,663,250	$6,284,593	$9,899,387	$5,533,584	$18,933,949	22%	76%
1994	7	$16,616,090	$5,956,078	$6,313,539	$4,346,473	$6,040,075	$10,564,520	36%	64%
1992	7	$20,189,649	$8,779,085	$6,255,621	$5,154,943	$6,656,495	$13,423,902	33%	66%
1990	8	$9,046,667	$3,324,994	$5,721,673	N/A	$3,621,114	$5,424,153	40%	60%
Total	7	$124,989,404	$43,546,758	$37,764,498	$43,678,148	$33,323,625	$90,581,784	27%	72%

†These numbers show how the industry ranks in total campaign giving as compared to more than 80 other industries. Rankings are shown only for industries (such as the Automotive Industry) -- not for widely encompassing "sectors" (such as Transportation) or more detailed "categories" (like car dealers).

METHODOLOGY: The numbers on this page are based on contributions to federal candidates and political parties from PACs, soft money donors, and individuals giving $200 or more, as reported to the Federal Election Commission. While election cycles are shown in charts as 1996, 1998, 2000 etc. they actually represent two-year periods. For example, the 2000 election cycle runs from January 1, 1999 to December 31, 2000. Data for the current election cycle were released by the Federal Election Commission on Monday, April 02, 2001. Feel free to distribute or cite this material, but please credit the Center for Responsive Politics.

NOTE Soft money contributions were not publicly disclosed until the 1991-92 election cycle.

Source: Center for Responsive Politics. *www.opensecrets.org* "Oil and Gas: Long-Term Contribution Trends," May 24, 2001.

Mike's Message: Why Don't We All Just Cut the Crap Right Now; The Sequel: The Crap Ends Here

Michael Moore

Dear friends,

Well, the mail has been pouring in since my last letter. It's been running about 5 to 1 in support of my view that Bush's "reversals" of Clinton's last-minute orders were not only made possible by Clinton's 8-year postponement of them, but were not even reversals—as Bush is only continuing the same regulations that have been in effect during the entire Clinton/Gore administration.

Obviously, thousands of you have been feeling the same way. But a number of you have written to me making some very passionate points and asking me some very pointed questions. I feel you deserve some answers. But this is going to be my last letter on Clinton/Gore until I—and you—get busy and focus on the present and the difficult work ahead of us: trying to stop the damage George W. Bush intends to wreak upon the planet earth.

What follows are the concerns some of you have raised and my responses to them:

1. "Why do you keep bashing Clinton and Gore? Don't you know they were under attack for 8 years by a rabid right wing? Aren't you just playing into the Republicans' hands with these criticisms?"

A: I voted for Clinton in 1992. I did so with much hope, as I felt here was someone from the working class who I believed, in his heart, wanted to do the right thing. But the promise that was held out to us was never realized. His pushing NAFTA through into law—something Poppy Bush and Reagan had been unable to do—helped to drive the final nail in the coffin of my hometown, Flint, Michigan. More GM jobs were lost in Flint under Clinton/Gore than during the entire 12 years of Reagan/Bush. Clinton's decision to help companies like GM destroy the lives of my friends and neighbors was so personal to me that—and I hope you forgive me for this—I will never be able to vote for anyone who made this law possible. Perhaps I should be looking at all the good things Clinton did do. But this hit so close to home that, sadly, I can't.

I do not hate Clinton. I actually like him as a person. And I like Al Gore. These are not bad men like the ones who now illegally occupy 1600 Pennsylvania Avenue. I love Hillary, and worked to get her elected in November—even though I do not agree with her

Source: Michael Moore, "Mike's Message: Why Don't We All Cut the Crap Right Now; The Sequel: The Crap Ends Here." *http://www.michaelmoore.com*, May 1, 5, 2001.

on many issues. I am not opposed to compromise and do not expect any candidate to stand for everything I do. I thoroughly resented the abuse she and her husband suffered at the hands of the right wingnuts and aggressively fought against his impeachment.

I believe that at one time Bill and Al wanted to do good, but chose the path of expedience and excessive compromise. I wish they hadn't.

2. "How can you say that there is NO difference between Gore and Bush?"

A: This seems to be a popular mantra. I do not understand the motives of those who want to misrepresent or take out of context what I and others had to say about the "choice" in last November's election. It was NEVER stated in such simplistic, unsubstantiated language. From the first letter on the election that I sent out last July, I was VERY clear about where I stood: "The one outstanding difference between Bush and Gore is that one is evil and the other isn't."

Of course there's a difference between the two. There's a big difference between me and Ralph Nader. There's a "difference" between any two of anything!

Of course one of them is worse. One of any two choices is always "worse." *Temptation Island* is worse than *Survivor*. Hitler was worse than Mussolini. So what? Arguing over degrees of worseness is a waste of time. I'm worse than my wife. Big deal.

We can make lists all day about how Gore would have been better on any of a number of issues. Of course he would have! He's not the evil one!

But it was also Al Gore who, in the second debate, agreed with Bush's position on 32 major issues! Did I say 32? YES, THIRTY-TWO TIMES, GORE OR BUSH SAID, "I AGREE [WITH YOUR POSITION]!"

From moving American jobs to foreign sweatshops, to keeping the minimum wage low, to his unabashed support of the death penalty, to continuing the bombing and embargo of Iraq, to INCREASING the Pentagon budget (with Gore wanting a larger increase than Bush!), all the way down to both of them opposing the return of little Elian Gonzales to his father in Cuba, Gore and Bush did everything but ask each other out on a date. At one point, Gore moved so close to Bush, I thought he was going to lay a big Tipper wet one on him.

3. "But Bush is going to build the Star Wars missile shield! Gore wouldn't have!"

A: I get the feeling no one reads the paper any more. CLINTON/GORE tried to build the same damn missile shield! Billions were spent by their administration on this nonsense—billions that could have gone to fix every school in America. The tests failed so many times that they suspended the thing—REFUSED to kill it, thus leaving the door open for the Cheney Junta to keep the program going. Am I the only one who knows this? I mean, I'm not that smart, so somebody else must have noticed that Clinton not only promoted Star Wars, he reneged on three key provisions of the Kyoto agreement last October, effectively scuttling it, and did a lot of the things people now believe W. is instituting for the first time.

4. "So, it sounds like you hate Clinton and Gore more than Bush."

A: Quite the contrary. I and all other good Americans consider George W. Bush our mortal enemy. We're just disappointed in Bill Clinton and Al Gore. I and others fought for 37 days after November 7th to stop Bush's theft of the election. Gore IS the president. He got the most votes in the country and he got the most votes in Florida. He won. Some Nader supporters thought I shouldn't have been so vocal in my support of Gore's effort to assume the seat that was rightfully his. I told them that our drive to see that this country is run by the true will of the people has no integrity if we do not speak out loudly about the will of the people being subverted by Bush, his brother, his cousin at Fox News, and the Supreme Court. I wish more Nader supporters—and Ralph himself—had been more aggressive in fighting for what was right in November and December.

5. "So why on earth did you support Ralph Nader? There was no way he was going to win. He has a huge ego, he purposefully tried to hurt Gore more than Bush, and I heard he owns stock in the very companies he attacks!"

A: I believe one should always vote their conscience. The voting booth is not a negotiating table. It is the one place where every American needs to be completely honest so that whoever is elected is a true representation of what people want to see their government do. I do not believe in the lesser of two evils theory, even though I employ it in every other aspect of my daily life ("Let's see, I think the A train will not be as bad as the D train at rush hour" or "Drinking Coke will give me heart disease, drinking Diet Coke will give me MS and cancer. Hmmm. I'll take my chances with the heart attack."). In the voting booth, if you always end up settling for less, you will keep getting less and less with each election—because lowering your expectations only creates lower and lower candidates of any worth or integrity. With the lesser of two evils, either way, you still end up with evil.

Ralph Nader, of all the candidates, most closely represented how I felt on the issues. I believe every American should have health care, every college student should go to college for free, the minimum wage should be at least $8/hour, anti-abortion terrorists should be vigorously hunted down and prosecuted, and on and on. Why shouldn't I support the candidate who supports me?

Ralph Nader has many faults, as do all of us. But I've known him for a long time— and, trust me, having an inflated ego is NOT one of them. If anything, this guy needs more ego. I set up an interview with him and a *Nightline* crew. But he didn't want to do the interview. He preferred to sit in a room and rework his speech. Who would pass up a chance to be on *Nightline*? A guy who would rather make sure he gives a good speech to 10,000 than to talk in sound bytes to 10 million.

Ralph owns stock. I don't. Never have. To some people, I guess that makes me nuts, considering the boom of the past decade. But I do not judge others on things like this. I mean, I'm on AOL! What's important are your real actions and what you do with the money you may be blessed with. Ralph has put nearly every dime of what he makes into his projects. And he attacks those very companies he owns stock in, which, in turn, may prevent his stock from making any money. I'm not defending it, I just say to each his own.

Many signed on to the Nader campaign at the suggestion of Molly Ivins who wrote that, if you live in a state where Bush or Gore is already going to win by a big margin, then vote for Nader and make a statement with your vote. But if you live in a swing state, then it is your duty to stop George W. Bush.

Sometime in early October, the Nader campaign reversed itself and disavowed the "Ivins Rule," perhaps because it was becoming clear that they were not going to make the

5% threshold. Thus, they began an aggressive second campaign tour in the swing states of Wisconsin, Oregon, Washington State, and Florida. I declined to join that tour as I thought there was no reason to anger the very people we would have to work with after November.

In fact, I went down to Tallahassee on my own two weeks BEFORE the election and held a press conference. I also spoke at a gathering of thousands at Florida State. I said that it was easy for me to vote for Nader because I lived in a state where Gore was going to win by a huge margin. But you here in Florida have a different job to do. Your job is to stop George W. Bush. In the next two weeks, Ralph's poll numbers in Florida went from 6% to 1.7% on Election Day.

In the interests of full disclosure, I must admit that, in large part, it is for very personal reasons that I put in countless hours helping Ralph Nader. Yes, I supported his platform, but real life is not about platforms and policy statements. It's about people and what they mean to you on a personal level. In 1986, when I was broke and unemployed, Ralph Nader called and offered me a job. It didn't pay much but it got me through a tough time. He then made it possible for me to shoot "Roger & Me" while working out of his office over a two-year period. Without his support and the help of the people in his office, I don't know if that film would have ever been made.

I owed him so much, yet when the film came out and received this incredible response, Ralph felt slighted and ignored for the contribution he had made (suddenly he had some ego!) and attacked me in the *New York Times*. I was stunned. For a long time I just attributed it to his pettiness and eccentricity. But as time went on, I wanted to heal this wound, because the world wasn't getting any better, and it sure didn't help that Ralph Nader and I weren't talking to each other.

So, I invited him to the premier of "The Big One" and he came. I stood at the back and watched him laugh all the way through the film. Afterwards, I went up and apologized to him for any pain I may have caused him. I offered to give some of the proceeds from my film to his Center. He didn't know what to say, but his look said it all. Reconciliation is never a bad thing.

When he called last summer to ask for my help with his campaign, I felt it was a debt I needed to repay. It also didn't hurt that I agreed with every damn thing he had to say! But I had met Al Gore, and immediately liked him. So I wrote him a private letter asking him to explain why I should vote for him instead of Nader. He sent me back a four-page response. I decided I had to help Ralph.

6. "So, thanks to you and that little pity-party story you just told, you and Ralph put George W. Bush in the White House! Bastards!"

A: I have decided to come clean on this one. I've wasted a lot of time since November explaining how Ralph actually did quite poorly around the country (except among young people and people who earn under $15,000 a year, his two largest voting blocks that surpassed the 5% mark), and that he didn't hurt Al Gore because, in Florida, Al Gore won the election. Why aren't you angry at the Supreme Court and the political machine that rigged the whole damn thing? How odd you would go after someone who is your ally on so many issues when it was Al Gore, not Ralph Nader, who voted to put Antonin Scalia on the Supreme Court. And blah, blah, blah.

I told Ralph that, from now on, when he is accused of costing Gore the election, he should say, "You bet I did! It was all me!! I alone, the mighty Thor Nader, hold enough votes to deny him or any Democrat the White House or control of Congress should they not straighten up and fly right. If the Democrats don't stop acting like Republicans, we will deny them all power. If they start behaving like the true opposition party that fights for working people, women, minorities, the environment, and an equitable distribution of the wealth, then we shall allow them to enter the Promised Land!"

Of course, that would take too much ego—but I sure would like to hear Ralph deliver those words in the mighty voice of Thor!

7. "OK, enough of this! Baby Bush is destroying the country! What do we do to stop him?"

A: Well, I guess, seeing how we are responsible for this mess . . . I guess we better clean it up. In my next letter, I will propose a plan for what I think we need to do to stage our countercoup.

In the meantime, my good Democratic friends, let's stop the blame game and join forces for the common good. Blaming is the tool of the coward who is afraid to confront his or her own culpability. Don't blame Nader, blame yourself. I blame myself for not being able to persuade enough people to see that there was a better way to go. Al Gore needs to accept responsibility for blowing his own campaign and all three debates. How you could not defeat the dumbest man in America when you've been given a high IQ and three chances to do so is beyond me. Al, after you screwed up, I had to get my ass down to Florida to try and save yours. And I don't even believe in half of what you stand for! I just couldn't have it on my conscience that a Shrub would be running the country. My trip there, and all the notice it received around the state, cost Ralph, my friend, perhaps thousands of votes, most of which went to you!

But at least 537 didn't make the switch. So, I'll devote the next four years to being the biggest pain in the ass ol' George has had since that cop made him take a Breathalyzer. To the Gorestopo out there who still won't let up with their bellyaching and fingerpointing after this letter, let me remind you of one final thing. Those greens and activists you keep attacking for voting for Nader? Lay off 'em, 'cause they're your only hope.

THEY are the ones who will lead the marches, hold the sit-ins, organize door-to-door until they drop to protect our environment, fight for women's rights, and stand up against racism and war. You don't think the party hacks down at the local Democratic headquarters are going to risk going to jail or mobilize millions to stop the Bush tax cut or save the Alaskan wilderness, do you? You had better stop trashing the very people who are going to be doing all the work for you in the next four years. Disagree with their electoral choices, fine. But give 'em a bit of gratitude for always being the ones who fight the fights that need to be fought.

Enough. On to our mission. . . .

Yours,

Michael Moore
mmflint@aol.com
Michael Moore Home

PS. Thirty-one years ago today, four students were murdered at Kent State. Take a moment today to remember them and what they died for. Thanks.

VII. The Social Institution Education

Make This Natural Treasure a National Monument

President Jimmy Carter

ATLANTA—Rosalynn and I always look for opportunities to visit parks and wildlife areas in our travels. But nothing matches the spectacle of wildlife found on the coastal plain of America's Arctic National Wildlife Refuge in Alaska. To the north lay the Arctic Ocean; to the south, rolling foothills rose toward the glaciated peaks of the Brooks Range. At our feet was a mat of low tundra plant life, bursting with new growth, perched atop the permafrost.

As we watched, 80,000 caribou surged across the vast expanse around us. Called by instinct older than history, this Porcupine (River) caribou herd was in the midst of its annual migration. To witness this vast sea of caribou in an uncorrupted wilderness home, and the wolves, ptarmigan, grizzlies, polar bears, musk oxen and millions of migratory birds, was a profoundly humbling experience. We were reminded of our human dependence on the natural world.

Sadly, we were also forced to imagine what we might see if the caribou were replaced by smoke-belching oil rigs, highways and a pipeline that would destroy forever the plain's delicate and precious ecosystem.

Unfortunately, that scenario is far from imaginary. The reason the Alaskan coastal plain is home today to a pageant of wildlife is that there have been both Republican and Democratic presidents who cared about the environment. In 1960 President Dwight D. Eisenhower designated the coastal plain as part of a national wildlife refuge. Twenty years later, I signed legislation expanding the protected area to 18 million acres.

I listened to scientists who emphasized that the coastal plain is the ecological heart and soul of this, our greatest wildlife sanctuary. And I decided we should do everything possible to protect it and the stunning wildlife that it shelters. At my urging, the House twice voted to dedicate the coastal plain as statutorily protected wilderness.

Then, even more than today, much attention was focused on high energy prices; oil companies—playing an Americans' fears—sought the right to drill in protected areas. While the House held firm, the Senate forced a compromise, without ever putting the fate of the refuge to a vote. Thus, the law I signed 20 years ago did not permanently protect this

Source: President Jimmy Carter, "Make This Natural Treasure a National Monument," *The New York Times,* December 20, 2000. Op-Ed page.

Arctic wilderness. It did, however, block any oil company drilling until Congress votes otherwise. That is where the issue stands today.

The fate of the Arctic coastal plain was a subject of intense debate in the presidential campaign. But as the 106th Congress adjourned, a bill to safeguard the coastal plain by designating it as wilderness was blocked by parochial opposition from Alaska's congressional delegation. And there is little doubt that President-elect George W. Bush and Vice President-elect Dick Cheney will press Congress to open this area to oil companies. As oil industry veterans, they have unquestioning faith that drilling would have little impact.

The simple fact is, drilling is inherently incompatible with wilderness. The roar alone—of road-building, trucks, drilling and generators—would pollute the wild music of the Arctic and be as out of place there as it would be in the heart of Yellowstone or the Grand Canyon.

Some 95 percent of Alaska's oil-rich North Slope lands are already available for exploration or development. Our nation must choose what to do with the last 5 percent. Oil drilling or wilderness. We cannot have it both ways.

I am for the wilderness. That is why I urge President Clinton, who has been a champion for America's environment, to proclaim the coastal plain as a new Arctic Wildlife National Monument before he leaves office. It is vital to do so now, as the Arctic is threatened as never before.

National monuments are a unique form of recognition that presidents have used for nearly a century to single out the finest examples of America's natural heritage. Of course, Congress can undo a presidentially proclaimed monument. But that has never been done.

Teddy Roosevelt pioneered bold presidential action for conservation. He used the Antiquities Act to protect the Grand Canyon, urging Americans: "Leave it as it is. The ages have been at work on it, and man can only mar it. What you can do is keep it for your children, your children's children and for all who come after you."

Now it is President Clinton's turn. With the Arctic coastal plain facing very real peril, it is time for presidential foresight once again.

Jimmy Carter, the 39th president of the United States, is chairman of the Carter Center in Atlanta.

Right Answer, Wrong Score: Test Flaws Take Toll

Diane B. Henriques and Jacques Steinberg

One day last May, a few weeks before commencement, Jake Plumley was pulled out of the classroom at Harding High School in St. Paul and told to report to his guidance counselor.

The counselor closed the door and asked him to sit down. The news was grim. Jake, a senior, had failed a standardized test required for graduation. To try to salvage his diploma, he had to give up a promising job and go to summer school. "It changed my whole life, that test," Jake recalled.

In fact, Jake should have been elated. He actually had passed the test. But the company that scored it had made an error, giving Jake and 47,000 other Minnesota students lower scores than they deserved.

An error like this—made by NCS Pearson, the nation's biggest test scorer—is every testing company's worst nightmare. One executive called it "the equivalent of a plane crash for us."

But it was not an isolated incident. The testing industry is coming off its three most problem-plagued years. Its missteps have affected millions of students who took standardized proficiency tests in at least 20 states.

An examination of recent mistakes and interviews with more than 120 people involved in the testing process suggest that the industry cannot guarantee the kind of error-free, high-speed testing that parents, educators and politicians seem to take for granted.

Now President Bush is proposing a 50 percent increase in the workload of this tiny industry—a handful of giants with a few small rivals. The House could vote on the Bush plan this week, and if Congress signs off, every child in grades 3 to 8 will be tested each year in reading and math. Neither the Bush proposal nor the Congressional debate has addressed whether the industry can handle the daunting logistics of this additional business.

Already, a growing number of states use these so-called high-stakes exams—not to be confused with the SAT, the college entrance exam—to determine whether students in grades 3 to 12 can be promoted or granted a diploma. The tests are also used to evaluate teachers

Source: Diana B. Henriques and Jacques Steinberg, "Right Answer, Wrong Score: Test Flaws Take Toll." *The New York Times*, p. 1, 22–3, May 20, 2001.

and principals and to decide how much tax money school districts receive. How well schools perform on these tests can even affect property values in surrounding neighborhoods.

Each recent flaw had its own tortured history. But all occurred as the testing industry was struggling to meet demands from states to test more students, with custom-tailored tests of greater complexity, designed and scored faster than ever.

In recent years, the four testing companies that dominate the market have experienced serious breakdowns in quality control. Problems at NCS, for example, extend beyond Minnesota. In the last three years, the company produced a flawed answer key that incorrectly lowered multiple-choice scores for 12,000 Arizona students, erred in adding up scores of essay tests for students in Michigan and was forced with another company to rescore 204,000 essay tests in Washington because the state found the scores too generous. NCS also missed important deadlines for delivering test results in Florida and California.

"I wanted to just throw them out and hire a new company," said Christine Jax, Minnesota's top education official. "But then my testing director warned me that there isn't a blemish-free testing company out there. That really shocked me."

One error by another big company resulted in nearly 9,000 students in New York City being mistakenly assigned to summer school in 1999. In Kentucky, a mistake in 1997 by a smaller company, Measured Progress of Dover, N.H., denied $2 million in achievement awards to deserving schools. In California, test booklets have been delivered to schools too late for the scheduled test, were left out in the rain or arrived with missing pages.

Many industry executives attribute these errors to growing pains.

The boom in high-stakes tests "caught us somewhat by surprise," said Eugene T. Paslov, president of Harcourt Educational Measurement, one of the largest testing companies. "We've turned around, and responded to these issues, and made some dramatic improvements."

Despite the recent mistakes, the industry says, its error rate is infinitesimal on the millions of multiple-choice tests scored by machine annually. But that is only part of the picture. Today's tests rely more heavily on essay-style questions, which are more difficult to score. The number of multiple-choice answer sheets scored by NCS more than doubled from 1997 to 2000, but the number of essay-style questions more than quadrupled in that period, to 84.4 million from 20 million.

Even so, testing companies turn the scoring of these writing samples over to thousands of temporary workers earning as little as $9 an hour.

Several scorers, speaking publicly for the first time about problems they saw, complained in interviews that they were pressed to score student essays without adequate training and that they saw tests scored in an arbitrary and inconsistent manner.

"Lots of people don't even read the whole test—the time pressure and scoring pressure are just too great," said Artur Golczewski, a doctoral candidate, who said he has scored tests for NCS for two years, most recently in April.

NCS executives dispute his comments, saying that the company provides careful, accurate scoring of essay questions and that scorers are carefully supervised.

Because these tests are subject to error and subjective scoring, the testing industry's code of conduct specifies that they not be the basis for life-altering decisions about students. Yet many states continue to use them for that purpose, and the industry has done little to stop it.

When a serious mistake does occur, school districts rarely have the expertise to find it, putting them at the mercy of testing companies that may not be eager to disclose their failings. The surge in school testing in the last five years has left some companies struggling to find people to score tests and specialists to design them.

"They are stretched too thin," said Terry Bergeson, Washington State's top education official. "The politicians of this country have made education everybody's top priority, and everybody thinks testing is the answer for everything."

The Mistake: When 6 Wrongs Were Rights

The scoring mistake that plagued Jake Plumley and his Minnesota classmates is a window into the way even glaring errors can escape detection. In fact, NCS did not catch the error. A parent did.

Martin Swaden, a lawyer who lives in Mendota Heights, Minn., was concerned when his daughter, Sydney, failed the state's basic math test last spring. A sophomore with average grades, Sydney found math difficult and had failed the test before.

This time, Sydney failed by a single answer. Mr. Swaden wanted to know why, so he asked the state to see Sydney's test papers. "Then I could say, 'Syd, we gotta study maps and graphs,' or whatever," he explained.

But curiosity turned to anger when state education officials sent him boilerplate e-mail messages denying his request. After threatening a lawsuit, Mr. Swaden was finally given an appointment. On July 21, he was ushered into a conference room at the department's headquarters, where he and a state employee sat down to review the 68 questions on Sydney's test.

When they reached Question No. 41, Mr. Swaden immediately knew that his daughter's "wrong" answer was right.

The question showed a split-rail fence, and asked which parts of it were parallel. Sydney had correctly chosen two horizontal rails; the answer key picked one horizontal rail and one upright post.

"By the time we found the second scoring mistake, I knew she had passed," Mr. Swaden said. "By the third, I was concerned about just how bad this was."

After including questions that were being field-tested for future use, someone at NCS had failed to adjust the answer key, resulting in 6 wrong answers out of 68 questions. Even worse, two quality control checks that would have caught the errors were never done.

Eric Rud, an honor-roll student except in math, was one of those students mislabeled as having failed. Paralyzed in both legs at birth, Eric had achieved a fairly normal school life, playing wheelchair hockey and dreaming of becoming an architect. But when he was told he had failed, his spirits plummeted, his father, Rick Rud, said.

Kristle Glau, who moved to Minnesota in her senior year, did not give up on high school when she became pregnant. She persevered, and assumed she would graduate because she was confident she had passed the April test, as, in fact, she had.

"I had a graduation party, with lots of presents," she recalled angrily. "I had my cap and gown. My invitations were out." Finally, she said, her mother learned what her teachers did not have the heart to tell her; according to NCS, she had failed the test and would not graduate.

When the news of NCS's blunder reached Ms. Jax, the state schools commissioner, she wept. "I could not believe," she said, "how we could betray children that way."

But when she learned that the error would have been caught if NCS had done the quality control checks it had promised in its bid, she was furious. She summoned the chief executive of NCS, David W. Smith, to a news conference and publicly blamed the company for the mistake.

Mr. Smith made no excuses. "We messed up," he said. "We are extremely sorry this happened." NCS has offered a $1,000 tuition voucher to the seniors affected, and is covering the state's expenses for retesting. It also paid for a belated graduation ceremony at the State Capitol.

Jake Plumley and several other students are suing NCS on behalf of Minnesota teenagers who they say were emotionally injured by NCS's mistake. NCS has argued that its liability does not extend to emotional damages.

The court cases reflect a view that is common among parents and even among some education officials: that standardized testing should be, and can be, foolproof.

The Task: Trying to Grade 300 Million Test Sheets

The mistake that derailed Jake Plumley's graduation plans occurred in a bland building in a field just outside Iowa City. From the driveway on North Dodge Street, the structure looks like an overgrown suite of medical offices with a small warehouse in the back.

Casually dressed workers, most of them hired for the spring testing season, gather outside a loading dock to smoke, or wander out for lunch at Arby's.

This is ground zero for the testing industry, NCS's Measurement Services unit. More of the nation's standardized tests are scored here than anywhere else. Last year, nearly 300 million answer sheets coursed through this building, the vast majority without mishap. At this facility and at other smaller ones around the country, NCS scores a big chunk of the exams from other companies. What the company does in this building affects not only countless students, but the reputation of the entire industry.

Inside, machines make the soft sound of shuffling cards as they scan in student answers to multiple-choice questions. Handwritten answers are also scanned in, to be scored later by workers.

But behind the soft whirring and methodical procedures is an often frenzied rush to meet deadlines, a rush that left many people at the company feeling overwhelmed, current and former employees said.

"There was a lack of personnel, a lack of time, too many projects, too few people," sighed Nina Metzner, an education assessment consultant who worked at NCS. "People were spread very, very thin."

Those concerns were echoed by other current and former NCS employees, several of whom said those pressures had played a role in the Minnesota error and other problems at the company.

Mr. Smith, the NCS chief executive, disputed those reports. The company has sustained a high level of accuracy, he said, by matching its staffing to the volume of its business. The Minnesota mistake, he said, was not caused by the pressures of a heavy workload but by "pure human error caused by individuals who had the necessary time to perform a quality function they did not perform."

Betsy Hickok, a former NCS scoring director, said she had worked hard to ensure the accurate scoring of essays. But that became more difficult, she said, as she and her scorers were pressed into working 12-hour days, six days a week.

"I became concerned," Ms. Hickok said, "about my ability, and the ability of the scorers, to continue making sound decisions and keeping the best interest of the student in mind."

Mr. Smith said NCS was "committed to scoring every test accurately."

The Workers: Some Questions About Training

The pressures reported by NCS executives are affecting the temporary workers who score the essay questions in vogue today, said Mariah Steele, a former NCS scorer and a graduate student in Iowa City.

In today's tight labor markets, Ms. Steele is the testing industry's dream recruit. She is college-educated but does not have a full-time job; she lives near a major test-scoring center and is willing to work for $9 an hour.

For her first two evenings, she and nearly 100 other recruits were trained to score math tests from Washington State. This training is critical, scoring specialists say, to make sure that scorers consistently apply a state's specific standards, rather than their own.

But one evening in late July, as the Washington project was ending, Ms. Steele said, she was asked by her supervisor to stop grading math and switch to a reading test from another state, without any training.

"He just handed me a scoring rubric and said, 'Start scoring,'" Ms. Steele said. Perhaps a dozen of her co-workers were given similar instructions, she added, and were offered overtime as an inducement.

Baffled, Ms. Steele said she read through the scoring guide and scored tests for about 30 minutes. "Then I left, and didn't go back," she said. "I really was not confident in my ability to score that test."

Two other former scorers for NCS say they saw inconsistent grading.

Renée Brochu of Iowa City recalled when a supervisor explained that a certain response should be scored as a 2 on a two-point scale. "And someone would gasp and say, 'Oh, no, I've scored hundreds of those as a 1,'" Ms. Brochu said. "There was never the suggestion that we go back and change the ones already scored."

Another former scorer, Mr. Golczewski, accused supervisors of trying to manipulate results to match expectations. "One day you see an essay that is a 3, and the next day those are to be 2's because they say we need more 2's," he said.

He recalled that the pressure to produce worsened as deadlines neared. "We are actually told," he said, "to stop getting too involved or thinking too long about the score—to just score it on our first impressions."

Mr. Smith of NCS dismissed these anecdotes as aberrations that were probably caught by supervisors before they affected scores.

"Mistakes will occur," he said. "We do everything possible to eliminate those mistakes before they affect an individual test taker."

New York City did not use NCS to score its essay-style tests; instead, like a few other states, it used local teachers. But like the scorers in Iowa, they also complained that they had not been adequately trained.

One reading teacher said she was assigned to score eighth-grade math tests. "I said I hadn't been in eighth-grade math class since I was in eighth grade," she said.

Another teacher, she said, arrived late at the scoring session and was put right to work without any training.

Roseanne DeFabio, assistant education commissioner in New York State, said she thought the complaints were exaggerated. State audits each year of 10 percent of the tests do not show any major problems, she said, "so I think it's unlikely that there's any systemic problem with the scoring."

The Demand: States Pushing For More, Faster

Testing specialists argue that educators and politicians must share the blame for the rash of testing errors because they are asking too much of the industry.

They say schools want to test as late in the year as possible to maximize student performance, while using tests that take longer to score. Yet schools want the results before the school year ends so they can decide about school financing, teacher evaluations, summer school, promotions or graduation.

"The demands may just be impossible," said Edward D. Roeber, a former education official who is now vice president for external affairs for Measured Progress.

Case in point: California. On Oct. 9, 1997, Gov. Pete Wilson signed into law a bill that gave state education officials five weeks to choose and adopt a statewide achievement test, called the Standardized Testing and Reporting program.

The law's "unrealistic" deadlines, state auditors said later, contributed to the numerous quality control problems that plagued the test contractor, Harcourt Educational Measurement, for the next two years.

That state audit, and an audit done for Harcourt by Deloitte & Touche, paint a devastating portrait of what went wrong. There was not time to test the computer link between Harcourt, the test contractor, and NCS, the subcontractor. When needed, it did not work, causing delays. Some test materials were delivered so late that students could not take the tests on schedule.

It got worse. Pages in test booklets were duplicated, missing or out of order. One district's test booklets, more than two tons of paper, were dumped on the sidewalk outside the district offices at 5 P.M. on a Friday—in the rain. Test administrators were not adequately trained. When school districts got the computer disks from NCS that were supposed to contain the test results, some of the data was inaccurate and some of the disks were blank.

In 1998, nearly 700 of the state's 8,500 schools got inaccurate test results, and more than 750,000 students were not included in the statewide analysis of the test results.

Then, in 1999, Harcourt made a mistake entering demographic data into its computer. The resulting scores made it appear that students with a limited command of English were performing better in English than they actually were, a politically charged statistic in a state that had voted a year earlier to eliminate bilingual education in favor of a one-year intensive class in English.

"There's tremendous political pressure to get tests in place faster than is prudent," said Maureen G. DiMarco, a vice president at Houghton Mifflin, whose subsidiary, the Riverside Publishing Company, was one of the unsuccessful bidders for California's business.

Dr. Paslov, who became president of Harcourt Educational Measurement after the 1999 problems, said that the current testing season in California is going smoothly and that Harcourt has addressed concerns about errors and delays.

But California is still sprinting ahead.

In 1999, Gov. Gray Davis signed a bill directing state education officials to develop another statewide test, the California High School Exit Exam. Once again, industry executives said, speed seemed to trump all other considerations.

None of the major testing companies bid on the project because of what Ms. DiMarco called "impossible, unrealistic time lines."

With no bidders, the state asked the companies to draft their own proposals. "We had just 10 days to put it together," recalled George W. Bohrnstedt, senior vice president for research at the American Institutes for Research, which has done noneducational testing but is new to school testing.

Phil Spears, the state testing director, said A.I.R. faced a "monumental task, building and administering a test in 18 months."

"Most states," Mr. Spears said, "would take three-plus years to do that kind of test."

The new test was given for the first time this spring.

The Concern: Life Choices Based on a Score

States are not just demanding more speed; they are demanding more complicated exams. Test companies once had a steady business selling the same brand-name tests, like Harcourt's Stanford Achievement Test or Riverside's Iowa Test of Basic Skills, to school districts. These "shelf" tests, also called norm-referenced tests, are the testing equivalent of ready-to-wear clothing. Graded on a bell curve, they measure how a student is performing compared with other students taking the same tests.

But increasingly, states want custom tailoring, tests designed to fit their homegrown educational standards. These "criterion referenced" tests measure students against a fixed yardstick, not against each other.

That is exactly what Arizona wanted when it hired NCS and CTB/McGraw-Hill in December 1998. What it got was more than two years of errors, delays, escalating costs and angry disappointment on all sides.

Some of the problems Arizona encountered occurred because the state had established standards that, officials later conceded, were too rigorous. But the state blames other disruptions on NCS.

"You can't trust the quality assurance going on now," said Kelly Powell, the Arizona testing director, who is still wrangling with NCS.

For its part, NCS has thrown up its hands on Arizona. "We've given Arizona nearly $2 of service for every dollar they have paid us," said Jeffrey W. Taylor, a senior vice president of NCS. Mr. Taylor said NCS would not bid on future business in that state.

Each customized test a state orders must be designed, written, edited, reviewed by state educators, field-tested, checked for validity and bias, and calibrated to previous tests—an arduous process that requires a battery of people trained in educational statistics and psychometrics, the science of measuring mental function.

While the demand for such people is exploding, they are in extremely short supply despite salaries that can reach into the six figures, people in the industry said. "All of us in the business are very concerned about capacity," Mr. Bohrnstedt of A.I.R. said.

And academia will be little help, at least for a while, because promising candidates are going into other, more lucrative areas of statistics and computer programming, testing executives say.

Kurt Landgraf, president of the Educational Testing Service in Princeton, N.J., the titan of college admission tests but a newcomer to high-stakes state testing, estimated that there are about 20 good people coming into the field every year.

Already, the strain on the test-design process is showing. A supplemental math test that Harcourt developed for California in 1999 proved statistically unreliable, in part because it was too short. Harcourt had been urged to add five questions to the test, state auditors said, but that was never done.

Even more troubling, most test professionals say, is the willingness of states like Arizona to use standardized tests in ways that violate the testing industry's professional standards. For example, many states use test scores for determining whether students graduate. Yet the American Educational Research Association, the nation's largest educational research group, specifically warns educators against making high-stakes decisions based on a single test.

Among the reasons for this position, testing professionals say, is that some students are emotionally overcome by the pressure of taking standardized tests. And a test score, "like any other source of information about a student, is subject to error," noted the National Research Council in a comprehensive study of high-stakes testing in 1999.

But industry executives insist that, while they try to persuade schools to use tests appropriately, they are powerless to enforce industry standards when their customers are determined to do otherwise. A few executives say privately that they have refused to bid on state projects they thought professionally and legally indefensible.

"But we haven't come to the point yet, and I don't know if we will, where we are going to tell California—where we sell $44 million worth of business—'Nope! We don't like the way you people are using these instruments, so we're not going to sell you this test,'" Dr. Paslov said

Besides, as one executive said, "If I don't sell them, my competitors will."

The Expectations: Bush Proposal Raises the Bar

President Bush explained in a radio address on Jan. 24 why he wanted to require annual testing of students in grades 3 to 8 in reading, math and science. "Without yearly testing," he said, "we do not know who is falling behind and who needs our help."

While many children will clearly need help, so will the testing industry if it is called upon to carry out Mr. Bush's plan, education specialists said.

Currently, only 13 states test for reading and math in all six grades required by the Bush plan. If Mr. Bush's plan is carried out,—the industry's workload will grow by more than 50 percent.

Ms. Jax, Minnesota's top school official, says she is not close to being ready. "It's just impossible to find enough people," she said. "I will have to add at least four tests. I don't have the capacity for that, and I'm not convinced that the industry does either."

Certainly the industry has been generating revenues that could support some expansion. In 1999, its last full year as an independent company, NCS reported revenues of more than $620 million, up 30 percent from the previous year. The other major players, all corporate units, do not disclose revenues.

Several of the largest testing companies have assured the administration that the industry can handle the additional work. "It's taken the testing industry a while to gear up for this," said Dr. Paslov of Harcourt. "But we are ready."

Other executives are far less optimistic. "I don't know how anyone can say that we can do this now," said Mr. Landgraf of the Educational Testing Service.

Russell Hagen, chief executive of the Data Recognition Corporation, a midsize testing company in Maple Grove, Minn., worries that the added workload from the Bush proposal would create even more quality control problems, with increasingly serious consequences for students. "Take the Minnesota experience and put it in 50 states," he said.

The Minnesota experience is still a fresh fact of life for students like Jake Plumley, who is working nights for Federal Express and hoping to find another union job like the one he gave up last summer.

But despite his difficult experience, he does not oppose the kind of testing that derailed his post-graduation plans. "The high-stakes test—it keeps kids motivated. So I understand the idea of the test," he said. "But they need to do it right."

When a Test Fails the Schools, Careers and Reputations Suffer

Jacques Steinberg and Diana B. Henriques

Sitting in his cramped office in Fort Wayne, Ind., with his calculator running, John Kline became the first to suspect that a major test publisher had erred in computing the standardized test scores of thousands of his students.

As testing director for the local school system, Mr. Kline quickly alerted the company, CTB/McGraw-Hill, but it did not fully investigate his complaint at the time.

If it had, CTB would have discovered a crippling programming error in time to prevent it from upending the lives of students, parents and educators as it rippled across the nation over the first eight months of 1999. This mishap, the most far-reaching in the recent history of school testing, jolted school districts in at least six states, including New York City, where it mistakenly sent nearly 9,000 students packing off to summer school.

A post-mortem of how this error spread unimpeded for so long lays bare a basic truth of standardized testing: school districts lack the ability to uncover serious testing errors on their own, and must rely on the testing companies to do so voluntarily.

Because the testing industry has succeeded in fending off various proposals for federal oversight, the companies themselves decide what they will disclose and when.

CTB's error hit hardest in New York City, the nation's largest school system. Apart from the children, the most prominent victim may have been the city's schools chancellor, Rudy Crew. The error showed—incorrectly—that reading scores citywide had stagnated after rising for two years, raising questions about Dr. Crew's leadership. Within months, he was out of a job.

Before the mistake was discovered, Dr. Crew had been a leading advocate for using standardized tests to hold students and educators accountable. But now, as Congress is poised to vote on a presidential proposal that would sharply increase the nation's reliance on standardized testing, Dr. Crew says he has been chastened by his personal experience with the testing industry.

"The answer is not to use test scores as the sole source of information about a student's performance," he said. "These are human errors. They're going to happen again."

Source: Jacques Steinberg and Diana B. Henriques, "When a Test Fails the Schools, Careers and Reputations Suffer," *The New York Times*, p. 1, 10–11. May 21, 2001.

The issue, then, is how the test companies handle mistakes once they occur, educators say. A *New York Times* examination of CTB's error shows that the company had been warned repeatedly by testing officials in Indiana, New York City and other districts that their percentile scores seemed wrong. While CTB told each not to worry, the company did not mention the other complaints.

Then, after finding an error, CTB officials waited seven weeks before passing that critical information on to New York City and other school districts.

When told of these findings, Dr. Crew, who begins work next month at an education foundation in San Francisco, expressed disappointment and anger.

"What CTB did was lie," he said.

CTB officials say they did their best to uncover a deeply imbedded software problem. Once the problem was located, the officials say, they did not immediately alert any school districts because they wanted to be absolutely sure of the damage it had caused.

"It was hard to see this," David M. Taggart, the company president, said. "But, and I think this speaks to the integrity of our company, we didn't stop looking."

Robert Tobias, the longtime testing director in New York City, does not accept the company's explanation, particularly in light of the early warnings that CTB received.

"They clearly did not check carefully enough," he said. "It's that simple."

Dr. Crew sees a broader problem. "The largest testing companies are guilty of what most people accuse public schools of," he said. "They've actually got a monopoly."

In Indiana: The First Indication of a Costly Error

CTB has its headquarters in a tan fortress perched atop a hill overlooking California's idyllic Monterey Peninsula. Founded in 1926 by a Los Angeles public school official and his wife, CTB grew into an industry giant after being acquired in 1965 by McGraw-Hill, a financial information and publishing company.

CTB's biggest rival, NCS Pearson, might score more student tests—about one in every two nationwide—but CTB is an industry giant, too, providing test design as well as scoring. By 1998, nine million students were taking CTB tests annually, about 40 percent of the market.

Each spring, answer sheets descend on Monterey like a steady rain, with postmarks from as far away as American military bases in Japan. Once scored, the results are shipped back to the schools in boxes full of numbers that are regarded as the definitive educational measure of children and teachers and schools.

Though CTB's work is widely praised by educators, the company did make two errors in 1998: one resulted in wrong math scores for a number of Missouri school districts; the other affected the math scores of a small number of Florida students who took the company's tests.

Still, as the 1999 testing season began, CTB was the envy of the testing industry. The company could claim nearly 20 states as customers, all under contract for several years.

Indiana was one state that believed in CTB, hiring the company to test about 320,000 students in grades 3, 6, 8 and 10. But when Mr. Kline, the testing director in Fort Wayne, got his district's scores in early 1999, he saw that they had plunged unexpectedly.

"I felt sick," he said. "How am I going to explain it to the superintendent?" Although Indiana did not use the test to promote students, as many states do, the scores gave politicians and educators a yardstick to measure student progress. Bad test scores, Mr. Kline knew, would echo through the city like a tornado warning, causing parents to worry and teachers to wonder what they had done wrong.

Before releasing the bad news, Mr. Kline called half a dozen other testing directors to see how they fared. To his surprise, each described nearly identical drops in scoring. "It was almost unbelievable how similar the patterns were," Mr. Kline recalled.

It did not make sense, Mr. Kline thought, for so many students in so many places to fail by nearly the same margin. So he called the testing company.

CTB officials were not particularly alarmed to hear Mr. Kline's complaint, because they knew that when test scores drop, the first and easiest reaction of school officials is to blame the test.

But CTB did agree to look into Indiana's scores, and within days it found a problem. In trying to compare Indiana students with the rest of the country, CTB had used an old formula. When the problem was fixed, most student scores rose, some as much as 10 percentage points.

But Mr. Kline still was not satisfied. He and his colleagues told CTB that the error did not account for other large, unexplained drops. "Our feeling was, 'There is still more to it, there's something out there that no one's been able to explain,'" he said.

By now, Mr. Kline had come to suspect that the scoring drop could be traced to an arcane area of test design called equating.

This process is necessary so scores one year can be compared with those from previous years, even if different questions are used. States ask for new questions because they are worried the old questions will leak out.

CTB told Indiana that its sophisticated software program had insured that the current test was comparable, or equated, to the previous year's test. But just to be sure, the company agreed to take another look. This time, the company said it found nothing wrong. "Our confidence in the accuracy of the equating was reconfirmed," CTB told Indiana in a memorandum on Jan. 18, 1999.

CTB even sent its president, Mr. Taggart, to Indiana in early March, to personally assure educators that the test scores were solid. In a follow-up letter, though, the company said it was developing "procedures to improve quality control in the future."

Reluctantly, Fort Wayne distributed the results to its schools, but not before Mr. Kline had ordered them stamped: "May contain inaccurate scores."

Then, with no options left, Mr. Kline gave up, assuming he had heard the last of the matter.

In New York: Unearned Tickets to Summer School

In April, about the time Mr. Kline was conceding his fight, 300,000 students in New York City's public schools were taking their reading and math tests in grades 3, 5, 6 and 7. Those tests, too, were designed by CTB. And though many of the multiple-choice questions were different from Indiana's, both school systems drew some of their questions from the same versions of the company's flagship test, Terra Nova.

But the New York City Board of Education and its chancellor, Dr. Crew, had decided to attach a much greater value to CTB's tests than Indiana did. For the first time that spring, students in grades 3 and 6 were required to pass CTB's test, or attend summer school. And if they did poorly in summer school, they would be held back.

Making such decisions based on a single test score violates the testing industry's standards, and both CTB and city school officials agree that the company advised the city against putting such a premium on its test. But the board forged ahead anyway.

Dr. Crew raised the stakes not only for children but also for school principals and superintendents of the city's 32 neighborhood school districts. He announced that, for the first time, school officials would be judged by how well their students did on the CTB tests. Those educators whose students scored poorly faced the loss of their jobs.

Dr. Crew's future was also at stake. For two years, Dr. Crew had managed to do something that had eluded his predecessor, Ramon C. Cortines: forge a warm relationship with Mayor Rudolph W. Giuliani. But that was changing. The issue: school vouchers.

Mr. Giuliani said he believed that taxpayer money should help finance private-school tuition for thousands of students who were attending failing public schools. Dr. Crew disagreed with the mayor, and he did so publicly.

So long as test scores kept going up, Dr. Crew felt that he could defend his position. If the scores were bad, Dr. Crew's own job would be on the line.

When the eagerly awaited reading scores arrived from Monterey in early May, Mr. Tobias, the New York system's testing director, was among the first to see them.

The news was not good. As in Indiana, many of the students' scores had dipped sharply from the previous year—so steeply and uniformly as to appear improbable, Mr. Tobias thought. Knowing how high the stakes were this year, Mr. Tobias directed his staff to ask CTB whether it had made a mistake. The company's response, Mr. Tobias recalls, was as swift as it was definitive: "We can't find anything wrong."

Mr. Tobias continued to press CTB, eventually calling the company himself to make an argument the company had already heard: perhaps the tests from one year to the next were not quite equal. No one told him that he was echoing Indiana's earlier suspicions.

Still, CTB held firm. "If we were not comfortable, we would have advised them not to release the data," said Mr. Taggart, CTB's president.

Unsure of what to do, Mr. Tobias held off releasing the results until June 8, the last possible day the scores could be used to make summer-school assignments.

As the date approached, Mr. Tobias finally told Dr. Crew about his doubts. Dr. Crew says he seriously considered calling the press to disavow the results. But as a national spokesman for the movement toward standardized assessment, Dr. Crew decided his credibility would be lost. He thought he would be seen as a crybaby.

Mr. Tobias concurred.

"Errors of measurement are a fact of life in this business," Mr. Tobias said in an interview. "There are times you can explain them. Other times you just bite the bullet and accept the data as they are."

And so, Dr. Crew summoned reporters to deliver the disappointing news: two years of progress in reading had apparently stalled.

The mayor said he was "very alarmed and concerned." And Dr. Crew knew he had some homework to do.

In Tennessee: State Officials Seek Review of Test

Most school districts, including New York City, gauge progress by comparing students in a particular grade with their predecessors in the same grade a year earlier. But Tennessee has long used a more sophisticated approach: it compares a student's test scores as a first grader with that same student's scores as a second grader, third grader, and so on through school.

This approach was pioneered and overseen by William Sanders, a longtime professor at the University of Tennessee, who was curious about how class size and teaching styles influenced student performance.

In early May 1999, when Professor Sanders received Tennessee's scores from CTB, he knew from his own data that they could not be right, state testing officials said. The drops were much too sharp.

Again, state officials recall the company saying not to worry—the scores were accurate. But Tennessee had something that Indiana and New York City did not: a treasure trove of data on the performance of actual children going back six years or more. CTB's results broke patterns in individual students' scores that had been uninterrupted for years.

Professor Sanders was so insistent that there was a problem that he told the company he would call a news conference to challenge the results, Tennessee school officials said.

Then CTB did something that it would not do in any other state: it simply raised the comparative rankings of many Tennessee students, and lowered some others, to conform with Mr. Sanders's statistical models—even though the company could find no error to justify those changes.

The company made this adjustment in late May or early June, just as it was assuring New York City that its results were correct.

CTB did not tell any of its other customers what it had done for Tennessee. CTB considers its relationship with each state or district to be confidential, even if the products that state uses are similar to others, said Mr. Taggart, the company president.

Moreover, Mr. Taggart said, CTB's researchers had not yet detected any similarity in the complaints from New York City, Tennessee, Indiana and another state, Nevada, which had contacted the company around the same time. Finding a common thread was difficult, Mr. Taggart said, because each had used a customized version of the same basic test.

But after certifying New York City's results as accurate, and altering Tennessee's results, CTB began to have its own doubts, the company now says. In June and into July, unbeknown to its customers, CTB assigned an army of researchers to investigate its results.

The Results: School Districts Cope with Falling Scores

While CTB stepped up its inquiry, its clients were dealing with the consequences of the test results they had been given.

In Tennessee, the adjusted results were not distributed to teachers and principals until late summer, too late to play their customary role in many districts' decisions on summer school or student promotion.

In Indiana, the districts' very public concerns about the accuracy of the scores led teachers and principals to be wary about how much stock, if any, to put in those numbers. And so, educators there grew reluctant to use the test results to shape their lesson plans.

Nevada had voiced similar concerns to CTB. But state education officials nonetheless moved forward, branding a handful of schools as "inadequate" based on their poor scores. One of them was Cambeiro Elementary, in the shadow of the Las Vegas strip, which was put under the supervision of a state oversight panel and awarded over $100,000 for remedial programs. School administrators felt more than a little humiliation.

"At bowling night and at church," Cenie Nelson, the school principal, said, "teachers were asked by other teachers and friends, 'Why would you want to be associated with a school not doing a good job?'"

But nowhere did CTB's scores have more impact than in New York City. Based solely on their performance on the test, Dr. Crew immediately ordered nearly 40,000 third and sixth graders to attend summer school.

"Your child must attend summer school," the superintendent in one district wrote to parents. "We feel that your child would benefit from this enriching experience."

Two weeks after releasing the test results, Dr. Crew took direct control of 43 failing schools, saying he intended to fire many of their principals. He also fired or eased out 5 of the 32 superintendents who preside over the city's neighborhood school districts, citing their failures as leaders as well as their students' test scores.

One of them was Robert Riccobono, then 54, who had brought rigorous literacy programs to one of the poorest districts in the city, No. 19 in East New York, Brooklyn. After four years as superintendent, Mr. Riccobono says, his efforts were starting to bear fruit when Dr. Crew fired him.

"Giuliani was talking tough," Mr. Riccobono said. "Crew felt the need to find victims."

The day after Dr. Crew announced his firing at a news conference broadcast live on local television, Mr. Riccobono attended his son's graduation from high school.

"I felt singled out and embarrassed," said Mr. Riccobono, who had known teachers at the school for a decade. "I was wondering where I had gone wrong."

The Inquiry: An Error Is Found Deep in the Software

While New York City was firing administrators and disrupting the summer vacations of students and teachers, CTB was closing in on evidence that would undermine those very decisions.

The company's focus was again on the equating process, which allows test scores to be compared year over year.

As it turned out, CTB—despite its assurances to Indiana and others—had done an incomplete job of reviewing test data. When a much larger sample was reviewed, a programming error surfaced.

The error had—erroneously—made the current test appear easier than the previous year's. To make the tests equal in difficulty, the computer had then compensated by making it harder for some students to do as well as they had last time. The error did not change students' right and wrong answers, but it did affect their comparative percentile scores.

On July 20, Wendy Yen, then the vice president of research for CTB, walked into the office of Mr. Taggart, the company president, and announced, "We have found something."

Mr. Taggart decided not to tell schools just yet about the problem, because, he says, he did not yet know how bad it was. "Would it be a positive impact, a negative impact, no impact?" Mr. Taggart said.

At the time the company found the error, New York City's students were just two weeks into a monthlong summer-school program, sweltering in a heat wave. Even classrooms with air-conditioners routinely registered 90 degrees on indoor thermometers.

Dr. Crew would later say that had he known what CTB knew—no matter how tentative—"we could have corrected the action midstream, and not put families through all that torment."

A month later on Aug. 24, after summer school had ended, Mr. Taggart traveled to New York City to hear, in person, the city's lingering concerns about the spring results.

"We're the largest school system in the country," Dr. Crew recalls saying. "You have got to get this right with us."

Again, Mr. Taggart promised to look into the city's complaints. And again, he did not tell them what he knew about the error.

Mr. Taggart had more to say when he called Mr. Tobias, the city's testing director, on the first day of school, Sept. 9, 1999.

"We have done further analysis into your concerns about the scoring," Mr. Tobias recalls being told. "And we have found a problem."

"It's a small problem," Mr. Tobias remembers the company president saying. "We don't believe it's going to have a huge impact on your scores."

Mr. Tobias quickly did a few calculations of his own.

It seemed, at first, that 3,000 students who had been sent to summer school in June had in fact scored well enough to have spent the summer as they wished. That number eventually grew to nearly 9,000—almost a quarter of the mandatory summer-school roster.

So much for "a small problem," Mr. Tobias thought.

But the real shock came when school officials learned what the corrected test scores meant for the entire city. Instead of reading scores stagnating over all, the citywide average had actually risen five percentage points—a substantial jump, particularly for an urban school district.

"I was feeling really horribly," Mr. Tobias said. "I realized that what was a bad story last spring really could have been a triumph for the chancellor."

Dr. Crew agreed.

"You've got the mayor and the political people saying you haven't done a damn thing," Dr. Crew said. "This was the beginning of the end for me. You can't go back and retrieve this."

The following week, Mr. Taggart flew back to New York City to tell a packed meeting of the New York City Board of Education that he was sorry. His voice shaking, Mr. Taggart said that CTB had "worked diligently" to find the problem, and had notified New York "as soon as those calculations were complete and verified."

Mr. Taggart also said it was not his company's idea to use CTB's test to decide who had to go to summer school. Even so, he said, "The test itself remains a valid measure of student performance."

William C. Thompson Jr., the president of the board, was disbelieving. "Why would I use your company after this?" he asked.

Two days later, Mr. Taggart appeared at the Indiana Board of Education, where he told a similar story and received a similar reception. It was his second trip to Indiana in six months, and he was armed with his company's third version of that state's test scores.

But this time, the corrected percentile scores virtually eliminated the unexplained drops that had troubled Mr. Kline, the Fort Wayne testing director. "It was just good to know we were right," Mr. Kline said.

Mr. Taggart did not travel to Nevada, but he called testing officials there. Careful readers of *The Las Vegas Sun* on Oct. 20, 1999, may have noticed the headline, "Cambeiro Elementary School Taken Off Academic Probation by State."

When CTB recalculated the results of the Nevada tests, students at Cambeiro, and another school, in Reno, were found to have exceeded the state's criteria for the label "inadequate." They were, in fact, "adequate."

The school was no longer entitled to the more than $100,000 in remedial money it had been given, but the money had already been spent. A cloud had lifted, but it was hard for the school to tell.

"You can't undo an 'inadequate,'" Ms. Nelson, the school principal, said. "It's not something that goes away."

CTB also called Tennessee, with word that it could finally explain the unexplainable dips in its rankings. Now the company could actually correct the percentile scores, rather than simply adjust them to meet what Professor Sanders thought they should have been.

The Future: Most School Districts Have Few Options

When Mr. Tobias first learned of the error, he says, he asked Mr. Taggart if any districts outside New York had been affected. Mr. Tobias was told that was proprietary information.

The press release issued in New York, written by CTB's parent company, McGraw-Hill, mentioned only New York. And a release issued the same day in Indiana referred only to Indiana.

While the company has since confirmed that in addition to Tennessee and Nevada, two other states were affected—Wisconsin and South Carolina—it has refused to identify two other school districts involved, or to say whether the districts ever alerted teachers and parents to the error.

Subsequent audits by Indiana and New York criticized CTB for lax supervision in the research department—the department that had created the error, and then was charged with finding and correcting it. The auditors wrote that managers were only "informally involved in the day-to-day work of subordinates."

Wendy Yen, the CTB official who oversaw the research department, has since left the company to work for the Educational Testing Service, which administers the SAT. Dr. Yen, through a spokesman at her current company, refused several interview requests.

But Benjamin Brown, Tennessee's testing director, said the problem went beyond research: he said CTB's greatest error was in treating each customer as if its problem was isolated, even after the company knew otherwise.

"It'd be like someone holding a barking dog and saying, 'This dog won't bite,' knowing he's bitten three neighbors in the previous month," Mr. Brown said.

Mr. Taggart said the company had since installed new quality controls to intercept such an error, and had put its employees through a customer relations course.

The New York City Board of Education voted to renew CTB's contract despite its record, although the board did negotiate financial penalties that totaled $500,000 on a multimillion-dollar agreement renewable over four years. Dr. Crew supported retaining CTB because the city had already spent years working with the company to create tests specifically designed for city students. Also, CTB's competitors had experienced their own quality control problems.

"There was no place else to go," Dr. Crew said.

Dr. Crew did not fare as well as CTB.

On Dec. 23, 1999, a board majority led by the mayor's appointees voted not to extend his contract, saying that after four years he had lost interest in his job.

Though he lamented that no one noticed the city's vastly improved scores, Dr. Crew refused to rehire the superintendents and principals whom he had fired, saying their problems went beyond bad test scores.

But New York State's education commissioner, Richard Mills, disagreed, at least in the case of Mr. Riccobono, the innovative superintendent from Brooklyn. Mr. Mills is taking steps to help Mr. Riccobono, who teaches part time at New York University, get his old job back.

"I suppose I felt vindicated," Mr. Riccobono said. "I am certain that had the correct scores been reported initially, I wouldn't have been fired."

But he says he still bears emotional scars from the experience. After his firing, he applied for at least 30 other superintendent jobs in New York State—and did not get one of them.

"Clearly standardized tests are a valid way of providing part of the picture," Mr. Riccobono said. "But they should not be the ultimate determinant of success."

New York City now uses multiple measures—teacher evaluations as well as test scores—to make summer-school assignments.

Indiana's contract with CTB expires this year, and the state is soliciting bidders. For the first time, the state is requiring bidders to list all errors made over the last two years and to promise, if hired, to disclose any new errors immediately.

The superintendent of education, Suellen Reed, has said she would consider rehiring CTB, particularly if it was the low bidder. But officials in Fort Wayne are not awaiting the outcome.

Mr. Kline and his superintendent, Thomas Fowler-Finn, have instead written their own tests for the district's students, to be administered in grades 3 through 9.

"I still believe in standardized testing," Mr. Kline said. "I just don't think the industry is ready to give us the tests we need."

VIII. Stratification and Class

The Super Rich Are Out of Sight

Michael Parenti

The super rich, the top 1% who earn the lion's share of the nation's income, go uncounted in most income distribution reports. Even those who study the question sometimes overlook the wealthiest among us. For instance, the Center on Budget and Policy Priorities, relying on the latest U.S. Census Bureau data, released a report in December 1997 showing that in the last two decades, "incomes of the richest fifth increased by 30% or nearly $27,000 after adjusting for inflation." The average income of the top 20% was $117,500, or almost 13 times larger than the $9,250 average income of the poorest 20%.

But where are the super rich? An average of $117,500 is an upper-middle income, not at all representative of a rich cohort, let alone a super-rich one. Many such reports about income distribution are based on U.S. Census Bureau surveys that regularly leave Big Money out of the picture. A few phone calls to the Census Bureau in Washington, D.C., revealed that for years the bureau never interviewed anyone who had an income higher than $300,000. Or if interviewed, they were never recorded as above the "reportable upper limit" of $300,000, the top figure allowed by the bureau's computer program. In 1994, the bureau lifted the upper limit to $1 million. This still excludes the richest 1%, the hundreds of billionaires and thousands of multimillionaires who make many times more than $1 million a year. The super rich simply have been computerized out of the Census Bureau's picture.

When asked why this procedure was used, an official said that the Census Bureau's computers could not handle higher amounts. A most improbable excuse, since once the bureau decided to raise the upper limit from $300,000 to $1 million it did so without any difficulty, and it could do so again. Another reason the official gave was "confidentiality." Given place coordinates, someone with a very high income might be identified. Furthermore, he said, high-income respondents usually understate their investment returns by about 40% to 50%. Finally, the official argued that since the super rich are so few, they are not likely to show up in a national sample. And since they are so few, including them would skew the sample, wouldn't it?

But by designating the (decapitated) top 20% of the entire nation as the "richest" quintile, the Census Bureau is including millions of people who make as little as $70,000. If you make over $100,000, you are in the top 4%. Now $100,000 is a tidy sum indeed, but

Source: Michael Parenti, "The Super Rich Are Out of Sight," *Dollars & Sense*, May–June 1998. #217, p. 36–8.

it's not super rich—as in Mellon, Morgan or Murdoch. The difference between Michael Eisner, the Disney CEO who pocketed $565 million in 1996, and the individuals who average $9,250 is not 13 to one—the reported spread between highest and lowest quintiles—but over 61,000 to one.

Much attention has been given to the top corporate managers who rake in tens of millions of dollars annually in salaries and perks. But little is said about the tens of billions that their corporations distribute to the top investor class each year, again that invisible 1% of the population. Media publicity that focuses exclusively on a handful of greedy top executives conveniently avoids any exposure of the super rich as a class. In fact, reining in the CEOs who cut into the corporate take would well serve the big shareholders' interests.

Two studies that do their best to muddy our understanding of wealth, conducted by the Rand Corporation and the Brookings Institution—and widely reported in the major media—found that individuals typically become rich not from inheritance but by maintaining their health and working hard. Most of their savings comes from their earnings and has nothing to do with inherited family wealth, the researchers would have us believe.

In typical social science fashion, they prefigured their findings by limiting the scope of their data. Both studies fail to note that achieving a high income is itself in large part due to inherited advantages. Those coming from upper-strata households have a far better opportunity to maintain their health and develop their performance, attend superior schools, and achieve the advanced professional training, contacts, and influence needed to land higher paying positions.

More importantly, both the Rand and Brookings studies failed to include the super rich, those who sit on immense and largely inherited fortunes. Instead, the investigators concentrated on upper middle class professionals and managers, most of whom earn in the $100,000 to $300,000 range—which indicates the researchers have no idea how rich the very rich really are.

When pressed on this point, they explain that there is a shortage of data on the very rich. Being such a tiny percentage, "they're an extremely difficult part of the population to survey," pleads Rand economist James P. Smith, offering the same excuse given by the Census Bureau officials. We should not overlook the fact that the existence of the super rich refutes Smith's findings about self-earned wealth merely because he finds the group difficult to survey. He seemed to admit as much when he told *The New York Times*, "This [study] shouldn't be taken as a statement that the Rockefellers didn't give to their kids and the Kennedys didn't give to their kids." Indeed, most of the really big money is inherited—and by a portion of the population that is so minuscule as to be judged statistically inaccessible.

The higher one goes up the income scale, the greater the rate of capital accumulation. Drawing on Congressional Budget Office data, economist Paul Krugman notes that not only have the top 20% grown more affluent compared with everyone below, the top 5% have grown richer compared with the next 15%. The top 1% have grown richer compared with the next 4%. And the top 0.25% have grown richer than the next 0.75%. (Even the CBO data isn't perfect. It supplements census surveys with IRS data on the wealthy's after-tax earnings. This leads to $374,000 as the figure for the average after-tax, post-tax shelter income of the top 1%—about the income of a successful opthamologist in San Francisco or New York.)

It has been estimated that if children's play blocks represented $1,000 each, over 98% of us would have incomes represented by piles of blocks that went not more than a few yards off the ground. The blocks of the top 1% would stack many times higher than the Eiffel Tower.

Marx's prediction about the growing gap between rich and poor still haunts the land—and the entire planet. The growing concentration of wealth creates still more poverty. As some few get ever richer, more people fall deeper into destitution, finding it increasingly difficult to emerge from it. The same pattern holds throughout much of the world. For years now, as the wealth of the few has been growing, the number of poor has been increasing at a faster rate than that of the earth's population. A rising tide sinks many boats.

To grasp the true extent of wealth and income inequality in the United States, we should stop treating the "top quintile"—the upper middle class—as the "richest" cohort in the country. And we need to look beyond the Census Bureau's cooked statistics. We need to catch sight of that tiny stratospheric apex that owns most of the world.

Michael Parenti's most recent books are *Blackshirts and Reds: Rational Fascism and the Overthrow of Communism*, and *America Besieged*, both published by City Lights Books.

Sources

"Pulling Apart: A State-by-State Analysis of Income Trends," Center for Budget and Policy Priorities (December 16, 1997); "Trends in the Distribution of After-Tax Income: An Analysis of Congressional Budget Office Data," Center for Budget and Policy Priorities (September 1997); *The New York Times*, July 7, 1995.

Types of Forced Labor

USA TODAY staff

The International Labor Organization says there are eight main forms of forced labor in the world today. ILO's definitions and the countries it cites as examples of where the practices exist:

Slavery	A "physical abduction" followed by forced labor.	Congo, Liberia, Mauritania, Sierra Leone and Sudan
Farm and rural debt bondage	When workers see all their wages go to paying for transportation, food and shelter because they've been "locked into debt" by unscrupulous job recruiters and landowners and they can't leave because of force, threats or the remote location of the worksites.	Benin, Bolivia, Brazil, Cote d'Ivoire, Dominican Republic, Guatemala, Haiti, Mexico, Paraguay, Peru, Togo
Bonded labor	Another form of debt bondage, it often starts with the worker agreeing to provide labor in exchange for a loan, but quickly develops into bondage as the employer adds more and more "debt" to the bargain.	Bangladesh, India, Nepal, Pakistan, Sri Lanka
People trafficking	When individuals are forced or tricked into going somewhere by someone who will profit from selling them or forcing them to work against their will, most often in sexual trades. Many countries are both "origins" and "destinations" for victims.	Albania, Belarus, Bosnia and Herzegovina, Brazil, China, Colombia, Cote d'Ivoire, Czech Republic, Dominican Republic, Ecuador, France, Ghana, Haiti, Honduras, Hungary, Israel, Italy, Republic of Korea, Laos, Latvia, Malaysia, Moldova, Myanmar, the Netherlands, Nepal, Nigeria, Philippines, Poland, Romania, Russia, Thailand, Ukraine, United Kingdom, United States, Vietnam, Yugoslavia

Source: USA TODAY staff. "Types of Forced Labor." *USA TODAY Magazine.* http://www.usatoday.com. May 24, 2001. Copyright © 2001 USA Today, a division of Gannett Co. Inc.

Abuse of domestic workers	When maids and other domestic servants are sold to their employers or bonded to them by debts.	Benin, Cote d'Ivoire, France, Haiti, throughout the Middle East
Prison labor	The contracting out of prison labor or forcing of prisoners to work for profit-making enterprises.	Australia, Austria, China, Cote d'Ivoire, France, Germany, New Zealand, Madagascar, Malaysia, United States
Compulsory work	When people are required by law to work on public construction projects such as roads and bridges.	Cambodia, the Central African Republic, Kenya, Burma (also known as Myanmar), Sierra Leone, Swaziland, Tanzania, Vietnam
Military labor	When civilians are forced to do work for government authorities or the military.	Burma (also known as Myanmar)

IX. Population and Demographics

Population Implosion
Worries a Graying Europe

Michael Specter

STOCKHOLM, SWEDEN—Mia Hulton is a true woman of the late 20th century. Soft-spoken, well-educated and thoughtful, she sings Renaissance music in a choral group, lives quietly with the man she loves and works like a demon seven days a week.

At 33, she is in full pursuit of an academic career. And despite the fact that she lives in Sweden—which provides more support for women who want families than any other country—Ms. Hulton doesn't see how she can possibly make room in her life for babies. Someday maybe, but certainly not soon.

"There are times when I think perhaps I will be missing something important if I don't have a child," she said slowly, trying to put her complicated desires into simple words. "But today women finally have so many chances to have the life they want. To travel and work and learn. It's exciting and demanding. I just find it hard to see where the children would fit in."

Ms. Hulton would never consider herself a radical, but she has become a cadre in one of the fundamental social revolutions of the century.

Driven largely by prosperity and freedom, millions of women throughout the developed world are having fewer children than ever before. They stay in school longer, put more emphasis on work and marry later. As a result, birth rates in many countries are now in a rapid, sustained decline.

Never before—except in times of plague, war and deep economic depression—have birth rates fallen so low, for so long.

What was once regarded universally as a cherished goal—incredibly low birth rates—have in the industrial world at least suddenly become a cause for alarm. With life expectancy rising at the same time that fertility drops, most developed countries may soon find themselves with lopsided societies that will be nearly impossible to sustain: a large number of elderly and not enough young people working to support them. The change will affect every program—from health care and education to pension plans and military spending—that requires public funds.

Source: Michael Specter, "Population Implosion Worries a Graying Europe," *The New York Times,* July 14, 1998, p. 1, 6. (map).

Falling Fertility Change in fertility rates from 1975 to 1995.

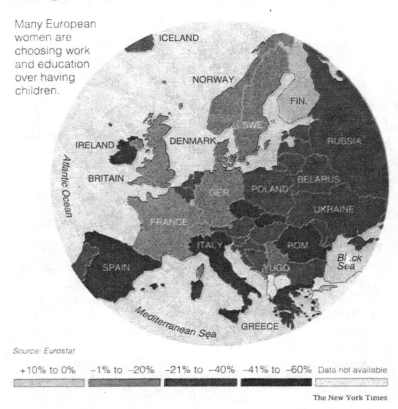

Many European women are choosing work and education over having children.

Source: Eurostat

+10% to 0%   –1% to –20%   –21% to –40%   –41% to –60%   Data not available

The New York Times

There is no longer a single country in Europe where people are having enough children to replace themselves when they die. Italy recently became the first nation in history where there are more people over the age of 60 than there are under the age of 20. This year Germany, Greece and Spain will probably all cross the same eerie divide.

"You can look at this in a philosophical way," said Jean-Claude Chesnais, director of research at France's National Institute for the Study of Demography. No country has worried more, or more publicly, about the implications of a low birth rate. Like so many other European nations, uneasy officials there see in current trends a world where populations of color—from Africa, India, Asia—are still growing, while their own is struggling to keep from shrinking.

"Europe is old and rigid," Chesnais said. "So it is fading. You can see that as the natural cycle of civilization, perhaps something inevitable. And in many ways, low population growth is wonderful. Certainly to control fertility in China, Bangladesh, much of Africa—that is an absolute triumph. Yet we must look beyond simple numbers. And here I think Europe may be in the vanguard of a very profound trend. Because you cannot have a successful world without children in it."

THE OUTLOOK: Worldwide Drop Confounds Experts

The effects of the shift will resonate far beyond Europe. Last year Japan's fertility rate—the number of children born to the average woman in a lifetime—fell to 1.39, the lowest level it has ever reached. In the United States, where a large pool of new immigrants helps keep the birth rate higher than in any other prosperous country, the figure is still slightly below an average of 2.1 children per woman—the magic number needed to keep the population from starting to shrink.

Even in the developing world, where overcrowding remains a major cause of desperation and disease, the pace of growth has slowed almost everywhere. Since 1965, according to United Nations population data, the birth rate in the Third World has been cut in half—from 6 children per woman to 3. In the last decade alone, for example, the figure in Bangladesh has fallen from 6.2 children per woman to 3.4. That's a bigger drop than in the previous two centuries.

Little more than 25 years have passed since a famous set of computer studies sponsored by the Club of Rome, the global think tank, showed that population pressures would devastate the world by the mid-1990s.

Nothing of the kind has come to pass. The authors of that dire forecast could not have foreseen 30 years ago that women in countries like Italy would by now be producing an average of fewer than 1.2 children, the lowest figure ever recorded among humans. Or that the Berlin Wall would disappear, creating economic uncertainties that have frozen the birth rate from the Black Forest to Vladivostok.

In a world where women work more than ever before and contraception remains readily available, it is hard to find somebody who believes that someday soon large families will make a comeback.

"I'm thinking of having children in the future, perhaps two," said Roberta Lenzi, 27, who is single and studies political science in Bologna, Italy, the city with the lowest birthrate in the world.

"I'm an only child and if I could, I'd have more than one child. But most couples I know wait until their 30s to have children. People want to have their own life, they want to have a successful career. When you see life in these terms, children are an impediment. At most you'll have one, more are rare."

There has long been an assumption that low birth rates were better than high birth rates. Fewer people put less strain on the resources of the planet. And anyway, as a country becomes richer its people always have fewer children. If more people are needed, immigration can be a solution—and in many places, specialists now think it's the only one left. But Europe, unlike the United States, has been resistant to immigration.

"What is happening now has simply never happened before in the history of the world," said Nicholas Eberstadt, a demographer based at the American Enterprise Institute in Washington. "This is terra incognita. If these trends continue, in a generation or two there may be countries where most people's only blood relatives will be their parents."

"Would it be a lonelier and sadder world?" he continued. "Yes, I think it would. But that might simply be the limits of my own imagination. Frankly, it's just impossible to really conceive of what this world will be like in 50 years. But when you come to the end of one era it's almost always impossible to see your way into the next."

THE WATERSHED: Birth Incentives No Longer Work

Perhaps no country has tried harder to change the future than Sweden.

Decades ago, with its birth rate dwindling, Sweden decided to support family life with a public generosity found nowhere else. Couples who both work and have small children enjoy cash payments, tax incentives and job leaves combined with incredible flexibility to work part time for as many as eight years after a child's birth.

Sweden spends 10 times as much as Italy or Spain on programs intended to support families. It spends nearly three times as much per person on such programs as the United States. So there should be no surprise that Sweden, despite its wealth, had the highest birth rate in Europe by 1991.

With 10 million mostly middle-class people, Sweden may have little in common with any other. But its experience clearly suggested that if countries wanted more babies they would have to pay for them, through tax incentives, parental leave programs and family support. At least that's what nearly all the experts thought it showed.

"We were a model for the world," said Marten Lagergren, under secretary in the Ministry of Social Health and Welfare, and the man responsible for figuring out what is happening with Sweden's birth rate. "They all came to examine us. People thought we had some secret. Unfortunately, it seems that we do not."

Sometime after 1990, the bottom dropped out of Sweden's baby boom. Between then and 1995, the birth rate fell sharply, from 2.12 to 1.6. Most people blamed the economy, which had turned sour and forced politicians to trim—so slightly—the country's benefit program. It is normal for people to put off having children when the future looks doubtful, so the change made sense.

But then, the economy got better and the birth rate fell faster and farther than ever. By March of this year the figure for Sweden was almost the same as that in Japan—1.42. And though it's too soon to say, officials here think it might be falling still.

"Nobody on earth can tell you what is going on here," said Mac Murray, a philosopher trained in statistics who is in charge of strategic planning for the nation's school system. "Sometimes I think it must be just a blip—we've had them before—and everything will turn out the way we expect it to. But I guess I don't really believe that. I believe we are seeing a fundamental shift in human behavior. We have lived for 200 years on the idea of progress. That the future will be better than the past. It's a universal belief—not just in our little country.

"But I think those days have ended now. I have no data to support my views. But young people now seem to have a sense that living for today is about the best they can do."

It is Murray's job to plan for the material implications of these changes. But it's not going to be easy. Sweden has 6,000 schools serving children from the ages of 6 to 18. This year there are more than 130,000 8-year-olds in the system—1990 was a boom year for births. They need classrooms and teachers and all the support that goes with them.

But in just three years the 8-year-old population will shrink drastically, to 75,000. "So what are we doing?" Murray asked rhetorically. "We are recruiting more teachers now than ever before and giving them raises that nobody else can hope to have. Have you ever tried to tell a politician to plan for something that's 20 years away?" It is a problem felt across Europe as the elderly supplant the young.

There used to be many more young people than old people in the world. Right now there are roughly equal numbers. But by 2050, according to data supplied by the European Union, there will be nearly twice as many old people as young people. Yet most governments' programs still encourage people to retire early.

"The whole system is backward," said Massimo Livi-Bacci, professor of demography at the University of Florence. "In Italy we are paying people to retire at an earlier age than ever before even though we know they are now going to live longer than ever before. We have the best pension system in Europe and the worst system for family support. Rich old people supported by the labor of poor young people. No wonder nobody wants to have a family."

THE PERCEPTION: The Good Life Is Top Priority

Ask dozens of people, and few of them even realize that the birth rate is dropping all across Europe. When they do think about it, most people see it as somebody else's problem.

"I am supposed to have an extra child to help the system?" said Jan Delaror, a recently married marketing expert for Erikkson AB, the Swedish telephone giant. Delaror says he has no children but expects to "if and when it makes sense, not because the government thinks it's a good idea."

Delaror was standing in the middle of the Sture Gallery, one of Stockholm's many exclusive malls. He was trying to decide whether to buy a box of Havana cigars, for several hundred dollars, or to wait until he traveled to London in a few weeks.

"It's not as easy to have children these days as it once was," he said, voicing a commonly held belief. "The sacrifices are not always acceptable."

In surveys, young couples almost always report that they want two children—but many also mention the future and their concerns for maintaining a good life. It doesn't seem to matter that materially at least—people in the developed world live better now than they ever have. There is a perception—shared even in vastly different countries like Sweden and Italy—that what was possible for previous generations is not possible for this one.

"I'd like to have a child but my work situation is unstable," said Francesca Casotti, 29, a lawyer in Rome who has been married nine months. "I'm at the office all day and it is difficult to think about having a child. People my age want their freedom. They see children as a burden, as an inconvenience. I'd like to have a stable job and I'd like to have more than one child. But there is the economic question."

"Children cost more than they used to," she continued. "Today you have to bring them to the pool and you need to get a nanny, and they have to learn a foreign language. Children have more needs. Parents just didn't think of all these things before."

Not everyone agrees, of course, that the need for pool memberships or foreign language tuition is responsible for such a remarkable drop in birth rates.

"We have become so selfish, so greedy," said Ninni Lundblad, 31, a biologist who works in Stockholm. Ms. Lundblad has no children but hopes that will soon change.

"Did your parents sit down with a spreadsheet and figure out whether they could afford to have two or three children?" she said, her bright eyes widening at the absurdity of her own statement. "No, of course not. Did this ever happen before anywhere? No, of course not. We live in the richest place and at the best time, and everyone is worrying whether they can afford to take their next vacation or buy a boat. It's kind of sickening, really."

THE EPICENTER: Bologna Focuses Help on Elderly

If there were a ground zero in the epidemic of low fertility it would have to be in the northern Italian city of Bologna, where women give birth to an average of fewer than one child (in 1997, the number was 0.8). The city has more highly educated women than any other in the country. Incomes average more than $16,500 a year. Produce is rich and cheap, food is wonderful and living is generally easy.

The local population has dropped steadily for two decades, but 1,500 people turn 75 every year. Fewer children and more elderly mean a greater need for health care programs and specialized housing and transportation. But that does nothing to help or encourage young couples to have families.

This year the budgets for retirees and children are roughly the same in Bologna, a city of 375,000. Next year 5 percent will be shifted from the young to the old. And that will happen every year for the next decade as the city becomes filled with elderly and starved for children.

How did Italy, a largely Roman Catholic country that has always been seen as the stereotypical land of big, close-knit families, become the place with the world's lowest level of fertility?

"Prosperity has strangled us," said Dr. Pierpaolo Donati, professor of sociology at the University of Bologna and a leading Catholic intellectual. "Comfort is now the only thing anybody believes in," he said. "The ethic of sacrifice for a family—one of the basic ideas of human societies—has become a historical notion. It is astonishing."

Where Donati sees selfishness, however, others see women who have been placed under monumental stress. To some minds, the women of Italy—and of other southern European countries like Spain and Portugal—have the worst of both worlds. They now work for a living in record numbers, but tremendous obstacles remain for balancing work and family life.

Far more than in places like Sweden, France, or even the United States, the Italian man still seeks a wife who will make his dinner every night and who takes complete charge of the family. Women have responded by realizing that with only 24 hours in each day something has to give. Children seem to have become that something.

Whatever the reasons, the changes, and what they will mean, are difficult to ignore. In 20 years, at present birth rates, for every child under the age of 5 in Bologna there will be 25 people over the age of 50—and 10 of them will be older than 80.

"It is impossible to have a human society built like this," Donati said. "Something simply has to change."

Walter Vitali agrees. The mayor of the longtime leftish town—its nickname Red Bologna still stands—Vitali is a former Communist who likes to invoke the name of the city's cardinal when talking about population figures.

"The cardinal says our lack of interest in families symbolizes our loss of faith in ourselves," he said. "It's sort of hard to disagree with that. Let's face it, something is going on here that is very troubling."

But exactly how troubling is it? And for whom? The birth rate is dropping, but there are still plenty of people on the earth. As a result, the world's total population is still growing rapidly, and that won't stop for at least another generation—when more than two thirds of all countries are at or below the replacement level. The fertility rate of Palestinians in the Gaza Strip, where population growth is viewed as a weapon of war against Israel, has soared to 8.8 children per woman. The 45 nations of East, West and Middle Africa average more than six births per woman.

Right now, the populations of Europe (including Russia) and Africa are about the same. If trends continue as they are now, by 2050 Africans will outnumber Europeans three to one. Between now and then, India will add more people to its labor force than currently live in all of Europe.

And in that same year, half of all residents of Italy will be over the age of 50. Half of the residents of Iraq will be under 25.

"The truth is there doesn't have to be a demographic catastrophe," said Lalla Golfarelli, the head of family planning in Bologna. "Look at a map. Look at Europe on that map. We are all only two to four hours away by boat or plane from many countries with many people. Open the gates. Immigration can solve this problem. If people would just open their minds they would realize there are enough people on this earth to go around."

In other words, either the developed world adapts—and that probably means large waves of immigration—or it gets pushed aside.

"The world is hardly about to disappear," said Jan Hoem, head of the demographics faculty at the University of Stockholm. "It's just becoming a very different place."

U.S. Population Has Biggest 10-Year Rise Ever

Eric Schmitt

The nation's population increased by more people in the 1990's than any other 10-year period in United States history, surpassing the growth between 1950 and 1960 at the peak of the baby boom, the Census Bureau reported today.

Even as many other industrial countries are suffering declining populations because of shrinking birth rates, the United States swelled by 32.7 million people in the last decade, to 281.4 million, the result of waves of young immigrants with families and a steady birth rate that outpaced deaths. The increase, which was greater than the country's population total during the Civil War, easily surpassed the previous record growth of 28 million in the 1950's.

The growth in the 1990's was notable for not only its size, but also its breadth. For the first time in the 20th century, the population of all 50 states increased, ranging from a half-percent rise in North Dakota to 66 percent in Nevada. Eighty percent of the nation's 3,141 counties and equivalent areas grew, compared with 55 percent in the 1980's.

Among the intriguing trends emerging from the 2000 head count was the convergence of two major demographic patterns. Sprawl from metropolitan areas accelerated through the 1990's to where it spilled into once rural areas, stemming decades-long population declines in many nonmetropolitan counties.

The two fastest-growing nonmetropolitan counties in the 1990's were both in Colorado: Elbert County, a farming area in the plains near Denver; and Park County, a cattle-grazing region nestled in the Rockies. Both counties more than doubled in size between 1990 and 2000.

"A lot of growth in nonmetropolitan areas in the last decade has come in counties that adjoin metropolitan areas, and is changing the character of those counties," said Calvin L. Beale, a senior demographer at the Agriculture Department who has analyzed population shifts in nonmetropolitan counties.

The nation grew faster and in more corners of the country than the Census Bureau projected. The number of people in metropolitan areas grew by 14 percent in the last

Source: Eric Schmitt, "U.S. Population Has Biggest 10-Year Rise Ever" (from series on U.S. census and population), *The New York Times*, April 3, 2001, p. A10 (map).

decade, narrowly exceeding nonmetropolitan counties, which grew by 10 percent. Four of five Americans still live in cities or suburbs.

Eight of the 10 largest cities gained population in the 1990's, with only Philadelphia and Detroit shrinking. New York, Los Angeles and Chicago remained the top three metropolises. But in a sign of the Sunbelt's pull on Americans and immigrants, Houston, Phoenix and San Diego were three of the next four largest cities. Despite its population loss, Philadelphia still ranks fifth, behind Houston and ahead of Phoenix.

As a result, the population center of the country, as calculated by the Census Bureau, moved to Edgar Springs, Mo., nearly 40 miles southwest of DeSoto, Mo., the population midpoint 10 years ago. The population center is determined as the place where an imaginary, flat, weightless map of the country would balance perfectly if all 281.4 million Americans were of identical weight.

The West grew by 19.7 percent and the South by 17.3 percent, compared with only 7.9 percent in the Midwest and 5.5 percent in the Northeast. These patterns revived states like Wyoming and Colorado that lost people in the 1980's with the downturn in the mining and energy industries.

Large swaths of the rural heartland continued to hollow out, from the Dakotas to western Texas, but the number of counties that dropped by 10 percent or more in some cases was far fewer than in the 1980's.

Moreover, several other Midwestern states experienced their fastest growth in decades. Missouri's 9 percent increase was the state's largest decade-to-decade lift since the period from 1890 to 1900. The Ozarks have attracted retirees and families moving out of cities who seek a better quality of life, Mr. Beale said.

The nation's middle-sized cities, ranging from 250,000 to slightly fewer than 2 million people, outpaced growth for the smallest and very largest cities. Again, much of this growth centered in the West, with Californians, in particular, heading not just to Phoenix and Denver but also Coeur d'Alene, Idaho, and western Colorado, said Marc J. Perry, a Census Bureau demographer.

John Long, chief of the Census Bureau's population division, said today that early data showed younger, non-Hispanic whites moving to urban areas, many seeking jobs and homes in the cities.

One prominent expert, Hugh B. Price, president of the Urban League, said that the reduction in city crime, coupled with quality housing and cultural diversity, had drawn many young white professionals back to urban settings that reminded them of their college years.

Demographics and Race
by Charts and Maps

The New York Times

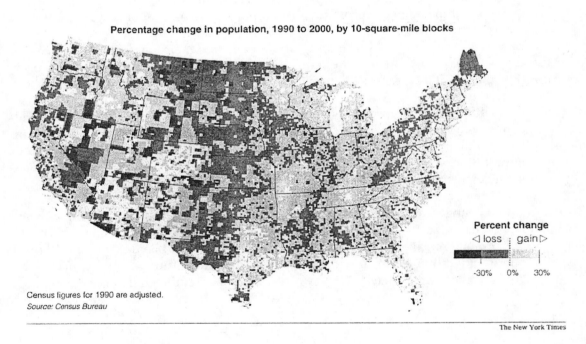

Percentage change in population, 1990 to 2000, by 10-square-mile blocks

Percent change

◁ loss ⋮ gain ▷

-30%   0%   30%

Census figures for 1990 are adjusted.
Source: Census Bureau

Source: The New York Times & U.S. Census on Population 2000, *Choosing the Mixed-Race Option*, March 8, 2001.

The New York Times
ON THE WEB

Choosing the Mixed-Race Option

The 2000 census was the first to give respondents a chance to
identify themselves as belonging to more than one racial category.
Younger blacks were more likely than older blacks to identify
themselves this way.

	IDENTIFYING THEMSELVES AS ...			
	BLACK AND ONE OR MORE OTHER RACES	BLACK ONLY	DIFFERENCE	DIFFERENCE AS A PERCENTAGE OF THE TOTAL
ALL AGES	36,419,434	34,658,190	1,761,244	4.8%
17 AND YOUNGER	11,845,257	10,885,696	959,561	8.1%
18 TO 29	6,656,205	6,353,405	302,800	4.6
30 TO 49	10,753,666	10,420,572	333,094	3.1
50 AND OLDER	7,164,306	6,998,517	165,789	2.3

Source: Census Bureau

The New York Times

A New Look at Race in America

Back to map

	1990 CENSUS	2000 CENSUS	
		NUMBER CHOOSING JUST ONE RACE, OR TOTAL	NUMBER CHOOSING THIS RACE WITH OTHER RACE(S)
CALIFORNIA	30,888,075	33,871,648	
Non-Hispanic			
White	17,280,076	15,816,790	721,701
Black	2,340,857	2,181,926	188,441
Asian or Pacific Islander	2,800,406	3,752,596	466,406
American Indian or Alaska Native	189,155	178,984	204,213
Other	57,249	71,681	296,487
Multiracial (not an option in 1990)		903,115	
Hispanic (may be of any race)	8,220,332	10,966,556	

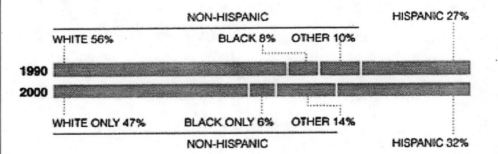

NON-HISPANIC — WHITE 56% — BLACK 8% — OTHER 10% — HISPANIC 27%

1990

2000

WHITE ONLY 47% — BLACK ONLY 6% — OTHER 14% — HISPANIC 32%

NON-HISPANIC

In the bar graphs for 2000, the "Other" category includes all but the two largest non-Hispanic racial categories for a given state.

Note: Percentages may not add to 100 because of rounding.

Source: Census Bureau

The New York Times

A New Look at Race in America

Back to map

	1990 CENSUS	2000 CENSUS	
		NUMBER CHOOSING JUST ONE RACE, OR TOTAL	NUMBER CHOOSING THIS RACE WITH OTHER RACE(S)
TEXAS	17,550,747	20,851,820	
Non-Hispanic			
White	10,522,862	10,933,313	188,004
Black	2,074,193	2,364,255	65,711
Asian or Pacific Islander	313,460	565,202	78,885
American Indian or Alaska Native	54,148	68,859	75,230
Other	22,582	19,958	68,359
Multiracial (not an option in 1990)		230,567	
Hispanic (may be of any race)	4,563,502	6,669,666	

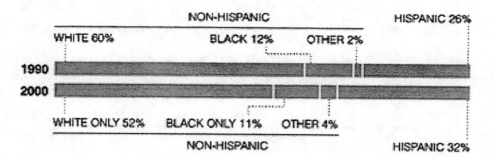

Note: Percentages may not add to 100 because of rounding.

Source: Census Bureau

The New York Times

A New Look at Race in America

 Back to map

	1990 CENSUS	2000 CENSUS	
		NUMBER CHOOSING JUST ONE RACE, OR TOTAL	NUMBER CHOOSING THIS RACE WITH OTHER RACE(S)
OREGON	2,898,058	3,421,399	
Non-Hispanic			
White	2,619,113	2,857,616	74,856
Black	49,200	53,325	14,859
Asian or Pacific Islander	69,744	107,731	31,410
American Indian or Alaska Native	37,029	40,130	35,735
Other	1,778	4,550	14,930
Multiracial (not an option in 1990)		82,733	
Hispanic (may be of any race)	121,194	275,314	

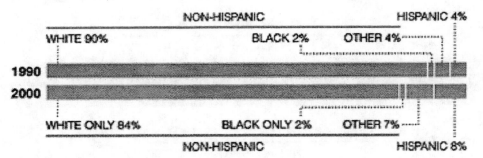

NON-HISPANIC — HISPANIC 4%
WHITE 90% — BLACK 2% — OTHER 4%
1990
2000
WHITE ONLY 84% — BLACK ONLY 2% — OTHER 7%
NON-HISPANIC — HISPANIC 8%

Note: Percentages may not add to 100 because of rounding.

Source: Census Bureau

The New York Times

A New Look at Race in America

 Back to map

	1990 CENSUS	2000 CENSUS	
		NUMBER CHOOSING JUST ONE RACE, OR TOTAL	NUMBER CHOOSING THIS RACE WITH OTHER RACE(S)
NEW YORK	18,304,414	18,976,457	
Non-Hispanic			
White	12,483,919	11,760,981	219,696
Black	2,730,427	2,812,623	150,239
Asian or Pacific Islander	725,074	1,041,156	126,070
American Indian or Alaska Native	51,506	52,499	66,588
Other	29,751	75,499	191,748
Multiracial (not an option in 1990)		366,116	
Hispanic (may be of any race)	2,283,737	2,867,583	

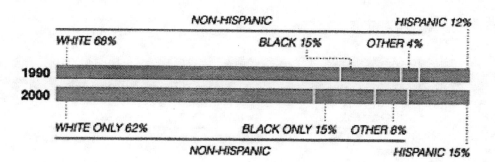

NON-HISPANIC

WHITE 68%   BLACK 15%   OTHER 4%   HISPANIC 12%

1990

2000

WHITE ONLY 62%   BLACK ONLY 15%   OTHER 8%

NON-HISPANIC   HISPANIC 15%

In the bar graphs for 2000, the "Other" category includes all but the two largest non-Hispanic racial categories for a given state.

Note: Percentages may not add to 100 because of rounding.

Source: Census Bureau

The New York Times

A New Look at Race in America

 Back to map

	1990 CENSUS	2000 CENSUS	
		NUMBER CHOOSING JUST ONE RACE, OR TOTAL	NUMBER CHOOSING THIS RACE WITH OTHER RACE(S)
FLORIDA	13,277,708	15,982,378	
Non-Hispanic			
White	9,666,104	10,458,509	151,247
Black	1,767,506	2,264,268	110,954
Asian or Pacific Islander	150,432	268,580	71,635
American Indian or Alaska Native	34,003	42,358	54,587
Other	8,582	28,994	99,153
Multiracial (not an option in 1990)		236,954	
Hispanic (may be of any race)	1,651,081	2,682,715	

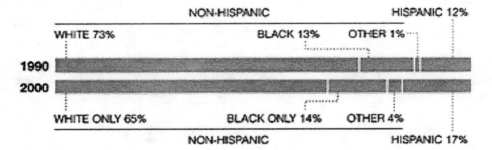

NON-HISPANIC HISPANIC 12%

WHITE 73% BLACK 13% OTHER 1%

1990

2000

WHITE ONLY 65% BLACK ONLY 14% OTHER 4%

NON-HISPANIC HISPANIC 17%

In the bar graphs for 2000, the "Other" category includes all but the two largest non-Hispanic racial categories for a given state.

Note: Percentages may not add to 100 because of rounding.

Source: Census Bureau

The New York Times

Population and Demographics • 221

A New Look at Race in America

 Back to map

	1990 CENSUS	2000 CENSUS	
		NUMBER CHOOSING JUST ONE RACE, OR TOTAL	NUMBER CHOOSING THIS RACE WITH OTHER RACE(S)
SOUTH CAROLINA	3,589,808	4,012,012	
Non-Hispanic			
White	2,457,238	2,652,291	26,945
Black	1,069,159	1,178,486	14,106
Asian or Pacific Islander	22,037	36,838	9,890
American Indian or Alaska Native	8,282	12,765	12,715
Other	869	3,266	6,062
Multiracial (not an option in 1990)		33,290	
Hispanic (may be of any race)	32,223	95,076	

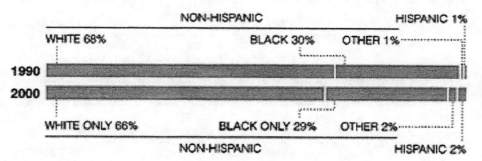

Note: Percentages may not add to 100 because of rounding.

Source: Census Bureau

The New York Times

A New Look at Race in America

Back
to map

	1990 CENSUS	2000 CENSUS NUMBER CHOOSING JUST ONE RACE, OR TOTAL	NUMBER CHOOSING THIS RACE WITH OTHER RACE(S)
MASSACHUSETTS	6,039,315	6,349,097	
Non-Hispanic			
White	5,278,697	5,198,359	78,719
Black	286,149	318,329	44,099
Asian or Pacific Islander	140,223	238,492	29,535
American Indian or Alaska Native	10,549	11,264	19,839
Other	23,120	43,586	55,087
Multiracial (not an option in 1990)		110,338	
Hispanic (may be of any race)	300,577	428,729	

NON-HISPANIC   HISPANIC 5%

WHITE 87%   BLACK 5%   OTHER 3%

1990

2000

WHITE ONLY 82%   BLACK ONLY 5%   OTHER 6%

NON-HISPANIC   HISPANIC 7%

In the bar graphs for 2000, the "Other" category includes all but the two largest non-Hispanic racial categories for a given state.

Note: Percentages may not add to 100 because of rounding.

Source: Census Bureau

The New York Times

A New Look at Race in America

Back to map

	1990 CENSUS	2000 CENSUS NUMBER CHOOSING JUST ONE RACE, OR TOTAL	NUMBER CHOOSING THIS RACE WITH OTHER RACE(S)
ILLINOIS	11,592,305	12,419,293	
Non-Hispanic			
White	8,614,847	8,424,140	127,729
Black	1,751,201	1,856,152	50,561
Asian or Pacific Islander	281,193	423,032	50,807
American Indian or Alaska Native	18,439	18,232	34,591
Other	8,660	13,479	53,445
Multiracial (not an option in 1990)		153,996	
Hispanic (may be of any race)	917,965	1,530,262	

NON-HISPANIC
WHITE 74%   BLACK 15%   OTHER 3%   HISPANIC 8%

1990

2000

WHITE ONLY 68%   BLACK ONLY 15%   OTHER 5%
NON-HISPANIC   HISPANIC 12%

Note: Percentages may not add to 100 because of rounding.

Source: Census Bureau

The New York Times

The New York Times
ON THE WEB

A Surge in Hispanic Population in Latest Census

Early data from the 2000 Census shows that the Hispanic population in the United States has grown by 61 percent since 1990 and Hispanics are now nearly even with blacks as the largest minority group.

The Hispanic population grew much faster than that of blacks ...

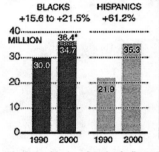

BLACKS
+15.6 to +21.5%

HISPANICS
+61.2%

... with the number of Hispanic men and women ages 30 to 49 growing the fastest.

AGE	MEN	WOMEN	TOTAL	MEN	WOMEN	TOTAL	PERCENTAGE CHANGE, 1990–2000
17 and younger	3.9	3.7	7.6	6.3	6.0	12.3	61.6%
18 to 29	2.9	2.5	5.3	4.4	3.7	8.1	52.1
30 to 49	3.0	2.9	5.9	5.2	4.8	10.0	68.9
50 and older	1.3	1.6	3.0	2.2	2.6	4.8	61.3
		1990			2000		

*Includes blacks who also indicated at least one other race.

Hispanics can be of any race.

Source: Census Bureau; Queens College Department of Sociology (1990 Hispanic count and age breakdown)

The New York Times

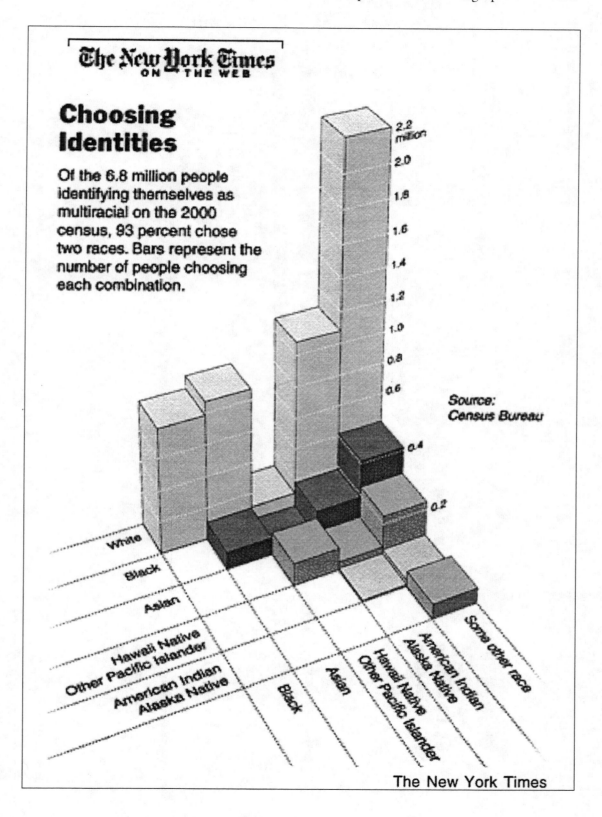

The New York Times
ON THE WEB

Choosing Identities

Of the 6.8 million people identifying themselves as multiracial on the 2000 census, 93 percent chose two races. Bars represent the number of people choosing each combination.

Source:
Census Bureau

The New York Times

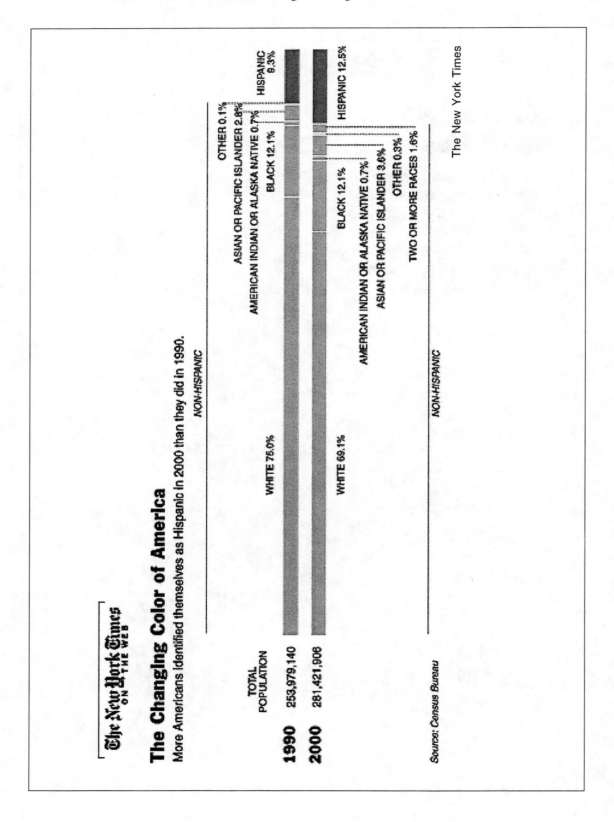

The New York Times on the WEB

The Changing Color of America

More Americans identified themselves as Hispanic in 2000 than they did in 1990.

	TOTAL POPULATION
1990	253,979,140
2000	281,421,908

NON-HISPANIC

1990
WHITE 76.0%
BLACK 12.1%
AMERICAN INDIAN OR ALASKA NATIVE 0.7%
ASIAN OR PACIFIC ISLANDER 2.9%
OTHER 0.1%
HISPANIC 9.3%

2000
WHITE 69.1%
BLACK 12.1%
AMERICAN INDIAN OR ALASKA NATIVE 0.7%
ASIAN OR PACIFIC ISLANDER 3.6%
OTHER 0.3%
TWO OR MORE RACES 1.6%
HISPANIC 12.5%

NON-HISPANIC

Source: Census Bureau

The New York Times

The New York Times
ON THE WEB

Tracking Sprawl

	URBAN	SUBURBAN	RURAL
PEOPLE PER SQ. MILE:	3,200 or more	320 to 3,200	Less than 320
PEOPLE PER ACRE:	About 5	About 1 to 5	About 1

1980

2000

Source: Census Bureau (data analyzed by The New York Times)
http://www.nytimes.com/images/2001/03/09/nyregion/010309_met_CENSA1.html

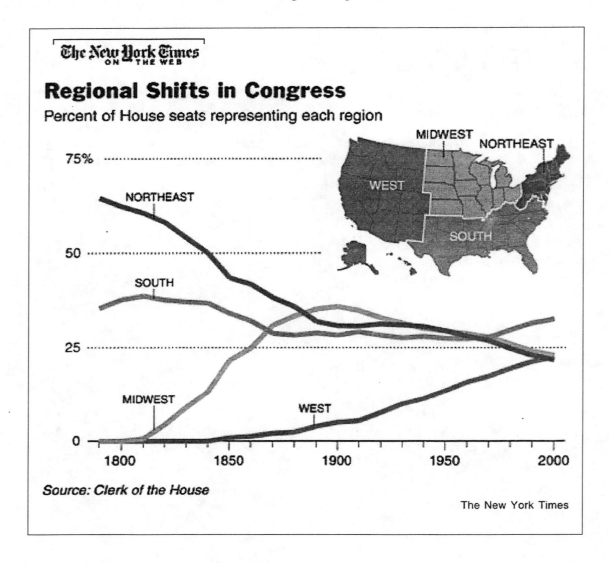

The New York Times
ON THE WEB

Regional Shifts in Congress

Percent of House seats representing each region

Source: Clerk of the House

The New York Times

The New York Times
ON THE WEB

The Shape Of America's Population

1800
POP. 5,096,908

1850
POP. 23,100,278

1900
POP. 74,685,943

1950
POP. 150,697,361

2000
POP. 281,421,906

The United States has 55 times more people today than it did in 1800. In these maps, called cartograms, each state is sized according to its number of residents as counted by the Census Bureau. Cartograms show the relationship between population and geography. States are included only after they gained statehood.

ANDREW PHILLIPS

Washington D.C. is too small to show.

Click on a year to see a Census portrait of the nation from that period.

VT. N.H.
CONN. MASS.
N.Y. R.I.
PA. N.J.
DEL.
KY. VA. MD.
TENN. N.C.
S.C.
GA.

▓ **Each square represents 100,000 residents**

Source: U.S. Census Bureau

The New York Times on the Web

Page: 1

The New York Times
ON THE WEB

The Shape Of America's Population

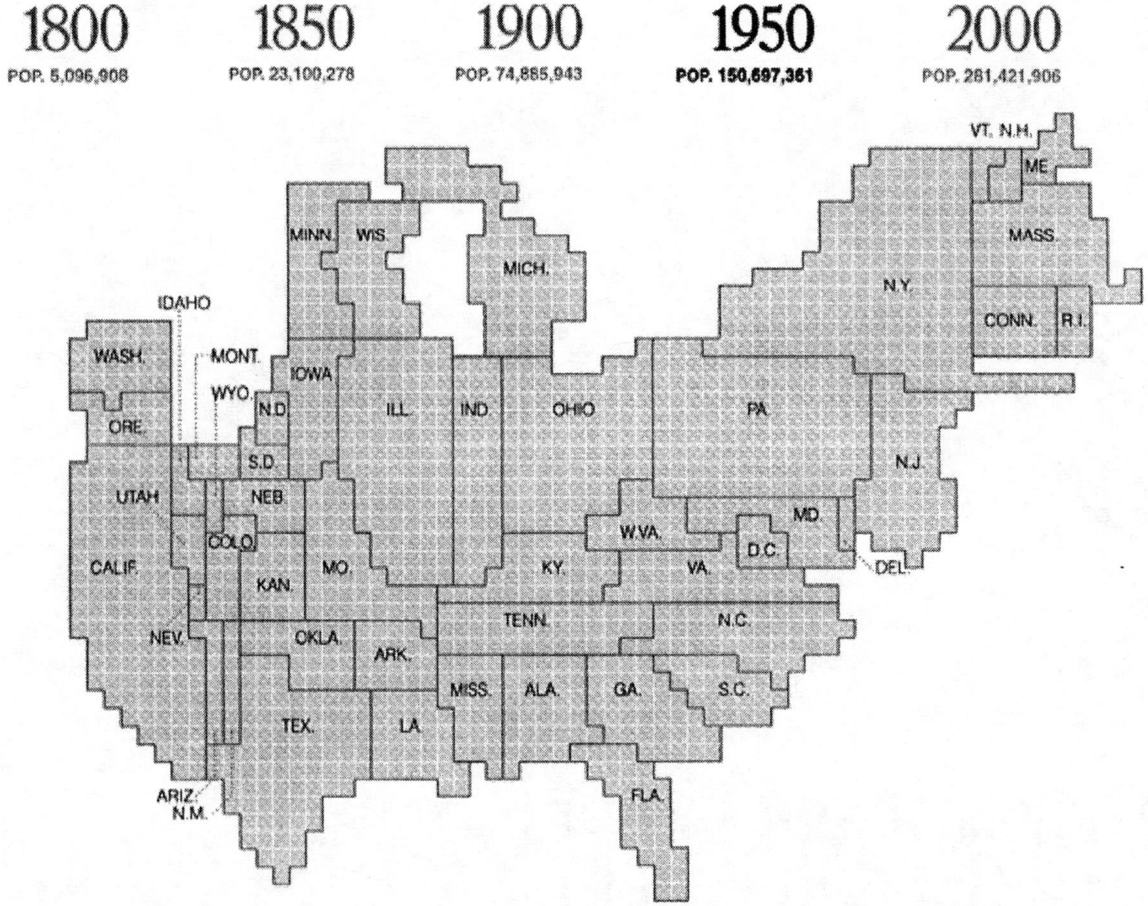

1800 POP. 5,096,968

1850 POP. 23,100,278

1900 POP. 74,865,943

1950 POP. 150,697,361

2000 POP. 281,421,906

Each square represents 100,000 residents

WASH. ORE. IDAHO MONT. WYO. N.D. S.D. NEB. MINN. WIS. MICH. ME VT, N.H. MASS. CONN. R.I. N.Y. PA. N.J. MD. D.C. DEL. UTAH NEV. CALIF. COLO. KAN. OKLA. TEX. ARIZ. N.M. MO. IOWA ILL. IND. OHIO W.VA. VA. KY. TENN. N.C. S.C. ARK. LA. MISS. ALA. GA. FLA.

The New York Times
ON THE WEB

The Shape Of America's Population

Change 1990 to 2000

INCREASE
- More than 30%
- 20 – 30%
- 10 – 20%
- 0 – 10%

☐ DECREASE

Nevada grew the most: 66.3%

Washington, D.C., lost residents, shrinking 5.7%

1800 POP. 5,096,908

1850 POP. 23,100,278

1900 POP. 74,885,943

1950 POP. 150,697,361

2000 POP. 281,421,906

ME
VT
N.H.
MASS.
R.I.
CONN.
N.Y.
N.J.
PA.
DEL.
MD.
D.C.
W.VA.
VA.
MICH.
OHIO
IND.
ILL.
KY.
TENN.
SC
ALA.
MISS.
WIS.
MINN.
IOWA
MO.
ARK.
LA.
N.D.
S.D.
NEB.
KAN.
OKLA.
MONT.
WYO.
COLO.
UTAH
NEV.
ARIZ.
CALIF.

ALASKA

X. Resource Tools in Sociology

Bookmarks, Current iSociology

85 Annotated Web Sites on the Internet

Resource Tools in the Social Sciences

General Statistical Sources—United States and Canada
The following is a selective guide to resources, both print and on the internet, for locating statistics about the United States and Canada.
http://www.columbia.edu/cu/libraries/indiv/dsc/stats/us.html

The Scout Report for Social Sciences—October 19, 1999
Each biweekly issue offers a selective collection of Internet resources covering topics in the field that have been chosen by librarians and content specialists in the given area of study. Copyright, University of Wisconsin Board of Regents, 1994–1999.
http://scout.cs.wisc.edu/report/socsci/current/index.html

Fedstats: Fast Facts
More than 70 agencies in the United States Federal Government produce statistics of interest to the public.
http://www.fedstats.gov/

Eitzen: In Conflict and Order 8/e
37 transparencies that illustrate concepts to be taught in sociology. The material covers wide ranges of various concepts.
http://www.abacon.com/eitzen2/trans.html

Software Gallery (Microsociology software)
A site for Macintosh users only from which you can download a number of programs (in "BinHex4 encoded self-expanding archives (.sea)" format). Hypercard is needed to view: games, simulations, utilities, animation, tutorials in sociology.
http://www.soc.umn.edu/~spitzer/softwaregallery.html

Source: "Bookmarks, Current iSociology: 85 Annotated Web Sites on the Internet"

W3C Technology & Society Domain

The explosive growth of technology has forced the entire Web community to look at society's ethical and legal issues from a new international perspective. The Society seeks to understand these issues in light of new technology-w3c.
http://www.w3.org/TandS/

Most Frequently Requested Dat Series

Up-to-date data on the state of the economy. T-bill rates, discount rates, price of crude oil, mortgages, house sales starts, electric poser use, GSP, GDP, etc.
http://www.economagic.com/popular.htm

ICPSR Homepage {Inst. for Social Research}

Access to the world's largest archive of computerized social science data.
http://www.icpsr.umich.edu/

Economics—The Dismal Scientist Thoughts: economic statistics, economic data, economic analysis

Guide to resources, both print and the internet, for locating statistics about the United States and Canada. Facts and figures about metro and state economies. Articles on contemporary issues. Historical & economic data shown on this site.
http://www.dismal.com/toolbox/sitemap.asp

Data Resources

Data Resources for Sociologists, provided by the American Sociological Association.
http://www.asanet.org/data.htm

Introducing Sociology

What Is Sociology?

The American Sociological Association gives a definition of the field of study.
http://www.asanet.org/public/what.html

SocioSite: SOCIOLOGISTS

A grid that lists and biographs 57 major sociological thinkers. Notation is made of a major work by each of these thinkers.
http://www.pscw.uva.nl/sociosite/TOPICS/Sociologists.html#REF

Quotes.html {sociosite}

Words to Remember: Quotes—They are old and new, familiar and obscure, humorous and pompous, ironic and maybe even a little profound. A light-hearted moment shared by Dutch sociologist in the Society for the Study of Social Problems.
http://www.pscw.uva.nl/sociosite/Quotes.html

Soc of Knowledge: Introductory essay

According to C. Wright Mills, there is a perspective called the "sociological imagination" that can be used to interpret how one sees social life. A healthy skepticism, a detector of that which is phony inside this world's social structures.
http://www.trinity.edu/~mkearl/knowledg.html

IIS99

"Multiple Modernities in an Era of Globalization," an international conference on sociology. Paper may be obtained via correspondence.
http://www.spirit.tau.ac.il/soc/IIS99/

Groups

Where to go from here . . . [Adolescent re-socialization]

Information about families, including marriage & dating, parenting, grandparents, and family problems like alcoholism, child abuse, and family violence. Editor: Nancy Darling. A site for people interested in Adolescent Peer Relations.
http://www.personal.psu.edu/faculty/n/x/nxd10/

UNRISD: Viewpoints

U.N. applied action research on topics regard social and human development.
http://www.unrisd.org/engindex/view.htm

A Sociological Social Psychology

Sociologists in Social Psych focus on understanding the relationships between group structures and processes; they are inclined to focus on individuals' social roles and social settings. The psychologist in SP atomizes man/the sociologist exams process.
http://www.Trinity.Edu/~mkearl/socpsy.html#in

Race, Gender and Class

Collectivities move toward Change

washington post.com: The Gender Revolution

FIVE ARTICLES. Men and women have declared a cease-fire in the war that raged between the sexes through much of the last half of this century. In its place, they face common new enemies < the stress, lack of time and financial pressure of modern life.
http://www.washingtonpost.com/wp-srv/national/longterm/ . . .

Social Development and Poverty Elimination Division Links:
Gender in Development/Tools for Gender Analysis and Mainstreaming

Social Development and Poverty Elimination Division Links: Gender in Development: Tools for Gender Analysis and Mainstreaming
http://www.sdnp.undp.org/~rlal/links/Gender in Development . . .

homepage.html (United Nations)

UNDP initiatives that demonstrate practical application of (a) gender mainstreaming in programs and institutional processes; and (b) women's empowerment.
http://www.undp.org/gender/homepage.html

Socioeconomic Status and Health Chartbook from Health, United States, 1998

The Socioeconomic Status and Health, the correlation between the two is measured in this report.
http://www.cdc.gov/nchswww/products/pubs/pubd/hus/201 . . .

American Pictures: Racism, Oppression, Multiculturalism, Ethnic and Cultural
Awareness, Black Underclass and Poverty

Focus: Race and Social Issues. Multi-media slide tape show, commercial success. Emotional piece, first-hand data can be obtained by contacting various colleges that presented the show and followed with workshop.
http://www.american-pictures.com/english/index.html

Radical Perspective/Conflict

From Eitzen to Seeley to Marx, etc.

Marxism Page

Marxist classics—Introductions to Marxist politics—Contemporary Marxist material—Interesting Graphics—Listen to The Internationale, read the lyrics or background to the song—Graduate research in Marxism and Search the Marxism Page.
http://www.anu.edu.au/polsci/marx/marx.html

Conflict Theory(ies)

Robert O. Keel: rok@umsl.edu Notes on Radical Conflict theory used in lecture at U of Missouri (St. Louis). Detailed, highlighted, can be displayed-email above.
http://www.umsl.edu/~rkeel/200/conflict.html

PSN HOME PAGE

A moderated list of academics who have displayed an interest in theoretical and political issues in sociology. Discussions are held by theoreticians on radical issues in sociology.
http://www.csf.colorado.edu/psn/

UNION RING
> A global network that is adding others to the union ring, so as to create a free web site. You are invited to join if you are interested in workplace, labor issues advocating a socialist perspective. Hundreds of union web pages are connected to this site.
> *http://www.geocities.com/CapitolHill/5202/unionring.html*

Economic Order

A social institution, its focus, the social interaction around the economy.

An Overview of Social Inequality
> The rich in America are getting richer, increased assets are in the hands of the top 1%.
> *http://www.trinity.edu/~mkearl/strat.html*

By the Sweat and Toil of Children—Volume V
> The fifth volume in a series of annual reports on child labor. This report was produced by the staff of the International Child Labor Program and published by the US Department of Labor (DOL).
> *http://www.dol.gov/dol/ilab/public/media/reports/icp.swel*

Labor Educational Module
> A site dedicated to the study of labor issues.
> *http://globetrotter.berkeley.edu/EdModule/labor/*

Human Rights Violations: Apartheid
> A site for human rights around the world.
> *http://globetrotter.berkeley.edu/violations/apartheid.html*

Corporate Predators by Mokhiber and Weissman
> "The incisive and sharply focused snapshots presented here give a telling portrait of some of the most dangerous forces undermining what is decent and hopeful in American and global society. A warning that should be taken very seriously."— Noam Chomsky
> *http://www.corporatepredators.org/*

Citizens for Tax Justice Home Page CTJ
> Citizens for Tax Justice is a nonpartisan, nonprofit research and advocacy organization dedicated to fair taxation at the federal, state, and local levels.
> *http://www.ctj.org/*

The Social Institution Education

NCES Site Map (Nat. Ctr. for Educ. Statist.)
A treasure-trove of institutional functionaries from K through 12 to graduate schools. Web links to research in all these areas.
http://www.nces.ed.gov/help/sitemap.asp

NatCenterEducStat.quick links (NCES Home Page, part of the US Department of Education
NCES is the primary federal entity for collecting and analyzing data that are related to education in the US and other nations.
http://www.nces.ed.gov/index.html

Family as an Institution

Which includes early childhood socialization

The Urban Institute & New Data on Sexual Behaviors of Teenage Males (Family & Children)
"The National Survey of Adolescent Males:" Preventing teenagers from having unplanned pregnancies is an important goal that has been pursued since the 1970s, when births to teenagers were first diagnosed as a major social problem.
http://www.urban.org/family/teenmale.htm

Federal Interagency Forum on Child and Family Statistics
This web site offers easy access to federal and state statistics and reports on children and their families, including: population and family characteristics, economic security, health, behavior and social environment and education.
http://www.childstats.gov/index.htm

Academic Affairs (College of Family Life, USU)
Across the US we are facing a serious shortage of professionals trained to solve critical problems confronting individuals and families. In the College of Family Life we address this shortage through preparation of professionals as problem solvers.
http://www.usu.edu/~famlife/academic/

Australian Institute of Family Studies (AIFS) Home Page Menu
The Institute is an authority to promote the identification and understanding of factors affecting marital and family stability in Australia. The following are links on the site: "What's New; Research; Information Resources."
http://www.aifs.org.au/

www.astr.ua.e . . . f-agnesi.html

Don't be put-off by the fact the site's written in French—there's also an English version. If you're looking for a basic introduction to Comte, the Man and His Ideas, this is probably as good a place as any to start.
http://www.astr.ua.edu/4000WS/witch-of-agnesi.html

left.htm

This is a link to 50 or more organizations promoting a specific value position on the family. This is not a neutral site, it sits in the political center and moves to the right of center in the current value spectrum. It is an import link to inspect.
http://www.afa.net/left.htm

Family Research Council Vision & Work

Develop and advocate legislative and public policy initiatives which strengthen and fortify the family and promote traditional family values. This link is not neutral but advocates a value position.
http://www.frc.org/whois/

Polity as an Institution

The political process and the functionaries of power.

Common Cause—Citizens Working to End Special-Interest Politics and Reform Government Ethics.

Citizens' lobbying group tracks the influence of money in congressional and presidential politics and advocates campaign finance reforms.
http://www.commoncause.org/

Digital Democracy: Contents

A Center for Responsive Politics report on the status of electronic campaign filing in the 50 states. Digital Democracy. A 50-State Report on computerizing Campaign Finance Disclosure.
http://www.opensecrets.org/pubs/digdem/index.htm

THOMAS—US Congress in the Internet

Includes searchable databases for bill status, sponsors of legislation, and committee actions. Congressional Record online, plus links to member and committee home pages, are also here.
http://www.thomas.loc.gov/

CRP: Political Parties

The biggest loophole in our campaign finance low is "soft money." A way around the legal limits set originally to individuals giving to parties.
http://www.opensecrets.org/parties/index.htm

Welcome to opensecrets.org

The Center for Responsive Politics is a non-partisan, non-profit research group based in Washington, D.C. that tracks money in politics, and its effect on elections and public policy.

http://www.opensecrets.org/home/index.asp

State of Illinois—Project Vote Smart

Illinois legislature report on issues taken by state leaders. Office phone numbers of state leaders.

http://www.vote-smart.org/ce/states/IL/

Power and Money in Illinois

This link examines the use of money and power in politics.

http://www.publicintegrity.org/illinoisproject.html

www.vote-smar. . . 599&checking=

College of DuPage Elected Officials. How to reach our political leaders.

http://www.vote-smart.org/districts.phtml?zip5=60137&zip4=6599&che

Illinois State Board of Elections

As an Ombudsman is how this organization fashions itself, this part of the link is focused on the state of Illinois. The focus is how power and money are buying influence in the state.

http://www.elections.state.il.us/

Candidate Search Page

Another Ombudsman organization; again, this part of the link is focused on the state of Illinois. The focus is how power and money are buying influence in the state.

http://www.elections.state.il.us/Cds/pages/CandSCrit.asp

US Senate

Main page of the US Senate. Committee hearing schedule, offices of the membership are given. Yesterday's floor activity is listed.

http://www.senate.gov/

Contacting the Congress

Important site to contact nearly the entire US Congress.

http://www.visi.com/juan/congress/

NCSLnet: Internet Sites of the State Legislatures
Constantly updated, this site links one to State Legislatures across the country. "The National Conference of State Legislatures" takes you to an in-depth search of each state.
http://www.nosl.org/public/sitesleg.htm

Project Vote Smart—A Voter's Self-Defense System
Tracking the performance of over 13,000 political leaders. Researcher hotline with an 800 number. Classroom assistance and data on congress.
http://www.vote-smart.org/

Belief System as a Social Institution

A social institution satisfies some of our long range essential needs. This institution focuses on Religion, Beliefs and even magic . . .

Mahayana Background page
A Buddhist sect.
http://www.-relg-studies.scu.edu/netcours/rs013/buddhism/mahayana/ba

American Religion Data Archive
The American Religion Data Archive (ARDA) is an Internet-based archive that stores and distributes quantitative data sets from the leading studies on American religion.
http://www.thearda.com/

Media Awareness Network—English Home Page
Project to counteract excesses of commercialism September 16, 1998—A new project counteracting commercialism was launched earlier this month by American consumer advocate Ralph Nader. Commercial Alert will serve as a clearing house for this concern.

Population and Demographic

The Social Science Data Analysis Network

Population Reference Bureau
Population has a profound effect on how we plan and realize our dreams; the PBR provides you with the facts you need to better understand our changing world. Population defines among other things our need for resource allocations (i.e.: roads, schools, etc.).
http://www.prb.org/

The Social Statistics Briefing Room

The purpose of this service is to provide easy access to current Federal Social statistics. It links to data produced by gov't agencies, regularly updated, most CURRENTLY available; includes color charts. Contains stats on: Crime, Pop, Ed. & Health.

http://www.whitehouse.gov/fsbr/ssbr.html

Children in the States: 1998 Data

Data includes a range of carefully chosen key indicators that measure critical aspects of children's lives; health and health care, personal achievement, economic status, family structure. Profiles are organized by states. USE: for live class sessions.

http://www.childrensdefense.org/states/data.html

Statistical Abstracts of the United States

"Statistical Abstracts of the United States: 1998" as well as 97, 96, & 95 are found on this site. PDF Adobe Reader (free) is used to view materials.

http://www.census.gov/prod/3/98pubs/98statab/cc98stab.htm

NCHS-Ser 2, NO. 128—Death Rates by Race and Hispanic-Origin: A Summary of Current Research

Research on the Quality of Death Rates by race in official mortality statistics of the US.

http://www.cdc.gov/nchswww/products/pubs/pubd/services/sr2/pre-121

1999—Annual Report on Nation's Health Spotlights Elderly Americans

"Health, United States, 1999," Report card on the nation's health produced by the Center for Disease Control (CDC). One out of five people will be over the age of 65 in the next millennium; the population is living longer.

http://www.cdc.gov/nchs/releases/99news/99news/hus99.htm

Atlas of United States Mortality

Released 4.97 this atlas shows leading causes of death by RACE & SEX for small US geo areas known as Health Service Areas HSA's 83% of all deaths. It accounts for age adjusted and region rates for each cause of death. GPO provides hard copy.

http://www.cdc.gov/nchs/products/pubs/pubd/other/atlas/atlas.htm

Social Science Data Analysis Network

The Social Science Data Analysis Network makes the US census surveys and demographic trends accessible to educators, policy makers, the media, and students at all levels.

http://www.psc.lsa.umich.edu/SSDAN/

Urban Collectivities

Sociologist E.K. Wilson refers to the urban collectivity as a source, symbol and locus of Social Change.

Saul Alinsky

Excerpts from Reveille for Radicals by Saul Alinsky
http://www.eng.uci.edu/~bchiu/Essays/alinsky.html

MP568 Community Development Theory

The community development approach: a democratic way of approaching citizens toward creating social change. A scholarly paper by James Cook.
http://muextension.missouri.edu/xplor/miscpubs/mp0568.htm

SSBR: Crime

FBI crime stats used by the westwing of government. Current and visual presentations.
http://www.whitehouse.gov/fsbr/crime.html

About the Urban Institute

Leaving politics to others, the Urban Institute brings three critical ingredients to public debates on domestic policy initiatives: accurate data, careful and objective analyses, and perspective. This policy research unit focuses on cosmopolitan concerns.
http://www.urban.org/news/newsinfo.htm

acs.htm

The American Community Survey is a new approach for collecting accurate, timely data on urban areas. Instead of once in 10 years it will update every year. See slide show that initiates the program for year 2000 and fully operational 2003 A.D.
http://www.census.gov/acs/www/acs.htm

State and Metropolitan Area Data Book—5th Edition

The Data Book contains a collection of statistics on social and economic conditions in the United States at the state and metropolitan area levels. Selected data for component counties and central cities of metropolitan areas are also included.
http://www.census.gov/statab/www/smadb.html

Gender Studies

www.ecofem.org

Sociologist Richard Twine's extensive, well-organized web site includes a definition of ecofeminism; a bibliography of books, journal articles, reviews, and videos; announcements of upcoming events; a review Twine wrote: and links to many related sites.
http://www.geocities.com/Wellesley/8385/ecofemlinks.html

Coalition Against Trafficking in Women

Website on a non-governmental organization dedicated to combating sexual exploitation, especially prostitution and trafficking in women. Includes publications, statements, testimony, fact sheets, links to related sites, and more.
http://www.uri.edu/artsci/wms/hughes/catw/

Welcome to the American Association of University Women

Contains info about AAUW publications, US congressional voting record on key issues, and much more.
http://www.aauw.org/home.html

Maven—The Portal Directory to the Jewish World

A careful examination of rabbinic texts reveals that within patriarchy there was distinct movement to extend to women more rights and benefits.
http://www.maven.co.il/subjects.asp?S=201

Matrix [women in religious societies]

The goal is "to document the participation of Christian women in the religion and society of medieval Europe." Includes biographies, community profiles, bibliography, glossary, archives of articles, an image library, and more."
http://www.matrix.divinity.yale.edu/MatrixWebData/matrix.html

Social Forces Moving Toward Social Change

Pro-active social forces moving toward Change

The Illinois Affiliate of the ACLU

This ACLU award winning web site has outstanding links and goes outside Illinois.
http://www.aclu-il.org/

National Gay and Lesbian Task Force (NGLTF) ONLINE!

Deviant groups in the American social structure.
http://www.ngltf.org/

FSM-A—The Free Speech Movement Archives Home Page

This is a home page to radical (1965) movements. The John Seeley speech "Quo Warranto" is found here and can be of interest to university students.
http://www.fsm-a.org/index.html

The Drug Reform Coordination Network

An advocacy group. The main purpose is drug policy reform.
http://drcnet.org

U.S. Census on Population 2000

Table T1. Resident Population of the United States
April 1, 2000 and April 1, 1990

Area	April 1, 2000	April 1, 1990	Numeric Change	Percent Change	State Rank as of April 1, 2000	State Rank as of April 1, 1990
Alabama	4,447,100	4,040,587	406,513	10.1	23	22
Alaska	626,932	550,043	76,889	14.0	48	49
Arizona	5,130,632	3,665,228	1,465,404	40.0	20	24
Arkansas	2,673,400	2,350,725	322,675	13.7	33	33
California	33,871,648	29,760,021	4,111,627	13.8	1	1
Colorado	4,301,261	3,294,394	1,006,867	30.6	24	26
Connecticut	3,405,565	3,287,116	118,449	3.6	29	27
Delaware	783,600	666,168	117,432	17.6	45	46
District of Columbia	572,059	606,900	−34,841	−5.7	(NA)	(NA)
Florida	15,982,378	12,937,926	3,044,452	23.5	4	4
Georgia	8,186,453	6,478,216	1,708,237	26.4	10	11
Hawaii	1,211,537	1,108,229	103,308	9.3	42	41
Idaho	1,293,953	1,006,749	287,204	28.5	39	42
Illinois	12,419,293	11,430,602	988,691	8.6	5	6
Indiana	6,080,485	5,544,159	536,326	9.7	14	14
Iowa	2,926,324	2,776,755	149,569	5.4	30	30
Kansas	2,688,418	2,477,574	210,844	8.5	32	32
Kentucky	4,041,769	3,685,296	356,473	9.7	25	23
Louisiana	4,468,976	4,219,973	249,003	5.9	22	21
Maine	1,274,923	1,227,928	46,995	3.8	40	38
Maryland	5,296,486	4,781,468	515,018	10.8	19	19
Massachusetts	6,349,097	6,016,425	332,672	5.5	13	13
Michigan	9,938,444	9,295,297	643,147	6.9	8	8
Minnesota	4,919,479	4,375,099	544,380	12.4	21	20
Mississippi	2,844,658	2,573,216	271,442	10.5	31	31
Missouri	5,595,211	5,117,073	478,138	9.3	17	15
Montana	902,195	799,065	103,130	12.9	44	44
Nebraska	1,711,263	1,578,385	132,878	8.4	38	36
Nevada	1,998,257	1,201,833	796,424	66.3	35	39
New Hampshire	1,235,786	1,109,252	126,534	11.4	41	40
New Jersey	8,414,350	7,730,188	684,162	8.9	9	9
New Mexico	1,819,046	1,515,069	303,977	20.1	36	37
New York	18,976,457	17,990,455	986,002	5.5	3	2
North Carolina	8,049,313	6,628,637	1,420,676	21.4	11	10
North Dakota	642,200	638,800	3,400	0.5	47	47
Ohio	11,353,140	10,847,115	506,025	4.7	7	7
Oklahoma	3,450,654	3,145,585	305,069	9.7	27	28
Oregon	3,421,399	2,842,321	579,078	20.4	28	29
Pennsylvania	12,281,054	11,881,643	399,411	3.4	6	5

Source: U.S. Census on Population 2000, Table T1. Resident Population of the United States, April 1, 2000 and April 1, 1990. Dept of Commerce, U.S. Census Bureau.

Area	April 1, 2000	April 1, 1990	Numeric Change	Percent Change	State Rank as of April 1, 2000	State Rank as of April 1, 1990
Rhode Island	1,048,319	1,003,464	44,855	4.5	43	43
South Carolina	4,012,012	3,486,703	525,309	15.1	26	25
South Dakota	754,844	696,004	58,840	8.5	46	45
Tennessee	5,689,283	4,877,185	812,098	16.7	16	17
Texas	20,851,820	16,986,510	3,865,310	22.8	2	3
Utah	2,233,169	1,722,850	510,319	29.6	34	35
Vermont	608,827	562,758	46,069	8.2	49	48
Virginia	7,078,515	6,187,358	891,157	14.4	12	12
Washington	5,894,121	4,866,692	1,027,429	21.1	15	18
West Virginia	1,808,344	1,793,477	14,867	0.8	37	34
Wisconsin	5,363,675	4,891,769	471,906	9.6	18	16
Wyoming	493,782	453,588	40,194	8.9	50	50
Total Resident Population[1]	**281,421,906**	**248,709,873**	**32,712,033**	**13.2**	**(NA)**	**(NA)**
Northeast	53,594,378	50,809,229	2,785,149	5.5	(NA)	(NA)
Midwest	64,392,776	59,668,632	4,724,144	7.9	(NA)	(NA)
South	100,236,820	85,445,930	14,790,890	17.3	(NA)	(NA)
West	63,197,932	52,786,082	10,411,850	19.7	(NA)	(NA)
Puerto Rico	3,808,610	3,522,037	286,573	8.1	(NA)	(NA)
Total Resident Population Including Puerto Rico	**285,230,516**	**252,231,910**	**32,998,606**	**13.1**	**(NA)**	**(NA)**

[1]Includes the population of the 50 states and the District of Columbia.
Source: U.S. Department of Commerce, U.S. Census Bureau
NA: Not Applicable

Defining Moments and Recurring Myths: A Reply

Seymour Martin Lipset

"DEFINING MOMENTS AND RECURRING MYTHS" is the most recent response, mainly by Canadians, to my efforts to describe and analyze differences, as well as similarities, between Canada and the United States. As an American, I seek to better understand the U.S. by comparing it to other countries. My writings bear on formative events, the institutions and values that derive from them, and the subsequent happenings which stem in some part from trajectories set in motion by the earlier events and the institutions and values they foster. Curiously most of my critics, though Canadian nationalists, usually seek to deprecate my conclusions that the variations in North American history and social and geographic environments gave rise to two peoples who differ in significant ways from each other, although as I have repeatedly stressed, they are more similar than different, particularly in comparison with other nations. My chief methodological argument for focusing on Canada in order to learn about the United States is precisely that the two nations have so much in common. Focusing on small differences between countries which are alike can be more fruitful for understanding cultural effects than on large ones among highly similar nations. The former permits holding constant many variables, which the units have in common.

I have found it necessary to note the obvious truism that statements about variations among groups or nations do not imply all or nothing relationships. Rather the differences often refer to somewhat more in one, somewhat less in another. Herbert Hyman noted a long time ago that small survey-based distinctions—55% in one population, 45% in another, or 15 compared to 10—are often discussed as if they are based on 100% to zero. There are always some rich socialists and poor conservatives. The social structure of the United States has frequently been described as egalitarian, that of Britain or Europe as ascriptive, aristocratic or post-feudal. Obviously those making such statements such as Tocqueville, do not challenge the existence of deep-rooted inequalities in the United States, or of considerable social mobility in Europe in the 19th century.

Source: Seymour Martin Lipset, "Defining Moments and Recurring Myths: A Reply. (Comparing Canada with the United States)" *The Canadian Review of Sociology and Anthropology,* Feb 2001, v38, i1, p. 97.

Comparative analyses are never simple. Joseph Schumpeter in his studies of social mobility concluded that all complex societies are characterized by much movement up and down the economic and social structures. He wrote that classes are like hotel rooms, looking the same, but occupied over time by different people. And the same patterns apply to nations. Max Weber, in describing the role of historical events in creating and institutionalizing social differences, noted that the process is like a dice game which begins with unloaded or unbiased dice, but that after each throw, the winning roll biases (not determines) the next one to come up the same way as the previous effort. In this way, institutionalization refers to a repetitive bias (Weber, 1949: 182–185). Thus it may be argued that the American Revolution pushed the U.S. in a classically liberal (laissez-faire) direction, but pressed the residual area of British North America to exhibit deference to the state.

In commenting on my work and that of others, my critics insist on attributing many ideas about cross-national differences to me, even though they occasionally mention, sometimes by name, usually not, the others as well. The idea that regional variations in latter-day behavior and values of North Americans can be linked to the social origins of the original settlers has been brilliantly explored in depth by David Hackett Fisher in Albion's Seed (1998). Unfortunately he did not extend his research to Canada, but his tracing of the ways the varying cultures of the original settlers became internalized in different sections of the U.S. and continues to show up centuries later is brilliant.

My critics reject the suggestion that the 40,000 loyalist emigres, who moved after the peace treaty to the portions of North America under British control, brought values and institutions with them which must have varied in systematic ways from those south of the new border. They cite various observers who reported that those who remained under the crown resembled most residents of the new republic in their behavior. There can be little doubt but that Anglophonic North American farmers or small towns-people were similar in many ways on both sides of the border, particularly when compared to the British or continental Europeans. Foreign, mainly English, observers had reported decades before the revolution that an American social type had emerged. The native-born Loyalists were Americans, more egalitarian. But I would insist that, on average, those who chose British North America had to be different in significant ways from those who did not, much as the Irish who immigrated to Canada varied greatly from those who moved to the U.S. The former, as my critics also note, were largely Protestant, the latter were overwhelmingly Catholic. We know, as my critics correctly assert, that the cross-border elites, both secular and religious, differed substantially in their beliefs and actions, the masses less so, but the masses are exposed from childhood to elite fostered beliefs.

I would have liked to document my arguments at length, but this would not be appropriate given the space limitation imposed by the editor. In any case, I think I have dealt with the issues in my most extensive writing on the subject, Continental Divide (1990). In it, I draw on the works of Canadian scholars like Harold Innis, Frank Underhill and S. D. Clark. Innis, Canada's greatest social scientist, like many historians, social scientists, and literary critics, including Underhill and Clark, referred to Canada as a "counter-revolutionary" country and derived many of its characteristics from that assumption: I would note that most of my writings on the counter-revolutionary image of Canada are cited by my critics, but they seem to have largely concentrated on one article, "Revolution and Counter-revolution—The United States and Canada," published originally in 1965. (They cite to a reprint in 1968.) But my most extensive and definitive work is Continental Divide, which discusses cross-national differences in literature, legal systems, governmental structures, e.g., monarchical versus populist, education, entrepreneurial values, ethnic and religious origins, political ethoses, criminal justice systems, and many others, as well as reports on abundant quantitative materials from sample surveys and aggregate data.

The varying institutions which have affected behavior, particularly government, religion, and economy, as well as geographic and demographic differences, were present from the beginning of the continental political divide. Anglo-Canadian religion, as Christopher Adamson (1994) brilliantly documented, has differed from American denominationalism. He stresses "the exceptionalism of religious development in the northern and western states of the American union by comparing it with religious development in the nearby British province of Upper Canada, [emphasizing] the effect of the triumph of Christian republicanism over Christian Loyalism" (418). The early strength of the state-linked and hierarchical Anglican church in Ontario led to the activities of the "state-supported clergyman . . . [who sought] to instruct people to control their passions, and to obey divinely sanctioned . . . civil authority." For its leader, John Strachan, "a Christian life could only be achieved by the alliance of church and state . . . Not just Strachan but all the key religious players in Upper Canada were oriented to the state . . ." (442–443). By contrast, American congregational, non-hierarchical, sectarian religion reflected republican and populist values, which they also reinforced. The post-Revolutionary differences in political institutions need not be elaborated on, one polity marked by constitutional checks and balances designed to weaken state power and the executive, the other retaining the British system of unified government under a strong and respected cabinet system which overwhelmed parliament and was legitimated by monarchy.

Frank Underhill, a great historian, emphasized that Canadians have felt it necessary for over 200 years to contrast their quiet and more law-oriented elitist culture to the more raucous vulgar populist one to the South. He noted that Canadians have been the largest and most continuing group of anti-Americans, that they sought to justify the great refusal of their ancestors by believing that Canada has the superior North American culture, way of life. Raymond Griffiths, the head of a Canadian think tank, recently was quoted by an American journalist explaining that the greater disdain for guns and violence by Canadians "lies in the origins of the two countries: one supporting armed rebellion, the other opposing it." And he reiterated a standard part of the Canadian self-image "myth" that "The Canadian slogan is peace, order and good government [as enunciated by the Fathers of Confederation], as opposed to life, liberty and the pursuit of happiness" proclaimed by the American founders. A Canadian professor of justice studies asked an American, "why is it that there are 10,976 firearm murders in your country in 1998, when there were 151 in Canada . . . If you look at Toronto, we had 17 gun murders . . . How do you explain 17 murders in a major city just 100 miles north of your border" (Brown, 2001: A14). These differences are not recent. Studies of the mining camps in California and British Columbia in the mid-nineteenth century show similar cross-border variations with respect to law and order. The native Americans recognized the difference. In June 1876, after defeating Custer and the American troops at Little Big Horn, Sitting Bull and his band of Lakotas marched north, crossed the border and surrendered to six Mounted Police. They knew that their rights under negotiated treaties often were ignored by the populist authorities below the 49th parallel, but were upheld by the Queen's representatives in the north.

Surely processes started in motion by the revolutionaries and counter-revolutionaries of 18th-century North America had something to do with all this. We should not ignore the validity of the big picture and the beliefs and behaviors which stem from varying origins.

References

Adamson, C. 1994. "God's continent divided: Politics and religion in Upper Canada and the Northern and Western United States, 1775 to 1841". *Comparative Studies in Society and History*. Vol. 36, No. 3, pp. 417–46.

Brown, DeNeenl. 2001. "Canada implements a law to track rifles, shotguns." *Washington Post*. Jan. 6, p. A14.

Fisher, D.H. 1989. *Albion's Seed: Four British Folkways in America*. New York: Oxford UP.

Lipset, S.M. 1990. *Continental Divide*. New York: Routledge.

Lipset, S.M. 1965. "Revolution and counter-revolution—The United States and Canada." *In The Revolutionary Theme in Contemporary America*. T. Ford (ed.). Lexington: University of Kentucky Press, pp. 21–64.

Weber, M. 1949. *The Methodology of the Social Sciences*. Glencoe, Ill.: The Free Press.

Mixed Paint

Louis Menand

America is less a mosaic than a can of paint whose colors are running together. But having enabled integration, liberalism has had to take the blame for the cultural antagonisms that integration has caused.

The "culture wars"—the metaphor into which campus hate-speech codes, school prayer, Afrocentric school curricula, abortion, politically correct language, family values, affirmative action, the racial distribution of intelligence, deconstructionist literary criticism, sexual harassment policy, the Great Books, hardcore pornography, publicly funded art, and many other fractious things, are currently stuffed—are misfigured. The term suggests two great armies, one "liberal" and permissivist and looking a lot like a horde of Michael Kinsleys with slightly more raffish beards, the other "conservative" and traditionalist and looking alarmingly like a horde of Patrick Buchanans with slightly less charm. And "in the cross fire": the soul of America.

This picture has two things wrong with it. First, there aren't two sides. There are a dozen sides, and the "war" has much less the character of the Battle of the Somme than that of a playground free-for-all. Second, "liberalism" is not one of these sides. Although the term has come to stand for state-sponsored cultural permissivism (i.e., the encouragement of deviant lifestyles and obscene art), liberalism, in its classic meaning, is a politics that brings nothing cultural to the table at all. Liberalism only tries to help people get what they want; it has nothing to say about what it is they ought to want, nor should it.

The best definition of classic liberalism is the one formulated by British political philosopher Isaiah Berlin in his 1958 essay, "Two Concepts of Liberty." Liberalism, in Berlin's terms, is a philosophy of "negative" liberty, which means freedom *from* coercion by others. This freedom is contentless. It takes different people's conceptions of the good life to be incommensurable. It doesn't take a Christian or an atheistic position on, for example, school prayer. It just says that since there is no way of satisfying both Christians *and* atheists on this matter, there shall be no school prayer, period. To take another case, feminists who want to ban pornography are not "liberals." They are, like fundamentalist Christians who want to ban pornography, people who *do* have a firm conception of the good life (and of the forces that militate against it) and who are willing to use public policy to help

Source: Louis Menand, "Mixed Paint," *Mother Jones,* May, 1995, *http://www.Motherjones.com/mother_jones/MA95/*

secure it. Liberals aren't so willing. This doesn't make liberals pro-pornography; it makes them anti-anti-free expression, which is a philosophically different thing.

The negative conception of liberty, which is very much the modern idea and the American idea, has always had to face the challenge of Berlin's second concept, "positive" liberty, which he describes as freedom *to*. Believers in positive liberty think freedom comes from directing one's actions toward some articulated conception of the good life. A certain, preferably benign, degree of coercion is therefore appropriate, since people need to know the right values from the wrong ones, and to be guided in their social doings toward those behaviors that will lead to self-realization and self-fulfillment. Schoolchildren will be better off praying; women will be better off without pornography.

In the mid-1990s United States, philosophies of positive liberty are in bloom all across the ideological spectrum. There have been challenges to liberalism before, but there has probably never been such a varied bouquet. Hillary Clinton's "politics of meaning," for example, a phrase she borrowed from Tikkun editor Michael Lerner, is a positive liberty philosophy. It seeks to infuse choices about values into the policy-making process in a manner alarming to classic liberalism. So does the communitarianism promoted by the sociologist Amitai Etzioni. Christopher Lasch's neopopulism, Allan Bloom's Straussianism, Catharine MacKinnon's "feminism unmodified," Patrick Buchanan's new nationalism, Dan Quayle's family values platform, Pat Robertson's Christian Coalition, Charles Murray's "clanism" (his solution to the problem of racial differences in IQ that he and Richard Herrnstein claim to have established in "The Bell Curve"): All base their appeal on the perception that liberalism's agnosticism about the nature of the good life has led to cultural breakdown.

If liberalism is now reduced by these competing moral doctrines to the position of an out-of-work gunfighter, hoping that things will get bad enough for its services to be in demand again, it has only itself to blame. For we are having these cultural brawls not because we fragmented, but because we integrated, and integration was a liberal accomplishment.

In 1964, Congress passed the Civil Rights Act. (It is profoundly symptomatic of the irrelevance of liberalism to the culture wars that the act's 30-year anniversary has gone by virtually without notice.) The act is the monument to the great equity movements of the 1960s, which began with the civil rights movement for African-Americans and led to the women's movement and, after 1969, to the gay liberation movement. The act mandated nondiscrimination by race, creed, and sex, and it has been the foundation of all civil rights progress—from the enforcement of voting rights to the equal funding of collegiate athletics for women—ever since.

The key to the act is neutrality: It doesn't propose that women or nonwhites are better than white men, worse than white men, or even different from white men; it and its subsequent interpretations and emendations say only that whatever difference sex and race may make, that difference shall be ignored when counting votes, serving customers at lunch counters, admitting applicants to educational institutions, interviewing candidates for jobs, selling houses, and generally passing around social resources.

Among its many consequences, the act enabled the realization of the meritocratic system of education. The symbol of this system is the Scholastic Aptitude Test, which represents the commitment made in postwar education, at every level, to reward only merit, regardless of race, sex, faith, or socioeconomic status, and to prevent class stratification in American life. Americans are supposed to feel that they have not been born into their social and economic positions, but can rise to whatever level their abilities permit (or even, I think most people hope, a notch or two higher).

But having established neutral standards, and having compelled adherence to nondiscriminatory procedures, liberalism can go no further. It must be satisfied with whatever these ostensibly neutral systems yield up. Liberalism's faith is that groups are fundamentally equal in capacity, so that bracketing race and gender to eliminate bias will produce demographically proportional results. There is no reason to believe that, in the cultural vacuum tests like the SATs are supposed to provide, people will score lower or higher just because they have breasts or darker skin. Holding cultural background constant, liberals believe we can measure, and reward, excellence and excellence alone.

The most pointed challenge to liberalism's neutrality is the movement known as "multiculturalism"—the notion that ignoring differences of race, ethnicity, gender, class, and sexual orientation is a covert method for continuing to oppress the different. For the very simple and disturbing point of multiculturalism is to suggest that there is no such thing as a cultural vacuum. This is not merely a theoretical proposition. It is based on, and draws its authority from, the experience of many of the women and nonwhites who showed up at the colleges and law firms integrated by the equality movements of the 1960s. Such people came to feel that although legal barriers to acceptance and advancement had been largely removed, cultural barriers remained.

For example, women in the academy (which was, until the late 1960s, one of the most overwhelmingly white and male places in America) found that although they might be paid on the same scale as male professors, and be free from discrimination in the legal sense, subtle impediments persisted, embedded in the institution's traditional folkways and attitudes. These women found it not implausible to conclude that as subtle male bias is to universities, blatant bias must be to mass commercial culture. Thus the exposure of sexism in American movies, television, music, and advertising, and the insistence on its oppressive consequences for women, became a major scholarly industry. And thus the belief that expressions demeaning to women (and to nonwhites, gays, and other marginalized groups) are deserving of censure, since such expressions, wherever they are allowed, inhibit members of these groups from participating as equals.

But most multiculturalism is not simply reactive. It also advocates the identification and celebration of subcultures for a positive reason: to instill a sense of pride and self-worth in people who, because of their race or gender or sexual orientation, have been reduced in, or erased from, mainstream versions of American history. Self-esteem is, multiculturalists think, a necessary condition of empowerment: People cannot take control of their own lives unless they are convinced of the merits of who they happen to be and where they happen to come from.

The great villain for multiculturalism, therefore, is liberalism. It is liberalism that defends the right of panders and bigots to purvey their sexist wares and to utter their racist epithets. It is liberalism that established sham categories like "merit" and "excellence," which have served as high-minded excuses for the exclusion, disparagement, and marginalization of "other" ways of knowing and achieving. And it is liberalism that insists on the majoritarian principles that permanently prevent minority groups—who will always be outvoted—from wielding power in America. Having enabled the integration of American institutions, liberalism has had to take the blame for the cultural antagonisms integration has caused.

The argument over multiculturalism now rages up and down the whole alphabet of American education, from K to Ph.D. It engages "culture" not only in the sense of "arts and letters," but in the very widest connotation of the term. Many multiculturalists propose not only that, say, women might take an interest in books not formerly read in literature classes; they also propose that women might actually have different modes of apprehension and analysis from men. Some multiculturalists claim that only women can teach books by women and only blacks can teach books by blacks, or that the standards of science and mathematics are not neutral and universal, but reflect a racial or sexual bias.

It isn't hard to see why these arguments drive many people to distraction—or, in the case of Arthur Schlesinger Jr., who attacked multiculturalism as an educational doctrine in "The Disuniting of America" (1992), and Robert Hughes, who attacked it as a plausible interpretation of culture in "Culture of Complaint" (1993), to the production of best-selling books about it. Writers like Schlesinger and Hughes insist on a distinction between their antagonism to multiculturalism, which they regard as a liberal one, and the sort of antagonism to multiculturalism associated with conservatives like Newt Gingrich and Patrick Buchanan—the sort of militant and nationalistic assimilationism that was the rhetorical feature of the 1992 Republican national convention, and that shows promise of becoming more than just the rhetorical feature of the 104th Congress.

But although the sort of work Schlesinger and Hughes would like to see culture do—in Schlesinger's case, to provide a common set of values for citizenship; in Hughes', to represent the finest in human accomplishment—is clearly very different from the sort of work Buchanan and Gingrich would like to see culture do, it is not quite correct to call this a distinction between a "liberal" attitude and a "conservative" one. For there can be no such thing as a "liberal" attitude toward culture, since liberalism has nothing substantive to say about culture. Liberals, like anyone else, have views about culture, but liberalism doesn't. And this is why, as shots ring out on Main Street, liberalism can only cool its heels and wait for the day when the townsfolk will decide that they have had enough and want the noise-makers run out of town. They don't look like having had enough any time soon.

The antagonists in the culture wars all seem to share two assumptions. One is that American society really is in a state of increasing fragmentation, that groups which once happily assimilated are now refusing, and are likely to continue to refuse, to melt. The second is that culture can be used instrumentally, either to glue the shards together (as the common-culturists hope) or to foster the self-esteem of members of America's constitutive groups (as the multiculturalists recommend).

The obsession with "culture" (as opposed to, say, economics) as the key to our national problems draws on an intellectual tradition which points to culture (high culture, indigenous culture, or folk culture, depending on the theorist) as the element of continuity and moral coherence in a world characterized precisely by its lack of respect for continuity and moral coherence. The trouble with this faith is that in addition to being socially and economically mobile and unstable, modern liberal societies are culturally mobile and unstable, as well. Capitalist democracies are not just permissive about cultural change; they actually thrive on it. A new taste means a new market. A free-for-all is exactly the sort of "culture war" capitalist societies produce.

Will the free-for-all end by bringing down the whole house?

Liberals can only stake the survival of their philosophy on a guess. The guess is that the cultural antagonisms that look like a new and dangerous tribalism are simply the epiphenomena, the shaking out, of an irreversible process of integration in American life. Contrary to most assertions, American society is becoming much less like a mosaic and much more like a can of mixed paint. The life-paths of women and men, and, to a lesser extent, of black and white Americans, are more likely to be congruent than at any time in history. Friction is not, after all, the consequence of separation.

But culture cannot be the organizer, blueprint, or palliative to this new and superficially diverse (though profoundly more unified) world, because culture is as fickle a hodgepodge of values, traditions, styles, and interpretations as anything else in modern life. It's not a foundation stone; it's only a Rubik's Cube of possibilities. And the history of cultural achievement in the 20th century—the examples of people who have made memorable contributions to modern life—demonstrates, over and over, that what's important isn't the "right" combination, but simply access to the cube. For everyone's combination must be different.

Almost everything we value in the way of individual achievement in the modern world has come when people have broken away from their traditions and made for themselves a new life out of materials their parents never knew. Almost nothing that we value has come from people submerging their identity into that of a group or trying to live facing backwards. But facing backwards has its appeal; and when Americans feel drawn to the notion, as they apparently do today, liberalism can only wait for them to get impatient with the results. They will.

Louis Menand teaches English at the Graduate Center of the City University of New York.

XI. Urban Collectivities

Are You Getting Enough Vitamin T?

Nicholas Albery

It's the miracle cure that can turn your neighborhood into a community

For most of human history, we have lived in small tribal groups of 50 to 250 people, and at an instinctual level we still crave bonds to people outside our immediate families. It's psychologically nourishing to feel connected to those we live among, not necessarily as close friends but as acquaintances with whom we can enjoy a regular chat and on whom we can depend in times of need or loneliness. Yet modern society, with its hectic pace and painstakingly scheduled round of activities and amusements, deprives us of these satisfying community bonds. The alienation and depression that typify modern life may stem in part from a deficiency of our basic requirements for what I call vitamin T—tribal connection.

I know that I'm deprived of vitamin T because I was lucky enough as a young man to take part in the rich community life of London's Notting Hill neighborhood when it was a center of countercultural ferment. Many of you might feel the same way about your college days when the air always seemed to crackle with the possibility of impromptu social encounters—a time when meeting friends did not involve phoning weeks ahead for an appointment or getting into a car. In my middle-aged isolation, I truly miss the convivial tradition of just dropping in on a neighbor for a conversation and a cup of coffee.

There's no word in the English language that quite means *lonely*—lonely despite having your happy nuclear family around you. A new word such as *kithless*—as in without kith and kin—is needed. Most urban dwellers, and perhaps even more people in the suburbs and country these days, know this feeling deep in themselves, but few can find an opening to talk about it. In the past, people no doubt felt trapped in the stultifying life of a village, seeing the same people every single day, but the pendulum has now swung too far the other way. We are overwhelmed with opportunities to escape the confines of our local world, from cars and jet planes to TV and the Internet, but we feel rootless and disconnected from our immediate surroundings.

Some folks convince themselves that their tribe consists of those who share the same interests or work in the same field, no matter how far away they might live. Yet Internet

Source: Nicholas Albery, "Are You Getting Enough Vitamin T?" *Utne Reader*, January–February, 2001, pp. 60–61.

connections, occasional get-togethers at conferences, or even workday relationships are no substitute for an actual face-to-face community. I believe we have a built-in, probably biologically rooted, need to live in proximity with a tribe, working and celebrating cooperatively within a geographical neighborhood.

There's mounting evidence that vitamin T is as essential for our health as vitamins A, B, C, and the others. Studies from Germany show that a strong social network is a better predictor of long life than smoking and drinking habits.

With the help of a group of friends, I created the following questionnaire to help people judge whether they are getting healthy levels of tribalism in their daily lives. Please note that in this questionnaire, "nuclear family" means you, your spouse, and your children. "Local" means within a 15-minute walk from your home. "Local people" means those other than your nuclear family. These questions focus on encounters in your neighborhood that take place within this 15-minute range of home and that are outside your nuclear family. It is a neighborhood rating, not a test of how many friends you have or how happy you are with your partner and family. Simply tally up the numbers to find out how much of the daily recommended allowance of tribalism you are getting. If it adds up to more than 100 percent, don't worry: You can't overdose on human connection.

A Quiz: What's Your Daily Diet of Tribal Connection?

- Roughly how many local people (nonfamily neighbors, local storekeepers and clerks, waiters, people at the bus stop, etc.) have you chatted with in the last week?

- Roughly how many people have you said "hi" or nodded to while passing on the street or another public place? (For scoring purposes, divide this total by 2.)

- How many local people would be likely to notice and regret your death, if you were to die tomorrow? (For scoring purposes, divide this total by 3.)

- If you were seriously ill, roughly how many local people could you count on to visit you? How many would volunteer to help with shopping and other tasks? (For scoring purposes, double this total.)

- How many households in your neighborhood do you feel you could drop in on for a chat or a meal, almost on impulse, without it being a big deal? (For scoring purposes, multiply this total by 5.)

- With how many local people would you feel comfortable discussing and sharing your deep personal fears and worries? (For scoring purposes, multiply this total by 10.)

- How many local people understand your goals in life and actively support you in trying to achieve them? (For scoring purposes, double this total.)

- Last week, how often did you engage in the equivalent of a tribal ritual?: a religious service, a meal with neighbors, a drink at the local tavern or coffee shop with friends—occasions, in other words, where there was active participation by all those present. (For scoring purposes, double this total.)

- In general, to what extent do you feel that you are part of a local community (or tribe) that cares for each other? (Score on a range from 0 to 20, where 20 means "one big extended family" and 0 means "no contact at all.")

If your score is low, you might want to supplement your social diet. How about initiating a get-together for your neighbors at your home or a local gathering spot, or maybe even an outdoor block party? We have an annual tea party on our street in Northwest London, meeting in a different house each year. Even this token event is beginning to boost our sense of community and increase our inclination to help each other out.

Nicholas Albery is one of the editors of www. globalideasbank.org, a Web site that presents awards for bright ideas about social improvements. He is also an editor of DoBe.org, a Web site for every city in the world that is using the Internet to promote group events in the real world. And he is one of the organizers of www.Internet-Free-Day.org (the first of these annual Web-free days is Sunday, January 28, 2001). He is interested in hearing comments on the questionnaire and on the idea of reviving neighborhood tribalism in our cities. Contact him at: Institute for Social Inventions. 20 Heber Road, London NW2 6AA. UK (e-mail: rhino@dial.pipex.com).

The 10 Most Underrated Towns in America

Peter Katz

Notes on 10 great places once dismissed as bad news or dullsville (or both)

Throughout the '80s and '90s, things looked mostly bad for American cities. Outside of a handful of coastal centers like San Francisco, New York, and Seattle, the overwhelming trend was people moving to the suburbs. Millions of middle-class families voted with their feet for open vistas, lower crime rates, newer schools, bigger yards, and shopping mega-complexes. But urban areas now seem to be staging a comeback. Evidence of this trend—good news for some, bad news for others—is escalating real estate prices in many urban neighborhoods across the country. Americans seem to be falling in love with cities again.

Worsening traffic congestion has convinced some suburbanites to trade 40-plus-mile freeway commutes for 10-minute strolls down city sidewalks. For others it's the realization, driven home by the Columbine High School shootings, that no community is immune to violence, drug abuse, and other woes once sense seen as exclusively urban problems. A lot of kids who hail from homogenous bedroom communities are coming to appreciate the appeal of city living. Many new dot-coms, for instance, find that edgy urban neighborhoods are potent lures for the young tech-savvy talent they're seeking. Cities are also increasingly attractive to suburban empty nesters—baby boomers with grown-up kids, who are eager to trade lawn mowing for theatergoing. And most important are the folks of all ages who never gave up on urban life, the ones who rolled up their sleeves to hold the line on urban decay and ultimately bring real improvements to their neighborhoods, even as suburban flight deprived cities of desperately needed tax dollars.

Not every city, and certainly not every neighborhood, has conquered its economic, environmental, social, and racial woes. Yet all around there is a new spirit of optimism—even in places where people once saw little hope. These 10 cities, which ranked low on most people's livability and economic vitality lists just a few years ago, still face very real problems, especially in their poorest districts, but they are also blessed with classic older neighborhoods, lively downtowns, and residents who are proudly working to make them great places to live.

Source: Peter Katz, "The Ten Most Underrated Towns in America," *Utne Reader,* January–February, 2001, pp. 62–65.

Milwaukee

A classic rust belt city that's made a fresh start • Mayor John O. Norquist understands what makes cities work as well as anyone in America • A freeway that cuts through the heart of the city is being torn down • **A thriving new neighborhood,** EastPointe, has been built on land cleared for another freeway that was never built • **A delightful river walk** lines the Milwaukee River downtown • **Great old industrial buildings** are being converted to offices and lofts • Miles and miles of **lakefront park** are lined by architecturally distinguished neighborhoods • A new ballpark and a dazzling addition to the city's art museum are in the works • A wonderful tradition of **ethnic festivals** enlivens the town throughout the summer • Strong neighborhood redevelopment initiatives, good housing stock, and the **best corner taverns** in North America.

West Palm Beach, Florida

Once the plain sister to ritzy Palm Beach, now a textbook example of how to revitalize a ho-hum town into a **bustling urban center** for a mostly suburbanized region • The downtown, moribund just a few years ago, now teems with restaurants and **street life** • Clematis Street hops every evening • A **Saturday market** and a thriving new **arts district** pull in folks from all over • A **superb urban master plan** drawn up by town planners Duany/Plater-Zyberk & Company (DPZ) helped to jump-start much of the excitement • CityPlace, a massive new retail/residential main street, followed on the heels of the DPZ plan. (Although CityPlace is a strong vote of confidence in the newly revitalized downtown, some fear that its glitz and gloss could overwhelm the fragile renaissance taking place just a short distance away.) • Close-in residential areas are a showcase of **classic Florida architecture** from the early decades of the 20th century • A big parks push has been proposed, featuring improvements to the waterfront connected to the "Turquoise Necklace"— a network of green space, **bike trails,** and waterways that will surround the city • Former mayor Nancy Graham and her successor, Joel Daves, have assembled one of the most visionary planning departments in America • Narrowed streets, **pedestrian arcades,** and **traffic-calming measures** have been incorporated along with state-of-the-art "typological" planning codes • The same kind of urban resurgence is under way in nearby Lake Worth, Boca Raton, and Del Ray Beach.

Louisville, Kentucky

A truly **comfortable town** where you can enjoy big-city advantages on a modest budget • It could become the next destination for those looking to cash out of expensive houses and harried careers in pricier coastal cities • An amazing calendar of **arts attractions** and events • The **most beautiful square in America,** St. James Court, will make you swear you're in Europe • Park DuValle, once a meanstreets public housing project, has been transformed into a thriving **mixed-income neighborhood** without booting the original residents • A recently designated state park and interpretive center across the Ohio River from downtown draws attention to the most prolific fossil bed on the continent • The Louisville Slugger factory and museum on Main Street is adjacent to an impressive stand of **19th-century cast-iron storefronts** (the grouping is the country's second largest, just after New York's

Soho district) • The **waterfront** is enjoying new life, and there's even talk of tearing down an ugly freeway there • The E-Main neighborhood is rebounding as a **work/live/play center** for young technology workers • Old Louisville is **one of America's most intact historic districts** • The Highlands, Crescent Hill, Beechmont, and other great neighborhoods from the streetcar era are linked by **Frederick Law Olmsted-designed parkways** • City and county governments recently voted to merge, hoping to bring greater efficiency and more streamlined planning to the greater Louisville area.

Washington, D.C.

Designed as America's Rome and now, after 200 years, beginning to act the part • It's becoming less a bureaucrats' town and more of a **blossoming cultural center** • The region is beginning to challenge Boston as the East Coast's leading technology center • Brutal traffic in outer Virginia and Maryland suburbs is driving some folks back to close-in neighborhoods • **Excellent subway** • Crime is dropping • Substantial **African American middle class** • Museum heaven • Many **beautiful streetscapes**—some leafy and genteel, others urban and hip • The Shaw, Mount Pleasant, and Howard University areas are at the forefront of a growing **neighborhood renaissance** • Capitol Hill and Logan Circle, once considered edgy, are now well established as comeback neighborhoods • Recalls a **Southern graciousness,** but balanced by a Yankee work ethic • Bouncing back from the Marion Barry era, although still hampered by a democracy deficit: ruled by Congress, pays taxes but has no voting representation on Capitol Hill.

Pittsburgh

The affordable San Francisco: great neighborhoods lining valleys and perched atop hills—and unlike San Francisco, it's not losing all its **working-class character** • Steel, once its lifeblood, is down to just a few thousand jobs, but the town has hung on and diversified • Downtown survived the '60s and '70s better than most, and still sports four major department stores (although a new plan to level some older buildings there warrants close scrutiny) • Hilly topography fosters **strong neighborhood identity** and cohesion • The city wisely kept its **streetcars,** upgrading them to light rail and adding **bus-only lanes** to improve transit • It passed on building a perimeter beltway and constructed fewer freeways than other cities • The **Andy Warhol Museum** helped to spark revitalization • A North Shore development replaces the outmoded Three Rivers stadium with a new football stadium, ballpark, housing, and office buildings • A New Urbanist community, now under construction, will extend the popular Squirrel Hill neighborhood across a mountain of industrial slag; it's the **ultimate brownfield reclamation** project • Chatham Village, a visionary workers' housing project built in the early 1900s, today ranks among Pittsburgh's most prestigious addresses • The stock of **old buildings** throughout the city is outstanding • A **unique tax system,** inspired by 19th-century economic theorist Henry George, assesses land at a higher rate than buildings, thus encouraging historic preservation, discouraging downtown parking lots, and reducing sprawl.

Spokane, Washington

Seattle's smaller country cousin, undeservedly overlooked for years, now attracting refugees from California and the Puget Sound region • Many **classic neighborhoods** offer shaded streets and **down-to-earth prices** on great old homes • A chain of parks, many laid out by the legendary Olmsted brothers, are scattered throughout the city • The centerpiece of the Olmsteds' 1913 plan, **Riverfront Park,** was finally reclaimed from abandoned rail and industrial facilities as the site of Spokane's Expo '74 • Now the park provides both a **green sanctuary** and dramatic views of the swift-running Spokane River right in the heart of the city • Downtown is a historic treasure with 80 blocks of mostly intact early-20th-century buildings • Strong local **tax incentives for historic preservation** are widely used • Sprawl to the east is a serious and growing problem, but there is earnest discussion of building a light rail line to link destinations there with downtown Spokane • There's easy access to the **great outdoors** all around for world-class skiing, kayaking, hiking, fishing, and pleasure boating.

Chicago

The quintessential American city full of robust neighborhoods, **rich ethnic diversity,** and the **best cheap restaurants** in the nation • **Elevated trains,** rumbling poetically above the streets, and a **great commuter-rail network** make car ownership optional • The site of the notorious and now partially demolished Cabrini-Green housing project abuts newly middle-class neighborhoods moving west from the prosperous lakefront • **Loft housing,** although it was invented in New York, has really found its home here as conversion of older buildings and construction of new ones struggle to keep up with demand in many revitalized sections of the city • The South Loop, once an industrial no-man's-land, is now a hot spot and home to mayor Richard Daley, who understands that little things make a big difference in urban life • Daley has planted tens of thousands of trees, installed a **rooftop garden** above city hall, and promotes key livability improvements like **traffic calming** • Miles and miles of **lakefront parks** are the city's number one warm-weather hangout.

Cincinnati

This old town has a **surprisingly big-city feel,** reflecting its 19th-century origins as one of America's preeminent metropolitan centers • A classy new **riverfront park** shows off the mighty Ohio River • A magnificent bridge built by John Augustus Roebling, who later designed the Brooklyn Bridge, crosses from downtown into the well-preserved German colony of Covington, Kentucky • They've sunk a **freeway below ground** to better connect the downtown streets with the "Banks," a new mixed-use neighborhood that features housing, a ballpark, football stadium, the National Underground Railroad Freedom Center museum, and other entertainment offerings • Mount Adams, high atop the river bluffs, is a charming **village within a city** • Over-the-Rhine, a Lower East Side-style neighborhood, is seeing some **hipster redevelopment** without major displacement (yet) of low-income residents.

Richmond, Virginia

After several decades of slumber, this old-line southern tobacco town seems finally to be hitting its stride • Happily, it was bypassed by much of the soulless '60s and '70s development, although a failed festival mall from that era still scars the city's downtown • T. K. Somanath, Indian-born executive director of the Richmond Better Housing Coalition, guides one of the country's most **successful efforts to improve low-income housing** • In redeveloping the Randolph Neighborhood, Somanath **involved residents in key planning decisions:** They wanted a classic Richmond neighborhood with alleys, parks, and houses with **front porches** and private backyards • Rejecting the usual fortress approach to public housing, the Randolph plan featured a true mix of housing (both market-rate and subsidized) and clear connections to surrounding neighborhoods and commercial streets • The nearby Fan district, once a case study in urban decay, has made a spectacular comeback • A **growing gay population** continues to play a significant role in Richmond's renaissance.

Dallas

On a quick walk through downtown, you might give Dallas up for dead, but a closer look reveals encouraging signs of life that could show the way for other sprawling sun belt cities • DART, a regional **light rail system** that succeeded against all odds, is helping to transform entire blocks around several stations • A once-rundown area just across the freeway from downtown, the St. Thomas/McKinney neighborhood, has been redeveloped largely through the efforts of one **visionary developer,** Post Properties (formerly Columbus Realty) • Post's solid low-scale apartment buildings combine to form streets and public spaces that have an almost European feel • Post has been so successful in the center city that suburban developers and municipalities have invited them to bring some sorely needed urban charm to the sterile corporate landscapes of Plano and Las Colinas • The Deep Ellum **warehouse district** is coming back, along with historic neighborhoods in East Dallas • The **Dallas Institute,** a unique think tank, continues to nurture the spirit of the city; its programs challenge citizens and the city's leaders to think about Dallas in bold and innovative new ways.

Peter Katz, author of *The New Urbanism: Toward an Architecture of Community* (McGraw-Hill, 1994), consults on urban design and real estate marketing from offices in Washington, D.C. He was founding executive director of the Congress of the New Urbanism and is now co-developer of a new traditional neighborhood, The Peninsula, in Iowa City. He is an associate member of the Citistates Group, a consortium of thinkers committed to the advancement of 21st-century metropolitan regions (www.citistates.com).

XII. Social Forces Moving Toward Social Change

Building Wealth

Lester C. Thurow

Abstract: *Knowledge has replaced natural resources as the basis for creating wealth. The growth of knowledge-based business opportunities in the US is a third industrial revolution that is creating an explosion of wealth. The new economic model requires brilliant individual entrepreneurs as well as public investments in education, research and development.*

One of the nation's most influential economists asks a few basic questions. How does knowledge create wealth? How can societies incubate entrepreneurs? What skills will the entrepreneurs need?

The old foundations of success are gone. For all of human history the source of success has been controlling natural resources—land, gold, oil. Suddenly the answer is "knowledge." The king of the knowledge economy, Bill Gates, owns no land, no gold or oil, no industrial processes. How does one use knowledge to build wealth? How do societies have to be reorganized to generate a wealth-enhancing knowledge environment? How do they incubate the entrepreneurs necessary to bring about change and create wealth? What skills are needed? The knowledge-based economy is asking new questions, giving new answers, and developing new rules for success.

No one ever becomes very rich by saving money.

THE rich see opportunities to work and invest in situations where great disequilibriums—imbalances or openings in the economy created by new circumstances—exist. Something, usually a new technology, has opened up opportunities to jump to new products with very different capabilities or to new processes with much higher levels of productivity. This was as true for John D. Rockefeller as it is for Bill Gates. For both of them lifetime savings constituted a small fraction of total wealth. Carefully saving money and investing in normal equilibrium situations can make one comfortable in old age but never really wealthy.

In what will come to be seen as the third industrial revolution, new technological opportunities are creating fortunes faster than ever before. The United States has created more billionaires in the past fifteen years than in its previous history—even correcting for inflation and changes in average per capita gross domestic product. Bill Gates might spend

Source: Lester C. Thurow, "Building Wealth. (knowledge as foundation of wealth)," *The Atlantic Monthly.* June 1999, Volume 283, No. 6, pp. 57–69.

close to $100 million on his house and still have only the second most expensive house under construction in the United States. The thirteen billionaires of 1982 had by last fall been joined by 176 others. Together these 189 people have well over a trillion dollars in wealth. An additional two dozen people would have been on the list if the assessments had been made in July rather than October, and with the recovery in the stock market they were probably back on the list by the end of the year. To be among the fifty wealthiest Americans last year required a minimum of $2.9 billion. The richest Americans don't hide their wealth; they actively seek to get their names on the list, and produce their financial records to prove that they belong there. They want to be seen as economic winners.

The slightly less wealthy exhibit their wealth in other ways. Conspicuous consumption is rising. Whereas since 1993 general consumption is up 29 percent, adventure travel is up 46 percent, sales of gourmet chocolates up 51 percent, pearls 73 percent, luxury cars 74 percent, and yachts 143 percent.

This wealth explosion isn't usual in America. In the 1950s, 1960s, and 1970s the economy was growing much faster (twice as fast from 1950 to 1970 as from 1970 to 1998), and average wealth was going up, but great wealth was not erupting. America did not suddenly give birth to a generation of super-Americans. Americans in the fifties, sixties, and seventies were no less talented, no less inventive, no less ambitious. Our political and economic systems—democracy and capitalism—were not different. The opportunities to become wealthy simply weren't there.

What we are seeing in America today was last seen in the 1890s, during the second industrial revolution. Two innovations were changing the nature of economic advancement then and opening up opportunities to build great wealth.

The first was the birth of the corporate research laboratory. In creating its chemical industry Germany established the concept of systematic industrial research and development. Technological advances did not just randomly happen; they could be systematically invented. Previously the economy had advanced on the brilliance of what we might call great entrepreneurial tinkerers—James Watt, Henry Bessemer, Richard Arkwright. Technological advances were not closely coupled to scientific advances. Bessemer, for example, never knew what chemistry made his blast furnace work. He just fiddled around until it worked.

Electricity was the other element behind the second industrial revolution. Electrification allowed a whole new set of industries to emerge (telephones, movies), and radically altered the production processes of every old industry. In the steam era a giant engine powered a central rotating shaft, and machine tools ran off pulleys in long linear factories. In the new electric model of production, small motors could be attached to each machine tool, and very different, more productive configurations of machinery could be arranged on the factory floor. It was an early industrial version of what is known today in the computer industry as distributive processing.

With the electric light bulb, night became day. The price-performance curve for the light bulb looked like the price-performance curve for today's computer. The lighting that can be had for thirty-three cents in a 100-watt bulb from Home Depot would have cost $1,445 in 1883 (adjusted for lumens emitted, length of bulb life, inflation, and changes in per capita income).

Being able to do something after dark changed basic habits. People had slept an average of nine hours a night; now they slept slightly more than seven hours. With electricity came transportation systems—underground and street railways—that allowed the emergence of the modern metropolis. Electricity powered the telephone communication system that allowed small local markets to become big national markets.

The second industrial revolution created a sharp discontinuity in economic affairs and opened up opportunities to do things never done before. Old things could also be done in new ways. The smart and the lucky did not have to content themselves with highly competitive businesses producing commodities that earned bond-market "equilibrium" rates of return. In the jargon of economists, high "disequilibrium returns" replaced low "equilibrium returns." America's first set of billionaires (in inflation-corrected dollars)—Rockefeller, Carnegie, Mellon, Morgan, Schwab—emerged.

Disequilibrium conditions always disappear eventually. New industries with high returns and high growth rates become old industries with much lower returns and normal growth rates. As technologies mature, costs stop falling faster than selling prices. Competitors arise to drive down selling prices. The new products reach saturation levels. Growth markets become replacement markets. But "eventually" often means several decades. It takes time to attract enough capital and people into new industries to turn them into mature industries with normal growth rates and normal rates of return. In the meantime, there are great fortunes to be made.

Although billionaires and market wealth dominate the headlines, there is another way to look at wealth creation that could generate a very different set of headlines if anyone wanted to pay attention. Real wealth is the ability to produce more with less—to generate a flow of goods and services without having to sacrifice something else of equal value. It is not created by taking time away from other activities and devoting it to money-making. Real wealth can be created by increases in what economists call labor productivity: the same time spent working generates more income (and hence wealth) than it did in the past.

But wealth can also be created by investing in plant and equipment. If one sacrifices consumption in order to save and invest, the sacrifice must be subtracted from the flow of income from that investment. Real wealth is ultimately not created by taking income away from consumption and devoting it to investment; it flows from increases in capital productivity—getting more out of the same capital resources or using fewer capital resources to generate the same levels of market wealth.

Sometimes successful businesses have to cannibalize themselves to save themselves.

BUSINESSES must be willing to destroy the old while it is still successful if they wish to build the new that will become successful. If they don't destroy themselves, others will destroy them.

Disequilibrium means great threats as well as great opportunities. Only six of what had been the twenty-five biggest firms in 1960 were still on the list in 1997. Most had been merged into other companies, but two of the twenty-five had gone out of business. Of what were the twelve largest American companies at the beginning of the twentieth century, eleven will not be around to see the beginning of the twenty-first. Technological breakthroughs occur, the economic environment changes, and they could not adjust.

Old big firms understand, and often even invent, the new technologies that transform the world, but they have a structural problem that is almost impossible to solve. When breakthrough technologies come along, such firms must destroy the old to build the new. Four of the five makers of vacuum tubes, for example, never successfully made transistors after transistors emerged to replace the vacuum tube—and the fifth is today not a player. When the microprocessor allowed the personal computer to replace the mainframe as the dominant growth market in the computer industry, the old industrial leader, IBM, fell off a cliff, and new leaders, Intel and Microsoft, emerged. IBM understood the new technology and wanted to compete but could not destroy its old (mainframe) business to build the new. In the 1980s IBM sold its 20 percent stake in Intel; if it still owned that stake today, IBM's total market value would be almost 30 percent greater than it is.

New firms have the great advantage of not having to destroy themselves to save themselves.

Two routes other than radical technological change can lead to high-growth, high-rate-of-return opportunities: sociological disequilibriums and developmental disequilibriums.

ENTREPRENEURS see sociological opportunities to change human habits. Starbucks persuaded Americans to replace their fifty-cent cup of coffee bought at a local restaurant with a $2.50 cup of coffee bought at a coffee bar. They turned a competitive commodity with widely distributed points of sale out of which no one made much money into a non-competitive differentiated product, and created a rapidly growing industry with high rates of return from which great fortunes could emerge.

The cruise industry took advantage of a shift in demographics: the relative purchasing power of the elderly had doubled in two decades. Seventy-year-olds twenty years earlier had cash incomes 40 percent below those of thirty-year-olds; suddenly seventy-year-olds had cash incomes 20 percent above those of thirty-year-olds. Cruises, known at least since the days of Cleopatra, became the perfect vacation for the elderly: We move you; you don't move. Some owners of cruise lines have become billionaires by exploiting sociological disequilibriums.

The problem with wealth generated this way is that sociological disequilibriums usually reflect a transfer of existing wealth rather than the generation of new wealth. Those who were selling conventional cups of coffee now sell fewer of them, and thousands of mom-and-pop restaurants make less money. The extra two dollars a cup that goes to Starbucks is two dollars that isn't spent somewhere else.

What might be called developmental disequilibrium exists whenever countries or entrepreneurs can replicate the activities of the developed world in the underdeveloped world.

A year or so before the hand-over of Hong Kong from Britain to China, I was sitting in the lounge at the Hong Kong airport eavesdropping on a conversation between two rich Chinese businessmen on their way to spend six months in Vancouver in order to get Canadian passports—their insurance policy in case things went wrong in Hong Kong. They were complaining about having to stay so long in Vancouver, because they could see no way of using their time there to make money. To hear them describe it, Vancouver was an economic desert. Why?

Vancouver, after all, is richer than Hong Kong.

The answer is to be found in the absence of developmental disequilibriums in Canada. In Hong Kong these businessmen had become rich by exploiting the differences between the developed world and poor, but now open, mainland China. They simply copied what was done in the developed world and replicated it in China. What were commodity operations with low rates of return and few growth prospects in the developed world were high-return, high-growth opportunities in China. These businessmen were skilled at replication and at knowing the exact time when mainland-Chinese conditions were ripe for any particular activity.

Vancouver held no replication opportunities. All the normal First World activities already existed there. To get rich in Vancouver one needed breakthrough technologies or new sociological concepts. The businessmen had neither. For them Vancouver truly was an economic desert.

Making capitalism work in a deflationary environment is much harder than making it work in an inflationary environment.

SYSTEMATIC deflation is not a certainty, but the third industrial revolution has made it likely enough that there's good reason to think about how standard economic operating procedures change when prices start to fall.

Globalization is forcing prices down. Production is being moved from high-cost to low-cost locations, and prices are falling as a result. Name any major product, calculate how much the world could produce if every factory were operating at capacity, subtract what the world is going to buy, and you'll find that the world's production potential exceeds expected consumption by at least a third. Cars, semiconductor chips, and oil are but three of many examples. With such an excess of production capacity, falling prices are no mystery. Firms have an enormous incentive to lower prices in an attempt to keep their facilities operating closer to capacity.

Globalization also brings pressure to bear to change work practices, to raise productivity, and to lower wages. BMW used its ability to set up a manufacturing plant in the United States as leverage with its unions to change work practices in Germany. Flexible shifts were introduced in Germany so that when demand was high, the plants could operate on weekends. This allowed capital costs to be cut by a quarter. BMW workers essentially have bank accounts in which their hours of work on weekends or after a normal shift can be deposited. When demand is low, workers who aren't needed can draw pay for the hours of work accumulated in their bank accounts. Overtime is not paid unless it is clear that total hours of work in a year will exceed the standard. The company is now spreading these practices to its Rover plants, in Britain. The British workers have been told that they must cut the productivity gap, of 30 percent, between themselves and the Germans. BMW does not have to threaten that if they don't, production will be moved elsewhere. Everyone knows that. With labor costs and wages down (the same pressures have been forcing down real weekly U.S. wages for the bottom two thirds of the work force at the rate of about a percentage point a year for the past twenty-five years), prices must eventually start to fall.

The Asian meltdown substantially increases the downward pressures on prices. Indonesia and Thailand have to export more, and can do so only by lowering prices. If their global competitors, mostly in the Third World, do not want to lose market share, they have no choice but to match the lower prices. In the developed world similar pressure comes from Korea and Japan.

New technologies, especially those affecting energy, minerals, and agricultural products, are also driving prices down very rapidly. Oil prices were at an all-time low early this year. Gold, that bellwether commodity, is also down dramatically from where it was just a few years ago. In every case new processes are dramatically cutting the costs of extracting value from nature.

Downsizing and outsourcing have also played a role in reducing prices. It is common in America for companies to have contracts with their suppliers that require annual price reductions. Auto-parts manufacturers, for example, have signed contracts with the major auto producers calling for price reductions of three percent a year. Outsourcing is largely responsible for these tough contracts, because it is easier to get tough with an outside supplier than it is with an inside supplier. If an outside supplier makes no money with the lower prices, that is his problem. But if an inside supplier makes no money, the corporation loses in one of its selling divisions what it gains in one of its buying divisions. It sees no gain in aggregate profits. Such practices led to a fall in new-car prices in the United States last year for the first time since the early 1970s.

In a deflationary world debt is to be avoided at all costs. Real interest rates (nominal money rates plus the rate of deflation) are very high and debts have to be repaid in dollars of greater value than the dollars that were borrowed. Those with debts want to repay them as quickly as possible, because debt burdens automatically grow larger in real terms over time. If prices fall by 10 percent, a $100 debt effectively becomes a $110 debt. And if debt reduction becomes the No. 1 priority, no one will invest in the things that cause growth.

There are no institutional substitutes for individual entrepreneurial change agents.

CAPITALISM is a process of creative destruction. The new destroys the old. Both the creation and the destruction are essential to driving the economy forward. Entrepreneurs are central to the process of creative destruction; they bring the new technologies and the new concepts into active commercial use. They are the change agents of capitalism.

The old patterns of powerful vested interests must be broken if the new is to exist, but those vested interests fight back. They are not willing to fade quietly into the pages of history. Entrepreneurs built the national companies that destroyed local companies at the end of the nineteenth century, and they are building the global companies that are destroying national companies at the end of the twentieth century.

History teaches us that it is only too easy to stamp out entrepreneurship. It is a fundamental human characteristic but, despite its creative and destructive powers, an extremely fragile one. Among most peoples in most times and most places entrepreneurs do not exist. The economic possibilities exist, but they are not seen, the energy to realize them is lacking, or the risks they involve seem too great.

When societies aren't organized so that the old vested interests can be brushed aside, entrepreneurs cannot emerge. Social systems have to be built in which entrepreneurs have the freedom to destroy the old. Yet destroying the old can too easily be seen as a step into chaos. Societies that aren't ready to break with the past aren't willing to let entrepreneurs come into existence.

Europe provides a good example of the importance of entrepreneurship. Europe saves and invests more than the United States, has a better-educated populace, and has a basic understanding of science that is just as good as that in the United States, yet it has created none of the new brainpower industries of the twenty-first century. Last year the production arm of the last indigenous European computer manufacturer, Siemens Nixdorf, was sold to Acer, of Taiwan. How can a region be a leader in the twenty-first century and be completely out of the computer business? The European entrepreneurs that should exist don't.

Sociology almost always dominates technology. Ideas often lie unused because people do not want to use them. The fact that something is possible does not mean that it will happen. Great persistence is needed to bring a truly new idea into the market. Steam toys have been unearthed in the archaeological exploration of ancient Greece, and the ancient Egyptians had steam-powered temple doors—yet the steam engine did not emerge as a source of power for economic production until the eighteenth century. The right sociology had to be in place for revolutionary new products to emerge.

No society that values order above all else will be creative; but without some degree of order creativity disappears.

CONSIDER China at the outset of the fifteenth century. Its curiosity, its instinct for exploration, and its drive to build had created all the technologies necessary to launch the Industrial Revolution—something that would not actually occur for another 400 years. It had the blast furnace and piston bellows for making steel (the amount of pig iron that China produced annually in the late eleventh century would not be matched anywhere in the world for 700 years); gunpowder and the cannon for military conquest; the compass and the rudder for exploration; paper and movable type for printing; the iron plough, the horse collar, rotary threshing machines, and mechanical seeders to generate agricultural surpluses; the ability to drill for natural gas; and in mathematics the decimal system, negative numbers, and the concept of zero, which put the Chinese far ahead of the Europeans. Large Chinese armadas—carrying as many as 28,000 men—were exploring Africa's east coast at about the same time that Portugal and Spain were sending much smaller expeditions down the west coast of Africa. Seven major Chinese expeditions explored the Indian Ocean with ships four times as large as those of Columbus.

But the geographic conquests and the industrial revolution that were possible did not happen. The Chinese rejected and ultimately forgot the technologies that could have given them world dominance. New technologies were perceived as threats rather than opportunities. Innovation was forbidden. Imperial edicts prohibited the building of new oceangoing ships and sailing away from the Chinese coastline. By the end of the fifteenth century the demand for order had overridden intrinsic human curiosity, the desire to explore, and the drive to build.

Consider the opposite case of Russia in the seventy-five years before the Russian Revolution. Creativity flourished in the chaos of a dying empire. Think of all the great authors: Tolstoy, Dostoevski, Chekhov, Turgenev, Gogol—the list goes on and on. Likewise in the world of music and the arts. Stravinsky, Tchaikovsky, Kandinsky, Kasimir, and many others are still played in our concert halls or admired in our museums. In science Russia was a leader. Wilhelm Ostwald was one of the first Nobel Prize winners in chemistry, for his work on the speed of chemical reactions. Ivan Pavlov, also a Nobel Prize winner, is perhaps the most famous physiologist ever. Dmitri Mendeleyev devised the periodic table of chemical elements. Markov chains—named for the mathematician Andrei Markov—have found a wide variety of applications in physics, biology, linguistics, and economics. Nikolai Lobachevski developed non-Euclidean geometry. Being skeptical and refusing to accept authority are the secrets of scientific advancement. Living in chaos, Russians could be skeptical. Compared with the dangers of political revolt against the Czar, the risks of scientific revolt against perceived wisdom were small.

Creativity flourished in the chaos, yes, but without some degree of order it was impossible for the Russians to use that creativity to develop a successful economy. Chaos led to more chaos, and ultimately to the Russian Revolution. Order was reimposed. Creativity died.

To advance and use knowledge a society needs the right combination of chaos and order. Too much order (China) does not work. Too much chaos (Russia) does not work. Although not as extreme, America and Japan are in many ways similar to Russia and China. America has more than enough chaos to be creative, but too little order to use its ideas in the most efficient ways. Japan has more than enough order to be efficient but too little chaos to be creative. Both could gain if each moved a little in the direction of the other. Successful societies create and manage a tension between order and chaos without letting either of them get out of hand. New ideas are easily frustrated if societies are not receptive to the chaos that comes from change, yet societies have to maintain an appropriate degree of order to take advantage of creative breakthroughs.

At the individual level these same forces show up as a tension between tradition and rebellion. Einstein dropped out of high school at the age of fifteen; renounced his citizenship a year later; lived on the margins socially, economically, and morally; and called himself a gypsy and was viewed as a bohemian. His life was in some sense a search for order in disorder, both scientifically and socially. Great creativity requires hard facts, wild imagination, and nonlogical jumps forward that are then proved to be right by working backward to known principles. Only the rebellious can do it.

Entrepreneurial and organizational skills, curiosity, the desire to explore, and the drive to build can be enhanced. Useful curiosity is a characteristic of individuals who have mastered the existing body of knowledge but are not paralyzed by it.

A successful knowledge-based economy requires large public investments in education, infrastructure, and research and development.

IT is not just a matter of brilliant individuals and aggressive entrepreneurs. The new economic game is simultaneously a team game and an individual sport. Without the support of the team the individual fails. Without individual initiative the team fails. Both are necessary.

Some countries are willing to invest in research and development; others are not. The right amount to invest is not obvious. The industrial world's four biggest economies spend very similar percentages of GDP on R&D: France and Germany spend 2.3 percent, Japan 2.8 percent, and the United States 2.5 percent. But the similarity derives more from a desire in each not to let the other three get ahead than from any proof that they are spending the right amount.

Most private American R&D, about four fifths, is done by big firms. Even among these big spenders, however, spending levels vary greatly: Boeing spends four percent of sales, Intel nine percent, Lucent 12 percent, and Microsoft 17 percent. Expenditure levels depend on the industry under consideration and on whether firms in that industry believe that the basic science is in place to make real progress in developing new goods or services. Virtually 100 percent of Intel's sales and profits come from products developed within the past three years, but only about 30 to 40 percent of IBM's profits come from recently developed products.

For countries or companies technological leadership is not the same thing as R&D spending. Europe spends its share on research, but if one looks at technological leadership, that spending does not seem to be paying off. To pay off, obviously, research has to be followed by the activities necessary to embed the newly developed technologies in the economy. Where America outclasses Europe is not so much in R&D spending on information technology, for example, as in investments in information hardware and software. As a fraction of GDP, U.S. investments were twice those of Germany or France in 1996. What has been learned isn't very different, but what is being done with the learning is quite different.

Private rates of return on R&D spending (the financial benefits that accrue to the firm doing the spending) average about 24 percent. But social rates of return on R&D spending (the economic benefits that accrue to the entire society) are about 66 percent (as computed by averaging eight different studies), with a range from 50 to 105 percent—almost three times as high as private rates. Two out of three dollars in net benefits generated do not accrue to those paying for the R&D. This result, never contradicted in the economic literature, provides powerful evidence that there are huge positive social spillovers from research and development. Left to themselves, private firms will spend too little, because they cannot capture all the benefits that flow from their activities.

Because the government doesn't care exactly which Americans reap the benefits, it has a very important role to play in R&D. Rates of return on R&D spending are far above those found elsewhere in the economy. Government now pays for about 30 percent of total R&D, but with a 66 percent rate of return it should be spending much more. Americans as a whole are investing too little in R&D. Put simply, the payoff from social investment in basic research is as clear as anything is ever going to be in economics.

Private returns are apt to be much more certain if one is looking for an extension of existing knowledge rather than for a major breakthrough; thus private firms tend to concentrate their money on the developmental end of the R&D process. Time lags are also shorter, and in the business world speed is everything.

Because of this proclivity in the private sector, government should focus its spending on long-tailed projects for advancing basic knowledge. This is where private firms won't invest, but it is also precisely where the breakthroughs that generate private business opportunities are made. That is why biotechnology had to be supported by the government. Where it did not receive government support—everywhere except the United States—it did not develop. No private company would have made the investments that the National Institutes of Health did, even if the company had known that success was certain, because money went in for more than twenty-five years before any salable products came out.

The biggest unknown for the individual in a knowledge-based economy is how to have a career in a system where there are no careers.

EDUCATION has always been a high-risk investment for the individual. More than 20 percent of all college graduates will end up making less than the average high school graduate. They invested and it did not pay off. But recently it has become even riskier. How does one plan the investments necessary to have a career in the face of corporate downsizings at profitable firms?

For my generation of high school graduates the concept of a career had meaning. During the 1950s in Montana, where I went to high school, many high school graduates started as laborers in the copper mines. Starting wages were good, and one could count on annual raises of two or three percent. There was a skill ladder. Laborers moved up to operating underground trains or other kinds of heavy equipment, learning the necessary skills by working as assistants to the operators. Someone who demonstrated intelligence and judgment could be given responsibility for setting off underground explosions. Each promotion meant higher hourly wages. When a worker reached his mid-thirties, he could expect to take the last step on the earnings ladder and become a contract miner, who was paid for each foot of tunnel dug rather than by the hour. He was no longer a wage slave. On this career ladder high school graduates could match college graduates in earnings.

But that's all gone now. Those mines were shut down. The thousands of people who worked there were laid off.

What used to be true only in declining industries—that skills suddenly become valueless—is now true everywhere. Downsizing is a way of life even in good times. In a global economy, if skills are cheaper somewhere else in the world, companies will move there to lower production costs. They aren't tied to any particular set of workers. When new knowledge makes old skills obsolete, firms want to employ workers who already have that knowledge. They don't want to pay for retraining. In the second half of this decade profitable American companies have laid off more than half a million workers each year despite the economic boom. The old career ladders are gone. The old lifetime employees are gone.

Explicitly or implicitly, today's high school graduate is given a message: "You are unlikely to have a lifetime career in any one company. You are going to have to learn to take responsibility for and manage your own career. Regular annual wage increases are a thing of the past. Paternalism is gone." If they are honest, employers themselves deliver the message. But how does anyone follow this advice?

If career ladders don't exist within any one company, maybe they exist across different companies. This would mean that a good initial performance at Company A would lead to training opportunities, a better job, and higher wages at Company B. But the world doesn't work that way for most employees. Companies don't tell other companies who their good employees are—even if they have no promotion opportunities to offer those employees. They don't want to lose them. And even if they did tell other companies, they wouldn't be believed. They would be suspected of trying to get rid of their bad workers. Similarly, they don't tell other companies about their bad employees. They don't want to open themselves up to lawsuits. If asked, and they seldom are, companies are willing to tell other companies just one thing about a worker seeking a new job: Yes, that person did work for us.

In this context a good performance at Company A doesn't matter, because it does not lead to opportunities for training and promotion at Company B. When workers move from one company to another, they simply start over at another entry-level job; there is no progress up a career ladder. The rational strategy is to keep moving until one finds a company that still has internal career ladders. But as such companies become fewer, the number of high school graduates with real career opportunities ahead of them declines to the vanishing point.

A cross-company career ladder runs into other problems. After age forty-five cross-company career moves are difficult, and after age fifty-five they are impossible. (Those tracking downsized workers find that after age fifty-five they seldom find good jobs with good companies.) Age-discrimination laws can protect older employees against being unfairly dismissed from their old firms, but they cannot get them a good job at a new company. Employers have the right to hire the best workers available. In a fast-changing world older employees too often bring obsolete experience and out-of-date skills. There are always a lot of young potential employees who look more promising.

The lack of career opportunities is dramatically visible in earnings data. The gains in real annual earnings of high school graduates aged twenty to forty are much smaller than they used to be. There are lots of jobs, and unemployment is low, but opportunities to acquire skills and the higher wages that go with them don't exist. As a result, earnings profiles are flatter. The lack of on-the-job opportunities to acquire new skills is another reason that the wage gap between high school graduates and college graduates has gotten much bigger in recent years.

Real wages have also been falling for most of the male labor force. Graduating from American high schools, these men don't initially have the same level of skills as their counterparts in the rest of the industrialized world, nor do they get the post-secondary skills training (apprenticeships, for example) that most of the rest of the world gives its non-college-bound labor force. At the same time, wage gains for those in the top 20 percent of the work force have never been larger. The widening disparity in earnings and wealth doesn't create problems for the economy (it simply produces more luxury goods and fewer middle-class goods), but it probably does create long-run political problems in a democracy. How does one preach political equality in an economy of ever-growing inequality?

The issue is not jobs. It is high wages and careers. If wages fall to be commensurate with skills, jobs are always available. That is what the American experience proves. Jobs have never been more plentiful than they are in the 1990s, yet wages have been falling for more than half of the work force. In contrast with jobs, careers are in very short supply in America.

With career ladders in place, the ambitious worker of the 1950s or the 1960s could figure out what skills were needed for advancement. He or she knew what to take in night school. But without career ladders, how does anyone rationally plan an educational investment? What skills will pay off? No one wants to waste investment funds on skills that will go unused.

Historically, on-the-job training has been central to skills acquisition for much of the population. But with downsizing, the days of extensive on-the-job training have ended. What replaces it? In economics textbooks workers start to pay employers for the training they used to get free, when they were expected to be lifetime employees, by working for wages below what they could get from an employer who was not providing training. This has not happened. Judging what skills to buy from one's employer is no simpler than judging what skills to buy from an outside institution.

Also missing from a downsizing environment is a sense of economic security. If workers are asked what factors are most important in a job, economic security always comes out ahead of maximum wages. This is not the answer that is supposed to be given by Homo economicus. He or she is supposed to be interested in lifetime income maximization, and not to be worried about the risks and uncertainties of economic life. But real live human beings like the feeling of a solid economic floor under them. Homo economicus does not worry about starving between jobs.

Paradoxically, just when one would think that firms would be building closer relationships with their key knowledge workers, in order to keep them committed to the firm, they are smashing the implicit social contract with these workers. Knowledge workers, like other workers, are now fired when not needed or when their skills become obsolete. They, too, see a reduction in their real wages when cheaper alternatives are found elsewhere in the world. Firms invest less in on-the-job training for knowledge workers even when they want them to stay around, because they know that in the future fewer of them will stay around. If workers are laid off when not needed, the smart ones know that they should leave whenever an even marginally better job opportunity presents itself.

As job uncertainty rises, the numbers of those with a strong interest in the success of their current employers dwindle. Surveys show that although attachment to their occupations has remained constant for American workers over the past two decades, the number of those with a strong attachment to their employers has gone down by a fifth. The system is evolving toward less commitment and less investment in skills just as it should be moving in the opposite direction.

The basic problem in the United States is that every employer wants a free ride in the training system. "You train, I'll hire" is the American way. Whenever unemployment is low, employers who themselves do no training bitterly complain about the shortage of trained workers. They see nothing strange about their complaints. As for the employees, without career ladders they cannot intelligently acquire the right skills on their own. Since they will be switching employers frequently, they don't know what skills they will need or how long those skills will be relevant to their earning opportunities. As a result—rationally—they don't invest in skills.

When it is clear that something must be done but rational individuals and companies won't do it, society has to reorganize itself to make what is individually irrational into something that is individually rational. There is a simple solution. For example, France levies a training tax of 1.5 percent of payroll. The purpose is not to collect taxes but to make it rational for every employer to train. Employers can deduct their expenditures for training from that 1.5 percent tax. Thus if they spend 1.5 percent of their sales on training their work force, they pay no tax. Since the money will be taken away from them if they don't train, training becomes a free good as far as the firm is concerned. No one tells employers what skills to teach their workers, but they are effectively being told that they must teach some skills. Such a system aids everyone. It makes employers invest as if there were career ladders even when these have been abolished. If all employers have to invest, no one gets a free ride.

Major unresolved problems

THE biggest problem of the third industrial revolution is as easy to enunciate as it is difficult to solve. Technology is creating a global economy that is rapidly supplanting our old national economies. National governments cannot control this new economy, yet no one, least of all Americans, wants to create the forms of global government that might be able to control it. As a result we are going to be living in a fundamentally unmanaged economic system. The difficulties of containing the 1997 Asian economic meltdown are just the first of many such difficulties we can expect.

National governments, which used to worry about managing and maintaining their economic systems, are slowly being pushed out of business. Changes in global finance overwhelm all but the largest governments. Governments have lost much of their influence over the movement of information and capital. They cannot control who crosses their borders either physically or culturally. They still have their armies, but they are afraid to use them when wars are also fought on television.

Conversely, the power—or perhaps we should say the freedom from government supervision—of global businesses is growing with companies' ability to move to the most advantageous locations and to play countries off against one another in bidding for attractive investment projects.

As national governments shrink and global corporations expand, a second major problem emerges. Almost everywhere we look we see rising economic inequalities among countries, among firms, among individuals. Returns to capital are up; returns to labor are down. Returns to skills are up; returns to unskilled labor are down. Firms will be global players or they will be niche players. The mid-sized national firm is a species in danger of extinction. Traditionally, national governments have acted to keep such inequalities under control. But having lost their ability to manage the system, they have also lost their ability to restrain economic inequalities. For at least a while we are simply going to live in a world with greater inequalities on a broad scale.

THE third industrial revolution is making obsolete old institutions and old modes of operation, requiring the individual, the firm, and the nation to change.

For individuals here are three words of advice: skills, skills, skills. The economic prospects of those without skills are bleak. What we now see—falling real wages for those without skills—is going to continue. In education the needs of the bottom two thirds of the labor force are particularly acute. In an age when brawn earns little and brains much, this part of the labor force simply has to be much better educated. Something is fundamentally wrong when the bottom quarter of South Korean eighth-grade students score, on average, higher than their American counterparts.

Entrepreneurial opportunities were few in the 1950s and 1960s. Today they are many. But for every success we read about in the paper, every new billionaire made, dozens of entrepreneurs will go broke unnoticed and unmourned. The downside risks are real.

Cannibalization is the challenge for old business firms. Can they aggressively seize the opportunities opened up by the third industrial revolution, even when that means deliberately destroying existing profitable activities? History is clear: few can, and those that don't are likely to die. For new firms the economic opportunities have never been better. The world is full of openings for businesses to grow in environments without established competitors.

Nations that are heavy investors in education, infrastructure, and R&D are going to tend to win. We need a national capital investment budget to remind ourselves of how we are spending our resources. The negative savings rates that we now have are not the route to success.

For those with skills and a fondness for risks, however, who are willing to cannibalize their old activities and are living in high-investment societies, the times have never been more favorable.

Lester C. Thurow ("Building Wealth") is a professor of management and economics at the Massachusetts Institute of Technology. His article in this issue will appear in somewhat different form in his book *Building Wealth: New Rules for Individuals, Companies, and Nations in a Knowledge-Based Economy,* which is to be published by Harper Business this month.

Globalization Theory: Lessons from the Exportation of McDonaldization and the New Means of Consumption

George Ritzer and Elizabeth L. Malone

Recent dramatic increases in the transnational flows of capital, people, goods, information, and culture have transformed the world. The consequences of these far-reaching economic, political, demographic, and cultural changes have elicited increasing political and civic concern over globalization, as evidenced in 1999 in the mass protests against the World Trade Organization in Seattle and in the spring of 2000 against the World Bank and International Monetary Fund in Washington, D.C. Globalization theory, which seeks to construct theoretical models to address these realities, emerged both from the social changes that it seeks to explain and internal developments in social theory, most notably as a reaction to earlier perspectives such as modernization theory and its western bias (although some globalization theorists [e.g., Galtung 1997; Giddens 1990; Hall 1997] retain this bias). It is not surprising, therefore, that globalization theory has emerged as one of the most widely discussed and hotly debated perspectives in contemporary social theory.

Given the vast expanse of globalization theory, it would be impossible in a single essay to address the full range of perspectives that it encompasses (for a sampling, see Lechner and Boli 2000). Nevertheless, although globalization theorists differ on a number of issues, they focus primarily upon the world as a system and devote most of their attention to global processes that transcend or operate more or less autonomously from individual societies or nations.

Theories of globalization can be classified on the basis of their emphasis on cultural, economic, political, and/or institutional factors, on the one hand, and whether they stress homogeneity or heterogeneity, on the other.

At the extremes, the globalization of culture can lead either to a trend toward common codes and practices (homogeneity) or to a situation in which many cultures interact to create a kind of pastiche or a blend leading to a variety of hybrids (heterogeneity). The trend toward homogeneity is often associated with cultural imperialism (see below). There

Source: George Ritzer and Elizabeth L. Malone, "Globalization Theory: Lessons from the Exportation of McDonaldization and the New Means of Consumption." *American Studies*, vol. 41, # 2/3, pp. 97–117.

are many varieties of cultural imperialism including associating it with American culture (Smith 1990), the West (Giddens 1990), or core countries (Hannerz 1990). Robertson (2001), although he doesn't use the term, seems to be describing a series of hybrids when he talks about the interpenetration of the universal and the particular, as well as in his discussion of the "glocal." Garcia Canclini (1995), Pieterse (1995), and others talk specifically about hybrids; Featherstone and Lash (1995), Abu-Lughod (1997), and Friedman (1994) describe a world characterized by a cultural pastiche. The pastiche may include a "global culture" (the world of jet setters and of international board rooms) that becomes yet another component of world culture.

Theorists who emphasize economic factors tend to focus on homogeneity (Harvey 1989; Piore and Sabel 1984; Wallerstein 1974). They generally see globalization as the spread of the market economy throughout the world. In a recent, more specific example, Chase-Dunn et al. (2000) have focused on the globalization of trade. While those who focus on economic issues tend to emphasize homogeneity, most acknowledge that some differentiation (heterogeneity) exists at the margins of the global economy. Other forms of heterogeneity involve, for example, the commodification of local cultures and the existence of flexible specialization that permits the tailoring of many products to the needs of various local specifications.

A political/institutional orientation, too, either emphasizes homogeneity or heterogeneity. Meyer et al. (1997), for example, focus on the nation-state, more specifically, the existence of worldwide models of the state and the emergence of isomorphic forms of governance. Keohane and Nye (1989) focus on the global influence of a multiplicity of institutions. Hobsbawm (1997) and Appadurai (1996) see transnational institutions and organizations greatly diminishing the power of both the nation-state and other, more local social structures to make a difference in people's lives. This is the phenomenon that Barber (1995) has termed "McWorld," the antithesis of which is "Jihad"—localized, ethnic, and reactionary political forces (including "rogue states") that involve an intensification of nationalism and lead to greater heterogeneity (Barber 1995; also Appadurai 1996).

Given the great scope of globalization theory, and the rate at which the literature is growing, we will not be able to address it in anything approaching its entirety in this essay. To make this discussion manageable we will focus on a recent statement by one of its foremost practitioners, Roland Robertson. Robertson is associated with the cultural approach to globalization and while he reaffirms that position in the essay, "Globalization Theory 2000+," (2001), he also seeks to deal with the significance of economic and political/institutional factors. In this context he seeks to identify and discuss the key problems in globalization theory. In this essay we will examine several of Robertson's ideas from the point of view of related processes that Ritzer (1998, 2000; Smart 1999; Alfino, Caputo and Wynyard 1998) has termed "McDonaldization" and the emergence of the "New Means of Consumption" (Ritzer 1999). This will allow us to analyze some of the strengths and weaknesses of globalization theory, at least as Robertson presents it.

While an important development, globalization theory is often presented as a series of broad generalizations that are not embedded in specific details of the social world. One of the things that the study of McDonaldization and the New Means of Consumption allows us to do is to examine some of the premises and assertions of globalization theory within the context of a specific set of developments about which much is known. It allows us to "test," at least in a very rough sense, some of the basic tenets of globalization theory.

We will see that while globalization theory has much to offer to our understanding of McDonaldization and the New Means of Consumption, the specifics of these processes make it clear that some of globalization theory's basic tenets need to be both tempered and made far more specific.

A Brief Introduction to McDonaldization and the New Means of Consumption

Before proceeding to a discussion of the relationship between globalization, McDonaldization, and the New Means of Consumption, we need a brief introduction to the latter two (to parallel the brief sketch of globalization theory offered above) in order to orient the ensuing discussion.

McDonaldization. This is the process by which the principles of the highly successful and revolutionary fast food restaurant are coming to dominate more and more sectors of American society and an increasing number of other societies throughout the world. The principles of the process are *efficiency, calculability, predictability,* and *control,* particularly through the *substitution of nonhuman for human technology;* also associated with McDonaldization are the seemingly inevitable *irrationalities of rationality.* The basic concept, as well as its fundamental dimensions, is derived from the German social theorist Max Weber's (1921/1968) work on formal rationality. Weber contended that the modern Western world was characterized by an increasing tendency towards the predominance of formally rational systems. Thus, the process of McDonaldization obviously predates the establishment and proliferation of McDonald's restaurants (Weber 1927/1981). However, the McDonald's franchise system and the principles upon which it has so successfully spread throughout the world represent the exemplar (as was the bureaucracy in Weber's model) of the contemporary development of rationalization. While the fast food restaurant is the paradigm of this process, the process of McDonaldization has by now affected most, if not all, social structures and institutions in the United States, and has penetrated most nations (at least those that are reasonably developed economically) in the world. Thus, the term McDonaldization is not restricted to the fast food industry or to the United States. Rather, it refers to a wide-ranging and far-reaching, but distinctive process, of social change.

The McDonaldization model has been applied well beyond the fast food restaurant and even everyday consumption to such disparate phenomena as higher education ("McUniversity") (Parker and Jary 1995), vegetarianism (Tester 1999), theme parks (Bryman 1995, 1999a; Ritzer and Liska 1998), southern folk art (Fine 1999), and politics (Turner 1999; Beilharz, 1999). (Bryman [1999b] has even recently proposed a process of "Disneyization" as a complement to McDonaldization.) McDonaldization is a broad social development. Even the processes surrounding birth and death increasingly conform to its principles (see Ritzer 2000, chapter 8).

Of course, not all systems are equally McDonaldized; McDonaldization is a matter of degree with some settings having been more McDonaldized than others. However, few contemporary social settings or institutions have been able to escape its influence altogether.

The relevance of the McDonaldization thesis to issues of globalization should be apparent, for, both implicitly and explicitly, it asserts that social systems in contemporary society are becoming increasingly McDonaldized and, more important, that the basic principles of efficiency, calculability, predictability, and control through the substitution of non-human for human technology that undergird it have been exported from the United States to much of the rest of the world. To the extent that these principles have been adopted and become defining features of institutions in other nations, they can be said to be undergoing the process of McDonaldization.

It is worth noting that when they have addressed the McDonaldization thesis and related ideas, some globalization theorists (e.g., Robertson 2001), especially those committed to the idea of heterogeneity, have tended to be critical of McDonaldization's focus on processes emanating from the United States and for its emphasis on its homogenizing impact on much of the rest of the world. Instead, they focus on diversity, the multi-directionality of global flows and the existence of global processes that are relatively autonomous of specific nation-states. While all of these processes exist and are significant, it is also the case that *some* aspects of globalization are best described as flowing from the United States and having a largely homogenizing effect on much of the rest of the world. We will return to the relationship between McDonaldization and globalization at a number of points in the ensuing discussion.

The thesis that the United States is undergoing a process of McDonaldization and that it is actively exporting manifestations of that process to much of the rest of the world is obviously a global perspective, but it is both less than and more than globalization theory. On the one hand, McDonaldization does not involve anything approaching the full range of global processes. For example, many of the economic, political, and institutional aspects of globalization are largely unrelated to McDonaldization. On the other hand, McDonaldization involves much more than an analysis of its global impact. For example, much of it involves the manifold transformations taking place within the United States, the source and still the center of this process. Thus, McDonaldization is not coterminous with globalization, nor is it solely a global process. Nonetheless, McDonaldization has global implications and can thus be a useful lens through which to examine globalization theory, or at least some of Robertson's perspectives on it.

The New Means of Consumption. There has been an almost dizzying creation and proliferation of settings that allow, encourage, and even compel us to consume innumerable goods and services. These settings, the New Means of Consumption, have come into existence, or taken revolutionary new forms, in the United States since the close of World War II. Building upon, but going beyond, earlier settings, they have dramatically transformed the nature of consumption.

The following are the major New Means of Consumption with notable examples and the years in which they began operations:

- Franchises (McDonald's, 1955)
- Shopping Malls (the first indoor mall, Edina, Minnesota, 1956)
- Mega-malls (West Edmonton Mall, 1981; Mall of America, 1992)
- Superstores (Toys R Us, 1957)
- Discounters (Target, 1962)
- Home Shopping Television (Home Shopping Network, 1985)
- Cybermalls (Wal-Mart, 1996)
- Theme Parks (Disneyland, 1955)

- Cruise Ships (Sunward, 1966)
- Casino-Hotels (Flamingo, 1946)
- Eatertainment (Hard Rock Cafe, 1971)

With the exception of mega-malls and the Edmonton Mall (created in Canada, but now supplanted by Mall of America as the leader in this area) and eatertainment and the Hard Rock Cafe (which was created in London, albeit to bring "American" food to England), all of these are American innovations that, in recent years, have been aggressively exported to the rest of the world; that is, they have become global phenomena.

Although all of the New Means of Consumption are highly McDonaldized (and McDonald's, fast food restaurants, and franchises are such new means)—that is, the underlying principles that we've enumerated above are essential to their operations—there is much more to these settings than simply their McDonaldized characteristics. The exportation of these New Means of Consumption must be considered, along with McDonaldization, in the context of a discussion of globalization.

The development and growth of the New Means of Consumption in the United States and their exportation to much of the rest of the world is also a global process. However, like McDonaldization (and for many of the same reasons) the exportation of the New Means of Consumption is, at once, more than and less than globalization, and it, too, offers an important perspective through which to view globalization theory.

With this background, we will address the issue of the relationship between globalization, McDonaldization, and the New Means of Consumption. To explore this relationship we will adopt as a framework, at least in part, some of the issues raised by Robertson (2001) about globalization: First, what are the driving forces of, and most important factors in, globalization? Second, what are the relationships between the global and the local and between homogeneity and heterogeneity? Third, does globalization imply the decline of the nation-state? Finally, is there any evidence of local and international resistance to globalization?

Key Factors in Globalization

Robertson is often accused by other globalization theorists of underestimating the importance of economic factors as driving forces in globalization. He acknowledges this and admits to downplaying their significance. While he continues to adhere to a view that emphasizes cultural factors, he concludes that globalization has no single motor force; such forces (politics is a third factor) will vary from one historical situation to another and must be studied empirically. Thus, the question of the relative importance of motor forces can only be answered empirically in cases like McDonaldization and the exportation of the New Means of Consumption.

The interaction of culture and economics is obviously central to the origins of McDonaldization. While Ritzer, like Robertson, emphasizes the importance of cultural factors (e.g., the fit between a culture that values efficiency and acceptance of McDonaldized systems), in the end he concludes that *material*—that is, economic—factors (especially profitability within a global capitalistic market) are the motor forces behind the spread of McDonaldization. Since McDonaldization involves a far more specific set of processes than globalization, it is possible to identify its driving force more precisely. For example, if we look at the paradigm for the process—the McDonald's restaurant—it is clear that no given restaurant, nor the entire chain itself, would exist were it not for the search for profits and that these enterprises are, and continue to be, profitable.

The spread of the McDonald's chain throughout the world represents the kind of specific empirical case suggested by Robertson. That is, it is an instance where one can study in historical detail the forces that caused, and continue to cause, the international expansion of the chain and assess the relative weight of economic, cultural, political (and other) factors. Robertson suggests the importance of comparative empirical research, and one could even do such a study comparing the origins of McDonald's to those of other chains that developed in the United States, or to chains that have emerged more recently in many other nations. One point to be made about the latter is that McDonald's itself has become a motor force in the rise of those chains. That is, it is the success of McDonald's, and the methods by which it achieved that success, that have facilitated the development of indigenous chains.

Perhaps the most important point, however, is that, just as Robertson views his work on globalization as part of the "cultural turn," the work on McDonaldization is of much the same genre. That is, even if economics is the motor force behind McDonald's, the process of McDonaldization is much more important culturally than it is economically (although, as Robertson points out, the two are increasingly difficult to distinguish from one another—the economic is becoming cultural, the cultural economic); the process of McDonaldization is transforming not only the culture of the United States, but also those of much of the rest of the world.

The most notable and more directly visible cultural impact is the way McDonald's is altering the manner in which much of the rest of the world eats. What and how people eat is a crucial component of almost all, if not all, cultures, but with the spread of the principles of McDonaldization virtually *everyone* in McDonaldized societies is devouring french fries (and virtually every other kind of food) and doing so quickly, often on the run (we will discuss some exceptions to this below). Of course, not just food, but many other sectors of many societies (health care, politics) are being McDonaldized and as a result the cultures of those societies, the way people live many aspects of their lives, are being transformed.

Much the same thing could be said about the New Means of Consumption. Each one of them, as well as the New Means of Consumption taken collectively, offers the possibility of an empirical test of the relationship between cultural, economic, political (and others) factors. The motor force is once again clearly economic—New Means of Consumption would not be created or survive were they not successful economically, and they would not be exported internationally were they not economically rewarding to the largely American corporations of which they are part. Yet, what is critical about all of the New Means of Consumption is that they are powerful representations of American culture and they all bring that culture to any nation to which they are exported. A good example is Disney World, which has been exported to Japan and France with other foreign ventures planned or in the discussion stage. On the one hand, Disney World is clearly a product of American culture, or at least Walt Disney's romanticized "Main Street" vision of that culture circa 1900. On the other, it brings American culture and some of its most famous icons (Mickey Mouse, Donald Duck) to those areas of the world to which it has been exported. Like most of the other New Means of Consumption (and McDonaldization), Disney has been welcomed by many in other countries, but its establishment abroad has also elicited extremely negative responses from critics concerned about its impact on national cultures. For example, at the opening of Euro Disney, a French politician said that it will "bombard France with uprooted creations that are to culture what fast food is to gastronomy" (Riding 1992, A10).

Both McDonaldization and the export of the New Means of Consumption tend to support Robertson's emphasis on cultural factors in the process of globalization. However, it is clear that neither process would have been begun without the expectation of economic rewards and both continue because they are enormously profitable. Nevertheless, the specifics of such case studies illustrate that there are other forces involved (such as McDonald's own success) as important factors in the international spread of McDonaldization. Much the same could be said for many of the other New Means of Consumption. For example, Disney is a similarly important international icon and its success has led to the creation of clones of its various enterprises throughout the world.

The Relationship between the Global/Local and Heterogeneity/Homogeneity

The relationship between global/local and heterogeneity/homogeneity is an area where there are fairly substantial differences between McDonaldization and the exportation of the New Means of Consumption and globalization, although they are mainly matters of emphasis. Robertson (2001) is at pains to argue that "globalization is not an all-encompassing process of homogenization but a complex mixture of homogenization and heterogenization." Featherstone (1990, 2) writes of global culture "in terms of the diversity, variety and richness of popular and local discourses, codes and practices which resist and play-back systemicity and order." Far from giving us a universally homogenous culture, globalization defines a space in which the world's cultures rub elbows and generate new, heterogeneous meanings and understandings. Featherstone and Lash (1995, 2) delineate a world in which "international social, political and cultural (for example the media) organizations are standing alongside and beginning to replace their national counterparts." They see every national culture in the mix, so that it is possible to discuss Americanization, Europeanization, Japanization—and even Brazilianization. Of more direct relevance to this discussion, Robertson (2001) argues: "the frequent talk about the McDonaldization of the world has to be strongly tempered by what is increasingly known about the ways in which such products or services are actually *the basis for localization*," and he cites approvingly James L. Watson's (1997) *Golden Arches East: McDonald's in East Asia*. Given its centrality to Robertson's argument, and to the larger issue of homogeneity/heterogeneity, Watson's book, a series of essays on the impact of McDonald's on a number of Asian cities, represents an appropriate place to view the relationship between globalization and McDonaldization and the New Means of Consumption. Watson (1997, 6) contends that "East Asian consumers have quietly, and in some cases stubbornly, transformed their neighborhood McDonald's into local institutions." McDonald's adapts to each distinctive cultural context and, as a result, is so modified that it is ultimately impossible to distinguish the local from the foreign. Thus, in China McDonald's is seen as much a Chinese phenomenon as it is an American phenomenon. In Japan, McDonald's is perceived by some as "*Americana as constructed* by the Japanese" (Ohnuki-Tierney 1997, 173). In Watson's terms, it is a "transnational" phenomenon. Rather than being monolithic, McDonald's, in Watson's view, is a "federation of semiautonomous enterprises." We begin with the evidence in support of this position (heterogeneity) and then turn to a discussion of the alternative view that McDonaldization is an imperialistic force (homogeneity).

McDonald's as a Local Phenomenon. There is no question that McDonald's (and other McDonaldized systems) adapt to local conditions, realities, and tastes. In fact, the president of McDonald's International says that the goal of the company is to "become as much a part of the local culture as possible" (Sullivan 1995, 1). Thus, while its basic menu remains intact, McDonald's has added local foods in many nations.

Even more adaptive in terms of foods are the smaller American food franchisers (Big Boy, Dairy Queen, Schlotzky's Delicatessen, Chesapeake Bagel) that have followed McDonald's and the other American giants overseas. In 1998 alone, these mini-chains opened 800 new restaurants overseas and as of that year there were more than 12,000 of them in existence around the world (Frank 2000). However, such mini-chains are far weaker than McDonald's and therefore must be even more responsive to local culture. Thus, Big Boy sells things like "country-style fried rice and pork omelette" and has added sugar and chile powder to make its burgers more palatable to its Thai customers. Because it caters to many European tourists, it has added Germanic foods like spatzle to its menu. Said the head franchiser for Big Boy in Thailand: "We thought we were bringing American food to the masses. . . . But now we're bringing Thai and European food to the tourists. It's strange, but you know what? It's working" (Frank 2000, B4).

McDonald's (as well as the mini-chains) also adapts to the local environment in the way it operates its outlets. In Beijing, the menu is identical to that in America, but the food is eaten more as a snack than as a meal. In spite of perceiving the food as a snack, Beijing customers (and those in other nations, as well) often linger for hours rather than eating quickly and leaving or taking their food with them as they depart the drive-through window, which undermines one of the principal dimensions of McDonaldization—efficiency. Perhaps the biggest difference, however, is that in Beijing McDonald's seeks to be more human by consciously presenting itself as a local company, as a place in which to "hang out" and celebrate important events and ceremonies (e.g., children's birthday parties) rather than simply a place to get in to and out of as quickly as possible. Personal interaction is emphasized by employing five to ten female receptionists, who are referred to as "Aunt McDonalds" (similarly, Ronald McDonald is known as "Uncle McDonald" in Taiwan), whose main tasks involve dealing with children and talking to parents.

Instead of discouraging the lingering of children, McDonald's in Hong Kong (and Taipei) tends to encourage it, especially for children on their way home from school. As in Beijing, McDonald's in Hong Kong is a more personalized setting where customers take about twice as much time as Americans to eat their food. It is a teenage hangout from three to six in the afternoon, and McDonald's makes no effort to limit table time. Overall, McDonald's feels more like "home."

Also in Hong Kong, McDonald's employees rarely smile at customers, but instead display the traits valued in that culture—"competence, directness, and unflappability" (Watson 1997a, 91). Those who eat in Hong Kong's McDonald's do not bus their own debris. In addition, napkins are dispensed one at a time because if they were placed in a public dispenser, they would disappear quickly. In Taipei, McDonald's is also a hangout for teenagers and more generally is treated as a home away from home; it is "familiar and indigenous"

(Wu 1997, 125). The same customers return over and over and come to know one another and the employees quite well.

Although there is considerable evidence that McDonald's (and other McDonaldized systems) adapts, and this adaptation has helped it to succeed overseas, an important question is whether this adaptation constitutes a threat to McDonald's because it goes against the very basis of the success of the system—its standardized foods and methods of operation (Barboza 1999). That is, if McDonald's adapts too much, "goes native," and loses its identity and uniformity, will it undermine the very source of its worldwide success? If local McDonald's around the world go their own way, will they eventually cease to be identifiable as McDonald's? Will the company itself (or at least its international operations) eventually be undermined, and perhaps destroyed, by such local adaptation? Moreover, will its surrender to these local practices that obviously undermine the efficiency that it achieves in the United States make it economically unprofitable?

McDonald's as Cultural Imperialism. In contrast to those who emphasize the local adaptation of American imports, others argue that McDonaldized systems are imposing themselves on local markets in other societies and in the process are transforming local economies and cultures. The enormous expansion of such systems in the international arena is one indication of this cultural imperialism. Second, while McDonald's may adapt to local realities in terms of the food and the way it runs its operations, the fact remains that not only the basic menu, but also—and more important—the fundamental operating procedures remain essentially the same everywhere in the world. Third, in many ways, it is not the existence of American chains (and other New Means of Consumption) in other countries that is the most important indicator of the spread of McDonaldization, but rather the existence of indigenous clones of those McDonaldized enterprises. After all, the importation of American products in other countries could simply be a manifestation of an invasion of isolated and superficial elements that represent no real and fundamental threat to the underlying realities of those countries. However, it is clear that the emergence of local variations on American consumption mechanisms reflects an underlying change—the McDonaldization of those societies.

The power of McDonald's to transform local restaurants is evident in Moscow. The initial success there of McDonald's restaurants, which were greeted with great fanfare and long lines (Ingwerson 1997, 1), led to the development of many imitators, indigenous enterprises such as Russkoye Bistro that now has over 100 outlets and serves 35,000 to 40,000 customers per day. Said Russkoye Bistro's deputy director, "'If McDonald's had not come to our country, then we probably wouldn't be here'" (Hockstader 1995, A13). Further, "'we need to create fast food here that fits our lifestyle and traditions. . . . We see McDonald's like an older brother. . . . We have a lot to learn from them'" (Hockstader 1995, A13). That is the central point: innumerable institutions throughout the world feel that there is much to learn from McDonald's and what is critical are the basic principles that the process of McDonaldization embodies.

In China, local restaurants copied the McDonaldized imports. For example, Ronghua Chicken and Xiangfei Roast Chicken emulated Kentucky Fried Chicken. The Beijing Fast Food Company has almost a thousand local restaurants and street stalls that sell local fare. Several of the company's executives are former employees of KFC or McDonald's, where they learned basic management techniques. They are applying the methods of those McDonaldized systems to the preparation and sale of local cuisine. Government officials and those from the restaurant and catering businesses often tour McDonald's restaurants. Even "the most famous restaurant in Beijing—Quanjude Roast Duck Restaurant—sent its management staff to McDonald's in 1993 and then introduced its own 'roast duck fast food' in early 1994" (Yan 1997, 75).

In Japan, the strongest competitor to McDonald's is Mos Burger (with 1,500 outlets) which serves "a sloppy-joe-style concoction of meat and chile sauce on a bun" (Ohnuki-Tierney 1997, 165). In Taipei, local establishments have become "fast food-style restaurants" (Wu 1997). In Seoul, competitors to McDonald's include Americana and Uncle Joe's Hamburger (the inventor of the *kimchi* burger featuring an important local condiment—spicy pickled cabbage).

However, the impact of McDonaldization is much more pronounced than minor changes in the operations of local restaurants alone; indeed, McDonaldization is likely to lead to changes in the customs of society as a whole. In Korea (and Japan) the individualism of a meal at McDonald's threatens the commensality of eating rice that is cooked in a common pot and of sharing side dishes. As in the United States, McDonald's in Hong Kong has helped to transform children into customers. Immigrants to the city are given a tour that *ends* at McDonald's! The clear implication is that this is the very best Hong Kong has to offer. In Japan, McDonald's is described as a new "local" phenomenon. One of the pieces of evidence for that is that a Japanese Boy Scout was surprised to find a McDonald's in Chicago; he thought it was a Japanese firm.

From our perspective these cultural transformations, like the development of indigenous McDonaldized settings, exemplify the power of McDonaldization. Its impact is far greater if it infiltrates a local culture and becomes a part of it than if it remains perceived as an American phenomenon superimposed on a local setting. As local residents come to see McDonaldized systems as their own, it seems certain that the process of McDonaldization will continue to expand and embed itself ever more deeply into the cultures and everyday realities of societies throughout the world.

This discussion of cultural transformation points to another important difference with the position taken by Robertson and other globalization theorists. In rejecting the idea of cultural imperialism and McDonaldization, Robertson argues that globally few goods and services are standardized. While this may be true, of far greater importance are the standardized *principles* by which McDonaldized systems, both global and local, operate. Thus, it is far less significant that in Russkoye Bistro blinis rather than hamburgers are sold than that the cooking, serving, and sale of both is based on a very similar set of standardized principles.

Consider Yan's conclusion to an essay on McDonald's in Beijing: "It is . . . tempting to predict that, twenty years from now, the 'American' associations that McDonald's carries today will become but dim memories for older residents. A new generation of Beijing consumers may treat the Big Mac, fries, and shakes simply as local products" (Yan 1997, 76). The author takes this to mean that the local will triumph over McDonaldization, Americanization, and globalization, but to us it represents the strongest possible evidence of the triumph of all three over the local.

Ohnuki-Tierney (1997) seems to take consolation that McDonald's has not really altered Japanese dinners or even lunches, and this is true elsewhere in Asia, as well. As we have seen, McDonald's food is viewed there more as snack food than as meal. Yet Ohnuki-Tierney also recognizes that something of great cultural importance—the way people eat—

is being altered. For example, the traditional Japanese taboo against eating while standing has been undermined by the fast food restaurant (the valuable real estate in Japan necessitates standing; in the United States larger restaurants that permit more seating can be built comparatively inexpensively). Also subverted to some degree is the cultural sanction against drinking directly from a can or bottle. She claims that the norm against eating with one's hands is holding up better (the Japanese typically eat their burgers in the wrappers so that their hands do not touch the food directly). Nevertheless, that deeply held norms are being transformed by McDonald's is evidence of the profound impact of McDonaldization.

While those who accept the cultural imperialism argument tend to emphasize the negative effects of McDonaldization on local customs, we must not forget that the imperialism of McDonaldized systems brings with it many advances over local ways of doing things. For example, in both Hong Kong and Taipei McDonald's virtually invented restaurant cleanliness and served as a catalyst for improving sanitary conditions at many other restaurants in the city.

While we argue in favor of the cultural imperialism position, at least in the case of McDonaldization, it is impossible to offer a single generalization that applies equally well to all nations. For example, in Korea, unlike other East Asian locales, there is a long history of anti-Americanism (co-existing with pro-American feelings), and there is great fear among Koreans of encroaching Americanism and the loss of Korean identity. Thus, one would anticipate greater opposition there to McDonaldization than in most other nations.

Finally, while a general threat to indigenous culture exists, there are counter-examples that demonstrate that McDonaldization has instead contributed to the revitalization of local traditions. For example, while fast food restaurants have boomed in Taipei, they have helped lead to the revival of indigenous food traditions such as the eating of betel nuts. More generally, in his book, *Jihad vs. McWorld*, Benjamin Barber (1995; see also, Friedman 1999) argues that the spread of "McWorld" brings with it the development of local fundamentalist movements ("Jihads") deeply opposed to McDonaldization.[1]

The New Means of Consumption, Localism, and Imperialism. Many of the same points apply to the New Means of Consumption more generally. For example, many have adapted to local cultures by altering what they sell and how they sell it. While many of the New Means of Consumption succeeded in entrenching themselves in many other countries, they have also given rise to indigenous versions that have adopted most of their underlying principles and methods of operations. Thus, for example, Europe has its own superstores that represent serious competition to the successful exportation of Wal-Mart and Costco. European television carries its own varieties of televised home shopping, obviously influenced by the American innovators in this area. American e-tailers and cybermalls are available throughout the world, but so are local clones of both. From our perspective, it makes little difference whether people utilize American-based or indigenous versions of superstores, home shopping networks, or e-tailers. While indigenous versions may manifest a variety of' inputs, by far the most powerful are those that emanate from the American pioneers and leaders in this area.

Take the case of Latin America's Rock in Rio Cafe. Its developers are very cognizant of American theme restaurants (eatertainment) and have made it clear that they have taken the lead from them in creating a spectacular chain of restaurants that include entry via monorail, changing projected imagery on the walls, and indoor fireworks (Friedland 1997). While Rock in Rio has its local touches, it is clearly heavily influenced by American theme restaurants. Its spread throughout Latin America may be expedited by those local touches and local ownership, but it is still bringing with it a very American approach to restaurants and eating with little emphasis on the nature and quality of the food and much on the spectacular nature of the setting. In some sense it matters little whether those in Rio de Janeiro eat in Rock in Rio or in Planet Hollywood since both are New Means of Consumption. But, in another sense, the seemingly local character of the former obscures its American roots and therefore poses an even greater threat to indigenous culture.

The more general point is that the American pattern of consumption—what may be termed "hyperconsumption,"—accompanies and undergirds both the exportation of the New Means of Consumption and the opening of indigenous versions of these American imports. These settings encourage people around the world not only to consume more, but also to consume more like Americans. That is, more and more people engage in mass consumption, spend most if not all of their available resources on consumption, and increasingly go into debt in order to support such a consumption pattern.

It is not just how much people consume that is being changed; it is also the ways in which people consume. Instead of paying cash for the things they consume, increasingly large numbers of people around the world follow large numbers of Americans into debt by using credit cards. The credit card (a mechanism that facilitates the use of the New Means of Consumption rather than itself being such a new means), which had its origins and still has its base in the United States, is also an American export (Ritzer 1995). Instead of the traditional method of shopping at a variety of local shops and stands, people around the world are increasingly embracing the American pattern of one-stop shopping at supermarkets, hypermarkets, superstores, and shopping malls. Instead of visiting shops where clerks and shopkeepers perform various tasks for consumers, people are increasingly following the American pattern of doing more and more things relating to consumption for themselves. Perhaps most important, the American pattern of making consumption less social is being adopted throughout the world. For example, instead of interacting with familiar shopkeepers on a regular basis, many are doing things for themselves in vast stores and malls, interacting only briefly and anonymously with robot-like clerks, or, in the most extreme case, interacting with nothing more than television and computer screens. Whether or not they consume in American-based means of consumption, others around the world are increasingly consuming like Americans. As with the case of McDonaldization, there is great variation in this from one locale to another, and the success of the New Means of Consumption is likely to lead to local counterreactions and perhaps even to a revival of traditional consumption settings. Nevertheless, it seems safe to say that the exportation of the New Means of Consumption, and the development of indigenous copies of these settings, are leading to a worldwide movement in the direction of American-style patterns of consumption. Thus, the cases of the exportation of the New Means of Consumption and McDonaldization point much more to cultural imperialism and homogeneity than they do to localism and heterogeneity.[2]

Globalization and the Nation-State

Robertson (2001) contends that, as a consequence of globalization, "the nation-state is being simultaneously weakened and strengthened." From the broad perspective of globalization theory, this is certainly accurate. However, when looked at through the lens of McDonaldization and the exportation of the New Means of Consumption, at least at this point in their historical development, two points are clear. First, both of these processes operate transnationally with little interference from the state. Such transnational flows serve, at least to some degree, to undermine the power of the state. For example, for obvious reasons the Chinese government (to take one example) may want to keep McDonald's or other New Means of Consumption out, but the public demand for them has made that impossible. By allowing McDonaldized systems based in the United States (and elsewhere) in, China is both admitting its weakness and further increasing that weakness. Chinese citizens and observers around the world see the inability of the Chinese to resist McDonaldization and they strive to further exploit that weakness. This is even clearer in the case of the Internet and the cybermalls and e-tailers that are such an increasing presence on it. Unable to keep the Internet out, the Chinese are therefore unable to keep out these New Means of Consumption and the types of consumption and consumer goods associated with them.

Second, while overall McDonaldization and the New Means of Consumption suggest the weakness of the state, they indicate again, at least at this point in history, the power of a *single* state—the United States. McDonald's, the process of McDonaldization it helped spawn, and the New Means of Consumption are distinctive products of American society, and their spread throughout the world enhances the global reach and power of the United States. Furthermore, a significant portion of the profits earned abroad return to American shores, and some find their way into the American treasury. However, while McDonaldization and the exportation of the New Means of Consumption work to the interests of the American state, it is also the case that the corporations involved in these processes operate largely independently of the U.S. government. In that sense, they can be said to undermine the power of the American state and the nation-state in general.

Thus, the study of McDonaldization and the New Means of Consumption points to the growing power of the corporation over the nation-state in the globalization process. Corporations have long operated at least semi-autonomously and to the detriment of state power, but this seems to be reaching new heights in contemporary corporations, especially those involved with McDonaldized systems and the New Means of Consumption. Increasingly, the corporation, not the state (even the American state), has become the most important actor on the world stage and the gap between these two entities is likely to grow in the future. This reality is captured in an anecdote that Friedman reports about a former U.S. ambassador to Israel who officiated at the opening of the first McDonald's in Jerusalem while wearing a baseball hat with the McDonald's golden arches logo:

> An Israeli teen-ager walked up to him, carrying his own McDonald's hat, which he handed to Ambassador Indyk with a pen and asked: "Are you the Ambassador? Can I have your autograph?" Somewhat sheepishly, Ambassador Indyk replied: "Sure. I've never been asked for my autograph before."
>
> As the Ambassador prepared to sign his name, the Israeli teen-ager said to him, "Wow, what's it like to be the ambassador from McDonald's, going around the world opening McDonald's restaurants everywhere?"
>
> Ambassador Indyk looked at the Israeli youth and said, "No, no. I'm the American ambassador—not the ambassador from McDonald's!" Ambassador Indyk described what happened next: "I said to him, 'Does this mean you don't want my autograph?' And the kid said, 'No, I don't want your autograph,' and he took his hat back and walked away." (Friedman 1999, 43–44)

Such actions challenge Robertson's (2001) assertion that "the nation-state remains the central and most formidable actor in world affairs generally."

On the other hand, the perspective that we are arguing is also at odds, at least in part, with the view of some globalization theorists, most notably Appadurai (1996), that what is most significant about globalization is the existence of global processes that operate independently of, and free of ties with, any given nation. While our previous discussion of the independence of corporations tends to support such a stance, the overall thrust of this essay is to stress the persistence of ties to the United States and American culture. Thus, while it is undeniable that there are global processes that operate free of any nation-state, one nation-state remains disproportionately important in globalization. The nation-state may, as Robertson suggests, not be as formidable as it once was, but, at least in the realms being discussed here, the United States remains a powerful presence.

Local and Global Resistance

One of the issues highlighted by the specifics of McDonaldization and the exportation of the New Means of Consumption is the nature of the resistance to them. Robertson discusses such resistance in terms of anti-global movements that themselves involve globalization. Once again, the specific issues of concern here allow us to examine the nature of this resistance much more concretely.

The global reach of McDonaldization and the exportation of the New Means of Consumption have given rise to reactions against these processes that are similarly transnational. For example, the exportation of McDonald's led to the infamous McLibel trial in Great Britain[3] and more important to a global McLibel movement against McDonald's franchises, as well as many other New Means of Consumption (Vidal 1997). Several million copies of the leaflet that led to the trial, "What's Wrong With McDonald's: Everything They Didn't Want You to Know," have been distributed around the world and it has been translated into a number of languages. More important, a website dedicated to opposing McDonald's and related phenomena (http://www.mcspotlight.org/), has reported an average of 1.75 million "hits" a month, a total of 65 million hits by March 1999. It acts as the repository for information on actions taken against local McDonald's throughout the world. It has become the heart of a worldwide movement in opposition to McDonald's, as well as other aspects of our McDonaldized world. For example, in one month it reported efforts to block the opening of new McDonald's restaurants in Surrey, England; Kerikeri, New Zealand; Torquay, Australia; and Edmonton, Canada. Among "McSpotlight's" other targets is the Body Shop, which is accused of using its "green" image to conceal that its products are detrimental to the environment, that it pays low wages, and that it encourages consumerism.

Another reaction against McDonaldization has been The Slow Food movement, which was initiated in the mid-1980s by an Italian food critic against the opening of a McDonald's in Rome. It is opposed to the homogenization of food styles and takes as its mission "to give voice to local cooking styles and small-time food producers." In addition to its anti-McDonald's stance, more recently it has taken on "fending off the homogenizing effects of European Union regulations on regional culinary treasures" (Richman 1998, M1). Its objective "to provide members from all different countries with an identity and [to propagate] convivia throughout the world" (Slow, 1998) reflects its anti-McDonaldization animus. It has over 400 chapters (called Convivia) and a membership of 40,000 people, mostly in

Europe, but also in 35 other nations. Among other things, the movement has a website (www.slowfood.com), publishes a handsome journal (*Slow*), and held its first biennial meeting, "Salone del Gusto: World Flavours in Piedmont," in Turin, Italy, in late 1998.

This is clearly a movement of a very different order from the McLibel group. The impoverished targets of the McDonald's libel suit are a far cry from the mainly well-heeled gourmets drawn to Slow Food. The Slow Food movement focuses on the issue of the poor quality of food (and, implicitly, almost all other products) in McDonaldized restaurants and food emporia, while McLibel focuses on threats to health (as does another movement, National Heart Savers), the environment, and workers. While there are differences in goals, methods, and in the social class backgrounds of most of the participants, these two groups share hostility to the McDonaldization of society (and the New Means of Consumption), and they are global in their reach.

Turning to other New Means of Consumption, Sprawl-Busters (info@sprawl-busters.com), founded by Al Norman, grew out of his successful effort to keep Wal-Mart out of his hometown, Greenfield, Masachusetts. Now the organization offers consulting services to local communities that want to keep McDonaldized superstores and chains out. For his efforts, the TV program "60 Minutes" called Norman "the guru of the anti-Wal-Mart movement." Among the services offered by the organization to local communities is help with overseeing media operations, raising money, referenda, data searches, and the like. Beyond Wal-Mart, organizations on Sprawl-Buster's "hit list" include Super Kmart, Home Depot, CVS, and Rite-Aid. The main objective is to keep out such superstores and chains—prime examples of the New Means of Consumption—in order to protect local businesses and the integrity of the local community.

Thus, this analysis suggests that while McDonaldization and the exportation of the New Means of Consumption are global in reach, they generate opposition movements that are similarly global. It is unlikely that these opposition movements will defeat the American-based forces that they oppose, but they are likely to force them to ameliorate their worst excesses.

Although there is general accord between Robertson and the perspective offered here on the global nature of resistance, one key difference is that while he sees the United States as the *"home of opposition and resistance to globalization,"* movements such as McLibel based in England and Slow Food in Italy indicate that in the specific case of McDonaldization opposition has emerged outside of the United States as well.

However, in our rush to focus on global opposition to these global changes, we must not lose sight of the wide variety of local and individual opposition efforts (although, as Robertson points out, these cannot be clearly separated from global processes) both within the United States and throughout the world. Thus, towns as widespread as Sanibel Island in Florida and Hove in England have succeeded in keeping out McDonaldized chains. Other towns and cities throughout the world have forced such chain restaurants to mute their structures and alter their menus. Beyond the local, there is individual opposition which can take such forms as refusing to patronize McDonaldized settings and New Means of Consumption, fleeing to areas free of such settings, or even escaping into a fantasy world free of these systems.

Thus, there are many ways to oppose the forces of McDonaldization and the New Means of Consumption. A discussion of these techniques highlights the global nature of some of them, but such a global perspective might lead us to ignore other more local and individual efforts. As is true of globalization in general, a focus on specific forms of opposition reveals much more than airy generalizations about this opposition. There is much more to the changing nature of the world than is caught by globalization theory and even by the globalization process.

Conclusion

Our objective in this essay has been to examine several of the basic tenets of globalization theory from the perspective of the processes of McDonaldization and the exportation of the New Means of Consumption. Our most general point is that while there is a role for broad generalizations about the nature and consequences of globalization, they need to be closely examined in case studies that focus on specific aspects of that process. Globalization has innumerable strands and interrelated developments; we have only been able to focus on two of them here. However, even the examination of these two processes has made it clear that generalizations about globalization need to be tempered and specified. What is true about some aspects of globalization is not necessarily true of other aspects of that process.

This essay has focused on four issues related to globalization theory derived, at least in part, from the recent work of one prominent globalization theorist, Roland Robertson. By looking at these issues through the lenses of McDonaldization and the New Means of Consumption, we have found some support, some lack of support, and in all cases a need for greater specificity.

First, the processes of McDonaldization and the exportation of the New Means of Consumption support Robertson's assertion that globalization is multifactorial, with economic and cultural factors being of prime importance. The evidence from these processes indicates that although they must be profitable to be undertaken and maintained, it is really their cultural character and cultural implications that are of utmost importance and significance. That is not to say that culture is the most important aspect of all elements of globalization. For example, the global financial system, and its many sub-components, are undoubtedly far more important economically than they are culturally.

Second, our greatest disagreement with Robertson is over the issue of homogeneity/heterogeneity or cultural imperialism/localism. While Robertson emphasizes heterogeneity and the coexistence of the global and the local, the cases of McDonaldization and the New Means of Consumption indicate the centrality of homogeneity, cultural imperialism, and the triumph over the local. Our evidence points much more to homogeneity than heterogeneity, even though in those cases where McDonaldization and the New Means of Consumption have been most successful in embedding themselves in indigenous cultures, elements of heterogeneity, the glocal and the local survive and may even be stimulated into reasserting themselves by the success of these imperialistic efforts. Again, however, other elements of globalization might well demonstrate the reverse. We need to look at what *each* of these aspects of globalization show and not be satisfied with generalizations about the process.

Third, our examination of McDonaldization and the New Means of Consumption adds nuance to Robertson's assertion that globalization simultaneously weakens and strengthens the nation-state. McDonaldization and the exportation of the New Means of Consumption serves to weaken, and to demonstrate the weakness of, the nation-state in that most are powerless to resist their incursion. However, these two processes serve to strengthen the *American* state through increased tax revenues generated by overseas successes and by furthering the proliferation of American culture throughout the world. Ultimately, however, these processes demonstrate the growing importance of the corporation vis-a-vis the state. It is really the corporations—the multinationals and transnational entities that lie at the base of McDonaldization and the New Means of Consumption—that benefit most from their success. These corporations operate largely on their own, free of state control. They are little interested in the success of their state of origin or of the other states in which they do business. In the end, distinctively American products such as McDonald's, Disney, Wal-Mart, the Gap, Amazon.com, and the like will remain based in the United States only so long as it suits their interests and bottom line to do so. When, and if, it makes more economic sense to base their operations elsewhere, or to sell out to some foreign-based conglomerate, they will do so without giving a second thought to the implications of these acts for the United States. What the cases of McDonaldization and the New Means of Consumption suggest is that it is the corporation, not the state, that is key actor on the world stage today.

Finally, the specific cases of McDonaldization and the New Means of Consumption illustrate the emergence of various types of resistance to them at the individual, local, and global levels. Theorizing about resistance to globalization at a general level is useful, but we learn a great deal more about resistance, and much else, if we look at the specific forms that they take in reaction to specific dimensions of globalization.

Notes

[1] However, it is worth noting that in the end Barber concludes that McWorld will win out over Jihad; to succeed on a large scale, fundamentalist movements themselves must begin to use highly rationalized, McDonaldized systems (e.g. e-mail, the Internet, television).

[2] However, we should reiterate that the realities of these cases do not contradict the idea that other global processes are producing greater heterogeneity around the world.

[3] McDonald's sued two impecunious young people associated with London Greenpeace for passing out anti-McDonald's pamphlets. In what became the longest libel trial in Great Britain's history, McDonald's won on most counts, but suffered an expensive public relations disaster (Vidal, 1997).

References

Abu-Lughod, Janet. 1997. "Going Beyond the Global Babble." In A.D. King, ed., *Culture, Globalization and the World-System*. Minneapolis.

Alfino, Mark, John S. Caputo and Robin Wynyard, eds. 1998. *McDonaldization Revisited*. Westport, Conn.

Appadurai, Arjun. 1996. *Modernity at Large: Cultural Dimensions of Globalization*. Minneapolis.

Barber, Benjamin. 1995. *Jihad vs. McWorld*. New York.

Barboza, David. 1999. "Pluralism under Golden Arches." *New York Times*, February 12.

Beilharz, Peter. 1999. "McFascism: Reading Ritzer, Bauman and the Holocaust." In Smart, ed., *Resisting McDonaldization*. London.

Bryman, Alan. 1995. *Disney and His Worlds*. London.

———1999a. "Theme Parks and McDonaldization." In Smart, ed., *Resisting McDonaldization*. London.

———1999b, The Disneyization of Society." *Sociological Review* 47, February.

Chase-Dunn, Christopher; Yukio Kawano; and Benjamin D. Brewer. 2000. "Trade Globalization since 1795: Waves of Integration in the World-System." *American Sociological Review* 65, February.

Featherstone, Mike. 1990. "Introduction." In M. Featherstone ed., *Global Culture: Nationalism, Globalization and Modernity*. London.

Featherstone, Mike and Scott Lash. 1995. "Globalization, Modernity and the Spatialization of Social Theory: An Introduction." In Featherstone, Lash and Robertson eds., *Global Modernities*. London.

Featherstone, Mike, Scott Lash and Roland Robertson eds. 1995. *Global Modernities*. London.

Fine, Gary. 1999. Art Centres: Southern Folk Art and the Splintering of a Hegemonic Market. In Smart, ed., *Resisting McDonaldization*. London.

Frank, Robert. "Big Boy's Adventures in Thailand." *Wall Street Journal*, April 12.

Friedland, J. 1997. "Can Yanks Export Good Times to Latins?" *Wall Street Journal*, March 6.

Friedman, Jonathan. 1994. *Cultural Identity and the Global Process*. London.

———1995. "Global System, Globalization and the Parameters of Modernity." In Featherstone, Lash and Robertson, eds., *Global Modernities*. London.

Friedman, Thomas. 1999. *The Lexus and Olive Tree: Understanding Globalization*. New York.

Galtung, Johan. 1997. "On the Social Costs of Modernization: Social Disintegration, Atomie/Anomie and Social Development." In Cynthia Hewitt de Alcántara, ed., *Social Futures, Global Vision*. Oxford, England.

Garcia Canclini, Nestor. 1995. *Hybrid Cultures: Strategies for Entering and Leaving Modernity*. Minneapolis.

Giddens, Anthony. 1990. *The Consequences of Modernity*. Stanford, Calif.

Hall, Stuart. 1997. "The Local and the Global: Globalization and Ethnicity." In A.D. King, ed., *Culture, Globalization and the World-System: Contemporary Conditions for the Representation of Identity*. Minneapolis.

Harvey, David. 1989. *The Condition of Postmodernity: An Inquiry into the Origins of Cultural Change*. Cambridge, Mass.

Hannerz, Ulf. 1990. "Cosmopolitans and Locals in World Culture." In Featherstone, ed., *Global Culture: Nationalism, Globalization and Modernity*. London.

Hobsbawm, Eric. 1997. "The Future of the State." In Cynthia Hewitt de Alcántara, ed., *Social Futures, Global Visions*. Oxford.

Hockstader, Lee. 1995. "Attack on Big Mac." *Washington Post*, August 8.

Ingwerson, Marshall. 1997. "That Golden Touch to the Arches in Russia." *Ohio Slavic and East European Newsletter* 25, Spring. (Originally published in the *Christian Science Monitor*, 1997.)

Keohane, Robert O. and Joseph S. Nye. 1977. *Power and Independence*. Boston.

Lechner, Frank J. and John Boli, eds., *The Globalization Reader*. Malden, Mass.

Meyer, John W., John Boli, George M. Thomas, and Francisco Ramirez. 1997. "World Society and the Nation-State." *American Journal of Sociology*, 65, February.

Ohnuki-Tierney, Emiko. 1997. "McDonald's in Japan: Changing Manners and Etiquette." In Watson, ed., *Golden Arches East*.

Parker, Martin and David Jary. 1995. "The McUniversity: Organization, Management and Academic Subjectivity." *Organization* 2.

Pieterse, Jan N. 1995. "Globalization as Hybridization." In Featherstone, Lash and Robertson, eds. *Global Modernities*. London.

Piore, Michael and Charles Sabel. 1984. *The Second Industrial Divide: Possibilities for Prosperity*. New York.

Richman, Phyllis. 1998. "Savoring Lunch in the Slow Lane." *Washington Post*, November 22.

Riding, Alan. 1992. "Only the French Elite Scorn Mickey's Debut." *New York Times*, April 13.

Ritzer, George. 1995. *Expressing America: A Critique of the Global Credit Card Society*. Thousand Oaks, Calif.

———1998. *The McDonaldization Thesis*. London.

———1999. *Enchanting a Disenchanted World: Revolutionizing the Means of Consumption*. Thousand Oaks, Calif.

———2000. *The McDonaldization of Society: New Century Edition*. Thousand Oaks, Calif.

———and Allan Liska. 1998. "'McDisneyization' and 'Post-Tourism'": Complementary Perspectives on Contemporary Tourism. In Chris Rojek and John Urry, eds. *Touring Cultures: Transformations in Travel and Theory*. London.

Robertson, Roland. 1992. *Globalization: Social Theory and Global Culture*. London.

———1995. "Glocalization: Time-Space and Homogeneity-Heterogeneity." In Featherstone, Lash and Robertson, eds. *Global Modernities*. London.

———2001. "Globalization Theory 2000+: Major Problematics." In George Ritzer and Barry Smart, eds. *Handbook of Social Theory*. London.

Slow. July–September, 1998.

Smart, Barry, ed. 1999. *Resisting McDonaldization*. London.

Smith, Anthony D. 1990. "Towards a Global Culture?" in Featherstone, ed. *Global Culture*. London.

Sullivan, Barbara. 1995. "McDonald's Sees India as Golden Opportunity." *Chicago Tribune-Business*, April 5.

Tester, Keith. 1999. "The Moral Malaise of McDonaldization." In Smart, ed. *Resisting McDonaldization*. London.

Turner, Bryan S. 1999. "McCitizens: Risk, Coolness and Irony in Contemporary Politics." In Barry Smart, ed. *Resisting McDonaldization*. London.

Vidal, John. 1997. *McLibel: Burger Culture on Trial*. New York.

Wallerstein, Immanuel. 1974. *The Modern World-System: Capitalist Agriculture and the Origins of the European World-Economy in the 16th Century*. New York.

Watson, James. 1997a. "Transnationalism, Localization, and Fast Foods in Asia." in Watson, ed. *Golden Arches East*. Stanford.

———1997b. "McDonald's in Hong Kong: Consumerism, Dietary Change, and the Rise of a Children's Culture." In Watson, ed. *Golden Arches East*. Stanford.

———, ed. 1997c. *Golden Arches East: McDonald's in East Asia*. Stanford.

Weber, Max. 1921/1968. *Economy and Society*. Totowa, N.J.

———1927/1981. *General Economic History*. New Brunswick, N.J.

Wu, David Y. H. 1997. "McDonald's in Taipei: Hamburgers, Betel Nuts, and National Identity." In Watson ed. *Golden Arches East*. Stanford.

Yan, Yunxiang. 1997. "McDonald's in Beijing: The Localization of Americana." In Watson, ed., *Golden Arches East*. Stanford.

The Culture of Liberty: An Agenda

Peter L. Berger

Cultural conflicts, such as those that trouble American society today, may sometimes appear to be less than serious squabbles between intellectuals who have nothing better to do. It is regrettably true, of course, that intellectuals have the tendency to think of themselves and their interests in grandiose terms; control of the English department, say, looks more important than control of the world's energy supplies. Yet culture is not a peripheral matter. In the final analysis, culture is the way in which a society understands itself. A society that no longer understands itself will be unable to act coherently on any problems facing it, including those that may superficially seem remote from cultural issues.

There are many "hard" issues—concerning economic policy, defense, foreign relations, crime, the reform of the welfare state. Cultural issues may look "soft" by comparison. They are not. Actually, a closer look at every one of the "hard" issues reveals that no recommended program can bypass fundamental questions about the society's self-understanding. The future of American society depends on how Americans will understand themselves. The formulation of a clear and plausible agenda on the cultural issues is anything but an academic project.

Every human society must achieve a measure of consensus concerning two fundamental questions: "Who are we?," and "How are we to live together?" Culture embodies the consensus as to how these questions are to be answered. This consensus will never be unanimous, but when it breaks down in a massive way, the survival of the society is threatened. Both social philosophers and social scientists have long agreed that there can be no order in human affairs without such a consensus. Some analysts have argued that a modern society no longer needs this, that it can dispense with a common morality and can function on the basis of rational self-interest expressed in various contractual arrangements. Morality is then replaced by procedure. Such a society would resemble a gigantic traffic system. In modern urban traffic most people stop at red and go at green, not because they have deep moral convictions about this behavior, also not because they are afraid of the traffic police; rather, they do so because it is in their common interest. This very image suggests the weakness of a traffic-system notion of society: The average driver will obey the

Source: Peter L. Berger, "The Culture of Liberty: An Agenda, (issues that rouse cultural conflicts)," *Society,* Jan–Feb 1998, vol. 35, #2, pp. 407–9.

traffic laws in the normal course of events; he will break them in an emergency (say, he must get to a hospital quickly). By analogy, a "normal" society can function to some extent like a traffic system—and "normality" means a state of affairs when no grave external or internal perils exist. When such perils appear, however, the contractual regulation of the many interests is not enough; some moral claim to solidarity and sacrifice will become necessary. Otherwise the contractual procedures will break down: In an emergency everyone drives through a red light.

The cultural situation in America today (and indeed in all Western societies) is determined by the cultural earthquake of the nineteen-sixties, the consequences of which are very much in evidence. What began as a counter-culture only some thirty years ago has achieved dominance in elite culture and, from the bastions of the latter (in the educational system, the media, the higher reaches of the law, and key positions within government bureaucracy), has penetrated both popular culture and the corporate world. It is characterized by an amalgam of both sentiments and beliefs that cannot be easily catalogued, though terms like "progressive," "emancipators" or "liberationist" serve to describe it. Intellectually, this new culture is legitimated by a number of loosely connected ideologies—leftover Marxism, feminism and other sexual identity doctrines, racial and ethnic separatism, various brands of therapeutic gospels and of environmentalism. An underlying theme is antagonism toward Western culture in general and American culture in particular. A prevailing spirit is one of intolerance and a grim orthodoxy, precisely caught in the phrase "political correctness."

The great challenge that this situation presents for people (and that means most Americans) who are not committed to rigid ideological positions of either the Right or the Left is to find a viable cultural agenda. The term "viable" has two meanings in this context: The agenda must be viable in the sense of being intellectually and morally coherent; it must also be viable in the sense of having a good chance of being politically successful. The two need not always go together. Thus a number of observers of the American scene (this author emphatically included) would say that one of the most abhorrent developments in recent years has been the increasingly routine application of capital punishment in this country. An agenda that puts a high priority on reversing this development would certainly be morally viable; unfortunately, it is unlikely to be viable in a political sense at this time. In other words, one of the more depressing insights into the realities of the world is that virtue is often unrewarded. In the present context however, a more comforting observation may be made: On some of the key cultural issues that currently divide American society it is possible to formulate a vision that will be viable in both the aforementioned senses. It will have to be a vision capable of capturing the middle ground of American politics, which happens to be the ground on which most Americans, almost instinctively, locate themselves. Such a vision can only have one focus: America as the culture of liberty.

Max Weber has taught us (or, more accurately, should have taught us) that social science cannot serve as the source of moral judgments. However, in the face of moral dilemmas such as the one facing American society today, social science can make two very useful contributions. First, social science can provide a societal "map" that allows one to assess what courses of action are likely to be empirically successful. Second, if social science is rightly understood, it fosters a distinctive attitude toward societal problems. It is an attitude of caution, shaped by an awareness of history and of the unintended consequences of all human action. By the same token, this attitude is suspicious of utopian ideologies and of radical programs of any political coloration. It is an attitude supremely useful in the currently over-heated cultural scene in America.

Culture cannot be simply a matter of politics, of course. Politics, after all, is concerned with influencing the institutions of the state and these are of limited use in affecting the culture. Not even the totalitarian state has been able to achieve the cultural goals it set itself (such as the creation of the "new Soviet man"); the democratic state is an even less likely agent of cultural change, and indeed, in the American tradition of democracy, it should not aim to be that. Consequently, a cultural agenda cannot be a political agenda only. It will have to be pursued in many different institutions, most importantly in the institutions of civil society. All the same, every one of the major cultural issues is also a political issue, because of the way in which the immense powers of the state have been used to promote various ideological purposes. The courts have played a quite deplorable role in this. Not surprisingly, then, much of American politics in recent decades has been over the so-called "social" or "values" issues, which in effect are cultural issues. That is, these issues have involved conflicts over the questions of who we are and how we are to live together.

The dynamics of the two-party system has been very unhelpful in the search for viable positions on the middle ground. Since the early nineteen-seventies the Democratic party has almost completely identified itself with the agenda of the cultural Left (considerably less so with other Left positions, such as those on economic or foreign policy). Given the importance of highly organized pressure groups, especially in the primary process, the captivity of the Democratic party to the culture of "the sixties" has been massive. The Republican picture is hardly more encouraging. An increasingly vocal segment of that party's constituency has taken radically anti-"progressive" positions on the cultural issues. And again, these groups have had an influence far beyond their numerical strength because of their strategic role in the mechanics of elections, especially on the primary level. Consequently, individuals taking less than "politically correct" positions, as defined by the respective orthodoxies, have found themselves to be pariahs in either party. It is safe to assume that both Democratic and Republican leaders have catered to these polarized groupings in a more or less cynical manner. Thus, for instance, traditionally Democratic labor officials are not very credible when they express enthusiasm for gay rights, neither are "country-club" Republicans when they voice outrage over abortion or the decline of sexual morality. Some party leaders have tried to avoid the problem by saying as little as possible about the cultural issues. This too, however, is a precarious tactic, because it assumes that voters don't really care about these issues, which is demonstrably not the case. If one is looking for political leaders taking sensible positions on the cultural issues, one may want to toss a coin as to which party one would look to. What is very clear is that any political figure in either party, who would want to run with such positions, would need to have a good deal of courage. Given what is known about the cultural inclinations of the majority of the electorate, it is likely that in the longer run such courage would be politically rewarded.

Most Americans are somewhere in the middle on these issues, equidistant from, say, the Christian Coalition and the National Organization of Women. While political candidates may get elected by keeping the support of the polarized groupings, who write cheques and stuff envelopes and ring doorbells, they will keep a vast number of Americans permanently frustrated in matters of great importance to them. This is an unhappy state of affairs for a democracy. Eventually politicians will have to come out and speak on the cultural issues in such a way as to capture this vast middle-ground. It is on this middle ground that the battle over American culture will be lost or won.

So far the cultural issues have been mentioned in very general terms. It is time to be more specific. While even the "hardest" issues involve questions of our identity and our moral convictions, there are five currently salient issues that involve the culture in a more direct way. These are the issues of multiculturalism, affirmative action, the public place of religion, abortion and homosexual rights. The agenda here is not simply to articulate sensible positions on each of these issues, but to make clear that these positions cohere in a principled way. Contrary to conventional "moderate" opinion, the principle cannot be just constitutional formalism or faith in the market. Contrary to the Religious Right, it cannot be the "Judaeo-Christian tradition" in religious terms. The latter principle would exclude the large number of people who are religiously indifferent (not to mention the growing number of those whose religion is neither Christian nor Jewish); the former principle will appeal to a rather limited constituency of legal scholars, economic determinists and admirers of Ayn Rand. The only possible principle capable of providing coherence on these issues in real American society is the principle of liberty. It can be shown that each of the aforementioned five issues raises vital questions about America as the culture of liberty.

Multiculturalism.—The real issue is not what Americans feel about other cultures, but what they feel about their own. For this reason one might argue that this issue is the most fundamental of all. As James Hunter has put it in his analysis of the "culture wars," this issue is over how to define America. Two affirmations must be made concerning this: That America is rooted in Western civilization. And that at the core of this civilization, and especially its American version, are the values of liberty.

The term "multiculturalism," as it is used in current controversies, is ambiguous. If it refers to the presence in America of people from many different cultures, it simply states an empirical fact. If it is intended to express respect for all human cultures, this is a value that any reflective person should approve of. But "multiculturalism" today also expresses sentiments of a very different sort—anti-Western and anti-American ones—and these ought to be vigorously repudiated.

To affirm Western civilization does not presuppose smug self-satisfaction or disdain of other civilizations. There are enough horrors in Western history to put to rest any notion of its moral superiority; the Holocaust, all by itself, will suffice. Of course Western civilization has made enormous contributions to mankind, but so have other civilizations. There is, however, one contribution that stands out beyond all others. It can be called, quite simply, the discovery of the unique worth of every human individual. To be sure, there are non-Western varieties of "individualism" as in the seeker of enlightenment in India and in the cultivated gentleman in China; the Biblical understanding of the individual standing alone in his responsibility before God has also continued in an Islamic form. But it is only in the West, drawing from its two historic sources in ancient Israel and ancient Greece, that the freedom and the rights of the individual have not only been "democratized" as referring to all human beings (in a somewhat different way that has also happened with Islam), but that this understanding has been institutionalized in the legal and political orders. The values of liberty are founded on this understanding of the individual. Of course this does not imply a denial of community or a glorification of deracinated selves. But all human cultures have had some ideas concerning the liberty of a community as against other communities—say, the right of tribe X to be free from domination by tribe Y. The West is distinctive in having come to assert the liberty of the individual against his own community. And America is unique in having made this assertion an essential component of the nation's self-definition. Perhaps the most common American phrase is "It's a free country"—usually pronounced in the context of an individual's maintaining the right to do something unorthodox or unconventional.

If America is defined as the culture of liberty, this has the implication of insisting that an allegiance to America means allegiance to this culture. Two areas of public policy affected by this principle are education and immigration. This is not to spell out specifics of education and immigration policy, but the principle obviously means that every new generation should be reared in these American values and that all new citizens, wherever they may come from, should be expected to affirm these values. The expanded pluralism of American society is no obstacle to the continuing realization of this principle. To see that this can be done successfully one only has to visit Hawaii, an emphatically American place, with a great majority of the population deriving from non-Western cultures. If "multiculturalism" then means no more than a further enhancement of the time-honored American idea of pluralism, that is all to the good. If, on the other hand, "multiculturalism" means a repudiation of the American culture of liberty and the Balkanization of American society, then it must be resisted on every front where it makes its appearance.

The most debilitating consequence of the cultural transformation of "the sixties" has been the entrenchment of an anti-Western animus in the institutions of elite culture. It is actually of little import whether this animus is expressed in this or that ideological jargon. Western civilization and American society may be denounced for being exploitatively capitalistic, sexist, racist, or despoiling of the environment. "Multiculturalism" then means admiration of any non-Western culture or anti-American movement, real or often imagined. It is ironic that these sentiments have arisen and taken hold among the most privileged members of the society. The phenomenon is not unique in history. It is adequately covered by the category of decadence—a society, and especially its elite, turning against itself. The future of a decadent society must be very much in doubt.

A viable cultural agenda will have to be in large measure a resistance against decadence. It is of great importance that such resistance avoid the extremes of jingoism and xenophobia, both for moral reasons and for the political reason of recovering the middle ground.

It is worth noting that this struggle over the definition of America has broad international implications as well. One does not have to agree with everything in Samuel Huntington's recent work on the "clash of civilizations," but he is certainly correct that the United States is the "core state" of Western civilization today. If America no longer has confidence in its own key values, it is unlikely to be confident as an international leader. Once again, though, the problem is not just political. American culture today enjoys a virtual hegemony in most of the world, both in its more sophisticated and its popular expressions. It follows that cultural developments in America will necessarily have huge consequences abroad. Put simply, the fate of America's culture of liberty will affect the fate of liberty everywhere.

Affirmative action.—This issue raises in the sharpest possible way whether the American culture of liberty pertains to individuals or to individuals as members of this or that collectivity. Put simply, the question is whether affirmative action is going to be a vehicle to create in America a strange modern version of the Hindu caste system.

Affirmative action began as part of the thoroughly admirable effort to eradicate the most monstrous injustice in American history—namely, the injustice committed against African slaves and their descendants. There can be no doubt about the moral legitimacy of this effort. This legitimacy became shakier as other ethnic groups were added to blacks as candidates for affirmative action, even shakier as women of any race or ethnicity were added. Suddenly more than half the population were now defined as victims of oppression, upper-middle-class white housewives alongside unemployed black sharecroppers. The moral status of affirmative action was finally nullified with the introduction of quotas. It is difficult to think of a more un-American idea of liberty—the "liberty" of every individual in America being coerced into an official registry of racial and sexual categories. The irony of this, given the history of the civil rights struggle, is exquisite: A racial caste system set up by government in the name of eradicating racism. It is a telling symptom of the decadence rampant in America that large numbers of high-minded and well-educated people who would not themselves benefit from these quotas (such as white male law professors at prestigious universities) are fervent supporters of this aberration.

Affirmative action as it has developed over the years can be criticized on many grounds: The injustice of reverse discrimination against people (notably white males) who have had no part in the evils that affirmative action is supposed to remedy. The fact that only a minority within the groups defined as victims actually benefits from it (notably middle-class women and middle-class blacks). The surreal illogic of the official classification system (just who is a "Hispanic"?—how is the offspring of a "Caucasian" and a "Pacific Islander" to be classified?—can American government officials master such metaphysical distinctions without the help of bureaucrats of the apartheid regime in South Africa, for whom a special immigration quota might have to be established?). The inevitable fact that the enforcement of these quotas has led to a quantum jump in both racial antagonisms and misogyny. While all such criticisms are very much to the point, there is an overriding reason why affirmative action as now practiced ought to be emphatically rejected: It constitutes a fundamental offence against the American culture of liberty.

Almost from its beginnings America was the country to which people could come from anywhere and from any background, and be treated equally as individuals on their own terms. To treat every human being as an individual endowed with inalienable rights, and not as a nameless member of some collectivity, has been the American value par excellence. Much of American history has been a struggle to realize this value in fact as well as in theory, with the civil rights struggle in this century marking a certain climax in this history. It is staggering that the very rhetoric of this struggle should now be used to defend a practice that denies its central purpose as defined by Martin Luther King—that individuals should be judged by their character and not by the color of their skin (to which one may add—and not by their gender or by the language spoken by their grandparents).

Given the vested interests that have coalesced around affirmative action, the demented quality that has marked so many recent actions of the courts, and the enthusiastic support of leading figures in both the cultural and corporate elites, it will not be easy to reverse this development. The effort to do so will gain, both morally and politically, if it is accompanied by serious ideas on how to deal with the major problem that affirmative action is, falsely, supposed to address—namely, the continuing presence of a largely black underclass. What is very clear, however, is that a dismantling of the affirmative-action system is supported by a majority of the electorate (and by no means only by allegedly angry white males). It can very plausibly be an important part of a viable cultural agenda intent on capturing the middle ground of American politics. This issue, incidentally, is useful in making clear that, in order to capture this middle ground, it is not always a matter of proposing a middling position—in this case, a position somewhere halfway between those who support and those who oppose affirmative action. A viable cultural agenda should be, and can successfully be, in unambiguous opposition, on some issues.

This issue too has implications for the position of the United States on the world scene. It is not only that the American example is important for other societies trying to deal with inequities stemming from historic injustices (India is one such case, which can also serve as a warning signal, with its ever-expanding system of "reservations" applied first to the lower castes and to tribal groups, then adding ever new people under the wondrous category of "other backward classes"). More generally, however, the American rhetoric on human rights will appear very hollow if the same government that proclaims the rights of the individual abroad negates this value at home.

The public place of religion.—This is the issue that is conventionally called "separation of church and state." But there is no significant body of opinion in America (this includes most of the Religious Right) that would do away with the separation of church and state. Rather, beyond disagreements on the meaning of the first amendment to the constitution, there is the question of the place of religion in public life. Put differently, in defining who we are, what is the place of religion in this self-definition? William Lee Miller, in his study of religion in American political history, spoke of freedom of religion as the "first liberty." This can be taken as simply a statement of historical fact: The most important first immigrants came to America in search of religious liberty for themselves. But one can also take Miller's phrase as a statement of principle: Religious liberty as the foundation of all other liberties.

Religious liberty in its Western sense is much more than an expression of tolerance. Indeed, most other religious traditions—Islam, Hinduism, Buddhism, the religions of China—have exhibited more tolerance toward other faiths than has Western Christianity. But religious liberty in its Western sense, at least since the Reformation and then the Enlightenment, is based on a profound respect for the right of every individual to give meaning to his own life, even if this means breaking with the tradition of his community, and to express this meaning freely. Religious liberty also expresses a profoundly Western (originally Biblical) view of the limits of political power; it touches on the core mystery of the human condition, before which the state should draw back. This is the liberty out of which the Hebrew prophets addressed the mightiest kings and which is implied in Jesus's saying about giving to Caesar no more than is Caesar's; it is at least analogous to the liberty out of which Socrates allowed his reason to question everything, including those things which his community would have him take for granted. The "first liberty" indeed: Touch that, and every other liberty is in danger.

These considerations certainly affect one's understanding of the separation of church and state in the American polity. And here there is another case of elite culture (this time even before "the sixties") coming into conflict with the values of large numbers of non-elite people. This conflict has resulted in a paradox: By any empirical measurement, America (with the possible exception of Ireland) is the most religious among Western democracies; yet the American courts have in recent decades interpreted the separation of church and state in more radically secularist terms than any other Western democracy, barring religion from the public sphere in a way that deviates sharply from earlier American practice. France used to be known for its rigid conception of a religion-free republic; the French word "laique" denotes this conception. Yet the United States, thanks to the federal courts, is today more "laique" than France, for example in the provisions barring government support for religiously defined schools. Most historians think that the separation of church and state mandated by the first amendment was intended to prevent the state from favoring one religious group over another, not to make the state antiseptically free of any "taint" of religion. In other words, the "no establishment" clause of the amendment was ancillary to the "free exercise" clause. What the federal courts have done is to alter this logic, setting up what Richard John Neuhaus has aptly called a "naked public square," expressed, for instance, in the banning of Christmas displays from public properties. It is not surprising that this move has made many religious people feel that they have been marginalized and that their own government is hostile to their most cherished beliefs. This is a dangerous situation for a democracy to be in.

A viable cultural agenda must seek to reverse this development. This in no way implies that the American state should be based in Christianity, or even on some synthetic "Judaeo-Christian tradition." Nor does it imply going back on the separation of church and state in its traditional constitutional sense, nor giving up the most careful protection of the individual's rights of conscience (for example, protecting children in public schools from being coerced into religious activities that offend their or their families' values). It is also clear that the presence of religious functionaries and symbols at public events should reflect the splendid pluralism of the American religious scene—as has actually been done at such events as presidential inaugurations. However, the definition of the place of religion in public life should be guided by the insight, as valid today as it was when Alexis de Tocqueville stated it, that the vibrancy of American religion is a great asset of American democracy. Most important, what has to be reversed is the de facto establishment of secularism as the American civil religion.

Abortion.—This is the most divisive issue in America today, arousing profound passions on both sides and serving as a symbol of other aspects of the "culture wars," such as the understanding of the family and of acceptable sexual mores. But it is also the issue that touches most directly on one of the most awesome questions of human existence—the origins of the self, and thus implicitly the very nature of the self. This issue cannot be evaded in a viable cultural agenda: If one proposes that the culture of liberty must focus on the individual, one must be clear just who or what this latter entity is. In other words, one must address the question as to whether the fetus is an individual to whom the rights of liberty belong.

Americans sharply divide on the answer to this question. There is a sizable group that answers the question in the affirmative: Yes, the fetus is an individual from the moment of conception; therefore, abortion is homicide. This group, in the main inspired by religious convictions, is, of course, in the pro-life camp, and it is very vocal indeed. There is the equally vocal pro-choice camp, which perceives the issue exclusively in terms of a woman's right to control her own body. It is not unfair to observe that this group generally ignores the awesome question that lies at the heart of the issue. The empirical evidence indicates that the majority of Americans is somewhere in the middle and is rather confused about the matter. If one pushes people in this group to confront the question of the human status of the fetus, they are likely to say that they do not know the answer. The present author must confess to a similar agnosticism. What is more relevant here, though, is that the only position likely to succeed politically is one that can occupy this middle ground. On this issue, unlike some of the others, a middle-ground position will also be a middling one.

As is so often the case, the rhetoric of the conflict is obfuscating. "Pro-choice" is obfuscating: Of course a woman has the right over her own body; but the question is where her own body ends and that of another human being begins; and a woman does not have the right to destroy her child one month after birth—may she do so one month before birth? "Pro-life" is just as obfuscating: Of course a fetus is "human life"; the question is whether it is a human person. The phrase "sanctity of life," commonly used in anti-abortion rhetoric, is also misleading. It is a phrase that more properly belongs to the vocabulary of radical environmentalism, where it is used to advocate the rights of animals if not trees against the needs of human beings. The core Western value here, rooted in both the Biblical and Hellenic traditions, is the sanctity of the human person—the same value, as was argued earlier, that must be upheld in the debates over multiculturalism and affirmative action. But this human person is and remains a mystery. It is a mystery precisely because it is more than just "life," because it cannot be equated with a particular collection of genes.

If one is not blessed with certitude in this matter (and this, to reiterate, is the case with most Americans), one is faced with the necessity of formulating a position in a state of considerable ignorance. There is nothing immoral about admitting this. Nor is it only on this issue that one finds oneself compelled to search for a morally defensible course of action while one is ignorant about important aspects of the matter at hand. One must begin with being clear about the parameters of one's ignorance. It is not plausible to assert that a fetus in the eighth month of pregnancy has the moral status of a wart on the mother's body. It is also not plausible to assert that a fetus one month after conception is a person with rights fully equal to those of the mother. The mystery remains as to just when in all those months between conception and birth the moral status of the fetus changes. A viable position can be one that acknowledges one's ignorance before this mystery and then charts a morally responsible course accordingly.

Such a position will indeed be somewhere in the middle. It will be based on respect for the valid moral concerns of the opposing camps—on the one hand, the horror at the possibility that a human being is destroyed—on the other hand, an awareness of the suffering (and not only of pregnant women) caused by unwanted children and illegal abortions. Reflections of this kind lead in the direction of what in Europe has been called the "stages solution" (Fristenloesung in Germany). This means that a decisive moral and legal distinction is made between abortions performed early or late in a pregnancy. In the early stages, where one can feel reasonably secure that another person is not involved, the decision to abort or not should clearly be the woman's choice—"abortion on demand," if you will—on the presumption that only her body is involved in the decision. This choice should be progressively restricted and finally prohibited in the later stages of pregnancy. Of course the line drawn between "early" and "late" will be arbitrary, and as such subject to negotiation, as will be the rules and exceptions to govern abortions in the later stages.

To put it somewhat polemically, one should not be uneasy to take a middle position that denies a compelling choice between moral fundamentalism and moral nihilism. It will not please everyone. The evidence suggests, however, that such a position, articulated honestly, can command majority support in America. And there are politically sophisticated people in both camps (including the Religious Right) who would be willing to settle for half a loaf,

312 • Views from the Left: Fresh Sociological Insights

at least for the time being: Even people who claim certitude can understand that politics is the art of the possible.

Homosexual rights.—This issue does not excite as many people as the abortion issue, and is therefore less divisive, but clearly Americans are also divided on how to view homosexuality. Possibly a majority does not particularly care about it one way or another, seeing it as a matter of taste rather than morality; others regard homosexuality as morally reprehensible; yet others as a legitimate, perhaps even superior way of life. There is no compelling necessity why a viable cultural agenda should take a definitive position on this. What such an agenda should do, however, is to shift the terms of the debate from homosexual rights to the rights of the family. This is not a matter of political tactics; rather it follows logically from the guiding principle of such an agenda, which, to repeat once more, is the culture of liberty: The family, in the sense that is now commonly called "traditional," is an essential component of the culture of liberty.

This is not by any means to set aside the preceding question, that of the rights of homosexuals; it is simply to say that the question of the family must be more important. The rhetoric and tactics of the gay movement can easily turn off even the most sympathetic heterosexual. This should not obscure the fact that homosexuals have been treated in barbaric fashion for a very long time, especially in the English-speaking societies. Their grievances are well-founded. What is more, one of the rather few attractive consequences of "the sixties" has been greater tolerance in sexual matters. It should not be a goal to return to the grim puritanism of an earlier period; grim puritanism should be conceded to the doctrinaire Left, where it is evidently most at home. On many matters that concern homosexuals—such as protection against discrimination or the financial rights of homosexual partners—there should be greater openness.

To pronounce the phrase "the family" immediately brings up the key question: Just what sort of family is one talking about? Up to the recent cultural conflicts, of course, the meaning of the phrase was clear—"the family" meant a man and a woman, married to each other, with children or the prospect of children. This meaning is no longer taken for granted. This fact exploded into public view when the Carter administration convoked a White House Conference on the Family and was successfully pressured to change the name to White House Conference on Families, which now could cover just about any domestic arrangement. This event led to a walkout by an outraged minority of participants and in turn helped create a network of conservative "pro-family" organizations. It is noteworthy that the assault on the conventional understanding of the family did not come primarily from gay and lesbian advocates, but from mainstream feminists for whom it has been a major target of attack. The feminist denigration of the allegedly "patriarchal" family has become more muted since then. Ironically, the currently most salient item on the agenda of the gay movement is the legal recognition of homosexual marriage: Far from attacking the conventional understanding of the family, homosexuals are now insisting that their own domestic arrangements be included in that understanding. Or perhaps more accurately: While homosexuals used to criticize the conventional view of the family for ignoring their difference, they now criticize it for ignoring their sameness.

It has become common to speak of the "traditional family" as referring to the pre-nineteen-sixties norm. This is somewhat misleading. The "tradition" is not all that old. It pertains to a specific form of the family that arose in Western society in tandem with the rise of the bourgeoisie. It has also, quite correctly, been called the "nuclear family." It probably has its origins much earlier in particular cultural patterns of northern Europe, but it only reached its present form in the nineteenth century. Contrary to the claims of many in the "pro-family" movement, this family type is vastly different from the family as it was understood in early Jewish and Christian teachings, not to mention Biblical ones. The "traditional" family of current parlance is the modern bourgeois family. It is characterized by its small size (hence "nuclear"), its relative isolation from extended kinship groupings, its isolation from the processes of economic production (a community, not of producers, but of consumers), its legitimation in terms of an ideal of personal affection, increasing equality of the spouses within the household (which, contrary to feminist claims, has often led to the dominance of the woman in the household), and, most importantly, by a historically unprecedented solicitude for the welfare and education of children.

There is no need to romanticize this family type. As with all cultural constructions, there have been costs to this one (the modern profession of psychotherapy at least partly exists thanks to these costs). However, the bourgeois family has one enormously important achievement to its credit: It has been a uniquely favorable environment for the raising of children who will grow up to be profiled, autonomous and responsible adults. Put simply, the bourgeois family has been historically, and continues to be today, the principal matrix of individuation. The most dramatic evidence for this assertion comes from the data on children who, for one reason or another, have had to grow up without this environment.

If one understands this, one will also understand why this form of the family—the "traditional family," if you will—is crucially linked to the culture of liberty. What is more, both democracy and the market economy have a great stake in the survival of this family type: Democracy needs citizens; the market economy needs entrepreneurs; neither grow on trees; both are characterized by high individuation—which is precisely what the bourgeois family is best qualified to produce. Therefore, both the law and public policy should have an unapologetic bias in favor of this family type. By the same token, the law and public policy should resist all efforts to disparage, diversify or relativize this concept of the family: It is the family—not "families."

The issue of homosexual rights should be seen in this much larger context. The defense of the family does not imply some sort of sexual orthodoxy or a disparagement of people who, for whatever reasons, choose other ways of life. And the private sexual behavior of adults should not be of public concern. Specifically, the defense of the family does not imply hostility to homosexuality or indifference to the valid concerns of homosexuals. However, the public legitimation of "alternative lifestyles" on par with the family is unacceptable. Therefore, both the law and public policy should resist the concept of "homosexual marriage." That phrase should be the oxymoron as which it was seen until very recently. It is not inconceivable that homosexuals, upon reflection, might themselves conclude that there is little point in insisting on an identity that has always referred to the very way of life in which they have chosen not to participate.

Needless to say, the five issues discussed here are not the only ones that a cultural agenda will want to address. However, they are key issues. The positions suggested here make up a "package" that is logically coherent and politically viable. Also, the thinking that leads to these positions can be applied to other issues. Some of the positions are somewhere in the middle between the contending militants, some are not in the middle; yet all, in a different meaning of the adjective, are capable of capturing the middle ground of American politics. The principle that makes the agenda coherent is dedication to the culture of liberty.

Today's cultural conflicts are marked by overheated rhetoric. Such rhetoric is instinctively uncongenial to people of non-doctrinaire views. They are prone to speak in quieter tones, take more qualified positions, and this may sometimes seem tepid or ineffectual. But the language of liberty is neither tepid nor ineffectual, even if it is uttered without shrillness. In recent years it has shown itself to be very powerful indeed in many parts of the world. There is every reason to think that the culture of liberty—the "American creed," as Gunnar Myrdal called it in his classic work on race relations—still rules the American imagination and, if articulated with conviction, can enlist the support of the American electorate. This fact constitutes a great challenge to those who aspire to political leadership in this society.

Peter L. Berger is director of the Institute for the Study of Economic Culture at Boston University. He has held professorships at Rutgers—The State University of New Jersey, and the New School of Social Research. Among his many books are *The Heretical Imperative: Contemporary Possibilities of Religious Affirmation, Social Construction of Reality: AQ Treatise in the Sociology of Knowledge* (with Thomas Luckmann), and *Pyramids of Sacrifice: Political Ethics and Social Change.*

Sovereign Corporations

William Greider

When NAFTA was adopted in 1993, Chapter 11 in the trade and investment agreement was too obscure to stir controversy. Eight years later, it's the smoking gun in the intensifying argument over whether globalization trumps national sovereignty. Chapter 11 established a new system of private arbitration for foreign investors to bring injury claims against governments. As the business claim and money awards accumulate, the warnings from astute critics are confirmed—NAFTA has enabled multinational corporations to usurp the sovereign powers of government, not to mention the rights of citizens and communities.

The issue has exquisite resonance with the present moment. On April 20 thirty-four heads of state gather in Quebec City to lead cheers for a Free Trade Area for the Americas. The FTAA negotiations are designed to expand NAFTA's rules to cover the entire Western Hemisphere. The Quebec meeting should provide good theater but not much substance. Tony Clarke of the Polaris Institute, in Ottawa, says the meeting is intended to be "a face lift for the whole global agenda, by portraying free trade as democracy." Protesting citizens will be in the streets, challenging 6,000 police and Mounties, with an opposite message: Democracy is threatened by the corporate vision of globalization.

Chapter 11 of NAFTA should become a defining issue for FTAA negotiations. Many, including Clarke, vice chairman of the Council of Canadians, believe corporate governance was and is the FTAA's intent. "There is a conquering spirit at the heart of all this," he says, adding that the corporations' attitude is: "We have to get into every nook and cranny of the world and make it ours."

Chapter 11 provides a model of how this might be accomplished. The operative principle is that foreign capital investing in Canada, Mexico and the United States may demand compensation if the profit-making potential of their ventures has been injured by government decisions—"tantamount to expropriation." Thus, foreign-based companies are given more rights than domestic businesses operating in their home country. For example:

[sections] California banned a methanol-based gasoline additive, MTBE, after the EPA reported potential cancer risks and at least 10,000 groundwater sites were found polluted by the substance. Methanex of Vancouver, British Columbia, the world's largest methanol producer, filed a $970 million claim against the United States. If the NAFTA

Source: William Greider, "Sovereign Corporations. (international bankruptcy law)," *The Nation*, April 30, 2001, v272, i17, p5. Copyright © 2001, The Nation Company L.P.

panel rules for the company, many similar complaints are expected, since at least ten other states followed California's lead. The federal government would have to pay the awards. California State Senator Sheila Kuehl and others have asked the US Trade Representative to explain how this squares with a state's sovereign right to protect health and the environment.

[sections] In Mexico, a US waste-disposal company, Metalclad, was awarded $16.7 million in damages after the state of San Luis Potosi blocked its waste site in the village of Guadalcazar. Local residents complained that the Mexican government was not enforcing environmental standards and that the project threatened their water supply. Metalclad's victory established that NAFTA's dispute mechanism reaches to subnational governments, including municipalities.

[sections] In Canada, the government banned another gasoline additive, MMT as a suspected health hazard and one that damages catalytic converters, according to auto makers. The Ethyl Corporation of Virginia, producer of MMT, filed a $250 million claim but settled for $13 million after Canada agreed to withdraw its ban and apologize.

[sections] The Loewen Group Inc., a Canadian operator of far-flung funeral homes, lodged a $750 million complaint against the United States, claiming that a Biloxi, Mississippi jury made an excessive award of $500 million when it found Loewen liable for contract fraud against a small local competitor.

[sections] Sunbelt Water Inc. of California has filed the largest and most audacious claim—seeking $10.5 billion from Canada for revoking its license to export water by supertanker from British Columbia to water-scarce areas of the United States.

[sections] Canada's Mondev International is claiming $50 million from the United States because the City of Boston canceled a sales contract for an office building with a shopping mall. Boston invoked sovereign immunity against such lawsuits and was upheld by a local judge and the Massachusetts Supreme Court. The US Supreme Court declined to hear the appeal, so the company turned to NAFTA for relief.

"When just the threat of a Chapter 11 action may suffice to wrest a financial settlement from a government, investors have unprecedented leverage against states," Lydia Lazar, a Chicago attorney who has worked in global commerce, wrote in *Global Financial Markets* magazine. Mexico, Canada and the United States effectively waived the doctrine of sovereign immunity, she explained, when they signed NAFTA.

As many as fifteen cases have been launched to date, but no one can be sure of the number, since there's no requirement to inform the public. The contesting parties choose the judges who will arbitrate, choose which issues and legal principles are to apply and also decide whether the public has any access to the proceedings. The design follows the format for private arbitration cases between contesting business interests. With the same arrogance that designed the WTO and other international trade forums, it is assumed that these disputes are none of the public's business—even though public laws are under attack and taxpayers' money will pay the fines. The core legal issue is described as damage to an investor's property—property in the form of anticipated profits. The NAFTA logic thus establishes the "regulatory takings" doctrine the right has promoted unsuccessfully for two decades—a retrograde version of property rights designed to cripple or even dismantle the administrative state's regulatory powers. "NAFTA is really an end run around the Constitution," says Lazar.

The fundamental difference in Chapter 11, unlike other trade agreements, is that the global corporations are free to litigate on their own without having to ask national governments to act on their behalf in global forums. Clearly, some of the business complaints so far are more exotic than anyone probably anticipated. These initial cases will set precedents, however, that major global firms can apply later. If nobody stops this process, the national identity of multinationals will become even weaker and less relevant, Lazar points out, since they have status to challenge government as "an open class of 'legal equals.'"

In Canada a private lawsuit was filed recently challenging the constitutionality of Chapter 11, since Canada's Constitution states that the government cannot delegate justice to other bodies. The Canadian government, itself embarrassed by the cases against it, expressed doubt that Chapter 11 should be included in the hemispheric agreement, though it appears to be backing away from outright opposition. In US localities, the cases are beginning to stir questions, but lawmakers and jurists are only beginning to learn the implications.

Does George W. Bush understand what he is proposing for the Americas? Did Bill Clinton and Bush the elder understand the fundamental shift in legal foundations buried in NAFTA's fine print? They knew this is what business and finance wanted. As the public learns more, the smoking gun should become a focal point in this year's trade debate, confronting politicians with embarrassing questions about global governance. Who voted to shoot down national sovereignty? Who crowned the corporate investors the new monarchs of public values?

William Greider is *The Nation*'s national affairs correspondent.